Sales and Inventory Planning with SAP® APO

 PRESS

SAP PRESS is a joint initiative of SAP and Galileo Press. The know-how offered by SAP specialists combined with the expertise of the publishing house Galileo Press offers the reader expert books in the field. SAP PRESS features first-hand information and expert advice, and provides useful skills for professional decision-making.

SAP PRESS offers a variety of books on technical and business related topics for the SAP user. For further information, please visit our website: *www.sap-press.com*.

Martin Murray
SAP Warehouse Management: Functionality and Technical Configuration
2007, approx. 500 pp.
ISBN 978-1-59229-133-5

Sachin Sethi
Enhancing Procurement with SAP SRM
2007, approx. 400 pp.
ISBN 978-1-59229-068-0

Marc Hoppe
Inventory Optimization with SAP
2006, 483 pp.
ISBN 978-1-59229-097-0

Jörg Thomas Dickersbach, Gerhard Keller, Klaus Weihrauch
Production Planning and Control with SAP
2007, 477 pp.
ISBN 978-1-59229-106-9

Jochen Balla, Frank Layer
Production Planning with SAP APO-PP/DS
2007, 336 pp.
ISBN 978-1-59229-113-7

Marc Hoppe

Sales and Inventory Planning
with SAP® APO

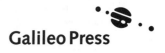

Bonn • Boston

ISBN 978-1-59229-123-6

1st edition 2007

Editor Frank Paschen
Copy Editor Nancy Etscovitz, UCG, Inc., Boston, MA
Cover Design Silke Braun
Layout Design Vera Brauner
Production Bernadette Blümel
Typesetting SatzPro, Krefeld
Printed and bound in Germany

For planners around the world:

Declaring the end from the beginning,
and from ancient times things that are not yet done;
saying: 'My counsel shall stand,
and all My pleasure will I do';
Calling ... the man of My counsel ...
I have purposed, I will also do it.
Old Testament, Isiah 46, 10 + 11

Contents at a Glance

1 Introduction 15

2 Overview of SAP APO 21

3 Demand Planning with SAP APO-DP
   —Basic Principles 41

4 Demand Planning with SAP APO-DP
   —Implementation 77

5 Inventory Planning with SAP APO-SNP
   —Basic Principles 199

6 Inventory Planning with SAP APO-SNP
   —Implementation 231

7 SAP APO—Integration and Architecture 383

8 Implementation Process 393

A Literature 409

B List of Acronyms 411

C Glossary 415

D The Author 433

Contents

1 Introduction **15**

1.1 Definition of Supply Chain Management (SCM) 15
1.2 Market Challenges Facing the Supply Chain 15
1.3 From Material Requirements Planning (MRP) to
    Supply Chain Management 16
1.4 Planning as a Critical Process 19
1.5 Target Group and Structure of this Book 19

2 Overview of SAP APO **21**

2.1 Requirements of Supply Chain Networks 21
2.2 Key Functions of SAP SCM 22
   2.2.1 Planning 23
   2.2.2 Execution 27
   2.2.3 Coordination 29
   2.2.4 Collaboration 29
2.3 Demand Planning (DP) 30
   2.3.1 Multi-Level Planning 31
   2.3.2 Forecasts 31
   2.3.3 Lifecycle Management 32
   2.3.4 Promotion Planning 33
2.4 Inventory Planning (in Supply Network Planning) 33
   2.4.1 Safety Stock Planning 34
   2.4.2 Inventory Planning 34
   2.4.3 Distribution Resource Planning 36
2.5 Integrated Supply Chain Planning 38
2.6 Summary 40

3 Demand Planning with SAP APO-DP
— Basic Principles **41**

3.1 Overview of the Administration of Demand Planning 41
3.2 Configuring the Administrator Workbench 43
   3.2.1 Overview 43
   3.2.2 InfoObjects and Other Relevant Terms from
         SAP NetWeaver BI 45
   3.2.3 InfoCubes 48

3.2.4   Saving Key Figures and Characteristics in
the InfoCube 51
3.3   Configuring the S&DP Administrator Workbench 52
3.3.1   Overview 52
3.3.2   Creating the Basic Planning Object Structure 53
3.3.3   Creating Characteristic Value Combinations 54
3.3.4   Configuring the Planning Area 58
3.4   Planning Books 64
3.4.1   Creating Planning Books 66
3.4.2   Assigning Users to a Planning Book 70
3.5   Advanced Macros 71
3.6   Summary 76

**4   Demand Planning with SAP APO-DP
—Implementation 77**

4.1   Creating a Demand Forecast 78
4.1.1   Interactive Demand Planning 78
4.1.2   Carrying Out Demand Planning (Sample Case) 84
4.2   Forecasts 103
4.2.1   Aggregation and Disaggregation 103
4.2.2   Introduction to the Different Forecasting
Techniques 108
4.2.3   Quantitative Forecasting Techniques in Detail 112
4.3   Monitoring the Forecast Quality 145
4.3.1   Introduction 146
4.3.2   Forecast Error 147
4.3.3   Causal Forecast Errors (MLR) 155
4.3.4   Forecast Errors in SAP APO—Summary 158
4.3.5   Alert Monitor 159
4.4   Lifecycle Planning 161
4.4.1   Introduction 161
4.4.2   Like Profiles 164
4.4.3   Phase-In/Phase-Out Profiles 165
4.4.4   Product Interchangeability 168
4.5   Promotion Planning 175
4.5.1   Overview 175
4.5.2   Creating a Promotion 176
4.5.3   Promotion Base 179
4.6   Collaborative Demand Planning 180
4.6.1   Overview 180

4.6.2   CLP Architecture and Data Transfer 181

4.6.3   Process Flow for Collaborative Demand Planning 182

4.7   Forecasting with BOMs 183

4.7.1   Overview 183

4.7.2   Process Flow 184

4.8   Result of the Demand Planning 190

4.8.1   Transfer to Program Planning in SAP ERP 191

4.8.2   Transfer to Supply Network Planning 192

4.8.3   Sample Results 192

4.9   Realignment 196

4.9.1   Areas of Use 196

4.9.2   Realignment 197

4.9.3   Copying Data 198

4.10   Summary 198

5   Inventory Planning with SAP APO-SNP —Basic Principles 199

5.1   Supply Network Planning Process 200

5.2   Configuring the Supply and Demand Planning
        Administration Workbench 203

5.2.1   Overview 203

5.2.2   Master Planning Object Structure 204

5.2.3   Configuring the Planning Area 205

5.3   Planning Books 207

5.3.1   Standard Planning Books 207

5.3.2   Individual Planning Books 208

5.4   Advanced Macros 208

5.5   SNP Master Data 209

5.5.1   Locations 209

5.5.2   Products 210

5.5.3   Resources 215

5.5.4   Production Process Model (PPM) 218

5.5.5   Production Data Structure (PDS) 222

5.5.6   Transportation Lanes 223

5.5.7   Master Data for Hierarchical Planning 227

5.5.8   Setting Up the SCM Model 229

5.6   Summary 230

6 Inventory Planning with SAP APO-SNP —Implementation 231

6.1	Desktop for Interactive SNP Planning		231
	6.1.1	Selection Area	232
	6.1.2	Work Area	234
6.2	Planning Method: Heuristic-Based Planning		235
	6.2.1	Operation of the Heuristic Run	235
	6.2.2	Heuristic Profiles	237
	6.2.3	Capacity Leveling	238
	6.2.4	Sample SNP Heuristic Planning with Capacity Leveling	240
	6.2.5	Procurement Scheduling Agreements in the Heuristic-Based SNP Planning	244
	6.2.6	Direct Delivery from the Production Plant to the Customer	248
6.3	Planning Method: Optimization in the SNP Planning		249
	6.3.1	Introduction to SNP Optimization	249
	6.3.2	Processing the Optimization Run	255
	6.3.3	Finite Planning with the SNP Optimizer	256
	6.3.4	Determining the Supply Source with the SNP Optimizer	263
	6.3.5	Lot-Size Planning with the SNP Optimizer	266
	6.3.6	Inventory Planning	273
	6.3.7	Optimization Profiles	279
	6.3.8	Executing the Optimizer in the Interactive Planning (Example)	281
6.4	Planning Method: Capable-to-Match (CTM)		288
	6.4.1	Possible Applications of CTM Planning	288
	6.4.2	CTM Planning Process	290
	6.4.3	Settings for the CTM Planning	291
	6.4.4	Planning Algorithm	302
6.5	Analyzing Planning Results		305
	6.5.1	Technical Aspects of the CTM Planning Run	306
	6.5.2	Evaluating the CTM Planning Results	307
6.6	Comparing the Planning Methods		309
6.7	Safety Stock Planning		311
	6.7.1	Simple and Enhanced Safety Stock Methods	314
	6.7.2	Standard Safety Stock Planning in SAP APO	315
	6.7.3	Enhanced Safety Stock Planning in SAP APO	322
	6.7.4	Conclusion	335

6.8   Deployment/Replenishment 336
   6.8.1 Deployment Heuristic 336
   6.8.2 Real-Time Deployment 344
   6.8.3 Deployment Optimization 344
6.9   Transport Load Builder (TLB) 354
   6.9.1 Grouping Transport Loads Using TLB 355
   6.9.2 Procedure for Remaining Quantities 356
   6.9.3 Setting Up the Master Data for TLB 357
6.10 Aggregated SNP Planning 365
   6.10.1 Prerequisites for Aggregated Planning 365
   6.10.2 Aggregated Safety Stock Planning 367
   6.10.3 Single-Level Assignment of Receipts and
         Requirements 368
   6.10.4 SNP Disaggregation 369
   6.10.5 SNP Aggregation 373
6.11 Product Interchangeability in SNP Planning 376
   6.11.1 Discontinuation of Products 377
   6.11.2 Supersession Chain 377
   6.11.3 Form-Fit-Function Class (FFF Class) 378
   6.11.4 Special Features When Using the SNP Optimizer 378
6.12 Transferring SNP Planning Results 379
   6.12.1 Releasing SNP Planning to Demand Planning 379
   6.12.2 Converting SNP Orders for Production Planning
         and Procurement into PP/DS Orders 379
6.13 Summary 381

7 SAP APO—Integration and Architecture 383

7.1   Integration with ERP Systems 383
   7.1.1 Plug-In (PI) 385
   7.1.2 Core Interface (CIF) 386
   7.1.3 Business Application Programming Interface (BAPI) 388
7.2   Integration with SAP NetWeaver BI 389
7.3   Architecture and System Landscape 390
   7.3.1 SAP Quick Sizer 390
   7.3.2 SAP liveCache 390
7.4   Summary 391

8 Implementation Process 393

8.1   Project Methodology 393
   8.1.1 Project Preparation 394

	8.1.2	Business Blueprint	394
	8.1.3	Realization	397
	8.1.4	Final Preparation	398
	8.1.5	Go Live & Support	398
8.2	SAP Solution Manager		398
8.3	Project Organization		401
	8.3.1	Project Management	401
	8.3.2	Steering Committee	402
	8.3.3	Project Core Team	402
	8.3.4	Business Process Owner	403
	8.3.5	Key Users	403
	8.3.6	Data Processing Team	404
8.4	Summary		405

Appendix **407**

A	Literature	409
B	List of Acronyms	411
C	Glossary	415
D	The Author	433

Index 435

Optimized supply chain management enables you to react flexibly and quickly on a global level to ever-changing market requirements. This chapter outlines the challenges and their solutions from the planning viewpoint, and also describes the structure of this book.

1 Introduction

1.1 Definition of Supply Chain Management (SCM)

The term *supply chain management* (SCM) refers to the inter-enterprise process of coordinating the flows of material and information along the entire logistics chain (or supply chain), throughout the entire value creation process. The objective of SCM is to structure the whole process—from raw materials acquisition to end-customer sales—in a manner that optimizes time and money. It ultimately involves intensified cooperation between all the parties involved in a supplier-customer relationship. The structure of this kind of relationship is usually more complex than a supply chain, as most suppliers have multiple customers, and most customers have multiple suppliers. Therefore, the term *supply networks* is also used. Nevertheless, information-processing systems are required to manage this level of complexity.

1.2 Market Challenges Facing the Supply Chain

As you know, economic and technological environments are continually changing. The current pace of change in the economy and enterprises has its roots in the ongoing process of globalization, the speed of development of information and communications technologies, and intensifying customer requirements.

These constant pressures are forcing enterprises to forge new paths: optimizing the whole value creation process throughout the enterprise, reducing product lifecycles, and expanding their range of products. Increasingly, enterprises, see themselves as using their specific core competencies to develop new services on an ongoing basis to create optimal customer benefit, instead of belonging to one specific industry.

In light of this trend, it is important for enterprises to be flexible and to be able to adapt internal company business processes to changing market conditions. At the same time, most innovations and new services cannot be created without integration and cooperation with business partners. Therefore, enterprises have to structure their supply chains in a global and flexible manner.

One business that reflects this kind of global and flexible supply chain perfectly is the international automobile production industry. This industry is based on a division of labor, and so, companies in different countries acquire parts from suppliers in their own country, and assemble these parts to form subassemblies or full assembly groups. These assemblies are then sent to one global location, where they are used to build the end product. This process requires that an incredibly high number of variants, suppliers, production processes, and procurement processes be coordinated and integrated. Moreover, this complex structure has to be able to react quickly to new market requirements, quality problems, and other external factors. This is just one of the many challenges that face enterprises today.

The primary goal of this supply chain (i.e., SCM) is to arrive at a global optimum. Ideally, this optimum maximizes the benefit to the customer in terms of price, service, and so on, while minimizing the costs to the enterprise.

There are still serious inefficiencies along the entire supply chain, especially within the interfaces between enterprises and departments. The biggest of these inefficiencies is the total duration of the manufacturing process, known as the *throughput time*. Ninety percent of this time is consumed by storage and transport. Another negative influence on cost is the so-called *bullwhip effect*, which refers to the element of uncertainty in demand forecasts that increases dramatically from one interface to the next when forecasts are managed separately for each enterprise or department. This uncertainty about expected sales incurs increased costs, due to the need to maintain safety stocks, delivery delays, poor capacity usage, and so on.

1.3 From Material Requirements Planning (MRP) to Supply Chain Management

The optimization potentials described in the previous section can be unlocked with a new information structure that enables the enterprise to make and implement enterprise-level decisions in real time. However, the

ERP systems that are most commonly used today are suitable for mapping these kinds of processes. This is where new technological solutions like SAP SCM come into play.

The first generation of *material requirements planning* (MRP) systems calculated material requirements by exploding the relevant bills of material (BOM) using the bill of material processor for MRP. This approach planned quantities and deadlines only. There was no resource allocation as such, and order processing was either nonexistent or only partially existent.

In most cases, independent, individual plans were created at each separate, unsynchronized level of planning and execution. The individual planning steps were carried out sequentially; that is, demand planning, followed by MRP, and then capacity requirements planning. Not only did this lead to long processing times in the planning stage, it also meant that contradictory goals existed concurrently, which made a unified and consultative approach to planning impossible. While the main goal of Production was to leverage capacities, the Sales department focused on ensuring deliverability by maintaining stocks. Often, procurement or production orders that had already been placed were postponed by shop floor control staff in the last planning stage, in order to optimize the operation sequence of the orders in accordance with production criteria. From this, we can discern that available capacities were taken into account very late in the production process, and all prior planning steps were based on limitless production capacities. Exact planning and production data from external suppliers and partners was likewise absent from the planning process.

Additional production resources were subsequently included in the planning phase with the extension of the MRP concept that is known as *MRP II*. As before, MRP was an important part of the approach, but now, this step was followed by other, sequentially executed steps such as capacity requirements planning and scheduling. Besides customer requirements, the anonymous planned independent requirements created in a production program were now also considered in calculating independent requirements. Cross-plant requirements planning and distribution planning were executed in other planning systems. It must be noted, however, that the MRP II planning concept has the following disadvantages:

▶ Long planning duration, because the planning steps are executed sequentially.

▶ Long planning cycles mean that planning results are out of date.

▶ Static throughput times increase the overall throughput time and lead to *thoughput time syndrome*.

▶ Planning and scheduling is based on unlimited resource availability.

▶ Poor capacity utilization, resulting in no sensible way of resolving bottlenecks.

▶ Special production principles (such as workshop production) are not properly supported.

Although the MRP II planning concept has been extended to include control stations, third-party advanced planning and scheduling (APS) systems, and concepts such as load-oriented order release, these new developments have not solved its structural planning problems. The disadvantages outlined above have therefore led to the emergence of a new generation of planning systems, known as *supply chain management* (SCM) systems. The concept of SCM is to process information and make it available in real time, and to use the Internet for information exchange.

The potential for success of SCM and SCM planning is based on the planning deficits of the *production planning and control* (PPC) and MRP II concepts. These deficits created a demand for certain functions, the most important of which are as follows:

▶ Cross-plant planning, including supplier and customer plants

▶ Simultaneous material and capacity requirements planning, i.e., capacity restrictions should be considered simultaneously rather than sequentially

▶ Extended planning functions with optimization tools for better capacity utilization, especially in bottlenecks

▶ Aggregation option for hierarchical planning

SAP responded to these demands by developing SAP Supply Chain Management (SAP SCM). With its component SAP Advanced Planner and Optimizer (SAP APO), SAP SCM is a complete *advanced planning and scheduling* (APS) system that facilitates simultaneous material and capacity requirements planning, and provides genuine optimization functions. Another of its benefits is that it enables close real-time integration with the back-end system, *SAP Enterprise Resource Planning* (SAP ERP).

1.4   Planning as a Critical Process

This book deals in detail with one of the critical processes of the complex world of supply chains: planning.

The planning phase is the one in which fundamental decisions are made about how and with what materials the challenges described in Section 1.2 are to be tackled and solved. While planning will never be an exact science, as it usually deals with assumptions about the future, it still makes sense to optimize it as much as possible, as the quality of the execution depends on the quality of the planning. The better the planning, the better the execution phase can react to ever-changing requirements. Also, the more reliable data there is about the future, the smaller the uncertainty factor.

A concept known as *rolling planning* is one answer to this need. Rolling planning is a generic instrument that is used in almost all planning processes and on almost all planning levels. When it is used, the planning process is repeated either at specific time intervals or when major data changes are made. The result is that there is always a plan that contains the most up-to-date information, which means that scenarios can be simulated and decisions can be made in advance. Because planning is repeated on an ongoing basis, the future is approached step by step, and new circumstances can therefore be taken into account with every repetition. The planning horizon (long-term, medium-term, or short-term; see Section 2.2.1) is also used in this process to anticipate changes in the distant future. If particular circumstances make this necessary, within a rolling planning, it is possible to take action on a short time frame.

1.5   Target Group and Structure of this Book

The focus of this book is on processes in demand planning and inventory planning. The SAP SCM solution, and its SAP APO component in particular, are used in this book to illustrate these processes and to explain them in detail, with the goal of enabling all parties involved in the planning processes to evaluate and use this planning tool in their own planning processes. Specifically, this book is aimed at department managers, MRP planners, demand planners, consultants, project leaders, and IT managers who are interested in the topic.

After this introductory chapter, **Chapter 2** briefly describes the SAP SCM solution and its SAP APO component.

Chapter 3 deals with the basics of demand planning with SAP APO-DP (Demand Planning). It describes the technical structure, master data, and components required to execute demand planning with SAP APO.

Chapter 4 describes the actual process of executing demand planning with SAP APO. This chapter explains the forecasting procedure, product lifecycle planning, promotion planning, and the other planning functions of SAP APO-DP.

Chapter 5 presents the basics of the SAP APO-SNP (Supply Network Planning) component. Here, you will learn about the settings, master data, and basic correlations between inventory, procurement, and distribution planning.

Chapter 6 focuses on supply network planning in detail. It deals with planning processes, the main planning procedures, safety stock planning, optimization measures, and final planning for customer delivery.

The technological architecture and other integration issues are described in **Chapter 7** in the context of the SAP SCM components.

The book concludes with **Chapter 8**, which provides an overview of the most important activities of implementation projects for the components SAP APO-DP and SAP APO-SNP.

The **appendices** include a list of acronyms and a comprehensive glossary.

Marc Hoppe
Hamburg, Germany, March 2007

Requirements of modern supply chains are increasing on an ongoing basis. SAP Advanced Planner and Optimizer (SAP APO), which is part of SAP Supply Chain Management (SAP SCM), provides a wide range of functions to fulfill these requirements. This chapter provides you with an overview of the key components of SAP APO.

2 Overview of SAP APO

2.1 Requirements of Supply Chain Networks

Supply Chain Management (SCM) is changing in accordance with ongoing efforts by enterprises to improve their responsiveness and customer service while keeping costs down. SCM solutions have to be able to support individual customer products like computers and cars with the same degree of quality that they exhibit to support global markets with local characteristics and suppliers. Despite this need, many SCM solutions are designed for linear, sequential, and controlled conditions. Such solutions are based on precise demand forecasts, but can do nothing with real-world demand data. This is because with these solutions, decisions are made centrally, and it can take days, weeks, or even months before they take effect. However, the truth of the matter is that it is becoming increasingly important for enterprises to be able to react within hours or even minutes. The future of SCM therefore depends on the ability of enterprises to react immediately, and on a global level, to changes in supply and demand and to important events in the extended supply chain processes. The faster a supply chain network can adapt itself to such changes, the greater the value creation. SAP Supply Chain Management (SAP SCM), part of the SAP Business Suite, enables you to react in a highly flexible manner to changing business processes—for example, by offering your customers new services—and thus to quickly adapt your enterprise as frequently as necessary to the latest market trends and changing customer requirements.

2.2   Key Functions of SAP SCM

The literature on SCM does not provide a single, consistent definition of the term. A very general definition describes SCM as an organizational and IT-based approach to structuring and coordinating logistical networks. SAP, for its part, defines SCM as a central element of extended logistics management. This includes optimizing the whole supply chain from sourcing raw materials, to delivering the product—which may have been produced in multiple intermediary steps—to the required end-customer services. Thus, SAP SCM gives you an extensive and integrated view of your supply chain and enables you to map almost all business processes, from budget planning and demand planning, to supply-demand distributions, to delivery and invoicing at the customer side (see Figure 2.1).

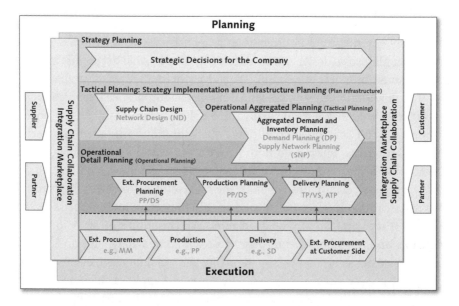

Figure 2.1 Correlations Between SAP Applications and Levels of Supply Chain Management

As we have seen, with SAP SCM, your supply chain processes can run in a fully integrated manner. You can also use SAP SCM to get started with the tactical planning of your supply chain design. To do this, you need to specify where you want to create supply chain locations in your enterprise. Aggregated demand planning and inventory planning functions enable you to reconcile and synchronize customer requirements with the available capacities. You can then plan your external procurement at the operational planning level, execute production planning, and plan your product deliveries.

The planning level is followed by the execution level, which includes purchase order handling in SAP Materials Management (MM), production execution, and the actual delivery to the customer. There is also the option, throughout the entire supply chain process, of collaborating with your business partners.

The process areas in SAP SCM can be roughly divided into the following four areas: planning, execution, coordination, and collaboration (see Figure 2.2). These four areas are described in detail in the following sections.

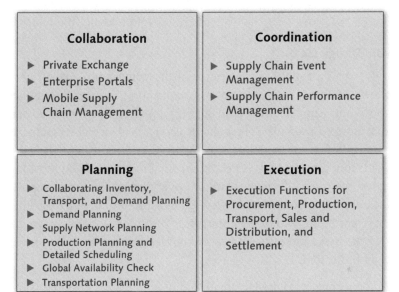

Figure 2.2 Four Process Areas of SAP SCM

2.2.1 Planning

The planning area covers three different planning horizons: long-term, medium-term, and short-term. *Long-term planning*, also known as *strategic planning*, is the basis of enterprise-wide, future-proof supply chain development. It involves designing and structuring a long-term supply chain over several years (up to a maximum of seven).

Medium-term planning, also known as *tactical planning*, involves planning activities for a horizon of between six months and three years. In this type of planning, repetitive processes are planned and optimized at regular intervals in terms of the quantity of information flows, financial flows, and resources along the supply chain.

Short-term planning, also known as *operational planning*, is specially designed for a time period of between a few minutes and three months. This type of planning has to be highly detailed and precise. Short-term planning considers constraints and is enhanced by the use of the following integrated APO components: *Supply Chain Cockpit* (for the supply chain design process), *Demand Planning*, and *Supply Network Planning* with deployment, production planning and detailed scheduling, transportation planning, and global availability check. These components are also described in more detail in the sections that follow. The demand planning and inventory planning functions, which this book describes in detail, are addressed in Sections 2.3 and 2.4.

Supply Chain Design (SCD)

SAP SCM gives you a centralized overview of the whole supply chain network, supports strategic and tactical enterprise planning, and enables you to monitor the whole supply chain management process. The *Supply Chain Design* (SCD) process uses the *Supply Chain Cockpit tool*, which contains a graphical user interface for modeling, representing, and controlling the supply chain. This tool consists of the Cockpit, the Engineer, and the Alert Monitor, and gives the user a detailed, graphical overview of the entire supply chain. It includes the various planning levels (demand, production, distribution, and transportation) within the enterprise. Multiple planners can simultaneously work, create forecasts, and carry out plans and performance measurements with this tool.

The *Supply Chain Engineer* is used to create and modify network models (supply chains in the direction of supplier to customer). The required data objects are transferred from the relevant source system to SAP APO. The transport relationship represents the links between the various locations (supplier, production plant, distribution center, customer). In a planning process, various versions of a plan are generated and evaluated for simulation purposes. Supply chain elements such as products, resources, production relationships, and transportation lanes are also mapped at this stage.

The *Alert Monitor* is the third component of the Supply Chain Cockpit. Its job is to show the status of a plan. If the figures for actual results and planned results vary, thereby indicating that a machine is overloaded, an alert is generated, signaling to the planner that the utilization of that machine needs to be optimized. The individual enterprise defines how alerts are displayed in the system, and this also depends on the version and model used.

Demand Planning (DP)

The *Demand Planning* (DP) component provides statistical forecasting techniques and demand planning indicators that help you to create precise forecasts and plans. Demand Planning is closely connected to SAP's Business Information Warehouse (SAP NetWeaver BI), which means that you have access to historical, planning and enterprise information for analysis purposes. Like the Supply Chain Cockpit, DP also uses the Alert Monitor. It does so to create alerts for orders that exceed or fall short of the forecast in cases where production is not adjusted accordingly, for example.

The DP component also enables you to carry out enterprise-wide forecasts. Forecast data can be gathered from a variety of sources and is stored in a general directory. This allows planners from the Marketing, Sales, Logistics, and Suppliers departments to collaborate on a consensus-based forecast. Specifically, you can use factors such as product substitution chain, substitution, and cannibalization to manage the lifecycles of your products. You can also model the effects of advertising measures in your Demand Planning function, measures that are based on your profitability goals, product availability, and previous results. For example, forecasts can be made about the extent to which price increases or decreases will affect future sales. For new products, you can develop precise forecasts that are based on models of similar products, sales histories, and other relevant factors. In addition, you can monitor new product releases and the end of product lifecycles by using point-of-sale data. Demand Planning also allows you to identify how factors such as demographic changes, environmental variables, and social and political issues influence your product sales. A selection of tools including multiple linear regression is used to analyze actual sales, and causal factors such as price are included in the analysis.

Supply Network Planning (SNP)

With the *Supply Network Planning* (SNP) component and its deployment functions, you can develop a model of your entire supply network with all its constraints. If you use this model, you can synchronize activities and plan the flow of materials along the entire supply chain. This, in turn, enables you to create plans for purchasing, production, inventory, and transportation. You can also carry out a precise requirement/delivery comparison. If you transfer this data to the liveCache, you can then use the deployment component to dynamically balance and optimize your distribution network. Furthermore, you are now in a better position to decide how and when the stock level should be distributed. To summarize, the SNP component and its deployment functions enable you to carry out your planning on an aggregated and detailed level, carry out "what-if" analyses, execute a dynamic requirement/delivery comparison that uses product substitutions, use vendor-managed inventory techniques, and determine the optimal stock level distribution to fulfill short-term requirements.

Production Planning and Detailed Scheduling (PP/DS)

To be able to react quickly to changing market requirements, you not only need a demand forecast, but also a solution that can meet the demand established by the forecast by providing adequate resources. As we saw in the previous section, SNP and deployment ensure an optimal flow of materials and resources along the supply chain. *Production Planning and Detailed Scheduling* (PP/DS) does the same at the individual plant level. PP/DS is integrated into SNP and deployment, and the result is an executable production plan that is implemented in a detailed schedule. PP/DS is a short-term planning concept and is used to fulfill product demand. Detailed capacity and material requirements plans can run simultaneously, and schedules can be synchronized at the various levels of the bill of material.

The central characteristics of this type of planning are as follows:

▶ Minimized setup times and better utilization of bottleneck resources
▶ Higher throughput due to better resource management
▶ Detailed production plans and schedules; overtime avoided
▶ No machine idle time
▶ Production delays avoided[1]

Another advantage of this type of planning is that optimized setup and throughput times create increased customer satisfaction (due to on-time delivery performance), which leads to higher profitability.

Transportation Planning and the TLB

Transportation Planning (TP), in the form of the *Transport Load Builder* (TLB), optimizes the delivery method, distribution across means of transport and carriers, and route planning on the basis of the lowest delivery costs, while at

---

1 See also the following SAP publication: *SAP Advanced Planner and Optimizer—Production Planning and Detailed Scheduling*, 2000, p. 3 ff.

the same time taking into account transport constraints. The goal of TP is to optimize the capacity of trucks, trains, ships, and aircraft.

Global Availability Check (G-ATP)

Companies that do business on a global level and have global production and manufacturing locations need to have business data and information available to them across system boundaries and at the touch of a button, so that their decision-making processes are optimally supported.

SAP's global availability check (known as *Global Available-to-Promise* (G-ATP)) is one of the most important core functions of SAP APO, as it is used to execute a multi-level component and capacity check in real time or in simulations. From a business viewpoint, it can be described as a comparison of supply and demand. A rule-based strategy (that is, a step-by-step availability check process that is controlled by defined rules) is used to ensure that such a check is always possible.

G-ATP can identify when and where a product is in stock in the system. If the product in question is not available, G-ATP searches for an alternative product. If the alternative is not available, the production process is triggered, thereby safeguarding the company's delivery obligations.

2.2.2   Execution

The supply chain execution area is where the business processes that were planned in advance are actually implemented. This is done at the document level in online transaction processing (OLTP) systems. The execution processes are important in triggering, recording the statistics of, and analyzing the physical execution of the supply chain and the associated material and financial flows. The following are the components of the execution area: materials management, production control, sales and distribution, transportation management, and warehouse management.

Materials Management (MM)

SAP SCM distributes precise information about stock levels and procurement orders throughout the whole supply chain network. The *Materials Management* (MM) component is the basic prerequisite for production goods procurement, inventory management, invoicing, and for maintaining a closed feedback loop between supply and demand.

Production Planning (PP)

SAP SCM supports all production processes including project manufacturing, make-to-order production, and make-to-stock production. *Production Planning* (PP) takes into account material and capacity bottlenecks, and ensures that design modifications and customer requests are implemented quickly and flexibly.

Sales and Distribution (SD)

As you have seen, SAP SCM contains a global availability check (G-ATP). The G-ATP function can be used in response to a request from order management or customer relationship management (CRM) systems to check the availability, costs, and delivery times of a product. Sales and Distribution (SD) functions are a vital link between order management, CRM, and planning.

Transportation Management (TM)

SAP SCM allows large enterprises with multiple locations to centralize their transportation management and to manage their processes either from a single point or from a number of business areas. With it, you can consolidate orders and optimize transportation while factoring constrictions.

Warehouse Management (WM)

Warehouse Management (WM) with SAP SCM provides extensive functions for both distribution centers and finished goods warehouses. WM manages the following main tasks:

▸ Inventory management
▸ Management of all relevant stock movements, such as goods receipts, goods issues, and intra-warehouse movements
▸ Physical inventory

WM therefore supports the user with the management of the total stock. It optimally processes all logistical processes within the warehouse and can map them in the system down to the storage bin level. WM gives the user an overview of the total quantity of each material and also allows him to identify the storage location at any time.

2.2.3   Coordination

The *coordination area* compares and synchronizes processes with suppliers, partners, and customers. It enables you to control events in the supply chain, to control output, and thus to ensure that all processes are running according to plan. The purpose of the coordination area is to ensure that logistics processes run smoothly by enabling users to monitor important processes (e.g., transport logistics or a procurement process) and to control them, both within SAP and in third-party applications, The coordination area consists of two components: *Supply Chain Event Management* and *Supply Chain Performance Management*.

Supply Chain Event Management (SCEM)

Supply Chain Event Management (SCEM) allows you to monitor processes, stock levels, and a variety of events along your supply chain. You can process information from heterogeneous systems and different suppliers, and recognize, analyze, and remove problems in a timely fashion, at all levels of the supply chain. If deviations occur at important points in the chain, you can use the system to issue alerts, recommend suitable measures, and create detailed status reports.

Supply Chain Performance Management (SCPM)

Supply Chain Performance Management (SCPM) is used to measure, monitor, and represent key figures in relation to logistics processes. It allows you to actively track the effectiveness of your extended supply chain and to analyze information in collaboration with business partners in order to jointly and continually improve the performance of the supply chain network.

2.2.4   Collaboration

Collaboration is about the Internet-based integration of business processes. Up-to-date technologies such as XML are intended to replace older ones such as Electronic Data Interchange (EDI), and using new technologies from scratch is also encouraged (e.g., innovative business processes such as business-to-consumer (B2C)).

Collaborative Planning, Forecasting and Replenishment (CPFR)

Collaborative Planning, Forecasting and Replenishment (CPFR) provides manufacturers with improved Internet-based options for cooperating with their strategic trading partners, and, in so doing, enables manufacturers to increase profits, improve service, and reduce stock levels and associated costs. The model consists of two phases: planning, and forecasting. In the planning phase, the general conditions of the partnership are agreed upon, while in the forecasting phase, a joint forecast is created that is then used as the basis for organizing goods supply in the replenishment phase.

Vendor-Managed Inventory (VMI)

With *Vendor-Managed Inventory* (VMI), SAP SCM supports a cross-enterprise process between manufacturers and customers that is used in several industries. VMI enables you to automate replenishment and distribution processes by simply allowing data on sold quantities and stock quantities to be exchanged over the Internet.

Supplier-Managed Inventory

SAP SCM supports suppliers with a ready-to-use *Supplier-Managed Inventory* process. In this process, the supplier is responsible for planning and executing replenishment at the manufacturer's premises. On the basis of contractual agreements, maximum and minimum stocks, and manufacturer's stock and demand data, the supplier plans replenishments and relieves the manufacturer of these tasks.

2.3   Demand Planning (DP)

Demand Planning (DP) is used to plan the quantities to be produced. SAP APO-DP comprises a range of statistical forecasting procedures and planning functions for calculating future demand precisely:

▶ Multi-level planning

▶ Forecasts

▶ Lifecycle management

▶ Promotion planning

DP also enables enterprises to collaborate with business partners. Internet-based user interfaces and technologies allow users to exchange information on particular events (such as promotions and marketing activities) and to compare and correct deviations in forecasts. Special forms of collaboration are also supported, such as VMI and CPFR.

2.3.1 Multi-Level Planning

Multi-level planning functions enable specific data to be displayed, forecasts to be created, and planning to be carried out at all levels and in any dimension:

▸ **Product-specific**
By product → product group → product family → brand

▸ **Regional**
By sales office → zip codes → city → region → country → continent

▸ **Time-dependent**
By day → week → month → quarter → year

2.3.2 Forecasts

Forecasts should be based solely on historical data that represents normal development and that can be extrapolated to the future. Therefore, you must first exclude all irregularities, which include the following:

▸ Missing values

▸ Outliers

▸ Structural changes to basic standards, trends, amplitudes, etc.

▸ Calendar-based irregularities (e.g., number of work days per month)

▸ Promotions

By excluding these kinds of irregularities, you can enhance the quality of the statistical forecast significantly. Demand Planning provides a range of standard methods that enable you to make these adjustments. However, the extended macros are an additional, easy means of making the required calculations in accordance with enterprise-specific definitions.

Irregularities occur throughout the entire lifecycle of a product, such as the common occurrence of a product range of a company including products that are at various stages of their lifecycle and that therefore have different sales profiles. Unfortunately, there is no general forecasting procedure that can be used to create equally precise statistical forecasts for established, fast-moving, and brand-new products. Forecasting approaches that attempt to cover most sales profiles are extremely complex and don't give forecasters much in the way of actual support. Genuinely precise forecasts can be achieved only by using a combination of a variety of methods. Demand planning features a range of practical and proven forecasting procedures, which can be divided into the following three categories (see Section 4.5):

▶ Univariate forecasting procedures

▶ Causal analyses

▶ Composite forecasts

2.3.3 Lifecycle Management

The lifecycle management function is contained in both Demand Planning and in Supply Network Planning. The planning strategies defined for a product in the demand planning process depend on the current phase of the product lifecycle.

The lifecycle of a product comprises the following phases:

▶ Product launch

▶ Growth

▶ Product maturity

▶ Product phase-out

In Demand Planning, the product launch, growth, and product phase-out phases can be mapped in what are known as the *phase-in* and *phase-out* profiles. A phase-in profile simulates the upward sales curve that is expected for the product launch and growth phases of the product. Similarly, a phase-out profile simulates the downward sales curve that can be expected when the product is in its final phase.

The decision-making process is supported by the analysis functions of the demand-planning component. These functions answer the following questions:

▶ Should a new product be introduced?

▶ When should a new product be introduced?

▶ What campaigns should be used to promote sales of the product in the various phases?

▶ Should a product be phased out, and if so, when?

▶ Should a follow-up product be launched?

▶ Should a product be re-activated, and if so, when?

▶ Will the launch of a new product cannibalize another product?

2.3.4 Promotion Planning

Promotions have long-term effects on the purchasing behavior of consumers. These effects must be calculated separately from the standard forecasting components, which are based on historical sales data. Components that are affected by promotions add up to form a baseline forecast. Demand planning is an extension of the classic, volume-based promotion planning. It can take product prices into account when a profitability analysis is being created for advertising calendars, for example. Promotions can be planned, aggregated, and disaggregated at all levels.

Reporting functions can be used to track promotional activities and their associated costs, which enables you to evaluate the effectiveness of advertising campaigns in your enterprise. You can also model how the promotion affects demand, using profitability goals, product availability, and historical patterns as a basis. Moreover, promotion patterns can be used to express in units of measure or percentages any sales increases that ensue because of promotions. The system can automatically identify any past promotion patterns on the basis of historical sales figures or calculations. These promotion patterns can be stored in a promotion catalog and re-used when the promotion is run again.

Also, SAP SCM Demand Planning is closely linked with SAP Customer Relationship Management (SAP CRM). Promotions that are planned using the SAP CRM Marketing Planner can also be taken into account in SAP SCM Demand Planning, thus enabling users to create optimized demand plans.

2.4 Inventory Planning (in Supply Network Planning)

The *Supply Network Planning* (SNP) component contains the inventory planning and distribution planning functions. With its extremely comprehensive functionality, SNP is a highly integrated component of SAP APO.

Once the demand has been defined in the demand planning stage and released to the inventory planning stage, this latter stage can carry out the net demand calculation, a calculation that includes stock levels. When doing this, the inventory planning stage can draw on the safety stock planning functionality. This means that safety stocks can be planned separately under certain conditions. After you have calculated the net demand and identified the associated requirement coverage elements (planned orders, order proposals, stock transfer proposals), the produced and procured products are distributed and delivered to the receiving distribution centers or customers with the help of the distribution plan. The next section deals explicitly with safety stock planning, inventory planning, and distribution planning.

2.4.1 Safety Stock Planning

Safety stock is the term given to extra stock that is procured and kept in storage in order to cover any unexpectedly high demand. Your enterprise's safety stock can be calculated and planned separately during any of the aforementioned planning procedures, which all carry out net demand calculations. The safety stock planning functions in SNP enable you to achieve an optimal level of readiness to deliver. When you use these functions, only the minimum level of safety stock for all intermediate parts and finished goods is stored at each location. Safety stock planning can be used to assign optimal safety stocks and target stock levels to all stocks within the supply chain network. The system carries out its safety stock calculations on the basis of lead times, forecast, supply fluctuations, and level of readiness to deliver.

Various inventory strategies and parameters can be assigned to products. You can carry out safety stock planning manually, or by using a key figure for time-dependent safety stock. Also, safety stock can be held at the location level or at the more detailed component or end-product level.

2.4.2 Inventory Planning

The SAP SCM Inventory Planning component includes aspects such as time-phased planning, distribution and material requirements, capacity constraints, and quotas.

It provides you with the following options:

▸ Stock replenishment on the basis of time-phased order logic

▸ Optimal procurement decision-making processes for planners

▸ Optimized product mix

▸ Synchronization planning between production runs and inventory costs

▶ Planning of optimal procurement paths in multi-level production environments

▶ Creation of delivery quotas for customers and sales partners

SAP SCM also provides you with three different options for net demand calculation within inventory planning: heuristics (empirical values) with capacity leveling, optimizers (exact procedures), and Capable-to-Match (prioritizing).

Heuristics carries out a demand planning run throughout the whole supply chain network in order to establish how your enterprise can best meet its customer requirements. This method uses local optimization methods on the basis of empirical values in order to increase the level of readiness to deliver while minimizing stock levels and synchronizing the material flow.

The Optimizer is a linear optimization procedure that uses algorithms, such as the following:

▶ All available data (using variables)

▶ Priority decomposition (the Optimizer first processes the process with the highest priority; then, it processes the rest in sequence)

▶ Period decompensation (the Optimizer first processes the process with the earliest period; then, it processes the rest in sequence)

The Capable-to-Match (CTM) functions compare several prioritized customer requirements and forecasts with a range of categorized quotations, taking into account current production and transportation options in a multi-level production environment. The preprocessing tools provide a range of categorized quotations and prioritized requirements as input for the CTM function which then carries out a quick check of production capacities. There are no constraints in terms of transport capacities. CTM categorizes requirements—such as sales orders or demand planning forecasts—according to priority, using characteristics such as customer priority, location, and product priority. Quotations are categorized on the basis of available supply and user-defined stock constraints; for example, stock quantity or planned deliveries. For every product, CTM considers a range of requirement characteristics and a list of prioritized substitute products. In doing so, it uses the G-ATP rules. Descriptive characteristics can also be assigned to orders. These characteristics are used to define the requirement priority. Then, the requirements are fulfilled in order of their priority, and the system attempts to guarantee a timely order processing. If timely order processing is not possible, the function for delayed order processing is used to schedule the orders for a later time, but before other requirements in the order list are addressed. CTM conducts this search before and after production. When searching before production, the system first looks for all quotation categories for finished or semifinished products before it triggers the production of the article. The search uses a top-down approach, which means that the system searches the production process model first for finished products, then for intermediate products, and lastly for raw materials. When searching after production, the system combs the categories after first attempting to produce the article.

2.4.3 Distribution Resource Planning

After production, distribution planning starts. This process distributes the produced quantities to the recipients. The recipients can be customers or distribution centers. SAP SCM provides two components for handling the distribution of supply and demand: *deployment* and the *Transport Load Builder* (TLB). Both support you by dynamically synchronizing and optimizing your distribution network. Furthermore, you are also in a better position to determine how and when the stock levels should be distributed.

Planning and optimization can be carried out for different planning horizons (short-term, medium-term, or long-term). SAP APO also allows you to plan independently of planning horizons using tables of periods. You can define the granularity of the tables of periods in accordance with your own requirements. In this process, data that is recorded over a number of days is compiled into a single column.

Planning goals are subject to several, various constraints, including transportation capacities, stock capacities, production capacities, calendars, costs, and profit. You can model different environments by defining planning strategies for a component. These strategies then affect production planning and how forecasts are handled. Examples of such strategies are make-to-stock production, order delivery, and make-to-order production (with or without final assembly).

Planning activities (such as interactive planning, heuristics, and optimization procedures) can be executed in simulation mode and then stored as separate versions. Later, these versions can be called, analyzed, and compared, and ultimately used as production planning data. If you modify plans, the system forwards the modifications to the whole network, thus considerably reducing planning cycles. The system supports interactive planning via online simulations and the integrated Alert Monitor.

There are two different approaches for finding the best solution to an optimization problem: exact procedure, and heuristics. Global exact procedures (such as the simplex method) identify the optimal solution using established algorithms. Heuristic procedures, on the other hand, use local improvement procedures that have proven themselves over time. Heuristics does not always provide the optimal solution; however, if effective heuristics are used, it can come acceptably close to finding it.

Deployment

The *deployment* function in SAP SCM Supply Network Planning identifies the optimal incoming and outgoing distribution for the available capacity in accordance with short-term requirements. These include sales orders, stock transfer requirements, and safety stock requirements. The deployment logic takes into account a wide range of short-term constraints, such as transportation, inventory turnover capacity, and calendar properties.

Deployment calculations use push logic if the *Available-to-Deploy* (ATD) quantity can cover the requirements in the system. The definition of a push rule establishes how the push logic is to be used. With *push distribution*, the deployment process immediately covers all requirements defined in the system. With *pull distribution*, on the other hand, the deployment process covers all requirements within the pull deployment horizon.

Distribution is carried out in accordance with the due dates/times defined in the distribution centers. With pull/push distribution, deployment immediately covers all requirements within the pull deployment horizon, without taking into account the due dates/times defined in the distribution centers.

If demand exceeds supply, the deployment calculation is carried out using fair-share logic based on the ATD quantity, the open sales orders, the safety stocks, and forecasts. Fair-share rules are defined in the product master data and describe how the fair-share logic is to be applied. The possibilities are as follows:

▶ Distribute stock proportionally to all distribution centers in accordance with requirements

▶ Increase stock levels in all distribution centers to correspond approximately to the percentage level of the target stock level

▶ Distribute stock in accordance with the priority of the requirements in the distribution centers

Also, priorities based on location and product can be assigned to individual orders (sales orders or forecasts). To do this, the requirement with the higher priority is first covered from the available capacity. If the requirement exceeds supply in a requirement class with the same priority, fair-share rules can be applied to this class.

Transport Load Builder (TLB)

The *Transport Load Builder* (TLB) uses the results of the deployment run (individual deployment stock transfers) to create transfer orders for multiple products.

The system optimizes the loading of the means of transport by grouping the available products in accordance with the deployment proposals. In this way, the TLB ensures that the means of transport are loaded to maximum capacity, and the delivery begins at the very earliest only once the minimum capacity is reached. Transportation costs are thus kept to a minimum.

Capacity can be defined in terms of volume, weight, and number of packages. The system checks the planned transfer orders to ensure that the minimum and maximum values that you defined are adhered to. If there are deviations, the system creates an alert, and you can then adjust the TLB plan as required.

The horizon for loading the means of transport can also be extended by what is known as the *pull-in horizon*. With this horizon, the TLB can meet certain requirements early, thus ensuring that the means of transport is optimally loaded.

2.5   Integrated Supply Chain Planning

The various functional areas of your enterprise (Sales, Planning, Purchasing, Production, Logistics) normally function in accordance with the goals that have been assigned to them. These goals can differ a lot; for example, Purchasing departments want to order large lots to minimize fixed order costs, while the Planning department—if it is responsible for stock and needs to keep stock costs down—will probably want to order only small lots. These contradictory goals often lead to *silo optimization*, that is, every functional area optimizes itself. An integrated supply chain removes these silos and creates an enterprise-wide transparency that reveals the interdependencies of the decision-making process. It is therefore possible to create a situation where every department is working for the same goals and is intent on achieving these goals through the transparency that has been established.

SAP APO enables you to create just such an integrated supply chain, as with it, all the relevant functional areas (Demand Planning, Planning, Purchasing, Logistics, Production) operate in an integrated manner. You also can choose to run these areas as standalone operations or as a group. If you're using several functional areas of SAP APO, you will need to ensure that a defined sequence is adhered to. Figure 2.3 shows the correct temporal sequence of the overall planning process.

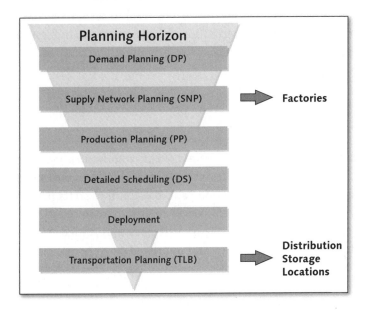

Figure 2.3 Planning Functionality with SAP APO

An enterprise that uses SAP APO carries out its flexible planning on the basis of constrictions. This means that when a production plan is created, any bottlenecks and real-world constraints that exist along the supply chain are recorded and analyzed so that the enterprise can take the appropriate countermeasures.

A precise and realistic mapping of the supply chain is a prerequisite for identifying these kinds of constraints and obtaining an accurate overview of resource availability at the right time. This reality-based planning is conducted at high speed and with good performance in a main memory location (SAP liveCache; see Section 7.3.2). If existing constraints change (e.g., if a defined threshold value is exceeded or undercut and an alert is generated in the system), a new plan can be created immediately via continual planning, and the results of the new planning run can then be transferred downstream (in the direction of the end user) and upstream (in the direction of the supplier). This continual and simultaneous planning can be carried out only if there is a globally networked structure of logistics partners who regularly exchange planning data with each other. One result of this approach is an increase in the supply of high-quality information along the supply chain, which, in turn, leads to an enhanced decision-making basis for planners. Simulations of various enterprise processes reduce the time and money required by test runs and potentially incorrect decisions based on wrongly analyzed information. What-if analyses can also be used to accurately simulate alternatives (for production or distribution, for example), and the results of these simulations can be better analyzed and proposed, and optimized at any time.

2.6   Summary

The results of integrated supply chain planning with an *advanced planning and scheduling* (APS) solution, and of integrating these results with the execution level, are flexible and effective planning and execution of strategic, tactical, and operational business decisions. These benefits are then reflected in a transparent, easily analyzed solution. The transparency thus gained ensures faster reactions to exceptional situations, and improved customer service. A process that is consistent throughout the enterprise means that cost-saving potentials can be exploited more easily. Overall, integrated supply chain management improves competitiveness and adaptability.

The configuration of demand planning and its planning books determines the manageability, the flexibility, and the performance of demand planning. A well thought-out concept will ultimately save a lot of time and money during implementation. This chapter will show you how to build the optimal technical foundations.

3 Demand Planning with SAP APO-DP — Basic Principles

3.1 Overview of the Administration of Demand Planning

The *Demand Planning* (DP) component of SAP Advanced Planner and Optimizer (SAP APO) is a complex, high-performance, and flexible instrument that supports the sales/requirements planning process in your company. User-specific planning layouts and interactive planning books allow not only the inclusion of various departments, but also of other companies, in the forecast creation process.

The configuration of demand planning is an important factor for a successful implementation of the system. This is performed, as it is also done for the Supply Network Planning component (see Chapter 5, *Inventory Planning with SAP APO-SNP—Basic Principles*), with the Supply and Demand Planning (S&DP) Administration Workbench.

The entire administration of the demand planning component and the components required for configuring the planning area are summarized in Figure 3.1.

First, we will give you a brief overview of the terms detailed in the figure and their relationships; then, they will be described in greater detail in the following sections.

1. Before you can begin the planning process, you must decide what *key figures* you want to use for demand planning. Key figures contain data that is shown as a numeric value—either a quantity or a monetary value. Examples of key figures that are used in demand planning are planned demand and historical sales. You can save key figures both in an InfoCube and in

the liveCache. You usually save key figures with historical data, that is, *actual key figures*, in the InfoCube. You save planning key figures in the liveCache. You also save those planning key figures that are to be *firmed* (i.e., fixed) in the InfoCube.

2. You must then decide what characteristics you want to use as planning levels and for selection. A *characteristic* is a planning object such as a product, location, brand, or region. The master data of the demand planning or the supply network planning comprise the allowed values of the characteristics, known as the *characteristic values*. Characteristic values are actual names. For example, the characteristic "Location" can have the values Hamburg, London, and New York. As part of the administration for Demand Planning (DP) and the Supply Network Planning (short description: S&DP Administration), you create a basic *planning object structure* for the characteristics that you want to use. A basic planning object structure contains all plannable characteristics for one or more planning areas. It is the structure on which all other planning object structures are based. The characteristics can be standard characteristics or those that you have created in the Administrator Workbench.

3. Once you have determined the key figures and characteristics, you must store additional information in the planning area. This includes, for example, the *storage buckets profile*, in which you determine the periods in which data is saved for a given planning area in the Demand Planning or in the Supply Network Planning; or the planning versions, in which different datasets can be saved for simulation purposes. Furthermore, you must ensure that the base unit of measure and the basic currency are assigned for the planning area.

4. You have defined the planning area when this information is assigned to the *planning area*.

5. You can then create individual user or department planning books. *Planning books* determine the content and layout of the interactive planning screen. You can use them to design the planning screen so that it corresponds to your planning requirements. A planning folder is based on a planning area.

6. Finally, you create the master data for Demand Planning (this cannot be seen in Figure 3.1). The master data of the Demand Planning determines the levels on which demand plans in your company are created, changed, aggregated, and disaggregated. For instance, your master data can comprise all products, product families, regions, and customers that are to be

planned in your company with the APO Demand Planning, as well as all corresponding combinations of these (e.g., which customers buy what products in which regions). Once you have created the master data, the implementation of the Demand Planning can begin.

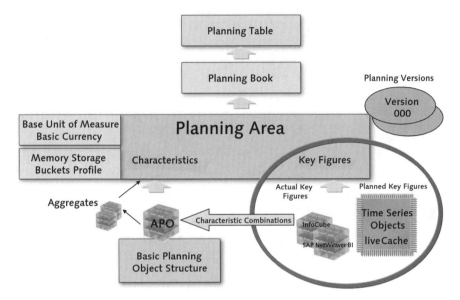

Figure 3.1 S&DP Administration (Source: SAP)

In the next section, we will describe in detail the configuration of the planning area with the Administrator Workbench.

3.2 Configuring the Administrator Workbench

The planning area and the corresponding key figures and characteristics are configured in the Administrator Workbench. In the following section, we will provide you with an overview of this tool. You will get to know the Info-Cube, the key element for Demand Planning, and you will learn how to save the required key figures and characteristics in the InfoCubes.

3.2.1 Overview

The Administrator Workbench is the tool for controlling, monitoring, and maintaining all processes linked to data procurement and processing in the SAP Business Information Warehouse (SAP NetWeaver BI, in former

Releases SAP BW); it is contained in SAP SCM 5.0. The InfoCubes are also created here (see Section 3.2.3). When you call the Administrator Workbench using the menu path **SAP APO · Demand Planning · Environment · Administrator Workbench**, a navigation menu appears to the left of the screen (see Figure 3.2).

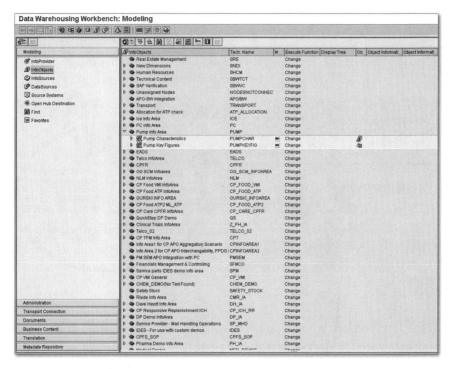

Figure 3.2 Administrator Workbench

With the buttons in the left navigation area, you can open the individual areas of the Administrator Workbench. The system will display the views and functions that are available in this area. By clicking on these views and functions, you can call them up in the right screen area.

The Administrator Workbench is used in SAP APO to create the data objects required for the Demand Planning, to enable data to be loaded from different data sources, and to monitor the data loading operations and the data updates. In this way, data extracted for the Demand Planning from different data sources (SAP ERP systems and SAP-external sources) can be imported into the SAP NetWeaver BI of the SAP APO system, which is then permanently stored in the data store. The Demand Planning can then access this data at any time.

By using the Business Content delivered by SAP, you can dispense with the bulk of the configuration work inherent in a business intelligence (BI) system, and therefore also for SAP NetWeaver BI in the SAP APO system. The Administrator Workbench is used to activate the Business Content delivered by SAP.

If it becomes necessary to create new SAP NetWeaver BI objects for specific requirements, this task can be easily executed with the functions of the Administrator Workbench. This may become necessary if special historical data from non-SAP systems is to be used for the Demand Planning. The integrated SAP NetWeaver BI component in SAP APO represents an important technical basis for integrating the most varied data sources into SAP APO in a very flexible way.

3.2.2 InfoObjects and Other Relevant Terms from SAP NetWeaver BI

The basic data storage medium in SAP NetWeaver BI[1] are the *InfoObjects*, which are business system evaluation objects (customers, sales, etc.). InfoObjects are divided into characteristics, key figures, units, time characteristics, and technical characteristics (such as request numbers, for example). They map the information necessary to build data targets in a structured form. You should therefore think of InfoObjects as a generic term for key figures and characteristics in SAP NetWeaver BI.

SAP NetWeaver BI InfoObjects (beginning with "0") and APO InfoObjects (beginning with "9A") are delivered in the standard SAP system. When you create your own InfoObjects, you can decide whether you want to create SAP NetWeaver BI or APO InfoObjects. While it is irrelevant whether you create SAP NetWeaver BI or APO InfoObjects for characteristics, this is not the case with key figures (i.e., you should create APO InfoObjects). Otherwise, you won't be able to fix any values or quantities for this key figure.

The *characteristics* of an InfoObject are reference objects (keys) whose dimensions generate relationships (e.g., "City" and "Country" are geographic dimensions of "Customer"). Characteristics can carry master data (texts, attributes, and hierarchies) that must be loaded from the source systems. *Time characteristics* are characteristics that are assigned to the dimension "Time", so their dependencies are already known, because the time in the system is predefined. The *technical characteristics* of an InfoObject have only

---

1 See also Egger, Fiechter, Rohlf: *SAP BW Data Modeling*. SAP PRESS, 2005.

an organizational significance within SAP NetWeaver BI. For example, the request number is taken when requests are loaded, so it helps to find the request again.

The *key figures* of an InfoObject form the data component, that is, they return the values to be evaluated. These are quantities, amounts, or numbers of items. We still require their *units of measure*, so that these values actually signify something.

Figure 3.3 illustrates the data flow over the InfoObjects from the source system SAP R/3-LIS into the Business Information Warehouse (BW) of the APO system, and from there into the APO component *Demand Planning*.

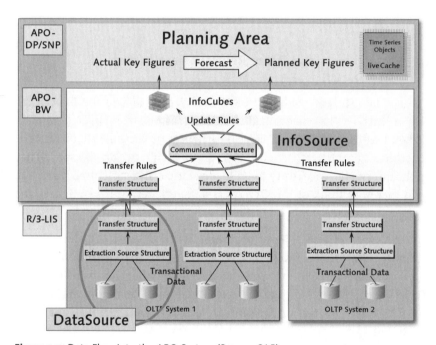

Figure 3.3 Data Flow into the APO System (Source: SAP)

1. First, we use the *DataSources*, which extract the data through an extraction structure from the source systems (in Figure 3.3, this is SAP R/3-LIS) and transfer it using a transfer structure into the target system.

2. By applying transfer rules, related InfoObjects are then logically grouped into *InfoSources* using a communication structure. Finally, the data is updated if necessary using update rules into the data targets (*InfoCubes*).

3. The data in the InfoCubes is the actual historical data, on which the SAP APO Demand Planning component bases its forecast in the *planning area*.

Other additional key terms are as follows:

▶ *InfoCatalogs* are user-definable and are used to organize characteristics and key figures.

▶ *Navigation attributes group and select actual and planned data.* Typical navigation attributes include the Material Requirements Planning (MRP) controller or customer group, which don't represent a separate planning level, but instead are used for the grouping. SAP NetWeaver BI navigation attributes can be used for the planning. You can only use SAP NetWeaver BI hierarchies for evaluation using SAP NetWeaver BI queries.

▶ *Data target* is a generic term for objects into which data is loaded. Data targets are the physical objects that are necessary for modeling the data model and loading the data.

▶ *InfoCubes* are data targets. They are assigned to an InfoArea and describe (from a reporting perspective) what is a self-contained dataset for an operational business area. They can also be *InfoProviders*, if reports and analyses are executed on them in SAP NetWeaver BI. InfoCubes are supplied with data from one or several InfoSources or *Operational Data Store* (ODS) objects (BasisCube), or from an external system (RemoteCube).

▶ *InfoAreas* help to organize the objects in the Business Information Warehouse.

   ▷ Every InfoCube is assigned to an InfoArea.

   ▷ InfoObjects can also be assigned to different InfoAreas via InfoObject catalogs.

▶ All systems that provide data for SAP NetWeaver BI are described as the *source system*. They can include the following:

   ▷ SAP systems from Basis Release 3.0D

   ▷ SAP NetWeaver BI systems

   ▷ Flat files for which the metadata is maintained manually and the data is copied to SAP NetWeaver BI through a data interface

   ▷ Database system into which data is loaded from a database supported by SAP without using an external extraction program through DB Connect

   ▷ External systems for which the data and metadata transfer is performed using staging *Business Application Programming Interfaces* (BAPIs)

You determine the type of source system in the Administrator Workbench in the source system tree with the function **Create**.

▶ An *InfoSource* in SAP NetWeaver BI describes the volume of all available data for a business transaction or a type of business transaction (e.g., cost center accounting). An InfoSource is a set of logically related information combined into a unit. InfoSources can comprise either transaction data or master data (attributes, texts, and hierarchies).

An InfoSource is always a set of logically related InfoObjects. The structure that stores these InfoObjects is called the *communications structure*.

When an InfoSource is activated, the transfer structure and the communication structure are created in APO-BW. Transfer structures always exist in pairs in a source system and the corresponding APO Data Mart system. Through the transfer structure, the data is transported from a source system in the format of the original application into an APO Data Mart and it is copied there using transformation rules to the communication structure of the InfoSource. The communication structure is source-system-independent and contains all fields of the InfoSource that it represents in the APO Data Mart.

▶ The *transaction data* that is copied into InfoCubes using extractors can come from very different modules. Because of the way the system has developed historically, very different extraction mechanisms are required for copying this transaction data.

3.2.3   InfoCubes

You save the actual data and archive planned data in the database in the Info-Cubes. If you have an external data warehouse such as SAP NetWeaver BI, you transfer the planning-relevant data to the InfoCubes of the Demand Planning (DP Data Mart). You can also extract the aggregated data from the SAP ERP system to import it from Excel, SAP NetWeaver BI, and legacy systems.

InfoCubes are essentially the data repository of the Demand Planning. Figure 3.4 shows three dimensions (of a possible total of 256):

▶ Period

▶ Customer

▶ Product (a product or master data hierarchy was created for this dimension)

InfoCubes create a multidimensional data model on the database server of the APO Data Mart. The multidimensional character of an InfoCube allows the user to filter data in many ways ("Slice & Dice" function). The facts are managed in separate fact tables and the dimensions are grouped in separate dimension tables. Both table types are relationally linked to each other. Individual dimension characteristic values can be subdivided in the form of master data tables. This ultimately creates a star-shaped arrangement of master data, classification data, and hierarchy data tables around the central fact table. During the analysis, the system first reads the data from the surrounding smaller tables, so that the access time for the large fact table is shortened.

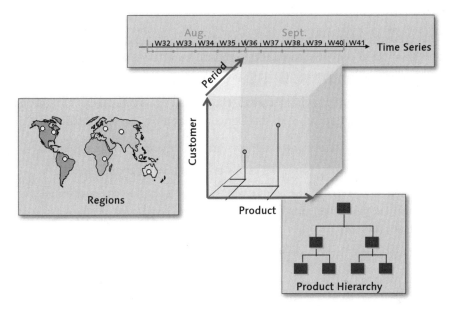

Figure 3.4 Data Structure of an InfoCube (Source: SAP)

The *fact table* contains the key figure data for the individual characteristic value combinations. Examples for key figures are currency, quantity, or number fields (e.g., order quantity and turnover).

The fact table is referenced using the "artificial" dimension key (DIM-ID). Because artificial keys are formed to link the dimension with the fact table, changes to the master data table can be made relatively easily, that is, without having to recreate the "natural" key each time. The evaluation produces a quantity, initially through the selections in the dimension tables. This quantity is then selected directly by the artificial key from the fact table.

Dimension tables enable you to structure the characteristics of an InfoCube. The characteristics should be distributed on the dimensions in such a way that the dimension tables are kept as small as possible and access to the fact table performs optimally (key reduction).

From a technical point of view, the characteristics of the dimension table form the "edges" of the "data die," which is saved as an InfoCube in the Data Mart. The dimensions are linked with the fact table through dimension keys. The data of the fact table is accessed through the selection of the characteristics and their (characteristic) values from the dimension table and by the generation of a corresponding SQL instruction, with which the fact table is accessed.

This database plan, which is described as a *star schema* (see Figure 3.5) guarantees efficient analysis possibilities and offers flexible solutions that can be adapted easily to changing operational requirements.

Note the following when considering what characteristics should be included in your InfoCube for the Demand Planning (see also Section 3.3):

▶ Characteristics determine the levels on which you can aggregate data.

▶ Characteristics determine the levels on which you can maintain data.

▶ The characteristics of the InfoCube must correspond to the planning levels of the Demand Planning (the InfoCube can contain more characteristics, but not fewer).

▶ Characteristic 9AVersion must be contained in the InfoCube.

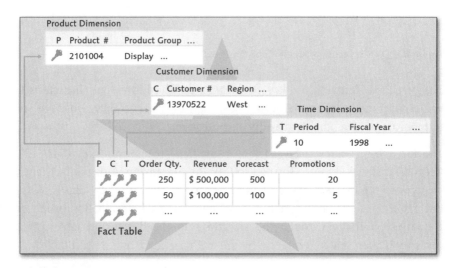

Figure 3.5 Star Schema of an InfoCube, Consisting of Fact and Dimension Tables (Source: SAP)

When you create an InfoCube, you must focus on the key figures and characteristics that you need for the planning. Then, you have to group your characteristics in dimensions (time dimension and quantity dimension). According to your entries, the system automatically generates a star schema in the database.

3.2.4 Saving Key Figures and Characteristics in the InfoCube

Once you have created the InfoCube(s) in the Administrator Workbench, you can save key figures and characteristics.

First you need to decide which key figures should be saved in InfoCubes and which key figures should be saved in the liveCache. Generally, you save the actual data of the Demand Planning in an InfoCube (together with old planned data) and the current planned data in the liveCache.

You then create the key figures that you want to use for the planning and that you have not already created in an InfoCube; to do this, in the Administrator Workbench, choose **Tools • Edit InfoObjects**. The screen shown in Figure 3.6 is displayed.

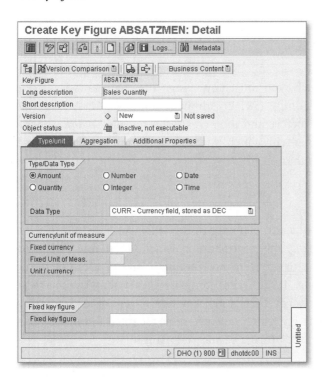

Figure 3.6 Fixed Key Figure

If you want to be able to fix the values of a key figure in the interactive planning, enter the key figure in which the fixed values are to be saved in the **Fixed key figure** field on the **Type/unit** tab.

The system is delivered with *standard characteristics*, for example:

▶ 9AMATNR for product

▶ 9ALOCNO for location

If you intend to use additional APO applications as well as the Demand Planning, you must work with these standard characteristics. If the characteristics that are delivered are insufficient for your requirements, you can create your own. To do this, in the Administrator Workbench, choose **Tools · Edit InfoObjects**.

For characteristics that you want to use for selection and navigation, but not as planning levels, create attributes and assign these to a characteristic that you want to use for planning. This procedure allows you to plan several characteristics with optimal system performance. For example, you assign the attributes *Sales Employee* and *Priority* to the characteristic Customer.

3.3   Configuring the S&DP Administrator Workbench

Once you have defined the general characteristics and key figures in the Administrator Workbench, you must now assign the characteristics in the Supply and Demand Planning (S&DP) Administration of SAP APO to the basic planning object structure and then create the so-called *planning area*. The planning environment in which you can perform the demand and requirement planning is then fixed.

3.3.1   Overview

You now configure the demand planning in the S&DP Administration. First you create a basic planning object structure in which you define all characteristics that are relevant for the Demand Planning. You can later determine several planning areas (e.g., for different company departments) from a basic planning object structure. You then assign key figures and other settings to the planning area. Ultimately, you have created the technical foundation that will enable you to begin the process of demand planning.

3.3.2 Creating the Basic Planning Object Structure

A basic *planning object structure* contains all plannable characteristics for one or more planning areas. In the Demand Planning, the characteristics can either be standard characteristics or characteristics that you have created yourself in the Administrator Workbench. Characteristics determine the levels on which you can plan and store data. Special characteristics are required for Supply Network Planning (SNP), for the characteristics planning, and for the forecast of secondary requirements; these characteristics can be included if required in the basic planning object structure.

The use of additional characteristics for SNP is not planned. The basic planning object structure 9ASNPBAS is an example of such a structure with the correct characteristics for SNP and can be used as a template.

The basic planning object structure is the structure on which all other planning object structures are based. Other planning object structures represent aggregates and standard SNP planning levels.

A basic planning object structure is an element of the definition of a planning area. The existence of a basic planning object structure is therefore a prerequisite for creating a planning area.

To edit basic planning object structures, you must branch into the administration for S&DP. To do this, choose **Demand Planning** or **Supply Network Planning • Environment • Current Settings • Administration Demand Planning and Supply Network Planning**. Here you can edit the planning areas and basic planning object structures.

To edit basic planning object structures, you must choose **Planning Object Structures** from the **F4** input help of the selection button on the top-left of the screen (see Figure 3.7).

You must perform the following steps to create the basic planning object structure:

1. In the context menu, choose **Create Basic Planning Object Structure** (cannot be seen in the figure). Enter the name of the new basic planning object structure and some descriptive text (see Figure 3.8).

2. On the **Configure Planning Object Structure** screen, you assign characteristics from the **Template** table to the **Planning Object Structure** table.

3. Save your basic planning object structure.

4. Finally, you must also activate the planning object structure using the context menu. The planning object structure is then available for your planning.

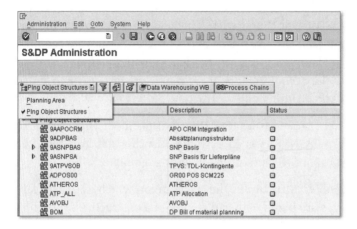

Figure 3.7 Calling the Planning Object Structure

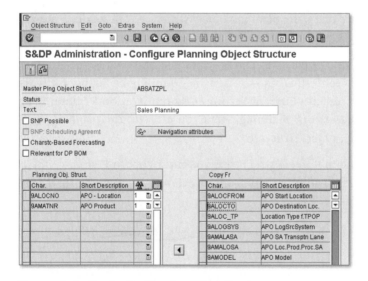

Figure 3.8 Configuring the Planning Object Structure

3.3.3 Creating Characteristic Value Combinations

A *characteristic value combination* is a group of characteristic values with which you want to plan. We also use the shorter term *characteristic combination* to describe this group of values. Data can only be planned if you have defined such a combination.

Characteristic value combinations are planned for basic planning object structures. The combinations then apply to all planning areas based on this planning object structure.

Under **Demand Planning** or **Supply Network Planning • Environment • Current Settings • Administration Demand Planning and Supply Network Planning**, you select the corresponding basic planning object structure and then choose from the context menu **Create Characteristic Combination**.

The **Maintain Planning-Relevant Characteristic Combinations** screen shown in Figure 3.9 is displayed.

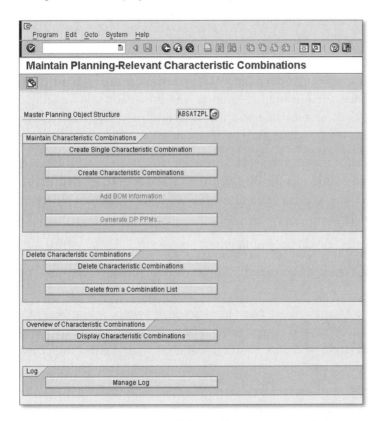

Figure 3.9 Maintaining Planning-Relevant Characteristic Combinations

Here you can perform the following activities, among others:

▶ **Create Single Characteristic Combination**
You use this option if no InfoCube contains suitable data, or the combination of the values is new, if you are dealing with a new product, for example.

► **Create Characteristic Combinations**
You use this option to create characteristic combinations that are based on the content of an InfoCube. The system checks what combinations of values are contained in the InfoCube and generates them for the basic planning object structure. What is important here is that the same characteristics are then finally contained in the InfoCube and in the basic planning object structure. The InfoCube can contain more characteristics than the basic planning object structure. Bearing in mind the aforementioned restriction, you can use every InfoCube you like to create combinations.

► **Delete Characteristic Combinations**

► **Display Characteristic Combinations**

► **Realignment** (not shown in the figure)
New characteristic value combinations can be formed during the course of business. For example, your company introduces new products, or products are manufactured in another location. SAP provides a tool for reorganizing data (realignment) that you use to create the new characteristic value combinations automatically (see Section 4.4).

Another method for maintaining several characteristic value combinations is to edit the combinations in a flat file (e.g., a Microsoft Excel file), upload this file into an InfoCube, and then use this InfoCube to create the characteristic value combinations.

To create characteristic value combinations, proceed as follows:

1. Click on the **Create Characteristic Value Combinations** button and the screen shown in Figure 3.10 opens.

2. In the **Create Characteristic Combinations** field group, select **Generate Immediately**. The system generates the new characteristic value combinations directly from the data source specified in the field group **Data Source**.

3. When you click on **Execute**, the system generates the characteristic combinations. You will then receive the message "Planning Object Successfully Created."

4. You can view the created characteristic combinations using the **Display Characteristic Combinations** button (see Figure 3.9 and Figure 3.11).

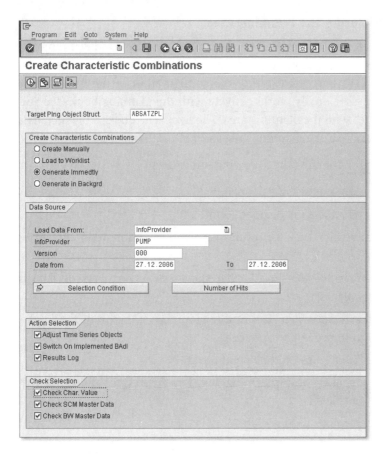

Figure 3.10 Creating Characteristic Combinations

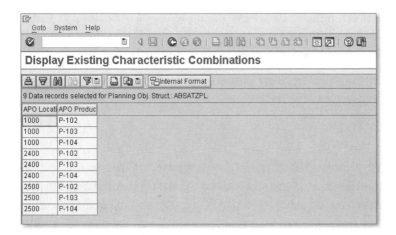

Figure 3.11 Displaying Existing Characteristic Combinations

3.3.4 Configuring the Planning Area

Planning areas form the central data structures for the Demand Planning and for the Supply Network Planning and are the foundation for planning books. The planning area is created during the configuration of the two components. The end user finally works actively with the planning book (see Section 3.4) and not with the planning area. The liveCache objects in which data is saved are based on the planning area and not on the planning book.

The planning area contains the following information:

▶ Unit of measure in which data is planned

▶ Currency in which data is planned (optional)

▶ Currency conversion type for displaying planned data in other currencies (optional)

▶ Memory storage buckets profile that specifies in what periods data is stored in this planning area

▶ Aggregate levels on which data can be stored (in addition to the lowest detail level) to improve performance

▶ Key figures that are used in this planning area

▶ Settings that specify how the individual key figures are disaggregated, aggregated, and saved

▶ Assigning key figures to aggregates

Supply Network Planning is delivered with predefined planning areas. You can also define your own planning areas.

You assign a planning area to a basic planning object structure, to which characteristics and aggregates are assigned. You then assign the key figures with which you want to work directly in the planning area.

You will now learn how to create period splits and planning areas, without which a planning area would be incomplete.

Period Split

There are two different period splits: One is for storing data (memory storage buckets profile), the other for planning the data (planning buckets profile). Both can be created using the SAP APO Easy Access menu and assigned to the planning area.

Creating the Memory Storage Buckets Profile

First create the storage buckets profile that determines the periods in which data is stored for a given planning area in the demand planning or in SPN. From the SAP APO Easy Access menu, choose **Demand Planning • Environment • Current Settings • Periodicities for Planning Area**. The screen shown in Figure 3.12 opens.

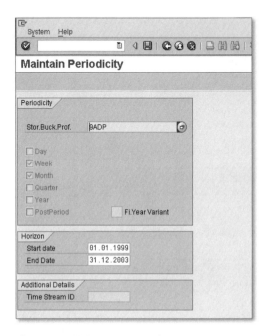

Figure 3.12 Maintaining Periodicity, Memory Storage Buckets Profile

---

Note

If you include months and weeks in the memory storage buckets profile, the data for those parts of a week that fall in different months are stored separately, e.g., data for the 30th and 31st of October (Monday and Tuesday) are stored in a different period than data for November 1st to the 3rd (Wednesday to Friday).

Creating the Planning Buckets Profile

The *planning buckets profile* defines the periods in which data is displayed and planned. You can use different planning buckets profiles for the past and the future. Specifically, the planning buckets profile defines the following:

▶ What time units are to be used for the planning

▶ How many periods of the individual time units are to be used

▶ The sequence in which you want to display the periods with the different time units in the planning table

Using the SAP APO Easy Access menu, create the planning time buckets profile with **Demand Planning · Environment · Current Settings · Maintain Time Buckets Profile for Demand Planning and Supply Network Planning** (see Figure 3.13).

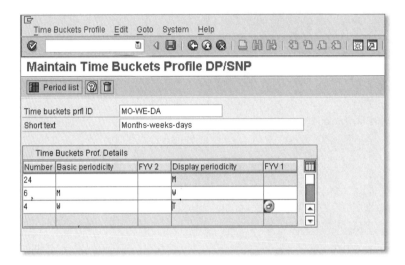

Figure 3.13 Maintaining Periodicity, Planning Buckets Profile

The time horizon comprises two years in the example shown. Of these two years, the first six months are shown in weeks. The first four weeks of the first month are shown in days. As we can see, the remaining 18 months are shown in months.

The first line defines the entire length of the time horizon. The following lines define the various sections of the horizon. You make entries in the columns **Number** and **Display periodicity**. The content of the other columns is displayed automatically as soon as you press **Enter**. If you want to see precisely what periods are displayed, click on the **Period list** button (see Figure 3.13).

Once you have created the planning buckets profile, you can use this profile to define the future planning horizon and the history horizon by entering them in a planning book. The system shows the horizon in the interactive demand planning; here it begins with the smallest period and ends with the largest. The future horizon begins with the smallest period, at the start date of the planning horizon, and ends—moving forward in time—with the largest period. The history horizon begins with the smallest period on the day before the beginning of the future horizon and ends—moving backward in time—with the largest period.

For a single planning book you may have several planning buckets profiles and thus several planning horizons. The planning buckets profile is linked to the data view within the planning book. You could for example have three data views for three users, with a different planning buckets profile applying for each view: Marketing plans in months, sales in months and weeks and logistics in weeks and days. To release the demand plan in daily periods to Supply Network Planning, you use a daily buckets profile, that is, a planning buckets profile, that only contains periods with the time unit "Day".

Creating the Planning Area

To now create the planning area, proceed as follows:

1. From the SAP APO Easy Access menu, choose **Demand planning · Environment · Current settings · Administration Demand Planning and Supply Network Planning**.

2. In the view that is displayed of the **Planning area**, choose the planning area node and from the context menu, choose **Create planning area**. The dialog window for creating the planning area opens (see Figure 3.14).

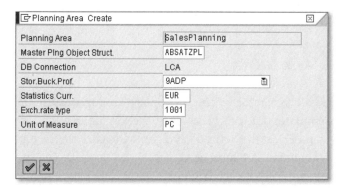

Figure 3.14 Creating the Planning Area

3. Assign a name for the new **Planning Area**, and enter the **Master Planning Object Structure**, a **Storage Buckets Profile** and a **Unit of Measure**. You can also specify a **Statistics Currency** and an **Exchange Rate Type**.

4. Click on **Execute**. You are then in the screen **Change Planning Area** (see Figure 3.15).

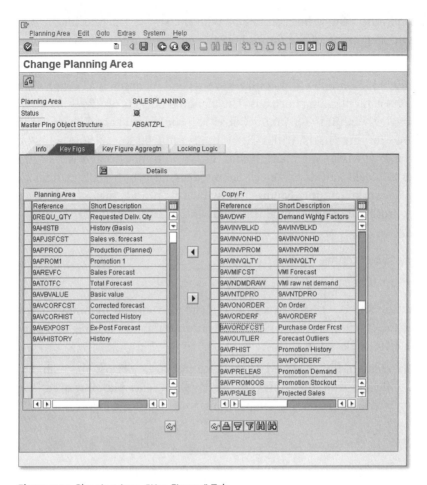

Figure 3.15 Planning Area, "Key Figures" Tab

5. On the **Key Figs** tab, you assign the key figures to the planning areas. In the right-hand table **Template**, you can view all of the key figures that are available in the system. Select the desired key figures and click on the top-most arrow to copy them to the **Planning Area** (table on the left). The system creates a planning object for each key figure at the detail level and on each aggregate level.

6. Save your entries.

You can change a planning area as long as you have not yet created any time series objects for the planning areas. Before you can work with a planning area, you must create time series objects. This process is also called "initializing the planning area." The system creates a network, consisting of characteristics and key figures in the liveCache.

Creating Time Series Objects

Proceed as follows to create time series objects:

1. Choose the desired planning area and from the context menu, select **Create time series objects**. The dialog box in Figure 3.16 opens.

2. In the **Create Time Series Objects** dialog box, enter the planning version and make your date entries.

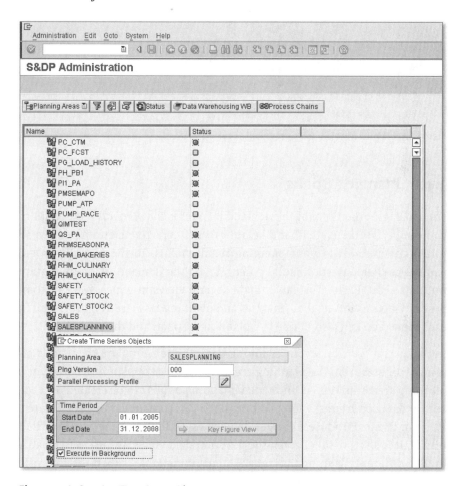

Figure 3.16 Creating Time Series Objects

3. Click on **Execute**, so that the time series objects are created. If the time series objects have been successfully created, the message "Planning version successfully initialized" appears, and the status symbol behind the planning area changes to "green" (see Figure 3.17).

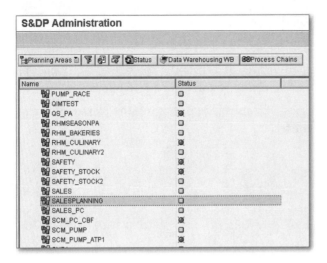

Figure 3.17 Time Series Objects Successfully Created

3.4 Planning Books

The most important tool of the demand planner is the *planning book*. With it, you can design the content and layout of the interactive planning screen so that it corresponds to your planning requirements. In the planning book, you select characteristics and key figures that the demand planners require for their tasks. Each book can contain several views in which you can compose key figures for detailed analyses and planning tasks (see Figure 3.18). In each view, you can also define the planning horizon and the period split.

You can create one or several planning books by selecting the characteristics and key figures from the planning area. The number of planning books for a planning area is unlimited. Individual planning books can be created for each user or for user groups. Each planning book can contain various key figures. This can in turn produce different data views on the planning area. For that reason, it is also possible, given the different data views, for users to be able to plan different planning horizons. The planning table is then the interface that the planner sees on the screen.

You can define the following elements in a planning book:

▶ Key figures

▶ Characteristics

▶ Functions and applications that can be called directly from this planning book

- User-specific planning horizons
- User-specific views of the planning book, including the initial column, number of planning tables (grids), and callability of the view by other users (the possible number of views within a planning book is not limited)

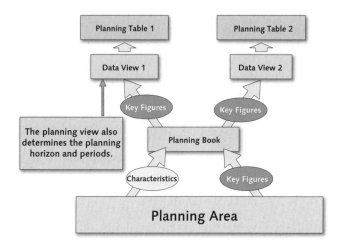

Figure 3.18 Planning Books and Data Views (Source: SAP)

You can configure these and additional elements of the interactive planning screen on the interactive planning screen (e.g., the order of columns and rows, the use of colors and symbols in rows, the hiding or showing of rows, the appearance of graphics and macros). For this configuration, you need to use the context menus in the interactive design mode.

In the planning book, you also define the functions with which you want to work. The APO demand planning is delivered with the following predefined views:

- Univariate forecast
- Causal analysis
- Combined forecast
- Promotion planning

You also define one or several separate views. You can perform the following in separate views:

- Define user-specific planning horizons
- Select different key figure subsets for different planning tasks
- Add rows for taking actual data from the current and/or prior year

▸ Configure the layout and use of individual rows and columns

▸ Define macros

Planning books support the online simulation of several planning scenarios, a consistent planning in the company as a whole (top-down, middle-out or bottom-up planning), as well as drill-up and drill-down functions, aggregation and disaggregation, the slice & dice technique, and the ad-hoc mapping of different planning situations.

Regardless of whether the demand planner is working with mass processing jobs or in interactive demand planning, she must always handle a planning book and particular data view from this book.

3.4.1 Creating Planning Books

Once you have created a planning area (see Section 3.3.4), the first step within the planning process is to create a planning book:

1. In the current settings or the Customizing of the demand planning, choose **Define Planning Book**. You can access this transaction by following the menu path **Demand Planning ▪ Environment ▪ Current Settings**. Later, in the design mode of the interactive demand planning, you can select **Change Planning Book** to modify a planning book. You will reach the planning book wizard (see Figure 3.19).

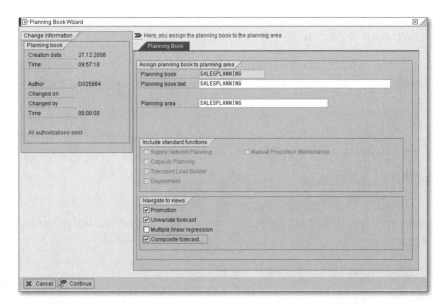

Figure 3.19 Planning Book Wizard, "Planning Book" Tab

2. Enter the following on the **Planning Book** tab:

   ▸ The **Planning area** on which the planning book is based

   ▸ The **Planning book text** for the planning book

   ▸ In the field group **Navigate to views**, enter the applications and functions that are to be callable from this planning book (in the example shown, the **Promotion**, the **Univariate forecast**, and the **Composite forecast**).

3. On the **Key Figures** tab, specify which key figures you want to work with in this planning book (see Figure 3.20).

   If you want to assign a key figure to the planning book, take the key figure from the **Planning Area** via drag & drop to the **Planning Book** (see left of the screen).

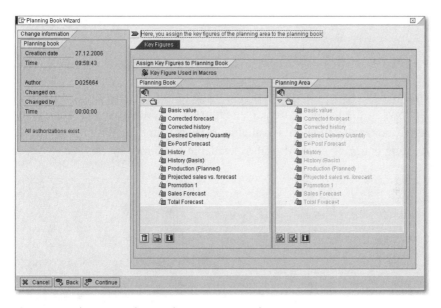

Figure 3.20 Planning Book Wizard, "Key Figures" Tab

4. On the **Characteristics** tab, specify which characteristics you want to assign to this planning book (see Figure 3.21).

   You select the characteristics you want from the basic planning object structure on which the planning area is based. If you want to add a characteristic, add it by dragging & dropping it onto the **Planning Book** symbol to the left of the screen. In the example shown, only two characteristics are required for the planning, namely, the **Location** and the **Product**. However, any number of characteristics is possible.

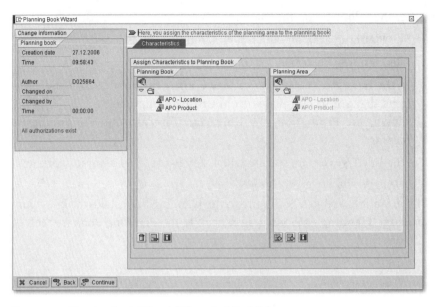

Figure 3.21 Planning Book Wizard, "Characteristics" Tab

5. On the **Key Figure Attributes** tab, you can define the attributes of particular rows in the planning book (see Figure 3.22). When you create a planning book, this tab is only available in **Display** mode. When you edit an existing planning book, the tab is available in **Change** mode.

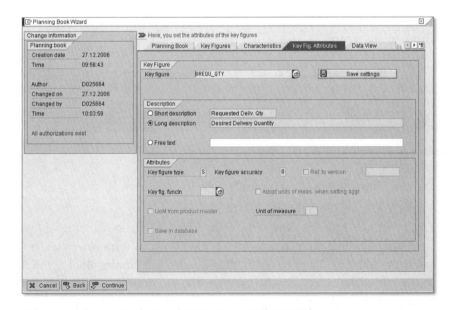

Figure 3.22 Planning Book Wizard, "Key Figure Attributes" Tab

On this tab, you can create auxiliary key figures that are not saved in the planning area, but which can be displayed as rows in the interactive planning. For a key figure you define yourself, you can specify that it should be saved in the database. You can use auxiliary key figures in the forecast and in macros. You cannot save any auxiliary key figures in the Demand Planning; however, you can do so in the database in the Supply Network Planning.

6. You create one or several data views for the planning book on the **Data View** tab (see Figure 3.23).

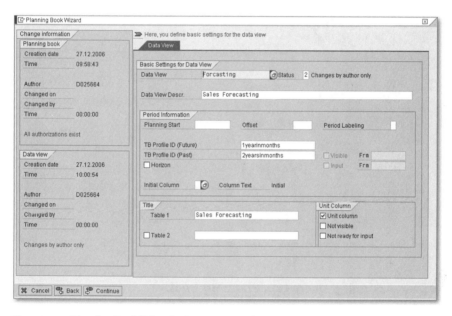

Figure 3.23 Planning Book Wizard, "Data View" Tab

You need at least one data view so that you can use a planning book. Several views can exist for several users within a planning book. In the data view, you enter the period split for the forecast period and the historical period. This means that time settings can be user-specific. In the example shown, a period of two years was chosen for the past and a period of one year for the future.

7. On the **Key Figures** (**Data View** area) tab shown in Figure 3.24, you indicate what key figures of the planning book are used by what users in this data view.

8. After the different tabs have been processed, you can save the planning book by clicking on the **Complete** button and confirming any messages that appear. The system saves the planning book and enhances the standard key figures that are required to perform the chosen applications and functions.

Figure 3.24 Planning Book Wizard, "Key Figures" ("Data View" Area) Tab

3.4.2 Assigning Users to a Planning Book

You can create individual planning books for each user or for user groups. In this way, the individual user groups in your planning book can plan different key figures, or see individual key figures and factor them in your planning. For example, you can create a planning book for the marketing planning, a planning book for the external sales force, and one for the demand planner. All three departments can then work in the same planning area on a uniform, consensus-based demand planning, but have different views of the planning and use different key figures for your planning.

In the SAP APO Easy Access menu, choose **Demand Planning • Environment • Current Settings • Assign User to Planning Book**. The table shown in Figure 3.25 appears. The assignments are visible here.

To create a new entry manually, click on the **New Entries** button and enter the required data.

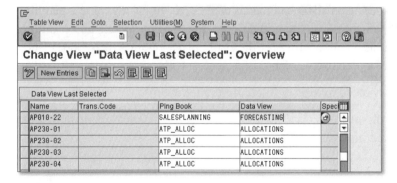

Figure 3.25 Assigning Users to a Planning Book

A user calls a planning book using various transactions. Examples for this include:

▶ /SAPAPO/SNP94 (Supply Network Planning interactive)

▶ /SAPAPO/SDP94 (Demand Planning interactive)

▶ /SAPAPO/SNPTLB (Transport Load Builder (TLB))

▶ /SAPAPO/MP34 (Promotion Planning)

For each of the transactions, you can manually assign a planning book and a data view to a user. If the user works in a data view when using one of these transactions, the system either creates the corresponding entries or updates them. As soon as the user calls the transaction again, the system automatically branches to this data view.

You can restrict the user access to just the planning or data view that is specified. To do this, set the identifier **Fixed Book**, if you want to limit a user's access to a single planning book. If you want to restrict a user's access to a single view in a particular planning book, set the identifier **Fixed View**.

3.5 Advanced Macros

Advanced macros allow you to perform complex calculations in the Demand Planning quickly and easily. Within the interactive planning, macros are either executed directly by the user, or automatically in the background at a specified time. In conjunction with SNP planning books, some macros are delivered in the standard system for stock and range.

You either define an advanced macro when creating or changing a planning book in the Customizing, or in the design mode of the interactive planning. You can define a macro either for the entire planning book or for a particular data view of a planning book.

With the advanced macros, you can do the following:

▶ Control the processing of the different macro steps with control instructions and conditions

▶ Create a macro that consists of one or several steps

▶ Control the calculation of results with control instructions and conditions

▶ Work with a broad spectrum of functions and operators

▶ Specify an offset so that, for example, the result for a given period is determined by a value in a previous period

▶ Restrict the horizon in which the macro is listed to a particular period or periods

▶ Write macro results either into a row, column, or cell

▶ Write the results of a macro step into a row, column, cell, or variable, and only use them in subsequent iterations, macro steps or macros

▶ Trigger an alert in the Alert Monitor that displays the result of a macro execution

The **Macro Workbench** (see Figure 3.26) is a tool for managing macro books and individual macros.

It allows you to quickly find macros books and the following functions:

▶ Copy macro books

▶ Start MacroBuilder

▶ Display macros in the macro book(s)

▶ Display code

▶ Change grouping of the macros book(s)

▶ Generate all macros of a book (activate)

▶ Start semantics checks for the books

▶ Delete macro books

▶ Transport macro books into another system

You write the macros themselves in the APO MacroBuilder (see Figure 3.27).

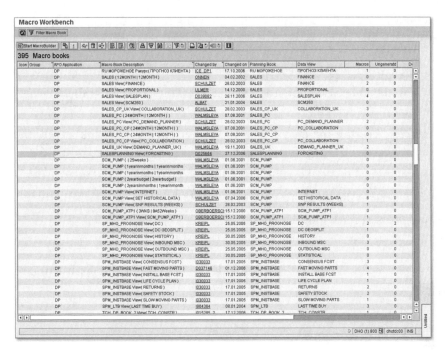

Figure 3.26 Macro Workbench

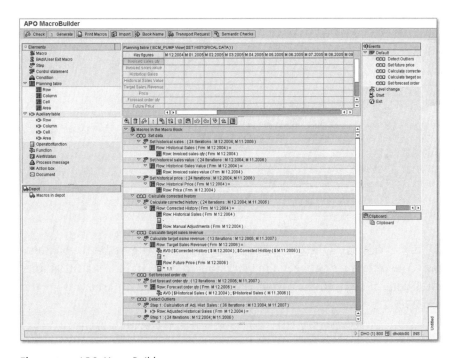

Figure 3.27 APO MacroBuilder

The *APO MacroBuilder* comprises the following screen areas:

► **Elements** in a tree to the top-left of the screen

► **Depot** with macros in depot to the bottom-left of the screen

► **Planning table** (also known as a demand planning table or grid) in the top-center of the screen

► Macro tree with the macro tools in the bottom-center of the screen (the area where you edit your **macros**)

► Standard macros in the top-right of the screen (**Events • Default**)

► **Clipboard** in the bottom-right of the screen

► Results area for **semantics checks**

► **Auxiliary table**

Now, you will see how the MacroBuilder works using a sample macro (see Figure 3.28).

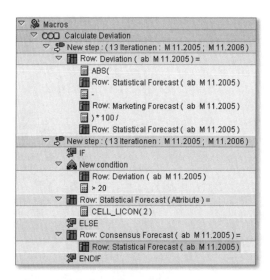

Figure 3.28 Sample Macro

This macro calculates the difference between two key figures in the planning book. The difference between the marketing forecast and the statistical forecast is determined and the system issues an alert if the difference is greater than 20 %.

The company XYZ produces the product ABC that—as a basic product—shows a stable demand over time. To create a consensus-based demand plan with all persons involved, the marketing forecast should be reconciled with the statistical forecast. For this reason, the two forecasts shouldn't differ too much, because, under normal circumstances, no sudden changes are to be expected. If the statistical forecast for a period is 100, but the marketing forecast for the same period was 60, this means that an exception exists of which the demand planner must be notified. This macro stores such exceptions, triggers an alert, and changes the color of the affected cell (CELL_LICON(2)). The planner can then take corresponding measures. If the marketing forecast does not differ significantly from the statistical forecast, the statistical forecast is converted to a consensus-based forecast.

You can specify that a macro be executed automatically for a particular planning book. Four options are available to execute a macro automatically (see Figure 3.29).

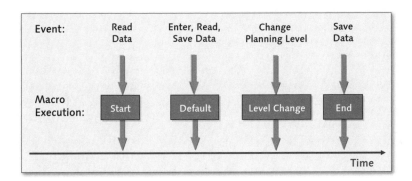

Figure 3.29 Automatic Macro Execution (Source: SAP)

▶ The *start macro* is always executed when the planning table is called.

▶ The *default macro* is always executed when the planning is regenerated (e.g., when you press **Enter**) as well as when you open or save the plan.

▶ A *level change macro* is always executed during drill-down or drill-up.

▶ The *end macro* is executed immediately before the data is saved.

If a macro is not set to be executed automatically, it can be executed directly in the interactive planning or the mass processing.

3.6   Summary

The configuration of the Demand Planning is an important factor for a successful implementation of the system. You decide what characteristics and key figures you use for the Demand Planning and where you want to save them. You then decide with what view your users are to work in the Demand Planning. Moreover, you give your users help tools in the form of intelligent planning books and advanced macros, in order to design the planning in as simple and effective a way as possible. Now that you are familiar with these basic configurations of the Demand Planning with SAP APO, we will describe their implementation in detail in the next chapter.

This chapter will focus on the application of demand planning. This includes, specifically, basic operational business principles, the functions of demand planning with SAP Advanced Planner and Optimizer (SAP APO), an explanation of the individual forecasting techniques and their error level, and a procedure for selecting the correct forecasting method.

4 Demand Planning with SAP APO-DP — Implementation

Once the planning environment of the demand planning has been configured and all necessary planning books and data views have been created, you can now perform the demand planning as the demand planner (see Section 4.1). Using the books, views, and the standard tools of the component SAP Advanced Planner and Optimizer-Demand Planning (APO-DP), you can create a forecast for different characteristics combinations (e.g., customers, customer groups, customer/product combinations, or simply for all products) based on the historical data from the InfoCubes (see Section 4.2). This can be executed both interactively and in the background. Lastly, you can then use analysis tools to check the quality of the forecast (see Section 4.3) and, if required, make corrections.

SAP APO-DP supports you here with many different tools and functions. What is most important here for the demand planning are the following:

▶ **Lifecycle Planning**
This allows you to schedule new products more easily or consider the special lifecycle of products (see Section 4.4).

▶ **Promotion Planning**
This allows you to schedule promotions and special events separately, first to keep an overview and then to be able to include particular promotions and events individually in the demand planning (see Section 4.5).

▶ **Demand Planning BOMs**
Demand planning BOMs make it easier for you to schedule promotion packs, generic articles, or product combinations. In this way, the multi-

stage nature (i.e., different levels during the planning cycle) of specific articles and products can be mapped automatically.

▸ **Collaborative Demand Planning**
You can also decide whether foreign subsidiaries or even customers can adjust their plans themselves using an Internet planning book. As the demand planner, you remain in full control here and, if you want to, you can override the planning of the external users at any time (see Section 4.6).

Once you have finalized the forecast, it must be passed on to the subsequent benefit areas. To do this, you can release the result of the demand planning to the Supply Network Planning in SAP APO (see Section 4.8). This concludes the demand planning process. In the next section, we will discuss the individual steps for performing a demand planning in detail.

4.1   Creating a Demand Forecast

You can perform the demand planning online in the interactive planning or offline in the background. The scheduling of the demand planning (i.e., online or offline) depends to a very large degree on the particular company and its process. We generally recommend that you run the demand planning in the background. As the demand planner, you should then intervene manually in the demand planning on the basis of alerts and exception situations. To understand what the background processing does, and to show the demand planner's options for manual planning, we will primarily focus on the interactive planning at this point. The functions of the different forecasting methods are described in Section 4.2.

4.1.1   Interactive Demand Planning

The interactive demand planning is the planning tool for the demand planner. Here the planner accesses the actual data, performs various functions, and changes the planned data manually at any time if necessary. You enter the interactive planning through the SAP menu path **Advanced Planning & Optimization • Demand Planning • Planning • Demand Planning interactive** (see Figure 4.1).

The interactive demand planning is the tool that enables you to directly view and edit planning data. The initial screen shows the two main components: the selection area and the work area.

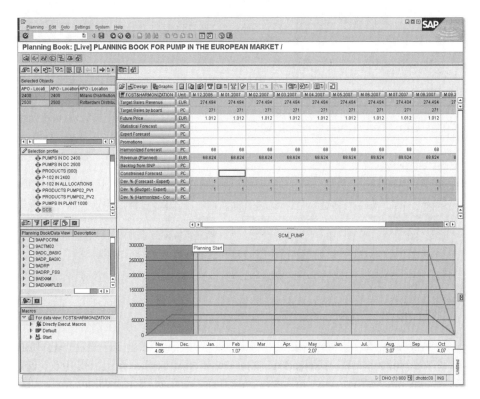

Figure 4.1 Interactive Demand Planning, Initial Screen

Selection Area (Selector)

The selection area (which is also referred to as the "selector") is the most important tool for searching, sorting, and organizing information. It is located to the left of Figure 4.1 and includes the following areas:

▶ **InfoObjects**
The InfoObjects area (see Figure 4.2) shows all characteristic values for which data can be planned and queried. InfoObjects in the demand planning are, for example, particular products, brands, sales organizations and customers. You can select the data for the InfoObjects area by opening the shuffler (see the next bullet point) and making a selection, or by choosing an existing selection from the selection profile.

▶ **Shuffler**
The shuffler (see Figure 4.3) is the window in which you choose the InfoObjects to be planned. Here you want to display, for example, all products in the APO—Planning Version 000 that belong to APO—Location 2500.

Figure 4.2 Selection Area "InfoObjects"

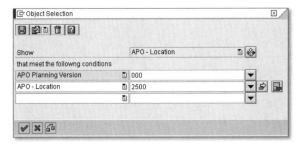

Figure 4.3 Selection Areas "Shuffler"

You can select several values of a characteristic with the standard function for multiple object selection. The lowest row is the most detailed level. This means that you can select only those characteristics values for which the previous selection criteria apply.

▶ **Selection Profile**
The selection profile (see Figure 4.4) shows the selection IDs with which the planner is currently working. The selection profile enables you to quickly access frequently used selections. If you want to add new selection IDs to the selection profile, click on the title bar **Selection profile**.

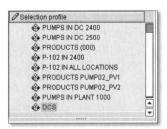

Figure 4.4 Selection Areas "Selection Profile"

▶ **Data Views**
In the Data View area (see Figure 4.5), you select your planning books and data views.

You can set a filter for the available planning books and views. In the demand planning, the display in the area of the data views depends on how the Customizing activity **Maintain Assignment User to Planning Book** has been configured. This activity allows you to set a standard planning book and view for a particular planner and to determine whether the planner can access all available planning books and views or only those that are his own. If the planner can display all available planning books, then he has access both to the books created for the demand planning and to those for Supply Network Planning.

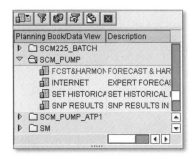

Figure 4.5 Selection Areas "Data Views"

▶ **Components**

The area of the components (see Figure 4.6) shows macros that are active both for all data views in this planning book and also for this data view.

Figure 4.6 Selection Area "Components"

Work Area

The work area is used for display and planning purposes. It is to the right of the screen (see Figure 4.1). Its elements are a **table** (also called a "grid") and a **graphic**. Only the table is displayed by default.

The work area has a pushbutton toolbar with symbols for various functions (see Figure 4.7).

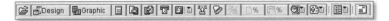

Figure 4.7 Pushbutton Toolbar for the Interactive Demand Planning, Detail from Figure 4.1

With this toolbar, you can:

▶ Change graphics settings

▶ Execute distribution functions

▶ Download data into an MS Excel Table or upload it from an MS Excel table

▶ Send the planning to another user by email

▶ Open the Alert Monitor

▶ Manage notes

▶ Show characteristics hierarchies

▶ Restrict the key performance indicator view

▶ Execute macros

The work area is divided into two different views: the standard view, with which the planner enters the planning each time, and the forecast view, with which the specific settings and information for the forecast are shown. We will present these views and others from the forecast area below.

Standard Views
In addition to the data views created by your company, you can work in one or more of the following standard SAP views. In the planning book, you can define the standard views that should be available to the demand planner.

Forecast View
If you select **Execute forecast**, an automatic forecast is performed immediately and you will reach the forecast view (see Figure 4.8).

To perform the forecast, the system uses either the model you have set up in the univariate forecast profile, or—if you have already performed the forecast for this selection ID—the model you last used in connection with this selection ID.

Once the forecast results are output at the top of the screen, you can analyze them using the various tabs in the lower part of the screen.

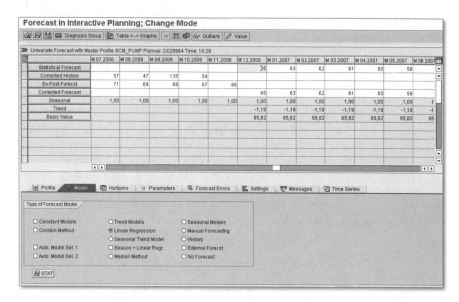

Figure 4.8 Forecast Views

If necessary, you can change the forecast profile, forecasting tehchnique, planning horizon, forecast parameters, or forecast settings. Which forecast parameters you can set depends on the forecasting technique. All forecasting techniques can be used (see Section 4.2).

Multiple Linear Regression (MLR) View

If you choose **Execute MLR forecast**, an automatic forecast is performed immediately. You reach the MLR forecast view.

If no profile has yet been assigned to this selection, the system of the forecast is based on the MLR profile that has been defined for this planning area.

Once the forecast results are output, you can use the buttons of the pushbutton toolbar to display the forecast messages and the alert situation and check the MLR Measures of Fit. The MLR Measures of Fit are defined by the parameter limits in the diagnosis group. While you cannot change the SAP diagnosis group, nevertheless, by creating your own parameter group, you can use different MLR limits. You can also display or hide the MLR parameters in the table.

Combined View

If you choose **combined forecast**, the system runs the forecast based on the combined profile.

As soon as the forecast results appear, you can display the forecast messages with the buttons on the pushbutton toolbar. You can also see what forecast profile has just been used, change the corresponding profile, or select a different profile.

Promotion Planning View

If you choose **Execute promotion planning**, the system jumps to the promotion planning. You will reach the promotion planning view (see Figure 4.9).

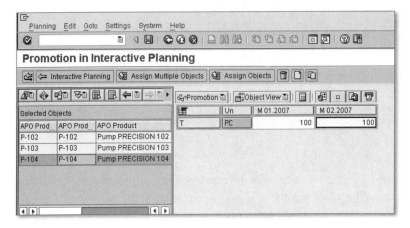

Figure 4.9 Promotion Planning View

Here you create promotions and edit them. Once you have saved the promotion, you return to the interactive planning by clicking on **Interactive Planning**.

4.1.2 Carrying Out Demand Planning (Sample Case)

Having introduced you to the composition of the interactive demand planning in the previous section, we would now like to discuss how to actually conduct the planning using a sample case.

The planner will first use the Supply Chain Cockpit to get an overview of the planning situation. He will then trigger an automatic forecast manually. Next, he will publish it to a business partner, who then can change his forecast. Furthermore, a promotion is also created, and the quality of the demand planning is finally analyzed. At the end of this planning, the result is passed on to the Supply Network Planning (SNP).

Supply Chain Cockpit

At the beginning of the demand planning, the planner can get an overview of the current state of the supply chain in the Supply Chain Cockpit. The Supply Chain Cockpit acts as the highest planning level, which also covers other planning areas such as manufacturing, requirements, sales and transport. With this tool, the planner can do the following:

▶ Supervise the entire supply chain in detail. Use the Cockpit to make it easier to handle large and complex supply chains. Because individual work areas are created, several planners can work on different parts of the supply chain at the same time.

▶ Reduce the many relationships between the components within the supply chain.

▶ Call up information from SAP APO using queries and thus simplify the planning function. For example, an APO query allows you to view the transport quantities aggregated by arrival time for a specific transportation lane.

▶ Measure the supply chain performance using key performance indicators (KPIs), which provide you with feedback on the actual performance. As a planner, you can follow the supply chain performance from the Cockpit in all areas—from the replenishment lead time through to the adherence to stock. You can therefore, for example, measure the resource efficiency for one of the plants or the service level of one of the suppliers.

▶ React quickly and accurately to new developments.

▶ Preserve the flexibility of the decision-making process.

To enter the Cockpit, choose **Supply Chain Monitoring • Supply Chain Cockpit** in the menu. Then, select the supply chain model and the planning version in which you want to work. The Supply Chain Cockpit screen is displayed (see Figure 4.10).

The Supply Chain Cockpit screen is divided into the following areas:

▶ The top-left area consists of a graphic interface that represents your current model.

▶ The top-center area is the monitor for some objects of your work area.

▶ The top-right area is the monitor for applications. It displays the alerts from the applications, if there are any.

- ▶ Various buttons are available in the central area with which you can select the objects for the work area.
- ▶ The bottom area consists of a tree overview containing all objects of the work area.

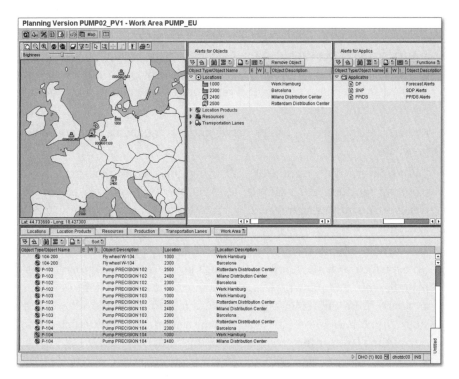

Figure 4.10 Supply Chain Cockpit

As a planner, you can now display the most important products (e.g., all A-products) and check the master data from here or jump directly into the requirement and stock list. With the context menu (right mouse button), you can view stock information on products or capacity evaluations for resources. You can also select alerts in your supply chain and jump directly into an application in order to eliminate the errors (e.g., stock shortages).

Outlier Corrections

As a planner, you want to check the historical data before you run a forecast. To do this, you double-click to go directly from the Supply Chain Cockpit into the interactive demand planning and select your products there. In Figure 4.11, you can see that on the one hand, the target sales defined by management are higher than the historical target sales. The targets from management have therefore risen by 10%. On the other hand, you can see that the historical sales in the last two years show an outlier in the month of September, in both cases. Outliers can distort the forecast results. You know that in September for both of the last two years there has been a special sale of old models. However, this is not planned, as yet, for this year. You must therefore now correct this outlier in the historical data before you perform the automatic forecast. To correct the outlier, you execute a previously defined macro (see Section 3.5) that corrects all outliers with a sales value of over 200 ST to the value of 200 ST. Figure 4.12 illustrates the results.

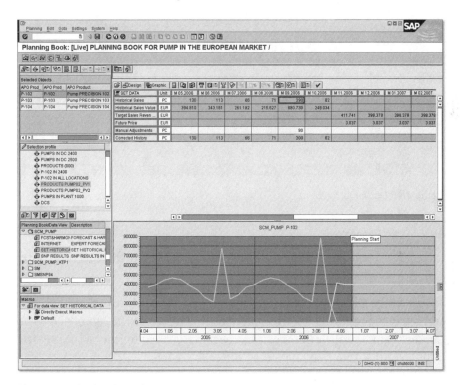

Figure 4.11 Outlier Control

In the **Manual Adjustments** row, the value has now been entered by which the row **Corrected History** is to be reduced. The **Corrected History** row provides the basis for the automatic forecasting in our case study.

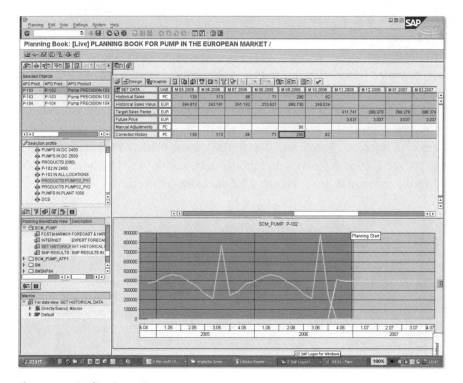

Figure 4.12 Outlier Correction

Automatic Forecast

Once you have corrected the historical data, you can run the automatic forecast.

Switch to the planning book from where you want to perform the forecast and select the products for which a forecast is to be run. In Figure 4.13, you can see that no statistical forecast has been performed for the product P-103 in the months from May 2006 (i.e., the cells are empty).

Now, click on the **Run Forecast** button.

Analyzing the Forecast

In the **Forecast** view (see Figure 4.14), you can now analyze the results of the forecast in detail.

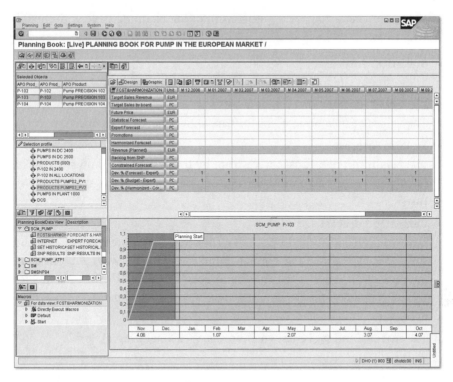

Figure 4.13 Automatic Forecast—Before It Is Run

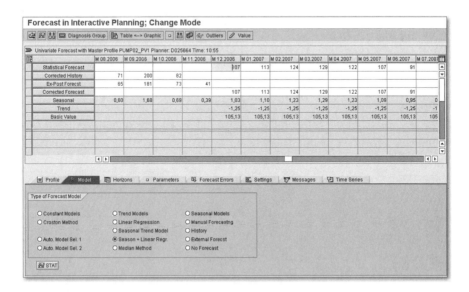

Figure 4.14 Automatic Forecast—Forecast View

In the upper chart, you see a special form of the planning table with the following rows:

▶ **Statistical Forecast**
The result of the forecast appears here.

▶ **Corrected History**
The values of the corrected history are shown here for comparison.

▶ **Ex-Post Forecast**
The results of the ex-post forecast run by the system are shown here. The ex-post forecast is an option for checking the quality of the statistical forecast.

▶ **Corrected Forecast**
Here you can adjust the forecast determined by the system once again and save it in a special key performance indicator. In this way, you can compare the corrected forecast and the forecast calculated by the system with the actual values and evaluate the quality of the adjustments.

▶ **Seasonal**
The seasonal index shows whether it is a seasonal progression.

▶ **Trend**
The trend value indicates whether a trend can be recorded in the forecast.

▶ **Basic Value**
The basic value shows the basic value of the forecast, which is determined by the ALPHA factor.

You can display more information on the forecast in the lower screen area of this forecast view. See the following tabs:

▶ **Profile**
Here you assign the selection an additional profile, or save the current settings as a forecast profile (see Figure 4.15).

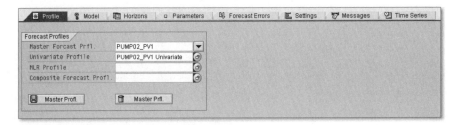

Figure 4.15 Forecast View, "Profile" Tab

▸ **Model**

Here you can see which forecast model has been chosen for the forecast, and you can choose a different type of model here (see Figure 4.16).

Figure 4.16 Forecast View, "Model" Tab

▸ **Horizons**

You can change the forecast and history horizons (see Figure 4.17).

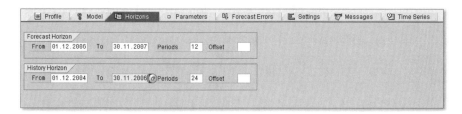

Figure 4.17 Forecast View, "Horizons" Tab

▸ **Parameters**

Here you can make the settings for the individual forecast procedures (see Figure 4.18). The settings that are possible here vary from model to model. You will find details in the F1 Help for the individual fields.

Figure 4.18 Forecast View, "Parameters" Tab

▶ **Forecast Errors**

Here you can see the chosen forecast error dimensions based on the ex-post forecast (see Figure 4.19). Note that some forecasting techniques do not calculate any ex-post forecasts and therefore cannot determine any forecast errors.

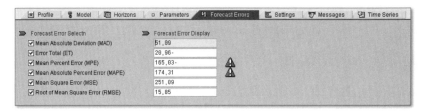

Figure 4.19 Forecast View, "Forecast Errors" Tab

▶ **Settings**

Here you can choose various options, e.g., outlier correction and LIKE profile. These settings (see Figure 4.20) don't depend on the selected forecast model.

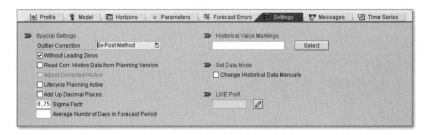

Figure 4.20 Forecast View, "Settings" Tab

▶ **Messages**

The system shows various forecast messages indicating the progress of the forecast while compiling it (see Figure 4.21).

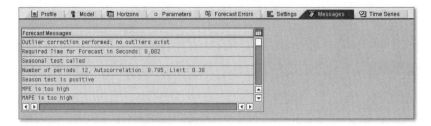

Figure 4.21 Forecast View, "Messages" Tab

▶ **Time Series**

On the tab shown in Figure 4.22, you can see the time series, which can be used as

▶ Phase-in/phase-out profiles

▶ Trend damping profiles

▶ Weighting groups

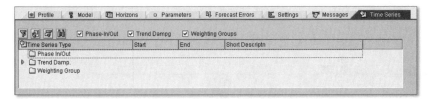

Figure 4.22 Forecast View, "Time Series" Tab

You can display individual profiles by double-clicking on the desired profile, or edit profiles from the context menu in each case.

Furthermore, from this forecast view, you can also start the forecast comparison using the **Forecast Comparison** button (see Figure 4.23).

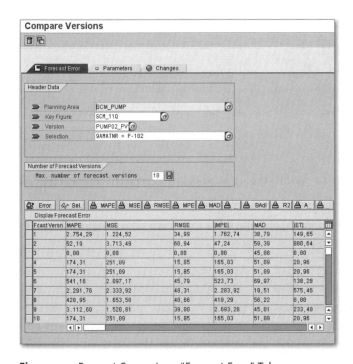

Figure 4.23 Forecast Comparison, "Forecast Error" Tab

Here you can compare the various forecast errors for different forecasts that you, as the planner, have performed and stored simulatively, in order to manually find the best forecast. You can also automate this comparison of forecasts in the forecasting models for the automatic model selection and the combined forecasts.

You can use the **Parameters** tab to compare the parameters from the simulative forecast runs with each other (see Figure 4.24).

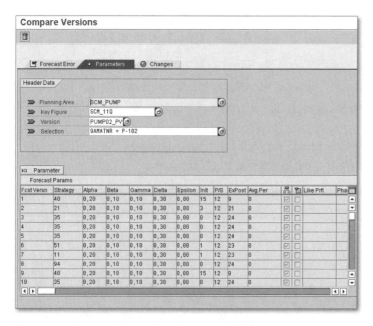

Figure 4.24 Forecast Comparison, "Parameters" Tab

Forecast Result

You can now view the result of the forecast in the interactive planning book (see Figure 4.25).

You can see that the periods as from May 2006 are now filled with values from the statistical forecast.

Now that you have performed the forecast manually, you should obtain an overview of the result by looking at a comparison of the key performance indicators: **Statistical Forecast**, the **Expert Forecast**, and their delta in % for all products and their locations. To do this, select the corresponding key performance indicators using the buttons from Figure 4.26 and sort the planning book using the pivot sorting.

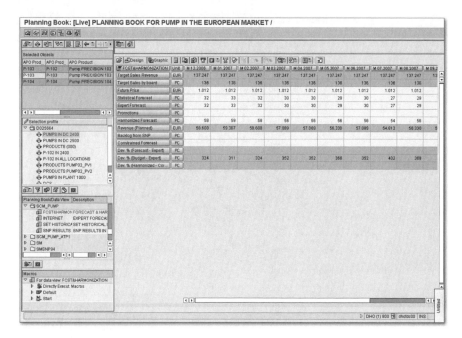

Figure 4.25 Automatic Forecast—After It Is Run

Figure 4.26 Pushbutton Toolbar for Selecting Key Performance Indicators and Characteristics

The result you get is the view shown in Figure 4.27.

Notes Management

In this example, you'll notice that the planner wants to add a note for the expert forecast for the product P-104 in the month of April. You now know that the Sales department plan a promotion here (see note in Figure 4.28) and can store this information as a note for the other persons involved in the planning process. To do this, select the corresponding field in which the note is to be stored and click on the **Create Note** button. A new screen appears at the bottom where you can enter and save your note (see Figure 4.28).

Every subsequent planner can easily ensure that a note has been entered, thanks to an icon in the relevant row (see Figure 4.29).

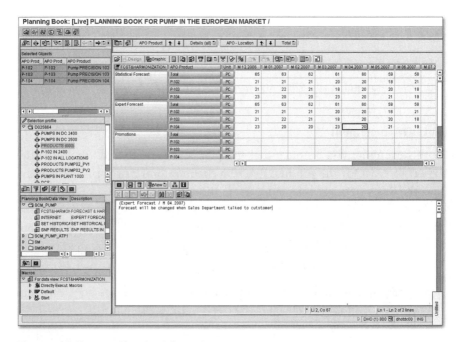

Figure 4.27 KPI Comparison by APO Location and APO Product

Figure 4.28 Notes as Planning Information

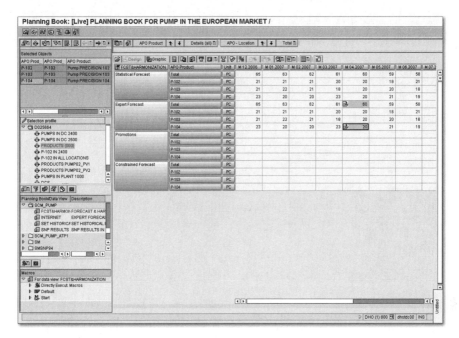

Figure 4.29 Note Icon in the Planning Book

Collaborative Demand Planning

Once you have run and checked the forecast, in the event of a previously agreed on collaborative demand planning, you can notify your business partner (here: the customer) of the result by email, so that she can check the forecast for her requirements and change them if necessary. You can send the email directly from the planning book using the **Customer mail ...** button (see Figure 4.30).

The customers receive the email in their inbox (see Figure 4.31).

Here, the customer is asked to confirm the joint demand plan or to amend it if necessary. The customer can now simply click on the link in the email and is then brought automatically through an Internet planning book into the SAP APO system of the demand planner (see Figure 4.32).

Once the customer has logged on with his username and password, this preset planning book will be displayed with the selection profiles activated for that customer. In this case, the customer can now change the expert forecast, for example, for the months of January and February. Here once again, the customer can explain this change in a note and store it in a way that is visible to the demand planner.

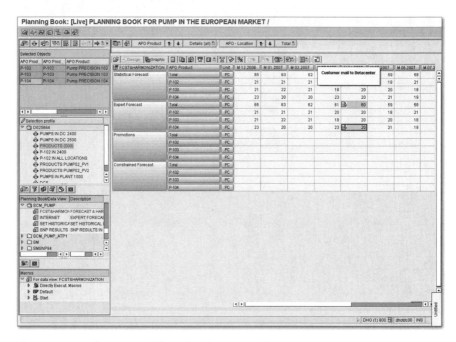

Figure 4.30 Sending an Email from the Planning Book

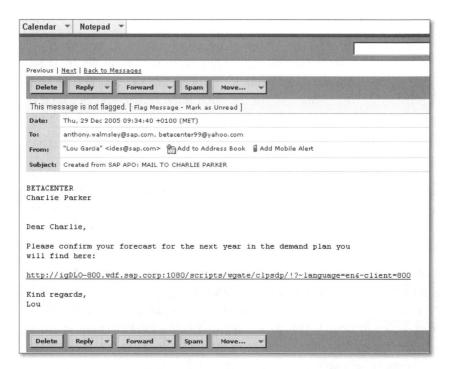

Figure 4.31 Email for Collaborative Demand Planning

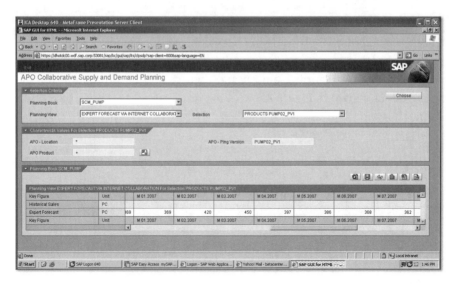

Figure 4.32 Collaborative Demand Planning

Once the customer has saved his changes, the change is immediately visible for the demand planner in his planning book (see Figure 4.33).

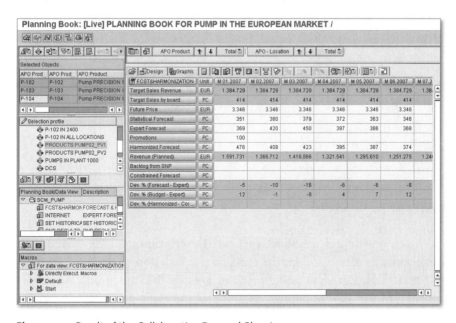

Figure 4.33 Result of the Collaborative Demand Planning

Promotion Planning

Once the collaborative planning has been completed, you must also schedule a promotion that is planned by the sales and marketing departments. Click on the **Promotion Planning** button and then create the promotion for the spring fair as shown in Figure 4.34.

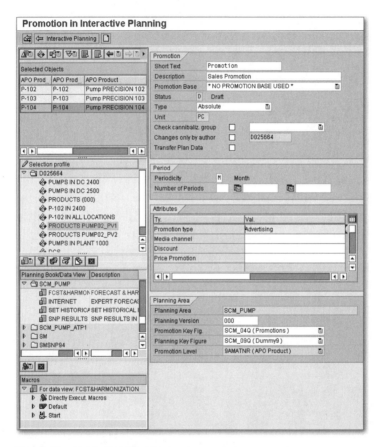

Figure 4.34 Promotion Planning

First, you must enter the **Short Text**, the **Description**, and the **Period**. You can optionally also maintain the remaining promotion attributes. You must also make an assignment to the planning area, so that the promotion can be assigned to the right planning version and the right planning key performance indicator. Once the promotion has been created, you must enter the quantity planned in the promotion (absolute or percentage) and assign the quantity to the relevant products (see Figure 4.35).

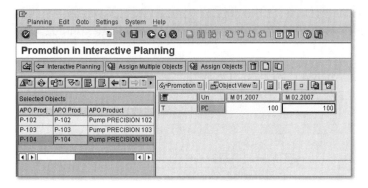

Figure 4.35 Assigning the Promotion

By selecting the **Interactive Planning** button, you can now jump back into the interactive demand planning, where you will see the scheduled promotion in the **Promotions** key performance indicator (see Figure 4.36).

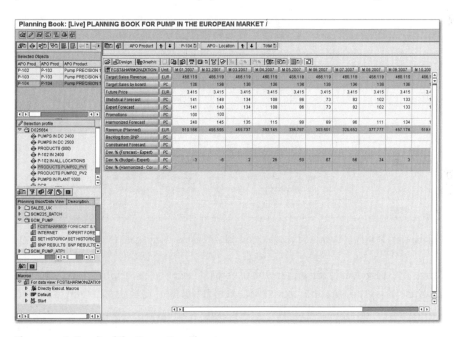

Figure 4.36 Result of the Promotion Planning

Once you have created the promotions and scheduled them accordingly, you can analyze the planning results again using the Business Explorer Analyzer (BEx Analyzer), before you release them to the Supply Network Planning. To call the BEx Analyzer, start transaction RRMX. To avoid having to navigate in the BEx Analyzer and search for the queries yourself, you can create a standard query as a favorite in the SAP Easy Access menu of the SAP Supply Chain Management (SAP SCM).

By calling the BEx Analyzer, you can display the aggregated view for all products (see Figure 4.37).

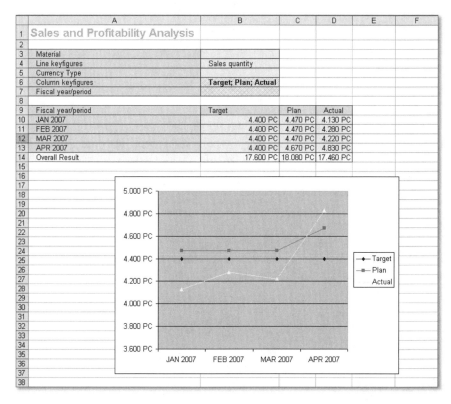

Figure 4.37 Planning Data Analysis with the BEx Analyzer (Aggregated View)

Since the BEx Analyzer generally uses MS Excel as its application, you can also use the graphic tools from MS Excel here. You can also display detailed information using the drill-down function (see Figure 4.38).

	A	B	C	D	E	F
1	Plan/Actual Comparison: Sales Quantity					
2						
3	Calendar Year/Month					
4	Sales Organization					
5	Division					
6	Material Group					
7	Sold-to party					
8	Structure					
9	Material					
10						
11	Material	Sales Organization	Qty in base UM	DPlan: quantity	Variance	Variance (%)
12	P-102	2400	4.476 PC		4.476 PC	
13		2500	5.334 PC		5.334 PC	
14		Result	9.810 PC		9.810 PC	
15	P-103	2400	3.601 PC		3.601 PC	
16		2500	3.965 PC		3.965 PC	
17		Result	7.566 PC		7.566 PC	
18	P-104	2400	4.917 PC		4.917 PC	
19		2500	5.698 PC		5.698 PC	
20		Result	10.615 PC		10.615 PC	
21	P-501	1000	186 PC		186 PC	
22		Result	186 PC		186 PC	
23	P182	1020	17.298 L		17.298 L	
24		Result	17.298 L		17.298 L	
25	P182-A	1020	48 CAN		48 CAN	
26		Result	48 CAN		48 CAN	
27	P192	1020	60 L		60 L	
28		Result	60 L		60 L	
29	R-1180	1000	1.084 PC		1.084 PC	
30		Result	1.084 PC		1.084 PC	
31	Overall Result		MIX		MIX	

Figure 4.38 Planning Data Analysis with the BEx Analyzer (Detail View)

4.2 Forecasts

There are many different forecasting procedures—each with its advantages and disadvantages—the most important of which are described below.

4.2.1 Aggregation and Disaggregation

Forecasts with SAP APO can be performed on any level. Depending on the level on which you want to perform a forecast, data is automatically aggregated or disaggregated.

Aggregation describes the function with which key performance indicator values at the lowest detail level are automatically totaled at runtime and are displayed or scheduled at a higher level. For example, if you forecast the requirement for a region in the interactive planning table, you'll see the requirement forecast for the various sales channels, product families, brands, and customers of the corresponding region that the system has added up.

Disaggregation describes the function that automatically details a key performance indicator value, which is located at a higher level at the lowest level. For example, if you forecast the requirement for a particular region, the system immediately breaks down this value by the various sales channels, product families, brands, and customers in this region.

Aggregation and disaggregation guarantee an integrated planning approach within your company's entire organization. The total of the details at the lowest level always corresponds to the total value at the higher level. Key performance indicator values are always saved at the lowest detail level. If there are aggregates, the data is also saved at the aggregate level.

If you perform the forecast at a high level, the historical data will be automatically aggregated (see Figure 4.39). The forecast results you receive are therefore different if the forecast is created at a high level, and the results are then disaggregated at the detail level from the results that are achieved at the detail level when the forecast is performed.

When you run the forecast in the background, you define the aggregation level in the mass-processing job. When designing your planning process, you must consider what aggregation level makes sense from a forecast point of view, for example, whether the forecast is to be created for individual products, product families, or customer-specific requirements.

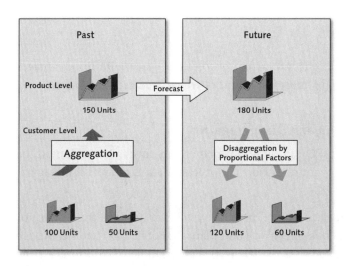

Figure 4.39 Automatic Aggregation of Historical Data (Source: SAP)

The aggregation and disaggregation of each key performance indicator depends on its calculation method and its time-based disaggregation type. While the calculation type defines the calculation basis for the disaggregation, the type of time-based disaggregation defines how planned data is disaggregated over time.

The following calculation types can be selected for the key performance indicator aggregation:

▶ **"S"—Pro Rata**
This calculation type is the proportional disaggregation. How this happens depends on whether you create or change the demand plan:

  ▶ If you create data on an aggregate level, the data is evenly distributed on the lowest detail level.

  ▶ If you change the data on an aggregate level, the values on the detail level change in such a way that each value shows the same percentage portion of the aggregated value as before.

▶ **"P"—Based on a Different Key Performance Indicator**
The data is distributed on the lowest detail level according to the portions that can be derived from the values of a different key performance indicator. For example, you can transfer the pro-rata distribution of the key performance indicator **Baseline/statistical forecast** for the key performance indicator **Manual correction**. Note, however, that pro-rata disaggregation is run if there are no values for the key performance indicator **Baseline/statistical forecast**.

If you enter "P", you must also specify the key performance indicator according to which the disaggregation is to run. You enter this key performance indicator in the **Time-Based Disaggreg.** field (see Figure 4.40).

▶ **"A"—(Key Figure) Average**
The average of the key figure values on the next-lowest aggregation level is shown as the result at runtime. You use this option for key figures to show percentage values (e.g., percentage difference between this year's forecast and last year's forecast) or to map sales prices (e.g., sales price per unit). If you input a value on an aggregation level, the system disaggregates the value by copying it into the details on the bottom level.

▶ **"D"—Average at the Lowest Detail Level**
Unlike the calculation type A, here the system uses the values at the most detailed level to form the average. This is the level for which a single value is assigned to each characteristic. Different numerical values may arise from this in comparison with calculation type A. The disaggregation is not different than that for calculation type A.

Because both average calculation types are generally used for descriptive purposes, for example, price per unit, you primarily use them with the time-based aggregation type N. However, if you are using the time-based aggregation/disaggregation, you may notice slight differences between calculation type A and calculation type B because of rounding.

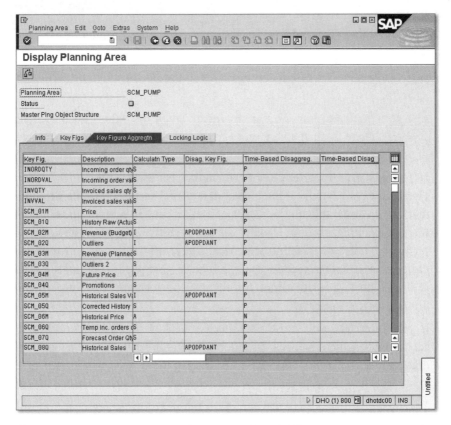

Figure 4.40 Key Figure Aggregation, Key Figures "P" and "N"

▶ **"N"—No Disaggregation**
Since disaggregation affects performance, you should ensure that you use this option for text lines, auxiliary rows, and other lines that don't have to be disaggregated.

▶ **"I"—Pro-Rata; If Initial: Based on a Different Key Performance Indicator**
If you create the data on an aggregate level, the data on the lowest detail level will be distributed according to the shares that can be derived from the values of another key performance indicator. For example, you can transfer the pro-rata distribution of the key performance indicator **Baseline/statistical forecast** for the key performance indicator **Manual correction**. If there is no value for the basic key figure, the values will be evenly disaggregated.

If you change the data on an aggregate level, the values on the detail level change in such as way that each value shows the same percentage portion of the aggregated value as before.

The following types of time-based disaggregation are available:

▶ **"P" — Proportional Distribution**
The data is distributed over time in such a way that the individual key fig-ure values in the smallest storage buckets proportionately display the same values as they did previously in the aggregate period.

If the key figure values prior to the distribution were zero, for example, and if a time stream ID is part of the storage buckets profile definition, then the system checks whether there are time-based weighting factors for this time stream. If there are, the data is distributed according to the time-based weighting factors of the time stream. If there are no factors present, the data is evenly distributed across the individual memory periods.

▶ **"E" — Equal Distribution**
The data is distributed equally onto the individual memory periods. This option is available only for key performance indicators that have not been defined as "firmable" in the Administrator Workbench (see Section 3.2.4).

▶ **"N" — No Time Distribution**
The value in the planning period is copied into the memory period, for example, a planned value of 100 Euro is copied for the month of June into the individual memory periods June 1–2, June 5–9, June 12–16, June 19–23 and June 26–30. If you display the planned value for June at runt-ime, the system will show the average of the memory periods. This option is only available for key performance indicators that have not been defined as firmable in the Administrator Workbench (see Section 3.2.4).

▶ **"K" — Based on a Different Key Performance Indicator**
This option essentially corresponds to the calculation type "P — Propor-tional distribution." The data is distributed on the lowest detail level according to the portions that can be derived from the values of a different key performance indicator. For example, you can transfer the pro-rata dis-tribution of the key performance indicator **Baseline/statistical forecast** for the key performance indicator **Manual correction**. Note, however, that no disaggregation is run if there are no values for the key perfor-mance indicator **Baseline/statistical forecast**. If you enter "K", you must also specify the key performance indicator on this screen according to which the disaggregation is to run. You enter this key performance indica-tor in the neighboring field **Disaggregation Key Figure**.

▶ **"L" — Reading: Value from Last Period; Write: No Distribution**
This aggregation type is intended for time series in Supply Network Plan-ning. If you aggregate in longer periods based on shorter periods (e.g.,

weeks or months), the system copies the value from the last period into the longer period. Alternatively, if you aggregate in shorter periods based on longer periods, the value is copied into all smaller periods.

4.2.2 Introduction to the Different Forecasting Techniques

For demand planners who use statistical forecasting techniques, it is very important to understand these mathematical forecasting methods and to know what they can and cannot be used for. In this chapter, we will therefore briefly describe the forecasting procedures, so that even readers who aren't mathematics experts can understand them. In addition to the brief description of the forecasting techniques, we will also explain how you can use these methods and provide some examples.

Basically, we can distinguish between qualitative and quantitative forecasting methods.

Qualitative Forecasting Techniques

Qualitative forecasting techniques are based on knowledge, experience, and instinct, and are applied in the absence of quantitative data. Some possible models are the Delphi method, expert surveys, and the scenario method. Since the Delphi method is the best-known method used, we will introduce it briefly below.

It is best used with long-term developments, the procurement of investment goods, or long-range forecasts. In these areas, qualitative methods have an advantage over quantitative methods. The procedure is as follows:

1. Selection of the forecast problem
2. Selection of staff for processing the problem
3. Individual interviews with the participants
4. Collecting the information
5. Anonymous evaluation of participants' answers
6. Written comment by experts on their own judgment as compared to that of the group
7. Distribution of (anonymous) results and comments
8. Step 3 is repeated ; forecast after three complete rounds with homogeneous answers

Quantitative Forecasting Techniques

Quantitative forecasting techniques are based on mathematical procedures (e.g., trend, time series analysis, indicator forecasts, and exponential smoothing) and have been used since the 1950s for business forecasts as well as for economic purposes (e.g., unemployment figures).

Their use in software modules enables the creation of forecasts for many different items within just a few seconds. The *Demand Planning* component in SAP APO also contains many statistical forecasting techniques and can be enhanced with additional customized forecast models without any problem.

Each of the quantitative methods tries to integrate historical key figures of a product into the forecast for future figures. However, there are two methods that are based on different foundations: the time series analysis and causal models.

Time Series Analysis (univariate forecasting technique)

The *time series analysis* is based on the assumption that demand follows a specific pattern. A forecasting technique is therefore intended to provide an estimate for that pattern by using historical observations. The forecasts can then be calculated based on this estimated pattern. The advantage of these methods is that they require only historical observations of the demand.

Univariate forecasts can be divided into the following types of time series progression:

▶ **Constant demand**
The demand deviates only slightly from a stable average value.

▶ **Trend demand**
The demand decreases or increases continuously over a longer period of time, with occasional fluctuations.

▶ **Seasonal demand**
Periodically recurring requirement peaks and slumps deviate substantially from a stable average value.

▶ **Seasonal trend demand**
Periodically recurring requirement peaks and slumps, however, with a constantly rising or falling average value.

▶ **Intermittent demand**
The demand is irregular.

▶ **No change compared to the previous year**
No forecast is carried out; instead, the system uses the actual data from the previous year.

These time series patterns are shown graphically in Figure 4.41.

These five time series patterns can be used for most forecasting models. In a *constant pattern*, the observed values fluctuate around a fixed value, whereas a *trend-like* or *seasonal trend pattern* is assumed to be based on a linear trend that rises or falls over a period of several years. In addition, the time series model with constant pattern can be regarded as a special case of the trend-like pattern in which the gradient of the trend line equals zero. The *seasonal pattern* is typical of everyday business where a season often corresponds to a calendar year. The degree of seasonal fluctuations frequently represents a multiplication of the trend level. An example of this seasonal demand is the pre-Christmas business that often causes December sales to increase by 20 % compared to the long-term trend. The *intermittent pattern*, on the other hand, is not very typical. It is characterized by the fact that only a few periods show values greater than zero.

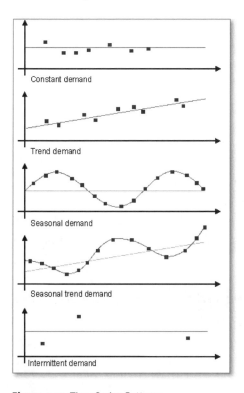

Figure 4.41 Time Series Patterns

Causal Models

Causal models are the second method for quantitative statistical forecasting. Causal models are based on the assumption that demand is determined by several known factors and by other factors that can be estimated. For example, the demand for ice cream depends on the temperature on a specific day. For this reason, the temperature is a so-called *main indicator* of the demand for ice cream. If a sufficient number of observations of the demand and the temperature are available, the underlying model can be estimated.

Because historical demand figures and a time series with indicators are required to estimate the parameters in causal models, the data quantity that is required is substantially bigger than it is for a time series analysis. Simple time series models can then generate better forecasts than complex causal models if stochastic (i.e., forecast-based) fluctuations are interpreted as "structures" and thus a systematic error creeps into the model. Therefore, you must pay special attention to the analysis and, if necessary, to the correction of the data basis when using causal models. But basically, we can say that causal models provide a more accurate forecast than time series models if a sufficient amount of historical data exists and the models are correctly used.

Naive Models

There are also the so-called *naïve models*, which do not take into account any of the historical data and calculate the forecast solely based on a basic value and a trend value.

Composite Forecast

The composite forecast is another forecast procedure. This is actually not another separate method but rather a combination of the methods described above, for instance of time series and causal models. Modern forecasting tools such as SAP APO enable you to create several forecasts simultaneously and to then generate a composite forecast from these individual forecasts. In this context, you can establish average values, but you can also select different weighting factors (e.g., 20 % time series analysis and 80 % causal model).

4.2.3   Quantitative Forecasting Techniques in Detail

Manual Forecasts (Strategy 70)

Definition

This forecasting strategy, which is also referred to as a manual or naïve forecast, enables you to manually input the basic value, trend value, trend dampening profile and/or seasonal indices in the interactive demand planning. Figure 4.42 illustrates a typical manual forecast in the image on the left. On the bottom right, the manual forecast shows a trend dampening of 5 %.

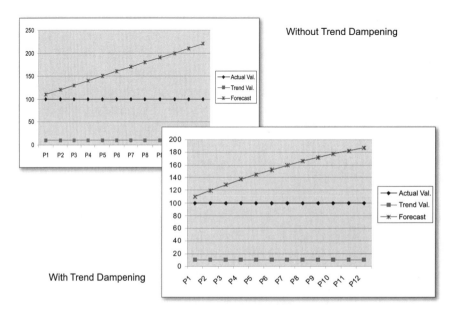

Figure 4.42 Manual Forecast with and without Trend Dampening

Application

These models are suited to products without a history, for instance, products that are newly introduced to the market. Nevertheless, to produce a successful model, you must be in a position to predict the trend value fairly accurately. The forecast is not calculated on the basis of historical values; rather, it is based on a basic value to be specified, and a trend value. Therefore, you should not use this model with mass data because the maintenance effort would be too high if you wanted to assign different basic and trend values for each individual product.

Copying Historical Data (Strategy 60)

Definition

Choose this method if the demand does not change and you want to use the least labor-intensive strategy or that which least affects the performance. In this case, there is no forecast calculation. Instead, the historical data from the previous year is copied as new planned values.

Application

This method can be used for products for which no changes to the demand pattern are anticipated, when compared to the previous year.

Moving Average Model (Strategy 13)

Definition

This strategy calculates the average of the time series values within a historical timeframe. The moving average model is used to exclude irregularities within a time series. As all historical data is equally weighted with the factor 1/n, it takes precisely n periods for the forecast to adapt to a possible level change. The accuracy of the forecast increases proportionately with the length of the time series you consider as the random deviations lose their significance accordingly. The moving average formula is displayed in Figure 4.43.

$$M = \frac{\sum\limits_{t=1}^{n} V(t)}{n}$$

Figure 4.43 Moving Average Formula

Application

The simple moving average model is used for products with a stable demand, that is, for time series that don't show a trend-like or season-like pattern. Thus the moving average model excludes random irregularities in the time series pattern.

If the demand level changes on a regular basis, this method does not provide any useful results. In addition, the information obtained in historical observations is lost in this procedure.

Weighted Moving Average Model (Strategy 14)

Definition

The weighted moving average model is similar to the simple moving average model, with the only difference being that each historical value is weighted with the factor from the weighting group in the univariate forecast profile.

When determining the average value, the weighted moving average model enables you to put a higher weight on younger historical data as opposed to older data. You can use this option if younger data is likely to correspond more closely to future requirements than older data. This means that a faster adaptation to level changes is possible. The weighted moving avarage formula is displayed in Figure 4.44.

$$M = \frac{\displaystyle\sum_{t=1}^{n} W_t * V_t}{\displaystyle\sum_{t=1}^{n} W_t}$$

M = Moving Average
V = Actual Value
W = Weighting Factor
n = Number of Periods in Weighting Group

Figure 4.44 Weighted Moving Average Formula

Application

The accuracy of this model strongly depends on the weighting factors you choose. If the time series pattern changes, you must adapt the weighting factors accordingly.

It remains questionable, however, whether these forecasting techniques (strategy 13 and strategy 14) can actually map a changing environment. The increasing level of competition requires that everything be up-to-date, flexibility, customer orientation, and a forward-looking approach. However, these criteria are not considered in the methods described so far as these methods update only historical values into the future. Keeping things up-to-date is an inherent problem in many quantitative procedures; for example, when you determine an average value, the forecast value for the month of June cannot be calculated until the end of May, when the actual values obtained are available. Even the second-order exponential smoothing method (see below) lags behind the periods, which can easily be calculated using $2(1-\alpha)/\alpha$ (speed at which the model adapts).

Models with First-Order Exponential Smoothing (11, 21, 41)

Definition

Exponential smoothing methods are currently the most common time series procedures. These methods are easier to grasp if you keep in mind that they were originally known as "exponentially weighted moving averages." The basic premise of simple exponential smoothing is that the sales values for younger periods have a greater influence on the forecast and therefore should be weighted more heavily, while the weighting of older periods exponentially declines. Since the calculations are based on data from the more recent sales history—in other words, a manageable period—we can also keep the data management to a minimum or at least keep it within limits.

Exponential smoothing of the first order (also known as *simple exponential smoothing*) works with a smoothing constant (alpha), which is assigned a value between 0 and 1. The higher its value is (i.e., the closer to 1), the more heavily the sales history of the last period will be weighted. A high alpha value (.8) is comparable to using a low number of periods (n) with a moving average model. A small value n allows a stronger weighting of the more recent periods. Conversely, a low alpha value (.1) corresponds to including a large number of periods with a moving average, because the influence of more recent periods is lower.

Advantages of the models based on exponential smoothing:

▸ Relatively easy to understand and manage

▸ Heavier weighting of more recent data periods

▸ No major data management required

▸ Relatively high accuracy for short-term forecasts (reaching from one to three periods into the future)

Disadvantages of models based on exponential smoothing:

▸ There may be a lot of effort required to determine the correct alpha value.

▸ Models are usually weak for medium- or long-term predictions (three periods and more).

▸ Forecast results may be highly inaccurate due to major random fluctuations with younger data. Since exponential smoothing models draw on historical data from a time series and a smoothing factor for the forecast, they are less able to forecast turning points with younger data. Usually, one to three periods are needed to factor extreme fluctuations that arise with newer data.

Application

The method of exponential smoothing of the first order is theoretically suitable if the data series shows a horizontal pattern (i.e., there is no trend). If first-order exponential smoothing is applied to a data series that shows a consistent trend, the forecasts remain behind this trend. Second-order exponential smoothing (also known as *linear exponential smoothing* after Holt, see further below in this section) avoids this problem by explicitly identifying the presence of a trend and taking it into account. A smoothed estimated value is created from the trend contained in the time series.

Constant Model with First-Order Exponential Smoothing (Strategy 10 + 11)

Definition

The consistent enhancement of the weighted moving average model takes us to the exponential smoothing model. The constant model with first-order exponential smoothing (strategy 10 + 11) is based on two fundamental ideas:

▶ The older the time series values, the less important they become for the calculation of the forecast.

▶ The current forecast error is taken into account in subsequent forecasts.

The exponential smoothing constant model can be derived from these considerations (see Figure 4.45 for the basic formula).

$$B(t) = \alpha V(t) + (1 - \alpha) B(t-1)$$

B (t)   = Current basic value for the current
              period (t)
B (t-1) = Basic value of the previous period
V (t)   = Actual requirement for the current
              period (t)
α = Smoothing for the basic value

Figure 4.45 Formula for the Constant Model

To determine the forecast value, the system uses the preceding forecast value, the last historical value, and the "alpha" smoothing factor. This smoothing factor weights the more recent historical values more than the less recent ones so they have a greater influence on the forecast.

How quickly the forecast reacts to a change in the time series pattern depends on the smoothing factor. If you choose 0 for alpha, the new average will be equal to the old one. In this case, the basic value calculated previously remains; that is, the forecast does not react to current data. If you choose 1 for the alpha value, the new average will equal the last value in the time series. Useful values for alpha therefore lie between 0.1 and 0.5. For example, an alpha value of 0.5 weights the historical values as follows:

▶ First historical value: 50 %

▶ Second historical value: 25 %

▶ Third historical value: 12.5 %

▶ Fourth historical value: 6.25 %

The weightings of the historical data can be changed by a single parameter. In this way, the system can react relatively easily to changes in the time series.

The following two methods are available to determine the smoothing factor: the use of empirical values and selection by the forecast error.

The suggested values in the bibliography (e.g., Tempelmeier 2003) lie between 0.1 and 0.3. You should choose a low factor if the random component has a major influence on the time series. The selection by forecast errors involves running simulations using various factors in order to calculate forecast errors. The factor that produces the smallest forecast error will be selected.

The example shown in Figure 4.46 illustrates the effects of the alpha value on the historical values.

Smoothing Principle
▶ Weighting the Current Value: Parameters α β γ
▶ Weighting the Previous Value: (1 – Parameter)

Examples of Weighting (in %):

Parameter	Current Period	1st Historical Period	2nd Historical Period	3rd Historical Period
0.1	10	9	8	7
0.3	30	21	15	10
0.5	50	25	13	6
0.7	70	21	6	2

Figure 4.46 Alpha Values of Exponential Smoothing

You can see that a low alpha value weights all periods the same, so that a coincidence in a period has little influence on the forecast. Alternatively, a high alpha value weights the periods very differently so that present coincidences can have a far greater influence.

Table 4.1 provides you with an overview of the effects of the alpha factor:

Criterion	Alpha = large	Alpha = small
Historical	low	high
New values	high	low
Smoothing	low	high
Adjustment	fast	slow

Table 4.1 Effects of the Alpha Factor

A large alpha factor puts less importance on the less recent past than on the more recent past. It has a minor influence on the forecast smoothing, but reacts more quickly to requirement adjustments.

In SAP APO, you can also automatically adjust the alpha factor in each historical period according to the mean absolute deviation (MAD) and the error total (ET).

Application

This model avoids a loss of information in case of a change in demand because it allocates different weightings to all observed data and includes those weightings in the forecast. The weighting for the observations declines exponentially into the past. In this way, the forecast values can better adjust to any changes to the demand pattern. However, the exponential smoothing method is only an appropriate method for short-term demand forecasts if the observed values fluctuate around an average value that is constant over time.

You should therefore use the constant model of first-order exponential smoothing for time series that neither show a trend-like pattern nor any seasonal fluctuations. The weightings of the historical data can be changed by a single parameter. In this way, the system can react relatively easily to changes in the time series. The more recent historical values have a greater influence on the forecast than the old values. The bigger a value is, the greater the influence of the latest observed value of the demand time series on the forecast value. The option of automatically adapting the alpha factor enables the automatic use of a known forecast error from the previous month in order to optimize the new forecast. This allows you to use an automatic error feedback function in your forecast, which helps you to achieve better results than in a first-order exponential smoothing process without adjusting the alpha factor.

The exponential smoothing with trend correction represents a modification of this method, which can take an existing trend into account.

Unlike the linear regression and moving average methods, the user can estimate and optimize one or more smoothing factors—depending on the algorithm—in the exponential smoothing models in order to obtain more accurate forecast results.

The optimized estimation of the smoothing factors automatically entails an optimization of the forecast values. Makridakis (1998, p. 172 f.) states that an optimization of the smoothing factors usually requires the same statistical key figures as those used to measure the forecast quality. Apart from that, when selecting the optimization variables, the interests of the user play a major role. If the user places an emphasis on relative forecast errors or information, the smoothing factors are estimated optimally if the mean absolute error percentage is minimal. Alternatively, the user can also focus on absolute errors. In this case, the most appropriate optimization variables are the mean quadratic and the mean absolute errors.

So far we have based the descriptions of our models on a linear trend; however, in everyday business this is not very realistic because the historical values usually show a saturation effect after a certain period of time. This phenomenon can be counteracted by using a dampening factor in order to dampen the future trend. For example, if you assume that the growth rate of a company's sales decreases by 10% every year due to the competitive situation in the market, the trend value of each future period will be dampened by 0.9.

Automatic Adjustment of the Alpha Factor (Strategy 12 + 23)

Definition
This model is used in forecast strategies 12 and 23; in both strategies, the system optimizes the alpha factor automatically.

In forecast strategy 12, the alpha factor within a defined interval is changed with a particular increment. A forecast is performed for each alpha value.

The system then chooses the value for which the chosen error measure is the smallest.

The minimum alpha factor in SAP APO is 0.05; the maximum alpha factor is 0.90.

In the univariate forecast profile, you specify the error measure to be used. The standard value is the Mean Absolute Deviation (MAD). You can also enter the start value and end value for alpha, along with a value for the increment. If you don't enter anything, the system uses the default values 0.1 as the start value, 0.5 as the end value, and 0.1 as the increment.

The system selects the alpha value with the lowest error measure.

In forecast strategy 23, the alpha factor in each ex-post period is adjusted according to the MAD and the error total (ET).

The minimum alpha factor is 0.05; the maximum alpha factor is 0.90.

The initial alpha factor (α_0) is either the default value of 0.3, or a value that you have specified in the univariate forecast profile.

To calculate the alpha factor in each ex-post period, the system uses an iterative formula (see Figure 4.47).

$$\alpha_1 = \alpha_{(i-1)} + 0.2 * [TS - \alpha_{(i-1)}]$$

Figure 4.47 Calculating the Automatic Adjustment of the Alpha Factor

Alpha Factor: Legend for the Formula
TS designates the tracking signal (error measure to evaluate forecasts)
TS = 0 if MAD(i) = 0
TS = ABS [ET (i) / MAD (i)] if MAD (i) ≠ 0
i = 1 … n, where n designates the number of periods in the ex-post forecast
α_i is used to calculate the ex-post forecast in the period i + 1

Application

Both of these models are useful if the historical data is valid and the planner does not want to assign the alpha value himself. In this case, the planner relies on the calculation quality of the forecast system.

Models with Second-Order Exponential Smoothing after Holt (Strategy 22 + 23)

Definition

The methods of the second-order exponential smoothing (also known as *linear exponential smoothing* after Holt) can be enhanced for trend models and multiplicational seasonal models. As early as 1957, Holt criticized first-order and second-order smoothing processes for not being flexible enough because they used only one smoothing parameter (alpha). So he proposed a model that today is referred to as the Holt procedure, in which both terms of the model—level *a* and the trend component *b*—are smoothed using different parameters α and β.

Here, a second-order exponential smoothing is therefore used. This involves using the same smoothing process once again for the time series of the forecast values, that is, for the average values that have been calculated in the first-order exponential smoothing procedure. As a result, you obtain second-order exponentially-smoothed average values, which are average values of the first-order average values.

The second-order exponential smoothing procedure is used in strategies 22 and 23; it is based on a linear trend and consists of two equations. The first equation is almost identical to the equation of the first-order exponential smoothing, with the exception of the bracketed indices. In the second equation, the values calculated in the first equation are used as initial values and smoothed a second time. You can see the formula in Figure 4.48.

$$B^{(1)}(t) = \alpha H^{(1)}(t) + (1 - \alpha) B^{(1)}(t-1)$$
$$B^{(2)}(t) = \alpha H^{(1)}(t) + (1 - \alpha) B^{(2)}(t-1)$$

$B^{(1)}$ = Singly Smoothed Basic Value
$B^{(2)}$ = Doubly Smoothed Basic Value
H = Historical Value
α = Smoothing Factor

Figure 4.48 Formula for Second-Order Exponential Smoothing

Application

If a time series shows a trend-like change of the average value across several periods, the forecast values calculated in the first-order exponential smoothing process always lag one or more periods behind the actual values. The second-order exponential smoothing method can then be used to achieve a faster adaptation of the forecast to the actual pattern of the consumption values.

Gardner (1980) compared this procedure with first-order exponential smoothing based on empirical time series and came to the conclusion that the Holt procedure provided better forecasts in many cases. This is not surprising because the additional parameter provides more influence capability, although it also has some problems with regard to its determination.

Trend/Seasonal Models with First-Order Exponential Smoothing after Winters (Strategy 20, 21, 30, 31, 40 + 41)

Definition
Winters introduced the trend/seasonal model of exponential smoothing, which is based on the Holt procedure. The Winters procedure is an efficient tool for predicting seasonal patterns as it smoothes the forecasts for the three parameters, *a* (for the axis section), *b* (for the gradient), and *c* (for the seasonal factors). Winters assumes a linear trend that is multiplicatively linked with the season. The basic value is smoothed using the smoothing factor, the trend value is smoothed using the gradient factor, and the seasonal index is smoothed using the seasonal factor.

The following formula is used in the forecast strategies 20, 21, 30, 31, 40 and 41 and in the forecast strategies 50 to 56, where a trend, seasonal, or trend/seasonal model is determined. The calculation takes into account both trend- and season-dependent changes. The basic value (alpha), trend value (beta), and seasonal index (gamma) are calculated on the basis of the initial period.

In Figure 4.49, you can see the formula for first-order exponential smoothing in a trend, seasonal, or trend/seasonal model. Figure 4.50 illustrates the difference between the three values.

Application
The demand for products is often subject to seasonal patterns, but this fact is rarely considered (if at all) in forecasting techniques, or, if it is included, then this is only done manually.

Example

Consider, for example, the manager of a shoe shop who needs a sales forecast for the coming two weeks in terms of daily periods. Since the sales figures are usually higher on Saturdays than they are on Mondays, when doing calculating his sales forecast, he must take into account the weekly "season."

Forecast Value for Period (t+i)

$$F(t+i) = (B(t) + i * T(t)) * S(t-L+i)$$

with:

Basic Value:
$$B(t) = B(t-1) + T(t-1) + \alpha \left[\frac{H(t)}{S(t-L)} - B(t-1) - T(t-1) \right]$$

Trend Value:
$$T(t) = T(t-1) + \beta \left[B(t) - (B(t-1) + T(t-1)) \right]$$

Seasonal Index:
$$S(t) = S(t-L) + \gamma \left[\frac{H(t)}{B(t)} - S(t-L) \right]$$

For Constant Model
$T(t) = 0$, $\beta = 0$, $S(t) = 1.0$, $\gamma = \text{Gamma} = 0$

For Trend Model
$S(t) = 1.0$, $\gamma = \text{Gamma} = 0$

For Seasonal Model
$T(t) = 0$, $\beta = 0$

$F(t+i)$ = Forecast calculated in current period (t) for period (t+i)

i   = Forecast Horizon

$B(t)$ = Current basic value for current period (t)

$B(t-1)$ = Old basic value from previous period

L   = Period Length (usually 12)

$H(t)$ = Actual (historical) requirement for current period (t)

$T(t)$ = Current basic value calculated for the current period

$T(t-1)$ = Old trend value from previous period

$S(t)$ = Seasonal index for period (t)

$S(t-L)$ = Old seasonal index for period (t)

α = Smoothing factor for basic value 'B',
            $0 < \alpha < 1$

β = Smoothing for trend value 'T',
            $0 < \beta < 1$

γ = Smoothing factor for seasonal index 'S',
            $0 < \gamma < 1$

Figure 4.49 Formula for Exponential Smoothing for Trend, Seasonal, or Trend/Seasonal Models

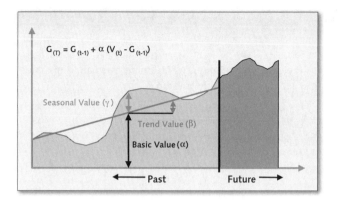

Figure 4.50 Exponential Smoothing with Basic, Trend, and Seasonal Index

According to Wagner, a reliable estimate of the seasonal coefficients requires the consideration of at least two cycles of the demand time series. This means that contrary to the previous two models, the seasonal model requires much more data to initialize the parameters.

According to Tempelmeier, another disadvantage is that each seasonal factor is not updated until after a complete seasonal cycle has ended. This means that substantial changes in the seasonal pattern are only identified and translated into new seasonal factor values at a very late stage.

A disadvantage of this method is the relatively late change of the seasonal indices because an observed value can only be used to adjust one seasonal index, although the entire seasonal pattern may have changed. Thus the Winters model is not able to completely identify the time series structure when structural interruptions occur. Structural interruptions describe an abrupt change in the time series values due to changes in the underlying causal foundations. Such structural interruptions can be caused by winning or losing major customers, the opening or closing of a subsidiary, the introduction or abandonment of a product variant, and so on.

Moreover, it is difficult to determine the three smoothing parameters. Due to the many possible combinations of the seasonal factor and seasonal cycle it is almost impossible to perform simple tests in the context of forecast simulations. However, Winters himself provides many different examples that show that the forecast error function has a flat progress when it is close to the optimal parameters, so that a rough optimization can already provide good results. For a more accurate approximation, you can use non-linear optimization methods and gradient methods; however, you should note that these methods don't provide any global optimum, but merely suboptimums that lie in the area of the default parameters a, b, and c.

You should use the trend, seasonal, or seasonal trend model of first-order exponential smoothing for time series showing a trend-like pattern and/or seasonal fluctuations.

Seasonal Linear Regression (Strategy 35)

Definition

Seasonal linear regression can be used as an alternative to forecast strategies 30 and 31, which provide high basic values if the seasonal index equals 0 or almost 0.

The linear regression can be described as a line that runs through a scatterplot, whereby the total of quadratic distances between the line and the historical values is minimal (see Figure 4.51).

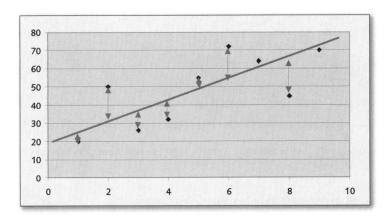

Figure 4.51 Linear Regression

The system calculates the seasonal linear regression as follows:

1. **Determination of seasonal factors on the basis of historical values**
   Figure 4.52 illustrates the first step of the seasonal linear regression. The most appropriate seasonal index is determined based on the seasonal history.

2. **Deseasonalization of historical values**
   The second step corrects the actual data on the basis of the seasonal indices calculated in Step 1 and converts them into a linear curve (see Figure 4.53).

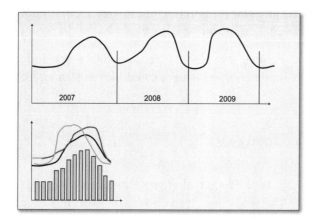

Figure 4.52 Seasonal Linear Regression, Step 1: Calculating Seasonal Index for the History

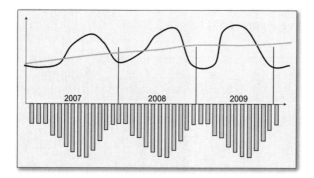

Figure 4.53 Seasonal Linear Regression, Step 2: Correcting Historical Data with Seasonal Index

3. **Determination of forecast values using linear regression**

   In the third step, the linear regression is now carried out for the non-seasonal historical values from Step 2. In Figure 4.54, the forecast for the year 2003 was obtained using this step.

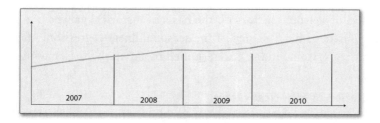

Figure 4.54 Seasonal Linear Regression, Step 3: Executing Linear Regression Based on the Now Linear History

4. **Seasonalization of forecast values**

In the fourth step, the seasonal indices are applied to the results of the linear regression calculation; this then again produces seasonal forecast results (see Figure 4.55).

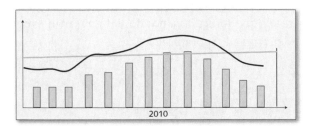

Figure 4.55 Seasonal Linear Regression, Step 4: Multiplying Seasonal Index with the Linear Result

Application

You should not use the linear regression method if your historical data shows a distinct trend-like pattern. Outliers must be corrected before you apply this method, so that the season is not corrupted. If the season from the history does not fit the possible future season because of errors in the historical data or changes in market trends, then you should observe this method very closely.

Croston Method (Strategy 80)

Definition

The Croston method is a univariate forecasting strategy for products with an irregular or sporadic demand. We call a time series sporadic if periods are observed without any demand. This demand pattern is typical for spare parts, but it can also occur if the subdivision of your periods is too detailed (e.g., daily periods). The use of statistical forecasting techniques would produce major errors for such items. An additional subjective forecast would not improve the quality because periods without a demand usually occur randomly and therefore cannot be predicted. Moreover, a sporadic demand mainly occurs for large quantities of inferior parts for which planners can only carry out low-cost forecasts that shouldn't be too time-consuming.

Efficient methods have therefore been developed for an automatic calculation of the forecasts for sporadic demand. These methods attempt to separately predict the two components "Occurrence of a period with positive demand" and "Volume of the demand."

The Croston method comprises two steps. First it uses the average requirement level to determine estimated values by applying the exponential smoothing procedure. Then it calculates the average amount of time that passes between the demands.

Figure 4.56 shows the sporadic history values on the left. On the right, it shows a possible forecast result; the forecast values do not appear in every period, but rather are also determined "sporadically."

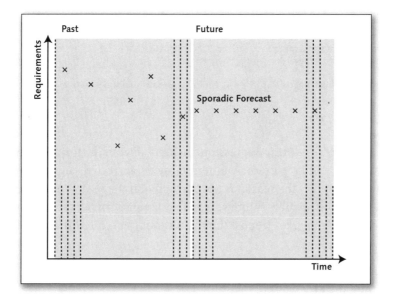

Figure 4.56 Croston Method

Application
In connection with inventory management systems, the exponential smoothing method is frequently used for forecasting the requirements. In the case of sporadic requirements, the use of this method almost always results in inadequate stocks.

The Croston method is suitable if the requirement occurs randomly, with there being no requirement in many periods, if not most of them; here the distribution of the demand, when it arises, is effectively independent of the duration since the last time a demand occurred. Such requirement patterns are described as "irregular" or "sporadic" requirements. The demand for spare parts is an example here as spare parts are usually ordered in large quantities to replenish the warehouse. Traditional forecasting models have great difficulties with these zero periods (i.e., historical values with periods of zero demand). Another advantage of the Croston method is that in addition to the requirements level, it also takes into account the intervals between demands, in other words, the average duration.

Median Method (Strategy 36)

Definition

This empirical method that is used in strategy 36 determines the median of the basic and trend parameters and of the seasonal index, if needed.

This method requires historical data of at least three preceding seasons. If the number of periods in a season is 1, the seasonal index is set to 1. A seasonal effect does not exist. In this case, the system needs three periods to determine the trend parameter and basic value. No initialization is required.

Because this method automatically excludes the influence of outliers, no outlier correction is necessary. The outlier correction function is not available in the context of the median method.

The system determines the difference between the first and second values of the historical data, between the second and third values, and so on until it reaches the end of the data series, and then generates a forecast (see Figure 4.57).

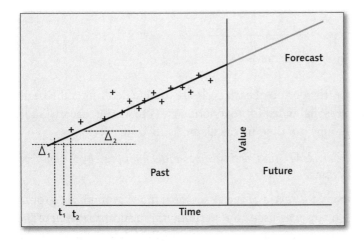

Figure 4.57 Median Method, Forecast

It then sorts the values, for example, in ascending order. Finally, the system selects the value that is located exactly in the middle of this list. This value is referred to as the *median value* (see Figure 4.58).

t_1	0.3
t_2	0.1
t_3	20.6
t_4	0.4
...	
t_{n-1}	Δ_{n-1}
t_n	Δ_n

Sorting

t_2	0.1
t_1	0.3
t_4	0.4
t_n	Δ_n
...	
t_{n-1}	Δ_{n-1}
t_3	20.6

Figure 4.58 Median Method, Selecting the Median Value

The method proceeds as follows to determine the trend parameter, the seasonal indices, and the basic value.

It creates groups of data for the first period in the cycle as well as for the second, third, and so on, as shown in Figure 4.59.

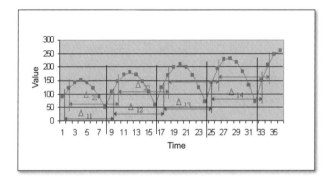

Figure 4.59 Median Method, Data Groups

The values from the first period of each cycle are used to determine the trend parameter T. The seasonal index for that period is set to 1. The seasonal indices for the other groups can then be calculated as follows:

The differences are divided by the trend parameter and multiplied by the number of periods in one season.

This produces as many estimates of the ith seasonal index as there are groups minus 1 (the first group was used to determine the trend parameter). The median value of each group represents the seasonal index for that group.

Application
The median method is suitable for time series that don't show any significant fluctuations. Here, the median method would also automatically correct the

outliers. The median method does not react strongly to fluctuations; instead, it supports a continuous curve pattern. As is the case with every forecast model, the median method cannot be used for all types of historical data. You should try to avoid the following situations:

▶ Time series that represent step functions
▶ Time series with several data points that have the same value

Automatic Model Selection

The automatic model selection is a mathematical method for choosing the best forecasting technique. With automatic model selection, we need to establish according to what criteria the most appropriate time series model should be selected using mathematical methods. To answer this question, various options are available to the developer. On the one hand, you can implement a strategy in which all possible models are calculated (i.e., adjusted to the available data), and then use a time series model for the forecast that provides the best forecast quality. Consequently, iterations occur in the model selection and adjustment phases. Although this solution is acceptable, in most cases the performance is quite poor because it processes all possible options completely and only then does it determine which forecasting technique should be used.

The second option that describes the forecasting process uses a series of significance tests that support and facilitate the decision in favor of a specific model. The simplest option here includes running a trend test and a seasonal test. However, there are some problems associated with this option. On the one hand, random fluctuations can lead to a successful seasonal test outcome during the initialization phase, resulting ultimately in the seasonal model, although the time series shows a long-term constant pattern, for example. The reason for this can be found in the higher number of parameters that are always available for adjusting the seasonal model as opposed to the constant model. A higher number of variables definitely facilitates the adjustment. Alternatively, a trend test that is based on the linear regression method is unable to identify an exponential trend, for instance. This means that the test selects the constant model although the values it provides are not as good as the ones provided by a time series model with a linear trend-like pattern. Contrary to the first option, the execution of several tests is much faster and is therefore better suited to the automatic model selection. However, the tests are much more difficult to implement because the developer has to deal with the described problems and may have to factor the number of parameters for the model adjustment when performing the significance tests.

High-quality historical data is a prerequisite for a successful automatic model selection. To obtain results from automatic model selection that approximate those of the manual selection, you must carry out the automatic model selection for each individual product. Often, the assumption is that only a forecast profile is used for all products because the automatic model selection uses all methods. First, this is not true. The automatic model selection does not use all methods. Secondly, the automatic model selection should use product-specific forecast horizons or history horizons. For products with different seasonal periods, for example, the difference must be considered in the automatic model selection. If you use only one forecast profile, the same number of historical periods is used for all products. In this way, the automatic model selection cannot reach the quality level of a product-specific model selection.

SAP APO contains two automatic model selection strategies. Both strategies are similar in that the system automatically performs the forecast on the basis of a constant pattern when no regular pattern can be identified with regard to the trend or seasonal components. These are automatic model selection procedure 1 and automatic model selection procedure 2.

Automatic Model Selection Procedure 1
Automatic model selection procedure 1 tests historical values with regard to constant, linear trend-like, seasonal, and seasonal trend developments. The seasonal test is performed based on the autocorrelation coefficient, while the regression analysis provides the basis for the trend test. After that, the system automatically uses the time series model for the forecast which, based on the results of the significance tests, seems to be the most appropriate one.

For example, if both the seasonal and the trend test are completed successfully, this strategy will select a seasonal trend model.

Automatic model selection procedure 1 is used in the forecast strategies 50, 51, 52, 53, 54 and 55.

▶ A seasonal test is carried out in forecasting strategies 50, 51, 53, and 54:
  ▶ Any trend-related influences on the historical time series that may exist are removed.
  ▶ An autocorrelation coefficient is calculated.
  ▶ A significance test is performed on the coefficient.

▶ A trend test is run in forecast strategies 50, 52, 53 and 55:

   ▶ Any seasonal influences on the historical time series are removed.

   ▶ A validation parameter is calculated according to the above formula.

   ▶ The system checks whether the historical data shows a noticeable trend-like pattern by checking the data against a value that depends on the number of periods.

Based on the seasonal and trend tests performed, the system identifies the most appropriate forecasting technique. It chooses from the constant model, trend model, seasonal model, and the seasonal trend model. Please note that at least two complete seasonal cycles must be available as historical data so that a seasonal test can be performed. It is useful to always provide at least two seasonal cycles and three periods as historical data. You should also execute the procedure 1 without an outlier control.

If you don't adhere to this recommendation, you cannot compare the results from procedure 1 with the results of the other procedures. This is because with procedure 1, the outlier control may be executed with a different procedure than the final forecast, because the characteristics of the time series can change after the outlier control. You should also note that the trend test depends on the number of periods per season. The trend test uses a history that is adjusted by the season, and this adjustment can depend largely on the number of seasonal periods. If you want to test only the trend, then you should set the number of periods per season to 1. If the number of periods you specify per season is greater than or equal to the number of existing historical values, you have practically terminated the trend test.

The **Periods per Season** value in the forecast profile plays a very important role. For example, if your historical data contains a season that consists of seven periods and you enter a value of "3" periods per season, the seasonal test will probably be negative. Unlike trend and constant models, seasonal models are not verified. You can make the setting in the forecast profile (see Figure 4.60). To do this, choose the menu path **SAP APO • Demand Planning • Planning • Demand Planning Interactive** and then click on the **Run Forecast** button, and select the **Parameters** tab.

Table 4.2 gives an overview of the strategies that automatic model selection 1 uses.

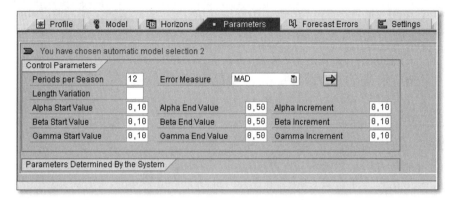

Figure 4.60 Settings in the Forecast Profile for the Automatic Model Selection in SAP APO

Automatic Model Selection Strategy	Positive Trend	Positive Season	Selected Model
50 – Automatic Selection 1	No	No	10 Constant
	Yes	No	20 Trend
	No	Yes	30 Season
	Yes	Yes	40 Seasonal trend
51 – Trend Test	Yes	N/A	30 Season
	No		10 Constant
52 – Seasonal Test	N/A	Yes	30 Season
		No	10 Constant
53 – Test for trend and season	No	No	10 Constant
	Yes	No	20 Trend
	No	Yes	30 Season
	Yes	Yes	40 Seasonal trend
54 – Seasonal model plus test for trend	No	Yes	30 Season
	Yes		40 Seasonal trend
55 – Trend model plus test for season	Yes	Yes	40 Seasonal trend
		No	20 Trend

Table 4.2 Strategies of the Automatic Model Selection 1

The automatic model selection procedure 1 thus does not consider any forecasts for sporadic requirements (Croston method), external forecasts, or regression procedures.

The described disadvantages clearly make one question whether the automatic model selection procedure 1 is really suited to providing an optimized selection process for the best forecasting method.

Automatic Model Selection Procedure 2

The *automatic model selection procedure 2* performs various tests to determine the model to be used (constant model, trend model, seasonal model, etc.). The system then varies the corresponding forecast parameters (alpha, beta, and gamma) in the intervals and with the increments you have previously specified in the forecast profile.

The procedure starts with the following initial values: alpha = 0.1, beta = 0.1, and gamma = 0.1. It applies the constant model, trend model, seasonal model, and the seasonal trend model, and then varies the individual parameters by increments of 0.1 until they reach a value of 0.5. You can also set the increment values manually. By default, the system then selects a model and parameter combination with the smallest mean absolute deviation (MAD).

You can also specify in the forecast profile which error is to be minimized. The use of a customer-specific error level is also possible; however, this doesn't mean that the system identifies the procedure or parameters where the error value is smallest. On the one hand, not all forecasting methods are tested; on the other hand, the system doesn't examine all parameter combinations due to the finite increments. For example, a constant model with alpha = 0.14 may have a smaller MAD value than the result of a forecast calculation using automatic model selection procedure 2, which has not even tested this parameter. Again with automatic model selection procedure 2, you must ensure that you provide at least two seasonal cycles plus three periods as the history. Furthermore, you must also bear in mind that if you use the outlier correction function, the results cannot be compared with those obtained in the individual procedures because the procedures used for the outlier correction and the final forecast can be different.

The automatic model selection procedure 2 is used in forecast strategy 56.

Table 4.3 gives an overview of the strategies that automatic model selection 2 uses.

	White Noise Test	Sporadic Data Test	Seasonal Test	Trend Test
Croston model		X		
Trend model				X
Seasonal model			X	
Seasonal trend model			A	A
Linear regression			o	X
Seasonal linear regression			A	A

Table 4.3 Strategies for Automatic Model Selection 2; Legend: X—The model will be used if the test is positive. A—The model will be used if all tests are positive. o—The model will be used if this test is negative.

From SCM Release 4.1 onward, the Croston method, the linear regression, and the seasonal linear regression are also included in the automatic model selection 2. A trend test, a seasonal test, and a test for white noise are also introduced into the automatic model selection 2. If the trend test is negative, no models or parameters (beta = 0) are tested that are assigned to a trend. If the seasonal test is negative, no models or parameters (gamma = 0) are tested that are assigned to a season. Whenever white noise is detected, the constant model will be used.

Drawbacks of Automatic Model Selection

The optimization of the smoothing factors is closely linked with the automatic model selection. This is carried out in the basic function module by using the grid search and increments of 0.01.

Based on the grid search, this strategy automatically selects the model with the smallest smoothed mean absolute error. You should note, however, that the system rarely identifies the model with the smallest MAD. One of the reasons for that is that not all possible model and parameter combinations are used. Moreover, the linear regression procedure is not used here. Another problem of that selection procedure is that the MAD shouldn't really be used as a criterion for comparisons.

The trend test that is based on the regression analysis, for example, only recognizes linear trends. But if a time series represents an exponential trend, the significance test will fail and reject a trend-like model. Consequently, the trend test proposes a constant model although it usually forecasts data of a poorer quality than a time series model with a trend-like pattern.

The same can happen in a seasonal test that is based on the autorelation coefficient. For example, if a time series shows several random fluctuations in the initialization phase, it may pass the significance test although the fluctuations are part of the random component, and not of the seasonal component.

For the automatic model selection procedure, you must therefore simply define the timeframe on which you want to base your calculations. The system examines all available statistical forecast procedures and parameter combinations, and selects a combination that provides the best forecast accuracy. Consequently, it provides the user with a list of the forecasting techniques and corresponding parameters for each item to be analyzed. Then, the planner must check if the model is appropriate for his needs. The planner can use the provided set of statistical methods as a black box.

According to Wagner (2000), the automatic model selection procedures described here have the following disadvantages:

▶ The time series is often too short when a demand planning process is introduced.

▶ The criterion used for evaluation purposes is often one of the forecast accuracy criteria previously described. However, those values don't provide any information on the robustness of the model results.

▶ Three periods of the demand series are required for the selection procedure:

  ▷ In the first period, the model components are initialized.

  ▷ In the second period, the parameter values are optimized.

  ▷ In the third period, the optimized parameters are used to obtain forecasts. These forecasts are evaluated based on the forecast accuracy. This degree of accuracy is then used as a selection criterion for choosing the best forecasting technique.

▶ The definition of the length of the individual periods has a significant influence on the model selection result. Usually, the user cannot change these settings. Users cannot even see them in the forecast software.

For this reason, the automatic model selection can optimally be used to provide some kind of indication when searching for the right method. However, experienced planners should under no circumstances use the automatic model selection as a black box.

In short, we don't recommend that you use the two automatic model selection procedures provided in SAP APO in your daily operations. But you can certainly use them for testing purposes, especially, if you want to get an idea of which forecasting technique you can possibly use before you start the actual selection procedure, or if you need some initial help for optimizing the smoothing parameters

Multilinear Regression (Causal Model)

Definition

If some factors can be identified that have a significant influence on the demand pattern, it is advisable to use causal models. The regression analysis is the standard method to use for estimating the parameter values in the causal model. Normally, linear relationships are considered that exist between the dependent variables (e.g., the demand) and the main factors (e.g., variables that are independent of each other, such as the temperature, expenditures for promotions, etc.). If several independent influencing factors exist, the model is called a *multiple regression model*.

The multiple linear regression procedure uses the method of the smallest squares to estimate the model parameters. This procedure minimizes the total of the squared difference between the actual and the forecasted demand that is determined by the model. Whereas the exponential smoothing procedure can take into account all historical values, the regression method is applied to a restricted set of data. The disadvantage of such a method is the loss of information, as is the case with the moving average method. Furthermore, the weight of all values considered is 1, which is why the model cannot react flexibly to changes in the demand pattern.

Application

Because the linear regression models require a significantly higher quantity of data, it is obvious that the effort is only worthwhile if you use the model for medium-term and long-term forecasts, or for important products only. The accuracy and plausibility of the historical data are decisive factors here.

The example shown in Figure 4.61 illustrates the use of the multiple linear regression for the consumption of beer, assuming that the owner of a beer garden observes the demand and the temperature over time.

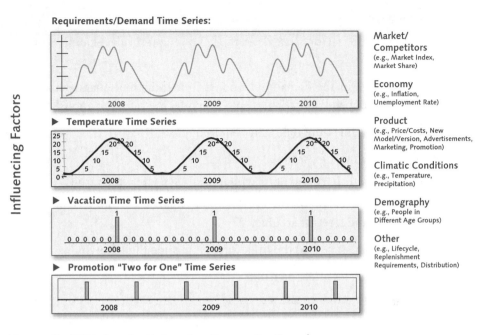

Figure 4.61 MLR Influencing Factors, Beer Consumption Example

The observed beer consumption is shown in the time series at the very top. The time series underneath shows the temperature pattern during the same consumption period. Below this is a time series for representing the vacation time series. Most vacations are of course taken during the summer months. The time series in the bottom illustration represents the sales values for those periods in which a special promotion ("two for one") was carried out.

As long as the owner of the beer garden is aware of the factors influencing the beer consumption, she won't be wholly surprised by changes in the consumer behavior, for example, if summer is exceptionally hot or cold.

The MLR forecast enables you to answer the following typical questions, for example:

▶ How can we achieve sales of x units?

▶ Which is the most cost-efficient solution?

▶ How will the market react if we (or one of our competitors) change the price by x%?

▶ How successful were the past advertising campaigns?

▶ How strongly does the demand depend on the climate (e.g., for ice cream and drinks)?

▶ To what extent does the economic cycle affect our sales?

▶ What are the factors that determine the long-term development of our sales?

The challenge for the demand planner is to identify and quantify the most important independent variables, and to model the causal relationship.

The data must meet the following requirements:

▶ Actual data must exist for all variables.

▶ Actual data from competitors would positively affect the result.

▶ The actual data for the independent variables is also important for the quality of the forecast accuracy.

The logical challenges for the MLR forecast include the following:

▶ Which variables affect demand?

▶ How do the variables affect demand?

▶ How are outliers, trend, and season modeled?

The following statistical problems must be considered:

▶ Correlation

▶ Autocorrelation

The advantages of the causal analysis are as follows:

▶ Complete modeling freedom

▶ Splitting of the overall problem into smaller, individual problems that are easier to estimate

▶ "What if?"simulations are possible

▶ Chances and risks are more transparent

The disadvantages are:

▶ It is difficult and requires a lot of effort to acquire the historical data for the variables

▶ Complex method that is one of the most difficult to grasp

▶ Needs the most processing time

▶ Demanding application

Assessment of the Causal Analysis

Several adaptation values are available to evaluate the quality of the MLR forecast, for instance Durbin-Watson and t-test. However, we would like to focus on the most important adaptation value for our purposes, namely, the adaptation value R square.

The R square is automatically calculated during the forecasting process. The R square always lies between 0 and 1. We can draw on the following intervals for the forecast quality:

- R square = 1: the MLR model perfectly describes the demand pattern
- R square = 0: the MLR model does not describe the demand pattern
- R square > 0.75: acceptable

Composite Forecasting techniques

Definition

The forecasting techniques described thus far can be combined with each other. For example, you can combine several different forecasting techniques on the basis of a constant or time-dependent weighting procedure (see Figure 4.62).

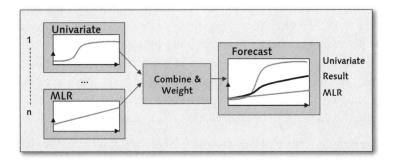

Figure 4.62 Combined Forecasting Technique

This way you can use the strengths of different methods simultaneously (e.g., you can use the trend and seasonal models based on short-term temperature influences).

Application

Experience has shown that composite forecasts that are based on different mathematical estimation procedures often have an advantage over the individual forecasts.

If you have opted to use the combined forecast, you must specify who should participate in the forecast. For example, do you want your demand planner to be joined by the S&D department, or do you want marketing to be involved as well when introducing new products? You should clearly decide on which areas and how many people from the respective areas you want to involve. In a composite forecast procedure, you can determine either the simple average or a weighted average of all forecasts involved. The example in Table 4.4 shows a possible weighting of the composite forecast.

Involved Party	Forecasting Technique	Weighting	Unit	Aug	Sep	Oct
Marketing	MLR	0.2	Units of 6	12,000	34,000	43,000
Sales and Distribution	Manual	0.4	Units of 6	20,000	40,000	60,000
Central planning	Median method	0.4	Units of 6	9,000	25,000	45,000
Total forecast	–	1	Units of 6	14,000	32,800	50,600

Table 4.4 Combined Forecast

The planners generate subjective forecasts based on their knowledge of the relevant data, such as historical figures, causal factors, and so on. Then they are confronted with forecasts that have been calculated using statistical methods. The planners then have the opportunity to improve their first estimate. It is not defined upfront to what extent the two components are integrated into the final forecast. This procedure often produces more accurate results than a simple evaluation without the help of statistical methods. Furthermore, it has the advantage that the planner has complete control.

Since the procedure described above assigns variable weightings to the two predictions, it is clear that these values are easy to influence. You can obtain a more objective result by combining the two values using a previously defined weighting schema. Even if you choose an equal distribution of the weightings, you will be able to obtain better results.

Many companies have adopted the habit of manually adjusting statistical forecasts in order to integrate the specific personal knowledge of the planner. However, the improvement process must be structured accordingly. This means that the adjustment must be based on signals that have already been set (e.g., promotions, weather, etc.).

Ex-post forecast

Definition

An ex-post forecast is a forecast that is run in past periods for which a history also exists with actual sales data. It calculates forecast accuracy measurements by comparing the differences between the actual values and the ex-post values. You use an ex-post forecast to obtain information about the different forecast errors.

Figure 4.63 shows two period blocks in the past: the initialization period, which is used as the history for the ex-post forecast and must be sufficiently long, and the ex-post period, in which an ex-post forecast is generated.

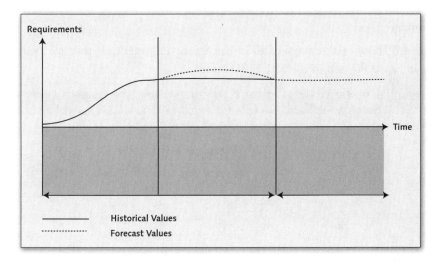

Figure 4.63 Ex-Post Forecast (Source: SAP)

Application

An ex-post forecast is automatically run as follows if sufficient historical data is available:

The historical values are divided into two groups:

▶ The first group, containing the older values, is used for initialization.

▶ An ex-post forecast is run for the more recent values in the second group.

The basic value, trend value, seasonal index, and mean absolute deviation (MAD) are modified in each ex-post period. These values are used to calculate forecasts for the future.

The system calculates the error total in the ex-post horizon. The error total is the total of the differences between the actual (historical) values and the planned values (in this example, the values in the ex-post forecast).

An ex-post forecast provides a sound foundation for evaluating the quality of the forecast, because it allows you to compare the forecast with the actual data before the next forecast interval. This is also very important for analyzing historical data and for selecting a suitable forecast procedure, for example.

The drawback of the ex-post forecast is that it can only be used for certain forecast procedures.

Summary

Table 4.5 shows a summary of all of the forecasting methods that are available in SAP APO and in the SAP ERP system.

Models	Methods	Strategies	Strategy
Univariate forecast	Constant	Constant model	10
		First-order exponential smoothing	11
		Constant model with automatic alpha adaptation and first-order exponential smoothing	12
		Moving average	13
		Weighted moving average	14
	Trend	Forecast using the trend model	20
		First-order exponential smoothing	21
		Second-order exponential smoothing	22
		Trend model with automatic alpha adaptation and second-order exponential smoothing	23
	Seasonal	Forecast using the seasonal model	30
		Winters' method	31
		Seasonal linear regression	35
	Seasonal trend model	Forecast using the seasonal trend model	40
		First-order exponential smoothing	41

Table 4.5 Forecasting Techniques in SAP APO

Models	Methods	Strategies	Strategy
	Automatic model selection 1	Forecast with automatic model selection Test for constant, trend, season, seasonal trend	50
		Trend test (model selection procedure 1)	51
		Seasonal test (model selection procedure 1)	52
		Trend test and seasonal test (model selection procedure 1)	53
	Manual model selection with a test for additional time series pattern	Seasonal model and trend test (model selection procedure 1)	54
	Manual model selection with a test for additional time series pattern	Trend model and seasonal test (model selection procedure 1)	55
	Automatic model selection 2	"Full parameter test"	56
	Actual data for the previous period	Transfer historical data	60
	Manual forecast	Manual forecast	70
	Sporadic	Croston method	80
	Linear regression	Simple linear regression	94
Causal forecast		Multilinear regression (MLR)	
Composite forecast	Combined forecasting technique	Combination of univariate and MLR possible	

Table 4.5 Forecasting Techniques in SAP APO (cont.)

4.3 Monitoring the Forecast Quality

To achieve a high level of forecast accuracy, you must know what your current forecast accuracy is. You can measure the accuracy (or quality, or rating) of a forecast using forecast errors. How you do this is described below.

145

4.3.1 Introduction

The selection of the correct forecasting technique plays a very important role in forecasting. You therefore need to know how to determine the best forecasting technique to meet your requirements. It is striking that the criteria for evaluating forecasts that have been developed in the relevant literature almost exclusively seek to analyze the forecast errors using measured values that compare the ex-post forecast values with the actual observed values. These forecast errors can be calculated automatically. Several forecasts are usually generated (using different parameters) for this purpose, based on historical data. The forecast errors are then calculated and the model with the fewest forecast errors is then selected. Next, the parameters of the selected forecast model are optimized. Forecasts are then generated for different parameters here and the forecast errors are compared.

Unfortunately, many companies don't have forecast tools that are capable of automatically calculating several forecasts and then selecting the best. Usually the demand planners determine their demand planning in Microsoft Excel. It is therefore simply not practical to compare forecasts for many products or to take forecast error deviations into account when choosing the forecasting technique to be used.

In this section, we will discuss three forecast controlling possibilities that are available with SAP APO:

▶ **Forecast errors, their significance and application**
After reading this section, you will be able to select appropriate forecast errors for your products and use them in your company.

▶ **Macro-dependent forecast alerts**
These alerts refer to customer-specific problems, for example, if a requirements forecast exceeds or falls short of a customer-specific key figure. You can also assign customized status messages to individual macro steps and have these messages displayed like alerts in the Alert Monitor. Section 3.5 shows a practical example of such a macro alert.

▶ **Forecast alerts in the Alert Monitor**
The system generates these alerts if the historical data, which the forecast is based on, is incorrectly described by the selected forecast models. For example, you have assumed that the demand rises constantly, but over time you find out that it depends on the season.

4.3.2   Forecast Error

Forecast errors are divided into two groups of alert types in SAP APO:

▶ **Alerts for the univariate forecast**

- ▹ Mean Absolute Deviation (MAD)
- ▹ Error Total (ET)
- ▹ Mean Absolute Percentage Error (MAPE)
- ▹ Mean Percentage Error (MPE)
- ▹ Mean Square Error (MSE)
- ▹ Root of the Mean Square Error (RMSE)

▶ **Alerts for the Multilinear Regression (MLR) forecast**

- ▹ R square
- ▹ Adjusted R square
- ▹ Durbin-h
- ▹ Durbin-Watson
- ▹ t-test
- ▹ Mean elasticity

Univariate Forecast Errors

The mathematical forecast errors for the univariate forecasting techniques are outlined below. They can be classified as follows:

- ▶ Percentage errors
- ▶ Relative errors
- ▶ Mean values
- ▶ Other errors

First, you will learn how to calculate percentage errors and relative errors. Next, you will learn about the methods for summarizing individual values (mean, median, and geometric mean). Lastly, you will be introduced to a number of other common errors.

Error Total (ET)

The deviations between the forecast value and the actual observed value in each period are added to calculate the error total:

Error total = $\Sigma |(C_t - F_t)|$
Legend: C_t = Consumption; F_t = Forecast

Table 4.6 shows the error for the error total for the above formula.

Actual Value	Forecast	Absolute Deviation	Error Total
120	110	10	
140	160	20	
			30

Table 4.6 Error Total Calculation

Mean Absolute Deviation (MAD)

The MAD is the average absolute error:

MAD = $^1/_n \, \Sigma (C_t - F_t)$
Legend: C_t = consumption; F_t = forecast, n = number of periods

Positive and negative deviations don't outweigh each other. The smaller the value, the better the forecast in a given period. A large value may signify a small percentage deviation in the case of a large volume. Therefore, volume should always be taken into account (see percentage errors).

By adding the differences between the forecast value and the actual value, positive and negative deviations are given equal weighting.

Table 4.7 shows the MAD error for our example.

Actual Value	Forecast	Absolute Deviation	MAD
120	110	10	
140	160	20	
			15

Table 4.7 Calculation of MAD

Mean Square Error (MSE)

The MSE is the square of the sum of the deviations across all periods, divided by the number of periods.

MSE = $^1/_n \, \Sigma (C_t - F_t)^2$
Legend: C_t = consumption; F_t = forecast, n = number of periods

Table 4.8 shows the MSE error for our above formula.

Actual Value	Forecast	Absolute Deviation	MSE
120	110	10	
140	160	20	
			250

Table 4.8 Calculation of MSE

Outliers in individual periods have a major influence on the MSE (the deviations within one period have a more significant effect on the result than the deviations in two periods divided by two). The current literature advises against using this key figure.

Root of the Mean Square Error (RMSE)

RMSE is the root of the mean square error (RMSE).

$$RMSE = \sqrt{1/_n} \; \Sigma \, (C_t - F_t)^2$$
Legend: C_t = consumption; F_t = forecast, n = number of periods

It was used very frequently in the past. More recently, however, it has been overtaken by other error calculations (see above). The current literature advises against using the RMSE to compare forecast models, because a small number of outliers have a significant effect on the RMSE.

Table 4.9 shows the RMSE error for our above formula.

Actual Value	Forecast	Absolute Deviation	RMSE
120	110	10	
140	160	20	
			15.81

Table 4.9 Calculation of RMSE

Absolute Percentage Error (APE)

The absolute percentage error (APE) indicates the degree to which the forecasts deviate from the actual values. The APE is calculated as a percentage. Positive and negative deviations don't outweigh each other, because the absolute error is always used:

$APE = (C_t-F_t)/C_t * 100$
Legend: C_t = consumption; F_t = forecast

The APE is therefore used very frequently in practice because it is easily understood and interpreted.

However, the APE has two distinct disadvantages. The first disadvantage is that it favors forecasts with values that are too low. In other words, it penalizes forecasts that are higher than the actual value to a greater degree than forecasts that are lower than the actual value. This behavior is also identified as an asymmetrical error. The lower limit is 100 % (forecast = 0), while there is no upper limit, that is, an error of more than 100 % is possible. In practice, this means that the forecast accuracy is greater if the forecast is conservative. However, this, in turn, could result in a loss of sales because planners who use this error to measure the forecast accuracy will tend to create forecasts with values that are too low.

The second disadvantage of the APE is that, if the actual values are zero or close to zero, the error becomes very large or cannot be calculated (division by zero).

Another disadvantage posed by the APE is the possibility of varying calculations. Because the APE is a percentage error, the actual value, as shown in the formula above, can be in the denominator. However, the actual value can also be in the numerator and the forecast value can be in the denominator. If the actual value is in the denominator, the APE favors forecast values that are too low, as mentioned above. If, on the other hand, the forecast is in the denominator, the APE favors forecast values that are too high. Table 4.10 shows an APE calculation.

Actual Value	Forecast	APE with Forecast Value in the Denominator	APE with Actual Value in the Denominator
120	100	20	16.67
140	160	12.50	14.29

Table 4.10 Calculation of APE

If you use this error in your company, you should therefore pay very close attention to the calculation methodology. Here, the same circumstances can be shown differently.

Due to its asymmetrical behavior, the APE should not be used if large error values are expected.

Adjusted Absolute Percentage Error (APE-A)

The adjusted APE was developed to counteract the disadvantages of the APE:

$APE\text{-}A = (C_t\text{-}F_t)/((C_t+F_t)/n)$
Legend: C_t = consumption; F_t = forecast

The difference between this adjusted version of APE and the absolute percentage error is that the average of the actual value plus the forecast value is used as the denominator, rather than the actual value. As a result, the APE-A produces comparable results, regardless of whether the forecast value exceeds the actual value, or the actual value exceeds the forecast value. It also returns a result if the actual value is equal to zero.

The APE-A is always between 0 and 2. Other values are not accepted. In contrast to the example shown above, the APE-A would calculate the following error (see Table 4.11).

Actual Value	Forecast	APE-A
120	100	0.18
140	160	0.13

Table 4.11 Calculation of APE-A

As a general rule, the smaller the value, the better the forecast with the APE-A.

Mean Absolute Percentage Error (MAPE)

The MAPE calculates the arithmetic mean of the percentage errors across several periods, based on the APE. First, the APE or APE-A is calculated for each period and the mean value of these errors is then calculated.

$MAPE = \Sigma((C_t\text{-}F_t)/C_t * 100)/n$
Legend: C_t = consumption; F_t = forecast, n = number of periods

Table 4.12 shows the MAPE error for our above formula.

Actual Value	Forecast	APE	MAPE
120	100	16.67	
140	160	14.29	
			15.48

Table 4.12 Calculation of MAPE

The advantage of the MAPE is that it provides a meaningful error value for a time series, because it calculates a mean value from all the errors in the individual periods.

However, the disadvantage is that it does not allow any conclusions to be drawn regarding effects on inventories. The MAPE thus cannot tell you whether a forecast is good or bad from the point of view of inventory management. The individual periods would have to be examined for this purpose. This applies to all forecast errors that calculate a mean value across several periods.

The following questions must be asked when interpreting the MAPE result:

▶ **For which products was a forecast created with the MAPE?**
The MAPE comprises the forecast results of various products. You should analyze precisely which products are included in the MAPE. Often the products don't even go together, so that a general forecast error is not useful.

▶ **Which periods are included in the MAPE?**
The monthly MAPE may be lower than the weekly MAPE.

▶ **What is your current MAPE?**
The development of the MAPE over time must be taken into account. This is often a much better indicator of forecast accuracy than a situation-specific MAPE.

Median Absolute Percentage Error (MdAPE)

The median value is the middle value in a list of figures sorted in ascending order. (With an even number of values, you take one of the two values in the middle of the sequence. If the two values differ, which is rare, you take the arithmetic mean of the two values.)

Example of an even number of values:

*10, 11, 15, **20**, **21**, 25, 30, 40 ⇒ Median = 20.5*

Example of an odd number of values:

*10, 11, 15, 20, **21**, 25, 30, 40, 100 ⇒ Median = 21*

First the APE is calculated for each period, and then the median is calculated according to the above logic.

The advantage of the median over the arithmetic mean is that it is robust against outliers, that is, against numbers that deviate to a significant degree from the norm. In this regard, MdAPE is preferable to MAPE.

The MdAPE is well suited for the selection of forecast models where sufficient data is available.

Relative Absolute Error (RAE)

With relative errors, two alternative forecasts are always compared with each other. The RAE formula is therefore as follows:

$RAE = (C_t - F_t)/1(C_t - F_{rw})$
Legend: C_t = consumption; F_t = forecast, F_{rw} = alternative forecast

Table 4.13 shows the RAE error for our above formula.

Actual Value	Forecast 1	Forecast 2	RAE
120	117	100	0.15
140	160	142	10

Table 4.13 Calculation of RAE

As you can see, the RAE is very large if the absolute error of the alternative forecast is very small. This favors the alternative forecast.

Since the RAE (like the APE and the APE-A) must be calculated for each period, only these periods can be compared with one another individually. A cumulation therefore results in an incorrect interpretation with the RAE.

Median Relative Absolute Error (MdRAE)

The MdRAE is the median RAE (for how the median is calculated, see the section above). It is well suited to the selection of forecast models where only a small amount of data is available (unlike the MdAPE). It is also robust against outliers.

Geometric Mean Relative Absolute Error (GMRAE)

The geometric mean of the RAE is used to summarize relative errors with marginal outliers.

The GMRAE summarizes the RAE for a time series. For example, it could provide you with a value for a period of 12 months. The GMRAE should be used if the parameters of a selected forecast model are to be optimized. The GMRAE is calculated as follows:

$$GMRAE = (RAE_1, RAE_2, ...RAE_n)^{1/n}$$

Tracking Signal

If you want to allow the forecast procedure to have a certain range of tolerance with regard to the error, you can use the tracking signal to define this range. In this case, normal distribution of deviation is assumed. Thus, if you wanted to allow the forecast model to have a tolerance range of 95 % of the mean value, you would use a standard deviation of approximately +/− 1.6.

The tracking signal is calculated as follows:

Tracking signal = |Error total/MAD|

Table 4.14 shows the MAD error for our above formula.

Actual Value	Forecast	Absolute Deviation	Error Total	MAD	Tracking Signal
120	110	10			
140	160	20			
			30	15	2

Table 4.14 Tracking Signal Calculation

Accordingly, the forecasting technique must be reset if the deviation signal is outside a certain interval of +/− 1.6.

So the tracking signal is not, strictly speaking, a forecast error. Rather, it is used to define a range of tolerance for an error, which is useful when you are creating a forecast.

Theil Coefficient

Nondimensional measures enable you to compare the forecast errors of different time series. If you divide the measures by the arithmetic mean, you can then interpret these as percentage errors.

The Theil coefficient is also not, strictly speaking, a forecast error. Rather, it helps the user to compare different forecasts.

Evaluating the Univariate Forecast Error

The current literature (see Marakidis; Armstrong) recommends the following error measures for univariate forecasts:

▶ The Median Relative Absolute Error (MdRAE) for selecting forecast models if only a small amount of historical data is available

▶ The Median Absolute Percentage Error (MdAPE), if a sufficient amount of historical data is available

▶ The Geometric Mean Relative Absolute Error (GMRAE), if the parameters of a selected forecast model are to be optimized

4.3.3 Causal Forecast Errors (MLR)

With multiple linear regression (MLR), you evaluate the effects of various causal factors on the forecast. A number of different functions are provided for this purpose. The system generates an alert if the statistical result of the calculation exceeds or falls short of the defined upper/lower limit.

R Square

With MLR, the R square indicates how well a certain combination of X variables (the drivers or independent variables of the model) explains the variation in Y (dependent variable).

The R square lies within the value range of 0 to 1. A value of 0 signifies that the MLR model cannot explain the variation in Y. A value of 1 means that the model is a perfect fit. A value of 0.9 or higher indicates an acceptable model.

R square is also known as the coefficient of determination or the measure of the "goodness-of-fit."

If you use this measure to compare two models, you must ensure that the same dependent variable is used.

Adjusted R Square

In a multiple linear regression model, the adjusted R square measures the percentage variation in the dependent variables that is accounted for by the explanatory independent variables. In contrast to the R square, the adjusted R square incorporates the degree of freedom associated with the sums of the squares. Even though the residual sum of squares may decrease or remain the same when new explanatory variables are added, this is not necessarily the case with the residual variance. Adjusted R square is therefore considered a more accurate measure of goodness of fit than R square.

Points to note in connection with adjusted R square:

▸ If the adjusted R square is significantly lower than R square, this usually means that one or more explanatory variables are missing. Without these variables, the variation in the dependent variables cannot be fully measured.

▸ If you use this measure to compare two models, you must ensure that the same dependent variable is used.

Durbin-h

This statistic checks for autocorrelation in time series where independent variables are delayed by one or more periods.

If Durbin-h is 1.96 or higher, it is very likely that autocorrelation exists. The Durbin-h test is suitable for large samples, that is, samples of 100 or more time series values.

Autocorrelation occurs if the error variables of a regression model are not independent, that is, if the values in the historical periods in the forecast model influence the values in the current periods. Time series with a marked seasonal or cyclical pattern are often highly correlated. A high degree of correlation means that MLR is not suitable as a forecasting technique if you're using the standard method of the smallest squares for the available data.

Durbin-Watson

Durbin-Watson is a measure used to test for first-order autocorrelation in time series in which independent variables are not delayed.

The Durbin-Watson statistic lies within a value range of 0 to 4. A value of 2 or thereabouts indicates that no first-order autocorrelation exists. Between 1.50 and 2.50 is an acceptable range.

In cases with consistently small error differences, the Durbin-Watson is low (< 1.50), which indicates positive autocorrelation. Positive autocorrelation is very common. In cases with consistently large error differences, the Durbin-Watson is high (> 2.50), which indicates negative autocorrelation. Negative autocorrelation is relatively uncommon.

In time series with delayed variables, the Durbin-Watson statistic is not reliable because it tends towards a value of 2.0.

t-Test

This test, which is also referred to as *t-statistic*, indicates whether an independent variable correlates with the dependent variable. This means it determines whether the independent variable contributes to the explanation of the dependent variable and thus it determines whether or not the independent variable should remain part of the model.

The t-test does not provide any information on the significance of the size and influence of an explanatory variable (for example, a t-test of around 4.6 has no greater significance than a t-test of 2.4). It simply means that the independent variables linked with the t-test are significant enough to explain why the deviation in the dependent variable exists. The size of this relationship is measured by the coefficient of the independent variable, including its unit of measurement.

The reference value for a t-test is +/–2.0. This value is used to determine whether the correlation between an independent variable and the dependent variable at a confidence level of 95 % is significant. However, empirical tests have shown that a t-test of +/–1.4 or higher is structurally significant at a confidence level of 90%. For this reason, SAP recommends keeping explanatory variables in the model if the t-test is +/–1.4 or higher.

Mean Elasticity

The elasticity measures the effect on the dependent variable caused by a change of 1 % to the explanatory variable. The elasticity is calculated as a percentage change of Y (dependent variable), divided by the percentage change of X (explanatory or independent variable). Elasticities often differ if they are measured at different points of the regression. The mean elasticity represents the average value of the elasticities measured at these different points.

Elasticities are useful because they aren't specified in any unit. For that reason, they provide a simpler option to interpret and describe the effects of causal variables, for example, for senior management. A high elasticity means that the dependent variable reacts sensitively to changes in the explanatory variable.

Other errors can be flexibly determined using macros (see Section 3.5).

4.3.4 Forecast Errors in SAP APO—Summary

Table 4.15 provides an overview of the aforementioned forecast errors. It also indicates which errors are supported in SAP APO.

Forecast Error	Description	Determining Formula	Univariate/ Causal	SAP APO Standard	SAP APO Macro
ET	Error total	$\sum |(C_t - F_t)|$	Univariate error	X	
MAD	Mean absolute deviation	$1/_n \sum (C_t - F_t)$	Univariate error	X	
MSE	Mean square error	$1/_n \sum (V_t - P_t)^2$	Univariate error	X	
RMSE	Root of the mean square error	$\sqrt{1/_n} \sum (C_t - F_t)^2$	Univariate error	X	
APE	Absolute percentage error	$(C_t - F_t)/ C_t * 100$	Univariate error		X
APE-A	Adjusted absolute percentage error	$(C_t - F_t)/ ((C_t + F_t)/n)$	Univariate error		X
MAPE	Mean absolute percentage error	$\sum ((C_t - F_t)/ C_t * 100)/n$	Univariate error	X	
MdAPE	Median absolute percentage error	Median of MAPE	Univariate error		X
RAE	Relative absolute error	$(C_t - F_t)/ (C_t - F_{rw})$	Univariate error		X
MdRAE	Median relative absolute error	Median of RAE	Univariate error		X
GMRAE	Geometric mean absolute error	$(RAE_1, RAE_2, ...RAE_n)^{1/n}$	Univariate error		X
Tracking signal		|Error total/MAD|	Support for univariate errors	X	
Theil coefficient			Support for univariate errors	X	
R square			Causal error	X	
Adjusted R square			Causal error	X	

Table 4.15 Forecast Errors in SAP APO

Forecast Error	Description	Determining Formula	Univariate/ Causal	SAP APO Standard	SAP APO Macro
Durbin-h			Causal error	X	
Durbin-Watson			Causal error	X	
t-test			Causal error	X	
Mean elasticity			Causal error	X	

Table 4.15 Forecast Errors in SAP APO (cont.)

4.3.5 Alert Monitor

In SAP APO, you can automate this interpretation of the forecast error. This is particularly useful when you have to create a forecast for many products. An alert system will then notify you when the selected forecasting technique doesn't provide any reliable values. The planner can individually define the threshold values and limits regarding the tolerance range of the forecast error.

The SAP APO Alert Monitor enables you to monitor the quality of your forecast during the planning process and to determine whether your plan can be carried out easily. For this purpose, you must define alert profiles for the applications that you want to use. These alert profiles store information on the situations in which the system notifies you of a problem, that is, it generates an alert.

It's not always possible for all planners involved to actively monitor the alerts in the Alert Monitor. However, you can use notification functions to ensure that each planner is notified of alerts in his or her respective area of responsibility.

In demand planning, the Alert Monitor distinguishes between macro-dependent alerts and forecast alerts.

The system generates forecast alerts if the historical data, which the forecast is based on, is incorrectly described by the selected forecast models. For example, let's say that you have assumed that the demand rises constantly, but over time you learn that the rate of demand depends on the season.

To navigate to the forecast alert maintenance, select **SAP APO • Supply Chain Monitoring • Alert Monitor** (see Figure 4.64).

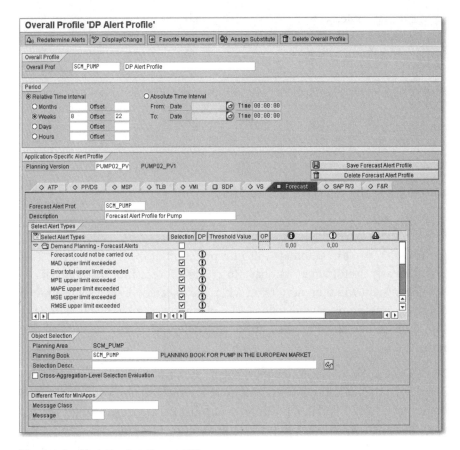

Figure 4.64 Alert Monitor, Forecast View

In the upper part of the screen, you can see the maintenance of the **Overall Profile** and the **Period** for which you want SAP APO to generate alerts. The center of the screen displays separate tabs that enable you to maintain the alerts for the individual SAP APO modules. You can maintain the forecast alerts in the **Forecast** tab.

Macro-dependent alerts refer to customer-specific problems, for example, if a requirements forecast exceeds or falls short of a customer-specific key figure. You can also assign customized status messages to individual macro steps and have these messages displayed like alerts in the Alert Monitor. Figure 4.65 shows an example of such a macro alert.

This macro calculates the difference between the forecasts of the current week and the previous week and generates an alert if the difference is larger than 20 %. **Forecast** and **Previous Forecast** are two key figures (two rows) in the planning table. The company XYZ produces the basic product ABC, which shows a stable demand over time. For this reason, the forecasts for the current and previous weeks shouldn't differ too much, because under normal circumstances no sudden changes are to be expected. If the forecast for period 3 in the current week is 100 and if it was 60 for the same period in the previous week, this represents an exception of which the demand planner must be notified. This macro records such exceptions, triggers an alert, and highlights the relevant cell in red. The planner can then take the necessary action.

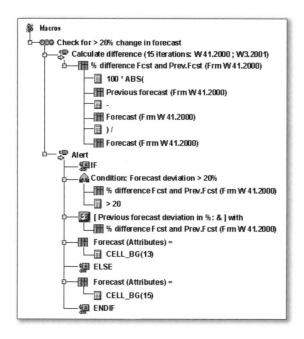

Figure 4.65 Example of a Macro-Dependent Forecast Alert

4.4 Lifecycle Planning

In the lifecycle planning, we can look at the different phases in a product's lifecycle from a planning point of view. We will describe how this happens in SAP APO.

4.4.1 Introduction

The lifecycle of a product is usually divided into the following stages: introduction, growth, maturity, saturation, and discontinuation (see Figure 4.66).

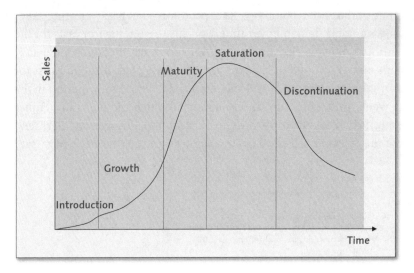

Figure 4.66 Product Lifecycle

In a product's growth period, demand will suddenly grow disproportionately higher than in the introduction phase. The forecasting technique for the growth phase will now no longer fit. The speed of the demand changes, which means that the speed of the forecasting technique must be adapted to that change as well.

The same applies to the next stage when the product leaves the maturity stage and enters the saturation stage. If demand planning does not account for this phase, its requirements forecasts will be too high and the stocks will increase inexorably. This change of the stages also requires that the forecasting technique be adjusted and in some cases replaced.

Products at the saturation stage have a long history and are the favorites of the demand planner. Here, we no longer expect any big surprises in the requirements pattern and the planner is in a good position to take into account any exceptional influences simply thanks to his or her experience with these products. A typical example is the product Coca Cola. Quantitative methods are best suited to these products,

The cannibalization of products is a phenomenon that is closely linked to the product lifecycle. This describes the mutual influence that two or more products may have on each other. The demand for a new product (at the introduction or growth stage) can sometimes affect the demand for existing products that are at the saturation or discontinuation stages.

Cannibalization: Example "Promotion action for ice cream"

A promotion action for ice cream is a classical example of cannibalization. Promotions are often supposed to advertise certain products, for example, chocolate ice cream. At the same time, the demand for vanilla ice cream will decrease because customers are influenced by the advertising campaign and will buy more chocolate ice cream than vanilla ice cream. In other words, the vanilla ice cream will be cannibalized by the chocolate ice cream.

You can counteract this problem by implementing phase-in and phase-out mechanisms. In a phase-in-/-out modeling process, the result of the statistical forecast is multiplied by a time-dependent factor. The result of this process is the final forecast. The time-dependent factor is stored in a phase-in or phase-out profile.

Phase-in/phase-out mechanisms: Example "white goods"

"White goods" are an example illustrating where this phase-in/phase-out mechanism would be applied. For instance, if a manufacturer of coffee machines has previously produced only white coffee machines and now introduces a coffee machine with an innovative green color instead of the white color onto the market, then the white coffee machine will be phased out while the green one is phased in. In phase-in profiles (for the green coffee machine), the factor increases over time, while it gets smaller in phase-out profiles (for the white coffee machine). These interdependencies (cannibalization) must be taken into account during the demand planning.

SAP APO offers various tools for modeling the lifecycle and cannibalizing a product in the demand planning. These functions can also be used for other characteristics. For example, if you introduce an existing product at a different location, you can use like profiles to base your calculations on historical data from the current locations, while with a phase-in profile, you can then reduce the forecast for the period of the introduction.

Lifecycle planning is integrated with the univariate forecast, the causal analysis, and the composite forecast.

Lifecycle planning in SAP APO comprises two functions—the like modeling and the phase-in-/phase-out modeling—which will be outlined for you below. Both functions enable you to forecast at detail level and at aggregate level.

4.4.2 Like Profiles

When you start creating a forecast for new characteristic values combinations, it is unlikely that historical data exists, which could be used as a basis for the forecast. However, there is the option of copying data from a different characteristic values combination using the realignment function, that is, by reorganizing the historical data, but that would result in an unnecessary increase in the amount of redundant data in the system. In a like modeling process, one characteristic value is replaced by one or more other values. This results in a new combination for which historical data exists. Based on this data, the system can then create a forecast.

Here the example that we have chosen is that of a new almond ice cream variety, which will be introduced with the product number T-FV300. For this new flavor, there is no historical sales data available, which could be used as a basis for the creation of a new forecast. For this reason, we will use the historical data (sales history) for the vanilla (T-FV100) and chocolate (T-FV200) flavors to simulate historical data for the new flavor. We can do this by using the like profile.

In SAP APO, you can maintain the like profile in the menu **SAP APO • Demand Planning • Environment • Life Cycle Planning**. You will get the input screen shown in Figure 4.67.

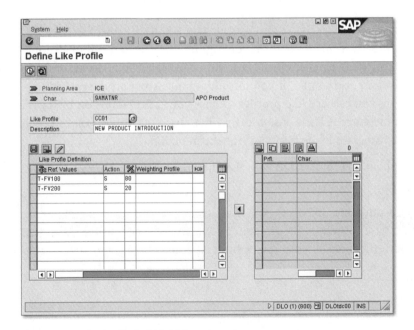

Figure 4.67 Like Profile in SAP APO

Specify a planning area and a characteristic, and assign a number and a description to the like profile.

In the **Reference Values** column, please maintain the materials that are to be drawn for the forecast of the new product T-FV300 (almond ice cream variety). In the above example the forecast for the new product, T-FV300, is thus based at 80% on the historical data of the T-FV100 product (vanilla), and at 20% on the historical values of the T-FV200 product (chocolate). Finally, the like profile must be assigned to the new product, T-FV300.

SAP APO therefore enables you to base your forecast on one or more similar products.

4.4.3 Phase-In/Phase-Out Profiles

The demand for an object (usually a product or a product group) in its introduction and discontinuation phases usually differs from the demand in the product's maturity phase. At the beginning, the demand rises with every period, whereas it decreases towards the end of the lifecycle. A statistical forecast that is based on the situation in the maturity phase cannot predict such a behavior. In a phase-in/phase-out modeling process, the result of the statistical forecast is multiplied by a time-dependent factor. The result of this process is the final forecast. The time-dependent factor is stored in a phase-in or phase-out profile. In phase-in profiles, the factor increases over time, while it gets smaller in phase-out profiles.

Here we have chosen an example where we now want the forecast for the new almond ice cream product to also take into account the lifecycle curve. For this purpose, we have chosen a time series that is supposed to map the product lifecycle influences. The time series must be assigned to the new ice cream flavor. After that, the forecast is multiplied by the time series in the respective periods so that the influences of the lifecycle can be integrated into the forecast.

In SAP APO, you can maintain the phase-in and phase-out profiles in the menu **SAP APO • Demand Planning • Environment • Life Cycle Planning**. Then click on the **Phase-in/out** button. You will get the input screen shown in Figure 4.68.

Select a planning area, assign a name (time series) and a description to the time series, and define the period for the phase-in or phase-out by entering the start and end dates. Select the required period by choosing the respective period identifier. In this case, in our ice cream scenario, we have defined a phase-in within a period of 10 weeks in which the sales figures increase by 10% in each week until sales of the new product reach a value of 100% above the basic value in week 10. Phase-in time series are entered in ascending order; phase-out time series are entered in descending order.

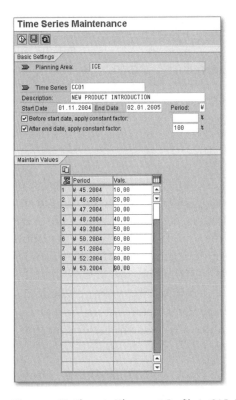

Figure 4.68 Phase-in/Phase-out Profile in SAP APO

Like the phase-out and like profiles, the phase-in profile must be assigned to a material, as shown in Figure 4.69.

This means that when you introduce a new product or discontinue an existing one, you should be aware that the demands will differ substantially from those in the product's maturity phase. The use of the phase-in/phase-out modeling function in SAP APO enables you to factor this behavior. To be fair, however, we should note that you cannot map a real lifecycle using the phase-in profile. Real-life requirements are often much too complex and cannot be fulfilled by a simple time series. Nevertheless, you can at least approach reality using this function. Additionally you can also map the lifecycle directly in the forecasting technique, as the example shown in Figure 4.69 illustrates.

Assign Life Cycle

⊕ Planning Area	ICE

No. of Assignments: 2

Profile Assignment for Life Cycle

APO Product	Like Profile	Phase-In Profile	Frm Date	To Date	Phase-Out Profile	Frm Date	To Date
T-FV100		CC01	01.06.2004	15.08.2004			
T-FV200					CC01	01.06.2004	15.08.2004

Figure 4.69 Assigning the Profiles for the Lifecycle

Cannibalization effects can also be observed during the promotion planning (see Section 4.5). It can happen that one and the same promotion affects the sales of some products positively and the sales of others negatively.

For example, a 5% discount on 32 ounce bottles of a peach shampoo can cause a sales increase of 30,000 units, whereas the sales of 8.5 ounce bottles decreases by 3,000 units and that of 17 ounce bottles by 5,000 units. This situation is depicted in Figure 4.70.

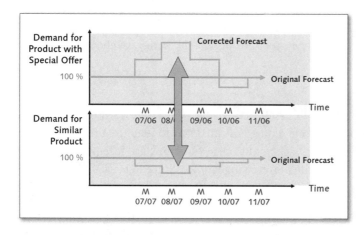

Figure 4.70 Cannibalization with Promotions (Source SAP)

In SAP APO you must determine the members of the cannibalization group and assign a factor to these members. The factor determines the amount by which the sales of the relevant product are influenced.

To do this, choose the menu **SAP APO • Demand Planning • Planning • Settings • Maintain Cannibalization Group**, and you will get the following input screen (see Figure 4.71).

Figure 4.71 Maintain Cannibalization Group

Enter a name (**Cannib. grp ID**) and a description for a cannibalization group. You then select the material that you want to assign to the cannibalization group. Enter a positive or negative figure for each material, depending on whether the sales of this product are positively or negatively influenced by the promotion.

4.4.4 Product Interchangeability

The demand planning offers a range of functions to map the product discontinuation and product replacement. These functions are integrated into the APO function of the product interchangeability. Since Release 4.0, the lifecycle planning has been fully integrated with the functions of the product interchangeability. Unlike the general demand planning, each product that you want to use with the functions of the product interchangeability must have a product master. Furthermore, these products must be assigned to the model you are using.

You must first create an interchangeability group under **SAP APO • Master Data • Maintain Interchangeability Group**. In Figure 4.72, you can see the interchangeability group that has been created.

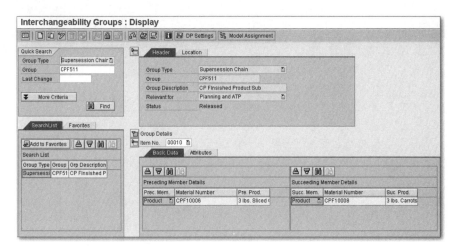

Figure 4.72 Interchangeability Group

In the upper part of the screen, you can see the group header data. This specifies that it is a supersession chain that is relevant for planning and the ATP availability check, and that the interchangeability group already has the status "Released".

In the bottom part of the screen, on the left, you can see the previous product and on the right you can see the follow-up product.

The demand planning is integrated with supersession chains. This is the only type of interchangeability group that is relevant for the demand planning. FFF classes (Form, Fit, Function classes) are not relevant for the demand planning because the planning of requirements takes place on a more general basis and the question, for instance, of the supplier from which a particular product is procured is not particularly important. The following types of supersession chain exist. The only one that is compatible with the demand planning is the product-product chain. Accordingly, only 1:1 relationships are possible. If you need more complex functions, you should use the standard demand planning functions, such as lifecycle planning or realignment (data reorganization).

When you click on the **DP Settings** button (see Figure 4.72), the **Product Interchangeability—Demand Planning** screen opens (see Figure 4.73).

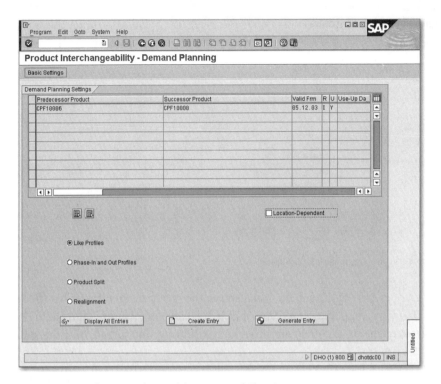

Figure 4.73 Product Interchangeability, Demand Planning

The demand planning has four functions that are linked with the initial and final phases of a product's manufacture:

▸ Like Profiles

▸ Phase-in and Out Profiles

▸ Product Split

▸ Realignment (data reorganization)

Since the demand planning is scheduled in periods, during the phase-out control, a change, for example, a phase-out step, applies to an entire period. This means that the demand planning cannot map the product phase-out as expected within a period. For example, if you are using a phase-out profile with monthly periods, and the phase-out date is the fifteenth of the month, the demand planning reduces the requirement for the successor product as from the first of the month. (In the case of a product assignment, the assignment then applies from the beginning of the next month.)

Since the demand planning doesn't work with actual stocks, the Use-Up indicator has no effect on supersession chains.

The product assignment function enables you to replace a product that you have planned in the demand planning with one or several products if you release the plan to the Supply Network Planning (SNP) and the production and detailed scheduling (PP/DS). This means that this function is primarily useful for the continued planning in SNP and PP-DS. It is of little significance, however, for the demand planning.

All of the functions available in the lifecycle planning apply to an individual phase-out combination. The phase-out combination comprises two products within a phase-out step—the preceding product and the follow-up product.

You first select a combination and then the profile or function that you want to edit.

Before you make the settings for the lifecycle planning, that is, for like profiles or phase-in/-out profiles, you must have implemented the basic settings for the planning area. If you want to update or check these settings, click on the **Basic Settings** button.

Three options are available here (see Figure 4.73):

▶ **Display All Entries**
The system shows all existing like-profiles, phase-in/-out profiles, the product assignment entries, or the corresponding realignment entries. You can choose an individual profile from the list and edit the details.

▶ **Create Entry**
You enter the planning area in a dialog window. The system then branches into the maintenance of the like- or phase-in/-out profiles of the planning area, so that you can create a profile for the follow-up product. To do this, you use the preceding and the follow-up product as reference products. For both reference products, the system sets the action "T— Total" and the factor 100%. This means that at the time that there is historical data for the follow-up product, this is taken into account during the forecast.

For the product assignment, the system automatically creates entries in the product assignment table, with the preceding product as the source product, the follow-up product as the target product, and a proportional factor of 1. It also creates an entry for the period until the next phase-out date.

During realignment, the system creates an entry with the source and target product as in the phase-out combination in the realignment table and displays the step in change mode.

▶ **Generate Entry**
The system automatically generates a like profile or a phase-in/-out profile for the phase-out combination.

During realignment, the system creates an entry with the source and target product as in the phase-out combination in the realignment table and displays the step in change mode.

The product interchangeability method for which you decide ultimately depends on your planning requirements.

Realignment (Data Reorganization)

Each time you want to plan a new product in the demand planning, you must have created the required characteristic values combinations before planning begins. The realignment (data reorganization) is a method that can be used for this; however, the realignment also copies the data from the source characteristic values combinations into the target combinations. Furthermore, it copies the notes and generated selections.

Because it takes considerably longer to copy the data than to create new characteristic values combinations, you should not use the realignment to create new combinations. The better method here is to edit the combinations in a spreadsheet file (MS Excel), upload the data into an InfoCube, and then generate the characteristic values combinations from the InfoCube.

The data of all key figures is transferred in a realignment run. For that reason, it may be necessary to first edit the transferred data before you actually work with the new product.

Since the realignment generally runs in regular intervals as a background job, once all entries have been made in the realignment table, this method cannot be used for rapid changes. It is not well suited to periodic product changes.

Instead, realignment is suitable for scenarios in which a product is replaced for technical reasons and you assume a requirement that corresponds closest to the requirement for the previous product.

Phase-In/Out with Like Modeling

The classical demand planning functions for the lifecycle planning offer you the most comprehensive options for creating a forecast.

Compared with the realignment, the like modeling reduces the dataset in the system; the historical data is only required for an individual characteristic value combination. It also allows for more complex processes to be mapped, for example, the totaling of the historical data of different existing products to generate the historical data for the new product, or the use of factors in a time series. Weighting factors like these allow you to include seasonal effects in such models.

Phase-in-/out models are the only option, aside from the macros, to use for mapping a gradual, controlled transition from one product to another.

Although a phase-out profile cannot prevent you from creating a requirement for a product being phased out, unlike other applications, it does not transfer the requirement to the successor product. To do this, you should use a product assignment.

Product Assignment

This is a flexible method for performing short-term changes. This function releases the data saved for a location product in the demand planning to one or several other products in the same location in Supply Network Planning (SNP). In the product assignment table, you can specify that a product assignment should only be valid for a limited period. In this way, you can plan short projects without having to create characteristic value combinations in the demand planning.

Since the product assignment does not take place until the release to SNP, you cannot see the changed data in the demand planning, unless you release the data from SNP back to the demand planning. However, this assumes that the required characteristic values combinations already exist in the demand planning, which means that the advantages of this method would not apply. It is not possible to map a curve for the follow-on product that is different to that for the previous product.

Example: Sporadic requirement

A scenario such as that shown in Figure 4.74 can be depicted with the product assignment without too much effort. To map this approach, you should consider using the promotion planning with cannibalization. Nevertheless, these functions cannot be called from the product interchangeability.

Example: Immediate switch

Figure 4.75 shows the classical product phase-out case. In this scenario, after a particular date we want no more requirements to be created for product 1. At the same date, the requirement for product 2 jumps from 0 to the forecast value.

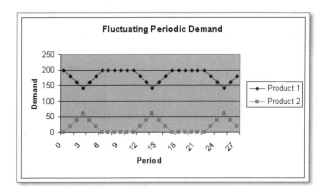

Figure 4.74 Product Interchangeability with Sporadic Requirement

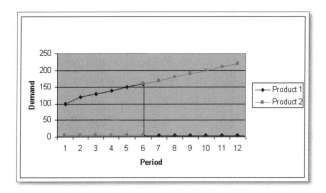

Figure 4.75 Product Interchangeability with Immediate Switch

To map the example shown in Figure 4.75 with SAP APO, you must make the following settings (see Figure 4.67, Figure 4.68, and Figure 4.69):

1. For the basic settings you set the indicator **Aggregated lifecycle planning with like profiles** and **Aggregated lifecycle planning with phase-in-/out profiles**.

2. Create a like profile, with product 1 and product 2 as reference products.

3. Assign the like profile to product 2 (as well as other characteristic values required).

4. Create a phase-in profile that is 100 % constant throughout the entire period. You can use a relatively short period. Set the required indicator so that a factor of 100 % is applied after the phase-in period.

5. Create a phase-out profile that is 0 % constant throughout the entire period. You can use a relatively short period. Set the required indicator so that a factor of 0 % is applied after the phase-in period.

6. Assign the phase-in profile to product 2 and the phase-out profile to product 1.

7. Perform the forecast in the interactive planning for both products together.

8. Select the corresponding product combination in the window **Product Interchangeability—Demand Planning**.

9. Select **Product Assignment** and choose **Create Entry**. The system will create two entries:

   ▸ For the period until the phase-out date

   ▸ As from the phase-out date

10. Check the entries, in particular, the date information and periods.

11. Release your requirements plan to SNP.

Planned independent requirements are created for the previous product until the phase-out date and for the follow-on product after this date.

4.5 Promotion Planning

In the following section, you will learn how to integrate promotions or special events into your planning in SAP APO.

4.5.1 Overview

With SAP APO demand planning, you can plan promotional measures and other initiatives, and other special events, separately from your remaining forecast activities. Use the promotion planning either to allow for a one time event or recurring events (e.g., quarterly advertising drives). Other examples of promotions include trade shows, trade discounts, and commissions, high-visibility sales, promotional actions including gift certificates, raffles or magazine supplements, competitive activities, market research, economic upswings and downturns, as well as major natural phenomena (hurricanes, tornados, etc.). The advantages of planning promotions separately are as follows:

▸ You can compare the forecast without promotions with the forecast with promotions.

▸ You can correct the historical sales data in such a way that you can exclude historical promotions and thus obtain historical data without promotional data for the baseline forecast.

▸ The process of creating baseline forecasts and the promotion planning process can be handled separately. For example, sales and distribution could create an initial forecast uploaded from Excel while marketing is responsible for the promotion planning.

The following steps describe a possible implementation of the promotion planning process.

1. The demand planner creates the baseline forecast by using mass processing.

2. The demand planner verifies the forecast results in interactive demand planning.

3. The required promotions are created in the promotion planning. For example, all promotions such as the marketing calendars that are filled with special offers, industry-specific promotions, and knowledge on the exit of a competitor are assigned to the "Sales" key figure. Promotion planning can be called via the interactive demand planning.

4. In interactive planning, the demand planner views the effects of all planned promotions on the forecasted overall demand and implements final corrections in the demand plan.

5. The demand plan (which represents the final result of the baseline forecast, promotion plan, and final corrections) is released to Supply Network Planning.

6. The constrained Supply Network Planning plan, which takes restrictions into account, is returned to demand planning.

7. The forecast accuracy is checked against actual data.

4.5.2   Creating a Promotion

To create a promotion, click on the **Promotion Planning** button in the interactive demand planning, or under **SAP Easy Access**, choose the menu path **Demand Planning • Planning • Promotion • Promotion Planning**. The **Promotion in Interactive Planning** window opens (see Figure 4.76).

Enter the following here:

▸ General information, such as the name of the promotion (**Short Text** field), and a descriptive text (**Description** field)

▸ The promotion type (**Type**); here you can enter absolute figures (items, kilograms) or percentages of the baseline figures.

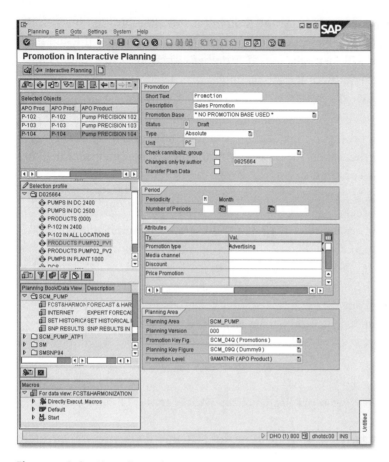

Figure 4.76 Creating a Promotion

▶ Specify whether a cannibalization group (**Check cannibaliz. group**) is to be used (and which one); a cannibalization group groups the products whose sales are influenced either positively or negatively by the same promotion.

▶ Whether only the author should be allowed to change the promotion (**Changes only by author**)

▶ The name of the **Promotion Base**, provided you want to use one

▶ Whether you want to copy the data from the key figure of the baseline planning into the promotion when creating the promotion (**Promotion Key Fig.**); this data forms the starting point for planning a promotion. You will see the status of the promotion (initially **Draft**) and the **Unit** that applies for the promotion.

▶ The Periodicity (e.g., day, week, month)

▸ The **Number of Periods** for the promotion and either the start date or the end date; alternatively, you can set both the start date and the end date. The system will then calculate the number of periods.

▸ Values for types of the promotion attributes; a promotion **attribute** groups promotions with the same attributes. Promotion attribute types are used as filters for selection and analysis purposes. You can select **promotions** according to their attributes in the shuffler; to do this, enter Promotion as the generic selection criterion and the promotion attribute types as the conditions.

Example for a Promotion Attribute Type

The promotion attribute type "Discount" has the following attributes:

▸ 20 % discount

▸ Two products for the price of one

▸ In the shuffler, you select all promotions with the attribute **Two products for the price of one**.

The promotion attribute type "Media channel" has the following attributes:

▸ Television

▸ Radio

▸ Internet

▸ In the shuffler, you select all promotions with the attribute **Internet**.

▸ The **Planning Area**, derived from the planning book you are currently working with; if you call the promotion planning directly (e.g., from the menu), then this is the planning book to which you are generally assigned, or the planning book that you call in the transaction /SAPAPO/MP34

▸ A **Planning Version** contained in the planning area

▸ A key figure in which the data for the promotion is to be saved (**Promotion Key Fig.**). This key figure should already be contained in the planning book. If you use a promotion base, the system automatically copies the key figure that was assigned to the promotion into this field. You cannot change this value here.

▸ A key figure into which the data is saved for the baseline forecast (i.e., the plan without the promotion) (**Planning Key Figure**). This key figure should already be contained in the planning book.

The **Promotion Level** field displays the characteristic on whose level the promotion is maintained. Here you see, for example, whether promotions are to be planned for a product or a location. This is the lowest plannable level.

Once you have entered all of the data, click on **Save**. The parameters now appear in the lower half of the screen as tabs. The top half of the screen shows the planning table as in the interactive planning (see Figure 4.77).

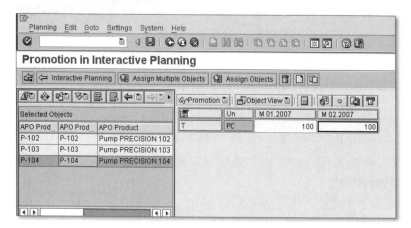

Figure 4.77 Promotion Planning View

4.5.3 Promotion Base

A promotion base forms the basis for a series of promotions. It specifies the characteristics that are used to plan promotions. A key figure is assigned to each promotion base.

When you use a promotion base to plan promotions, the effects of individual promotions can be more easily identified. It is also easier to plan promotions at detail level. A promotion base is set for a limited period of time. Two promotion bases can have the same period or overlapping periods, as well as the same characteristic combinations in the same planning area. However, their promotion key figures must be different.

Each promotion base contains at least one characteristic, the promotion level. Before you can define a promotion base for a planning area, you must have created a promotion level for this planning area.

You use a separate transaction to create and edit a promotion base (**SAP APO • Demand Planning • Planning • Promotion • Maintain Promotion Base**). This allows you to limit the number of users who are authorized to use this transaction. If you create a new promotion in the corresponding planning area, you can assign it to a promotion base. The system automatically loads the corresponding information from the promotion base. In particular, it determines the key figures in the promotion base and the promotion key figure. It is configured so that during the promotion planning, you cannot assign any values to characteristics that are not included in the promotion base.

In the transaction for promotion evaluations (**Demand Planning • Planning • Promotion • Maintain Settings for Evaluations**), you can create evaluations for individual promotions based on a promotion base.

4.6 Collaborative Demand Planning

The following section introduces you to the benefits of collaborative demand planning, and the procedures that you must adhere to.

4.6.1 Overview

The goal of SAP APO Collaborative Planning (CLP) is to help companies conduct their supply chain activities with their business partners. In this way, important input from business partners can be factored in order to synchronize the planning within the entire network, and optimized plans can be created based on data from the Supply Chain Network.

The Internet and related technologies such as XML have revolutionized internal operational business processes by allowing the seamless exchange of information between business partners. Large volumes of data can be transferred at minimal cost, and even small business partners can economically exchange information. Interactive online access to the different systems can be easily achieved using a conventional Internet browser.

SAP APO-CLP is the module with which companies can plan the logistical activities in cooperation with the business partners, beginning with the forecast all the way through to the transport planning. Collaborative Planning extends beyond the limits of Supply Chain Management, to integrate all relevant business partners and enable collaborative business processes in the entire network. The clear entities within this network, such as suppliers, manufacturers and retailers, can collaborate with each other and act as a single entity that can specialize in leveraging the added value for the customer, while costs in the chain as a whole are reduced.

SAP APO Collaborative Planning was designed to:

▶ Allow the exchange of required planning information with business partners

▶ Enable the use of a browser for reading and changing data

▶ Restrict user access to authorized data and activities

▶ Support the joint planning process

▶ Support the management in exceptional cases

There are two basic functions for using SAP APO Collaborative Planning:

▶ Collaboration Engine (CE) within/between APO systems

▶ Interactive use with the Internet Transaction Server (ITS)

4.6.2 CLP Architecture and Data Transfer

Figure 4.78 offers an overview of the architecture that is behind the solution of SAP APO-CLP, and illustrates how communication takes place between the various systems.

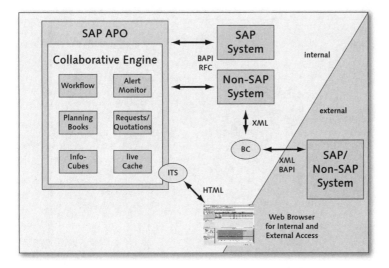

Figure 4.78 Architecture for Collaborative Planning with SAP APO

The figure clearly shows that there are two types of data transfer:

▶ Automatic data transfer with an incoming/outgoing interface to transfer time series and orders via EDI, BAPIs, and XML. This is controlled through the SAP middleware technology Business Connector (BC).

▶ Manual data transfer with the option of maintaining data via the browser interface, for which only an Internet access is required. The SAP middleware technology for Internet applications—the SAP Internet Transaction Server (ITS)—is used for this.

The goal of collaborative demand planning is to exchange period-based key figures between manufacturers and retailers in order to obtain a consensus-based forecast. The goal of collaborative inventory planning, on the other hand, is to exchange material requirements between manufacturers and suppliers at an early stage, so that all parties involved can adjust their delivery and production plans accordingly. You can exchange the key figures on various planning levels. We will now discuss collaborative demand planning in more detail.

4.6.3   Process Flow for Collaborative Demand Planning

There are many different possibilities for collaborative demand planning. The following example illustrates the use of collaborative demand planning (see also Figure 4.79).

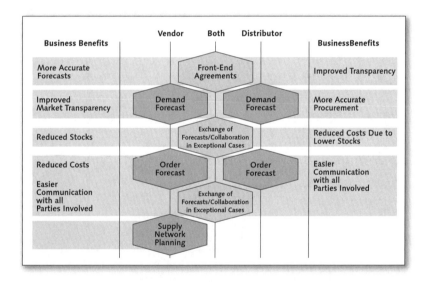

Figure 4.79 Collaborative Demand Planning Process

Within the collaborative demand planning, the buyer and seller develop a single forecast and refresh it based on common information from the Internet. It is a business-to-business workflow with a dynamic data interchange that was designed to reduce stocks in the entire supply chain. The basic workflow involves seven steps:

1. Agreement on the process: definition of the roles of the partners, fixing the data privacy level of common information; agreement on a procedure and on performance measurement

2. Creation of a joint plan and deciding on the products that are to be jointly administered; these include the category role, the strategy, and the tactics

3. Development of a forecast for customer requirements, based on common promotion calendars and an analysis of the Point of Sale (POS) and causal data

4. Identification and solving of exceptions in the forecast by planned/actual comparisons and determining of exception situations

5. Development of an order forecast that divides the demand forecast into time phases, while it complies with the stock and service goals of the business plan and adjusts corresponding capacity restrictions for manufacture and delivery

6. Identification and solving of the exceptions in the forecast, in particular exceptions relating to the manufacturer restrictions for delivering particular volumes; this produces an interactive loop for the revision of orders

7. Continue with the following planning steps.

4.7   Forecasting with BOMs

Another option in the demand planning is forecasting with BOMs to forecast secondary requirements.

4.7.1   Overview

You can forecast the secondary requirements in the demand planning. The system determines the components of finished products through the production process model (PPM) or the production data structure (PDS).

This can be beneficial if, in practice, material components have a restrictive effect on compiling the forecast at finished product level; in other words, the available set of components is fixed, but the components can be used for different finished products. This situation arises in the chemical industry, for example. The planner can see directly what effect the product forecast has on the level of the fixed components.

This process can also be applied in the consumer goods industry, for example, if we want to use the system to map the display space of a store with various products from a supplier. Both the display area (the "finished product") and the individual products (known as "components" in the demand planning) are released to Supply Network Planning.

In sectors such as the automotive industry, the important requirement for the OEMs only arises at component level, while the requirements for the finished product (e.g., the car) is only for the supplier's to make their forecast more transparent.

Example

For instance, if a cassette drive is installed in every car and we know that 1,000 cars are being manufactured, then the demand forecast of the supplier for cassette drives will also be 1,000.

The demand for the finished product is not released to Supply Network Planning. The PPM or the PDS of the demand planning (DP PPM/PDS) allows you to map this situation.

4.7.2 Process Flow

1. Create a production process model (PPM) with the usage D (BOM for Demand Planning (DP) and activate it (see Figure 4.80).

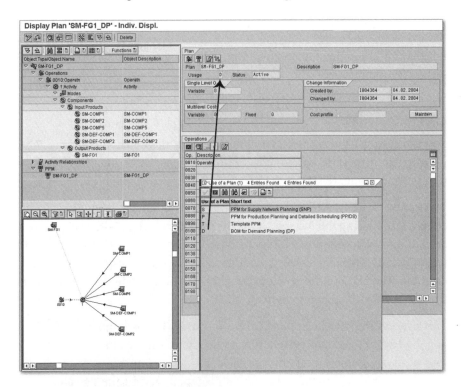

Figure 4.80 PPM for the Demand Planning

You can either create a PPM manually for the demand planning or generate a DP-PPM from an SNP-PPM or a PP/DS-PPM automatically. SAP recommends that you use single-level PPMs for this process, that is, PPMs for which all components of the finished product have been entered as inputs on one and the same level. This usually requires a number of calculations of input/output volumes in advance. If you generate a DP-PPM automatically, the system creates a single-level PPM, regardless of whether the PP/DS-PPM or the SNP-PPM is single-level or multilevel. You can also use production data structures (PDS). These should have been generated for DP or SNP.

2. Assign the PPM or the PDS to the supply chain model and the planning version with which you want to work (**Assign Model** button).

3. Create a basic planning object structure and select the option **Relevant for DP BOM**. This adds the characteristics 9AMATNR, 9ABOMID, 9ABOMIO, and 9APPMNAME to the basic planning object structure (see Figure 4.81). You can add other required characteristics.

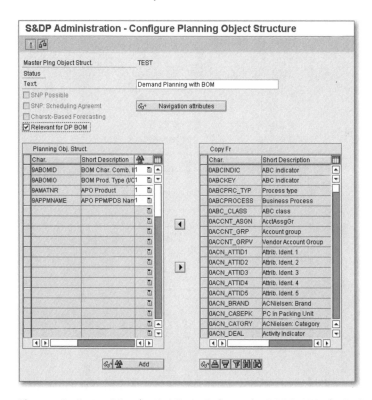

Figure 4.81 Customizing the Key Figure "relevant for DP BOM" in the Basic Planning Object Structure

4. Create a planning area and in it, take a key figure for planned independent requirement (finished product level) and a key figure for secondary requirement (BOM level). Perform the following steps for the key figure details:

▶ Configure key figures for the planned independent requirement and secondary requirement.

▶ Set linked semantic codes for the two key figures, for example, for the planned independent requirement key figure, set the **Key Figure Semantic 401** and for the secondary requirement key figure, set **Key Figure Semantic 501** (see Figure 4.82). Semantic code 401 is linked with 501, 402 with 502, etc. In each case, only use a semantic code for a key figure in a planning area once. If the planned independent requirement key figure/secondary requirement key figure exists more than once in the planning area, use a different semantic code for each pair.

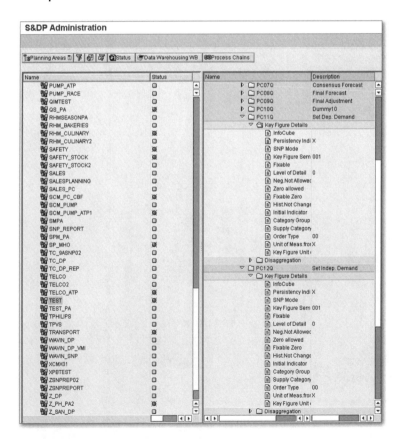

Figure 4.82 S&DP Administration: Planning Area—Key Figure Details for DP with BOMs

5. Create the master data for the demand planning, that is, the characteristic value combinations that are based on the basic planning object structure that is created.

6. Enter the PPM/PDS information in the master data of the demand planning by choosing the fourth option. Add BOM information and specify the version to which your PPMs/PDSs are assigned.

7. The system reads all characteristic value combinations and adds a PPM/PDS to the product combinations for which there is a PPM/PDS. This step generates additional characteristic values combinations for material components (as they are entered in the BOMs). Note that the input products in the standard system must have the same free characteristics as the output product. For instance, if output product 1 belongs to brand A, all input products must also belong to brand A. You should therefore be careful when deciding what characteristics should be used in the planning area. Consider using navigation attributes in cases where this could cause problems. From Release 4.0 onward, it is possible to change the free characteristics. To do this, implement the method COMBI_ENRICH of the BAdI /SAPAPO/SDP_MASTER.

8. Initialize the planning area and the version:

   ▶ From the current settings, choose **Administration Demand Planning** and **Supply Network Planning**.

   ▶ Right-click on the planning area you have created in Step 4.

   ▶ Choose **Create Time Series Objects**.

   ▶ Enter the version you have assigned in Step 2.

   ▶ Press **Enter**.

9. Configure the forecast settings for the planning area (right-click on the planning area).

10. Define a planning book view with two planning tables (grids): planning table 1 for finished products and planning table 2 for material components (see Figure 4.83).

11. In the interactive demand planning, you plan the requirement for the finished products in the upper table (this is the upper grid, i.e., Grid 1) (see Figure 4.84). If you've selected several products, drill-down to switch to the **All Details** level.

Figure 4.83 Planning Book with Two Grids

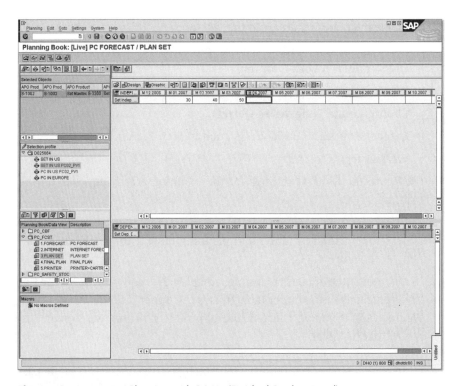

Figure 4.84 Interactive Planning with BOMs (Finished Product Level)

12. To see the secondary requirement in the bottom table (Grid 2), choose **Display Dependent Objects** in the upper table. The dependent components and their requirements are then shown in Grid 2 (see Figure 4.85).

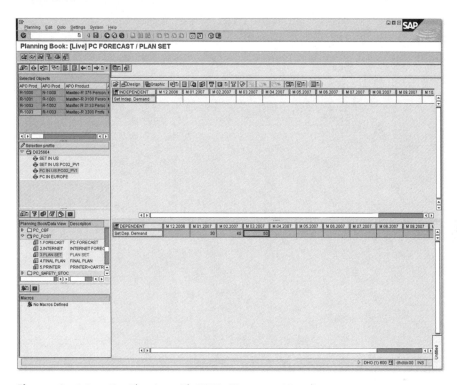

Figure 4.85 Interactive Planning with BOMs (Component Level)

13. If necessary, you can select a new sort sequence for the drill-down path in Grid 2 by right-clicking on the top-left cell of Grid 2 and choosing **Pivot Sorting**. To change the sort sequence, use drag & drop.

14. Release the requirement at the finished product level to Supply Network Planning, where the secondary requirement is then calculated based on SNP-PPMs.

15. In some sectors, you may want to release the material component requirement instead of the finished product requirement to SNP. This is the case if the components represent the products for which the requirement will be created.

16. In cases where there are both planned independent and secondary requirements for a product (e.g., consumer goods, which can also be part of a display area in a store), you can use a macro to add both types of the

requirement before you release them to Supply Network Planning. You can see both the independent and the dependent requirements in the planning book for the finished product (see Figure 4.86).

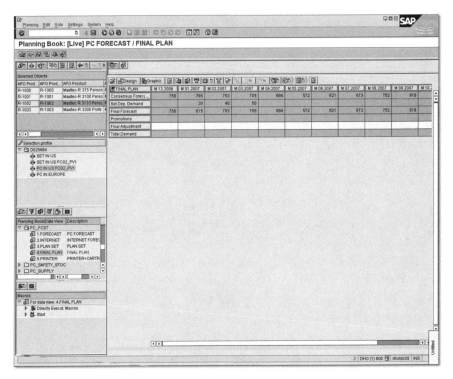

Figure 4.86 Interactive Planning with BOMs (Planned Independent Requirement and Secondary Requirement View)

4.8 Result of the Demand Planning

The result of the demand planning must be passed on to the next planning level. To ensure that the system does not simply transfer any version of the demand plan, you must explicitly release the version with which you want to continue working. This release is performed with the deliberate data transfer to the next planning level.

On the one hand, the demand plan can be passed on to the program planning in the ERP system if only the demand planning is used in SAP APO. On the other hand, the demand plan can be transferred to the Supply Network Planning if you continue planning in SAP APO. You can also copy the demand plan directly to the production planning in SAP APO PP/DS, if the next planning step is completed there; however, this is similar to the transfer to the SNP.

Both options will be discussed below.

4.8.1 Transfer to Program Planning in SAP ERP

This process transfers the SAP APO demand plan to the program planning in SAP ERP and generates a planned independent requirement there.

You must enter the following information (these values or inputs cannot be seen in the illustrations):

▸ The name of the planning area where the demand plan is located

▸ The InfoObject name of the key figure whose values you want to transfer to the SAP ERP program planning (This must be a quantity key figure.)

▸ The planned version from which the data is to be copied

▸ The InfoObject name of the characteristic that maps products in the planning area (If you leave this field empty, the system reads the data for the characteristic 9AMATNR.)

▸ The InfoObject name of the characteristic that maps locations in the planning area (If you leave this field empty, the system reads the data for the characteristic 9ALOCNO.)

▸ The requirements type that specifies the planning strategy of the product in SAP ERP
An entry in this field is optional. You don't need to enter anything in this field if the product master records in SAP ERP contain a planning group and if each of these planning groups in the SAP ERP Customizing has been assigned a strategy group. The system determines the requirements type from the main planning strategy, which is contained in every strategy group. You can also enter the requirements type from an alternative planning strategy in the same strategy group.

▸ The ID of the production program in SAP ERP (also called a (requirements) version number) to which the transfer is to be made
The version number allows us to determine the origin of the planned independent requirement, e.g., whether the production program originates in SAP ERP-SOP, in the SAP ERP material forecast, or the SAP APO demand planning.

▸ Select the Checkbox **Copy Planned Independent Requirements** if you want to take into account the planned independent requirements resulting from the transfer during the SAP ERP planning run. A version of the production program in SAP ERP can be active or inactive. Only active versions are included during a planning run.

4.8.2   Transfer to Supply Network Planning

This process gives the supply chain planner access to the demand plan if he or she uses Supply Network Planning. Depending on the horizons that were maintained for the relevant products, the process also provides the data in the production planning and detailed scheduling (PP/DS). In SNP, the supply chain planner can then make decisions on the sourcing, deployment, and transport based on the demand plan. The actual production is then planned in PP/DS.

From a technical point of view, you copy the data from the liveCache time series objects into a forecast category of the liveCache orders.

In a separate process, the supply chain planner releases the SNP plan to the demand planning. Certain data in the SNP plan that is created or changed by the supply chain planner is copied into a predefined key figure of a planning book in the demand planning. Here you can analyze the released data and, in particular, compare the original unconstrained demand plan with the constrained SNP plan.

There are two options for releasing data to SNP:

▶ **Online**
You can release small datasets using an online transaction.

▶ **In the background**
You schedule mass releases as background jobs, which can then be executed at times when there is a low level of system activity.

Four examples for the result of the demand planning are provided in the next section.

4.8.3   Sample Results

Example 1
You create a demand plan in months in the demand planning. The storage buckets profile contains weeks and months. The technical periods in which the data is saved are shown in Table 4.16.

Timespan for the Technical Period	Number of Days in the Technical Period	Planned Sales Quantity
Monday and Tuesday, February 28th and 29th	2	40
Wednesday, March 1st to Sunday, March 5th	5	100
Monday, March 6th to Sunday, March 12th	7	70
Monday, March 13th to Sunday, March 19th	7	70
Monday, March 20th to Sunday, March 26th	7	70
Monday, March 27th to Friday, March 31st	5	50
Saturday and Sunday, April 1st and 2nd	2	20
Monday and Tuesday, April 3rd and 4th	2	40

Table 4.16 Example 1: Sales Quantities for Release to SNP

For the release to Supply Network Planning, specify a release horizon from March 1st to March 31st. The system reads the following data and releases it to Supply Network Planning in the same periods. The location's shipping calendar indicates what days in Supply Network Planning are workdays. In this example, all days from Monday to Sunday are workdays. Please refer to Table 4.17 for the result of the transfer.

From Date	To Date	Planned Sales Quantity
March 1st	March 5th	100
March 6th	March 12th	70
March 13th	March 19th	70
March 20th	March 26th	70
March 27th	March 31st	50

Table 4.17 Example 1: Result

Example 2

You create a demand plan in months in the demand planning. The storage buckets profile contains weeks and months. The technical periods in which the data is saved are identical to those in Example 1.

For the release to Supply Network Planning, specify a daily buckets profile with twelve days. You set a release horizon from March 1st to March 31st. The system reads the following data in Table 4.18.

From Date	To Date	Planned Sales Quantity
March 1st	March 5th	100
March 6th	March 12th	70
March 13th	March 19th	70
March 20th	March 26th	70
March 27th	March 31st	50

Table 4.18 Example 2: Sales Quantities for Release to SNP

The requirements shown in Table 4.19 are then released to Supply Network Planning. The location's shipping calendar indicates what days in Supply Network Planning are workdays. In this example, all days from Monday to Sunday are workdays.

From Date	Planned Sales Quantity
March 1st	20
March 2nd	20
March 3rd	20
March 4th	20
March 5th	20
March 6th	10
March 7th	10
March 8th	10
March 9th	10
March 10th	10
March 11th	10
March 12th	10
March 13th to 19th	70
March 20th to 26th	70
March 27th to 31st	50

Table 4.19 Example 2: Result

Example 3

You create a demand plan in months in the demand planning. For the release to Supply Network Planning, specify a planning buckets profile that only contains months. You can only specify a planning buckets profile if you release data online. You set a release horizon from March 1st to March 31st. The system reads the following data from Table 4.20 and releases it to Supply Network Planning in the same period.

From Date	To Date	Planned Sales Quantity
March 1st	March 31st	360

Table 4.20 Example 3: Sales Quantities for Release to SNP

Example 4

You create a demand plan in months in the demand planning. For the release to Supply Network Planning, specify a planning buckets profile that only contains months, and a daily buckets profile with 12 days. You can only specify a planning buckets profile if you release data online. You set a release horizon from March 1st to March 31st. The system reads the following data from Table 4.21.

From Date	To Date	Planned Sales Quantity
March 1st	March 31st	360

Table 4.21 Example 4: Sales Quantities for Release to SNP

The following requirements in Table 4.22 are released to Supply Network Planning. The location's shipping calendar indicates what days in Supply Network Planning are workdays. In this example, all days from Monday to Sunday are workdays.

From Date	Planned Sales Quantity
March 1st	360/31 = 11,6
March 2nd	360/31 = 11,6
March 3rd	360/31 = 11,6
March 4th	360/31 = 11,6
March 5th	360/31 = 11,6

Table 4.22 Example 4: Result

From Date	Planned Sales Quantity
March 6th	360/31 = 11,6
March 7th	360/31 = 11,6
March 8th	360/31 = 11,6
March 9th	360/31 = 11,6
March 10th	360/31 = 11,6
March 11th	360/31 = 11,6
March 12th	360/31 = 11,6
March 13th to 31st	360–(12 * 11,6) = 220,8

Table 4.22 Example 4: Result (cont.)

The number of decimal places the system will round up to depends on the number of decimal places that is set for the unit of measure in the Customizing.

4.9   Realignment

Realignment allows you to flexibly and continuously adjust your master data to business processes.

4.9.1   Areas of Use

In today's business processes, master data is constantly changing. For instance, new projects may be introduced, organizational structures changed, or existing products manufactured at new production sites (locations). You must reflect these changes in your demand planning process.

Since it requires a lot of work to perform these steps manually, SAP offers corresponding functions for creating new characteristic value combinations and copying the data.

This is a twofold process in SAP APO:

▶ **Realignment (data reorganization)**
Characteristic value combinations are maintained for basic planning object structures. Realignment itself works on this level. The system creates new characteristic value combinations using selected values from

existing combinations. It then copies the data from the old combinations to the new ones. The data of all key figures in all planning areas that are based on the basic planning object structure is copied. If necessary, the old combinations will then be deleted together with the data.

▶ **Copy function**
The data itself is saved on the planning area level. If the characteristic value combinations already exist and you want to copy data from one combination to another, then use this function. Since the function's area of application is limited to the planning area, more selection options are available than for the basic planning object structure. The following is possible:

▶ Copying data between individual versions

▶ Choosing the key figures to be copied

▶ Limiting the period in which data is copied

A logging function is also available that offers extensive options.

4.9.2 Realignment

In this process, you can create new characteristic value combinations based on existing combinations and copy data from the source combinations into the new combinations. You can specify that the original values of both the characteristic values and the data should be deleted.

The process primarily involves two steps: Maintenance of the realignment table and the starting of the realignment run.

The system also performs the following activities:

▶ Copies notes into the target characteristic value combination, provided that this does not overwrite any existing note.

▶ Changes generated selections (no manually created selection IDs) in such a way that they correspond to the characteristic value combinations following a successful realignment.

▶ Copies promotions, provided that you delete the source characteristic values combination. When you perform a realignment for a promotion, it automatically receives the status "Draft" in the new characteristic values combination.

You cannot perform any realignment for characteristics of the characteristics planning (CP), including the characteristics planning of the product. The characteristics for the forecast profile, the forecast table, and the forecast row are not visible during realignment. You can use the product as a selection criterion. You can however use realignment for the non-CP-characteristics in a CP planning area. Consequently, you cannot perform any realignment for the DP BOM characteristics 9APPNAME, 9ABOMID, and 9ABOMIO. The last two characteristics are not visible during realignment. You can use the product and 9APPNAME as selection criteria.

4.9.3 Copying Data

This function allows you to copy data, within a planning area, for one or several characteristic values combinations into another combination. This function has many similarities with the realignment function; however, no characteristic values or combinations have been created. The copy steps only apply to a single planning area. Consequently, you can choose what versions and what key figures should be copied.

4.10 Summary

In this chapter, you learned about performing the demand planning with SAP APO. You are now able to choose and apply the forecasting methods that are available in SAP APO for your products. You can also make customer-specific settings in SAP APO. This means that you can create your own planning views and also monitor your forecast quality. In the next chapter, you'll learn about the basics of inventory planning with Supply Network Planning.

This chapter presents the basics of the SAP APO component Supply Network Planning. In doing so, it answers the following questions: How do I optimally configure the planning area and planning books? What master data do I need?

5 Inventory Planning with SAP APO—SNP—Basic Principles

The SAP Advanced Planner and Optimizer (SAP APO) component *Supply Network Planning* (SNP) integrates the Procurement, Production, Distribution, and Transportation areas. It therefore provides users with a global and consistent model for simulating and implementing comprehensive tactical planning decisions and options regarding source of supply. SNP uses sophisticated optimization procedures to plan the flow of products along the supply chain on the basis of constraints and penalty costs. The result is optimized procurement, production, and distribution decisions, reduced order processing times and stock levels, and improved customer service.

Using a demand plan as a basis, SNP calculates a feasible short-term to medium-term plan to address the estimated demand quantities. This plan covers both quantities that are to be transported between two locations (e.g., from the distribution center to the customer, or from the production location to the distribution center) using a means of transport, and quantities to be produced and procured. Once SNP has generated a proposed plan, the system compares all the logistical activities with the available capacity.

SNP's deployment function calculates when and how stock is to be delivered to distribution centers, customers, and Vendor-Managed Inventory (VMI) customers. It creates optimized distribution plans on the basis of constraints (such as transportation capacities) and business rules (such as minimum budget and replenishment strategies).

The *Transport Load Builder* (TLB) function maximizes the usage of transportation capacities by building transport loads in an optimal way. Also, its seamless integration with APO Demand Planning (DP) enhances the efficiency of the sales and operations planning process.

The basics that are outlined in this chapter are essential for successfully implementing SNP planning. We will first look at how to configure the administration function for *Supply and Demand Planning* (S&DP). Because we have already made the main settings in this context in Sections 3.2, 3.3, and 3.4, we will deal in Sections 5.2, 5.3, and 5.4 of this chapter with the SNP-specific settings only. This will be followed by a detailed description of SNP master data.

5.1 Supply Network Planning Process

SNP enables you to model your entire supply network and all its associated constraints. It also enables you to synchronize activities and to plan the flow of materials along the supply chain. You are therefore in a position to create feasible plans for procurement, production, stockholding, and transportation, and to reconcile supply and demand.

Figure 5.1 illustrates the SNP cycle and how it integrates with other SAP APO components.

In general, you can assume that the order of the procedures described here is the same as the order in which you should execute the cycle. However, you can also repeat specific steps or execute them in a different order, and not all activities are mandatory.

1. **Administrate the Planning Area**
   Execute all the steps required to set up your planning area. The planning area is the basis for all SNP activities and is a collection of parameters that specify the scope of all planning tasks.

2. **Configure the APO Master Data**
   SNP is a very data-intensive master component of SAP APO. Therefore, to achieve the desired results, you have to be very careful about configuring the master data. SNP master data includes locations, products, resources, production process models (PPMs), and transportation lanes.

3. **Create the Model or Version**
   Before you set up the model in the Supply Chain Engineer (SCE), you have to create a model name and assign the model to at least one version. You can assign the model to multiple different versions for simulation purposes. The version is also used to release the demand plan (final forecast) to the SNP component and vice versa.

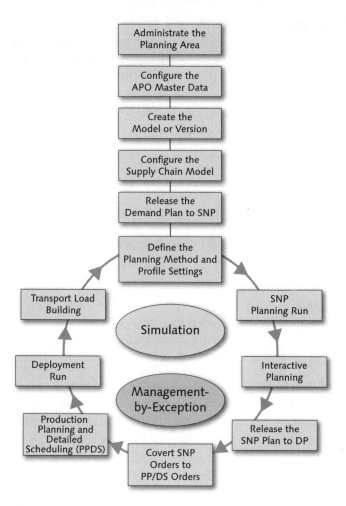

Figure 5.1 SNP Process Flow

4. **Configure the Supply Chain Model**
   The supply chain model for SNP must be configured in the SCE, which is where you assign locations, products, resources, and PPMs to a model. You then create the transportation lanes in order to connect the supply locations to the demand locations, and define quota arrangements.

5. **Release the Demand Plan to SNP**
   In this step, you release the demand plan from the DP application component to the SNP component. In many cases, the demand plan is not based on production and distribution constraints. This step can be carried out by the SNP planner or by the demand planner.

6. **Define the Planning Method and Profile Settings**
   In this step, you define which of the following methods are to be used for planning: optimization-based planning, heuristics-based planning, or supply and demand propagation. You also decide whether safety stock planning should be carried out before the SNP planning run. Then, you make the settings as required in the relevant profile of each individual method. You can still change these profiles during the planning process for simulation purposes. You may also have to define additional master data for the methods you use.

   ▸ **SNP Planning Run**
   You now carry out the planning process on the basis of the selected planning method, including all preparatory steps.
   If you are using heuristics, the Optimizer, or supply and demand propagation for the run, the result will be a medium-term production and distribution plan.

   ▸ **Interactive Planning**
   After the planning run, check the plan on the interactive planning desktop. If heuristics were used, you can also carry out capacity leveling from within the interactive planning table.

   ▸ **Release the SNP Plan to DP**
   In this step, you release the final SNP plan back to DP in order to compare the constraint-free demand plan with the constraint-based SNP plan. If there are major differences between the two plans, it may be necessary to regenerate the forecast and carry out a new planning run. For example, you may have to release the SNP plan back to DP if the available capacity cannot meet the demand created by a promotion, and you therefore have to make changes to the promotion planning strategy.

   ▸ **Convert SNP Orders to PP/DS Orders**
   This step is not part of the SNP process, as it can be executed in Production Planning and Detailed Scheduling (PP/DS) only. However, it is included in this cycle because it is usually executed before deployment and the Transport Load Builder (TLB).

   In PP/DS, then, by converting the SNP orders to PP/DS orders, you make them available to Production Planning and Detailed Scheduling.

   ▸ **Production Planning and Detailed Scheduling (PP/DS)**
   This step is not part of the SNP process, because it can be executed only in PP/DS. As before, however, it is included in this cycle, since

PP/DS is usually executed before deployment and the TLB, which belong to the SNP application component.

In PP/DS, create a feasible production plan on the basis of the planned orders generated in SNP.

▶ **Deployment Run**
Once production planning is completed and the system knows what will actually be produced (this information is automatically stored in the liveCache), the deployment run, which is responsible for distributing the produced quantities, generates what are known as deployment stock transfers. These are transfers that distribute the finished goods from the production plant to the distribution centers.

▶ **Transport Load Building**
The transport load building run combines the deployment stock transfers from deployment to form TLB transports. If you want, you can manually create TLB transports for transfers that could not be included in the TLB run due to the specified constraints.

5.2 Configuring the Supply and Demand Planning Administration Workbench

5.2.1 Overview

The configuration of the system environment is a central factor in the planning element of successful supply network planning. The first step in this configuration process is to manage the planning area.

1. Unlike DP, SAP provides predefined standard key figures and characteristics for SNP; in other words, you don't have to define any key figures or characteristics yourself. If the key figures provided with the system are not adequate for your purposes, you can create your own additional ones in the Administrator Workbench (to do this, open the Workbench and select **Administration · Demand Planning and Supply Network Planning** followed by **Tools · Edit InfoObjects** (see also Section 3.2.2).

2. To create storage bucket profiles, select **Periodicities for Planning Area** from the **Current Settings** menu of the SNP component (see also Section 3.3.4).

3. To create planning bucket profiles, select **Define Planning Buckets Profile** in the Customizing of the SNP component (see also Section 3.3.4).

4. Create the plan versions that you want to use for SNP and assign these to a supply chain model.

5. The SNP component comes with the 9ASNPBAS and 9ASNPSA (for scheduling agreement processing) master planning object structures as standard. You can also create your own master planning object structures, but there is no particular advantage in doing this rather than using the standard structures, because additional characteristics cannot be used in SNP. Also, you are not allowed to change the characteristics mentioned above. In particular, adding navigation attributes to characteristics is forbidden, as SNP cannot take these attributes into account (except the navigation attributes provided as standard).

6. Set up your SNP master data.

7. In SNP, standard planning books and data views are provided in accordance with the various planning types. We recommend that you use these standard planning books for SNP (see Section 5.3.1). It may be necessary to use the standard books as templates when creating additional planning books.

5.2.2 Master Planning Object Structure

A master planning object structure contains plannable characteristics for one or more planning areas. Characteristics determine the level on which you can plan and save data. In DP, characteristics can be standard or characteristics that you create yourself in the Administrator Workbench (see Section 3.3.2). SNP requires special characteristics that are contained in a standard master planning object structure. The master planning object structure 9ASNPBAS is the example provided with the correct characteristics for SNP.

The master planning object structure is the structure on which all other planning object structures are based. Other planning object structures are aggregates and standard SNP planning levels. A master planning object structure is part of the definition of a planning area. For that reason, the existence of a master planning object structure is a prerequisite for the creation of a planning area. It is not possible to use additional characteristics for SNP, and therefore, it isn't necessary to create a master planning object structure for SNP.

5.2.3   Configuring the Planning Area

SAP provides the following master planning areas for SNP:

▶ 9ASNP02 (order-based)

▶ 9ASNP01 (time series-based)

▶ 9ASNP03 (for scheduling agreement processing)

▶ 9ASNP04 (for time-specific constraints)

▶ 9ASNP05 (for safety stock planning)

You can also create your own planning areas by selecting **Administration •
Demand Planning and Supply Network Planning** from the **Current Settings**
menu of the SNP component, and then selecting **Planning Area** from the
pull-down menu on the top left-hand side of the screen.

To create an order-based SNP planning area, take an order-based SNP master
planning area as a template and make a copy of it. By doing this, you ensure
that your own planning area contains all the key figures and attributes
required in SNP. To create a time series-based SNP planning area, execute
the **Edit • SNP Time Series Object** menu function, which adds the SNP master
time series key figures to the planning area. You can also assign to your planning area additional key figures in which, for example, data that is calculated
via macros is stored. Make sure not to make any settings in the key figure
details of the additional key figures, as this creates these key figures in the
time-series objects of the liveCache (see also Section 3.3.4).

Because SNP planning areas can contain only the standard SNP characteristics, if DP is executed in your enterprise on the product level or on the product and location levels, you can use only one planning area that is intended
for both DP and SNP. If DP is to be carried out on other levels, such as brand
or region, separate planning areas will be required.

Every planning area can store the data in different areas. SNP gives you three
possible data storage areas:

▶ liveCache time series object (see Section 7.3.2)

▶ liveCache orders

▶ InfoCubes (see Section 3.2)

liveCache Time Series Objects

With this option, data is stored in periods without reference to orders. This storage method is suitable for tactical, aggregated planning and is normally used to store current DP data. It also supports the Sales and Operations Planning (SOP) process. The following functions are available for storing key figures in liveCache time series objects:

▶ Aggregation and disaggregation
▶ Upward and downward propagation of constraints (material constraints, capacity constraints, stock level constraints)
▶ Capable-to-Match (CTM)
▶ Deployment
▶ Single-level and multilevel infinite heuristics
▶ Freely-definable macros
▶ Capacity leveling
▶ Product allocation check
▶ Characteristics forecast
▶ Optimizer
▶ Vendor-Managed Inventory (VMI)

An example of SOP in which the time series storage method is used is contained in the standard APO system in planning book 9ASOP and here in planning area 9ASNP01 (transaction /SAPAPO/SNPSOP).

liveCache Orders

When you use this option, data is stored in relation to orders. This storage method is suitable for operational planning, such as the classic SNP environment. The following functions are available for storing key figures in liveCache orders:

▶ Real-time integration with SAP ERP
▶ Full pegging
▶ Freely-definable macros
▶ Single-level and multilevel infinite heuristics
▶ Capacity leveling
▶ MILP Optimizer
▶ Capable-to-Match (CTM)

- Deployment
- Real-time deployment
- Transport Load Builder (TLB)
- Vendor-Managed Inventory (VMI)

An example of SNP in which the order-based storage method is used is contained in the standard APO system in planning book 9ASNP94 and here in planning area 9ASNP02 (transaction /SAPAPO/SNP94).

InfoCubes

With this option, the data is stored in an InfoCube via the Administrator Workbench. This storage method is suitable for data backups, old planning data, and the demand history, which is used in DP to generate master data, and, as a basis for creating forecasts.

5.3 Planning Books

A planning book specifies the content and layout of the interactive planning screen. Planning books are used in both SNP and DP (see Section 3.4). They enable users to structure the planning screen in accordance with their individual requirements. A planning book is based on a planning area, and there are no restrictions on the number of planning books per planning area.

You can define one or more data views within the planning book. Data views can be used to adapt the way in which information is displayed for multiple users, for example (such as by displaying different key figures for different users).

5.3.1 Standard Planning Books

The SNP component comes with the following standard planning books:

- **9ASNP94 (Interactive Supply Network Planning and Transport Load Builder (TLB))**
  This planning book provides the standard functionality for executing interactive SNP and interactive TLB planning.
- **9ASOP (Sales and Operations Planning (SOP))**
  In this planning book, you execute the SNP planning procedure supply and demand propagation.

- ▶ **9ADRP (Distribution Resource Planning (DRP))**
  This planning book is almost identical to that of interactive SNP; however, in this case, you can also display distribution receipts and issues.

- ▶ **9AVMI (VMI Interactive)**
  Besides the typical SNP data, this planning book allows you to display the values for your VMI accesses and demand (planned, confirmed, and TLB-confirmed).

- ▶ **9ASA (Interactive Scheduling Agreements)**
  This planning book is used to display and modify all relevant data on scheduling agreement processing.

- ▶ **9ASNPHRPL (Hierarchical Planning)**
  This planning book is used to execute hierarchical (aggregated) planning.

- ▶ **9ASNP_PS (Product Interchangeability)**
  This planning book is used to execute planning into which you want to incorporate product interchangeability.

- ▶ **9ATSOPT**
  This planning book is used to specify time-specific constraints for optimization-based planning.

- ▶ **9ASNP_SSP**
  This planning book (or one based on it) is mandatory if you want to use specific standard methods of safety stock planning; you can use this planning book for extended safety stock planning as well.

5.3.2 Individual Planning Books

You can also create your own planning books and data views. You do this in SNP and DP in the Administration Workbench of Supply and Demand Planning. You can then assign these planning books and data views to individual users. When you create your own planning books, you should use the standard planning books as templates (see Section 3.4 for more information).

5.4 Advanced Macros

Advanced macros enable you to perform complex calculations quickly and easily (see Section 3.5). In interactive planning, macros are run either directly by the user, or automatically in the background at a specific point in time. You can also write your own macros if you wish.

Some standard macros for stock level and days' supply are provided along with SNP planning books. You can incorporate these into your own planning book by using one of the existing books as a template.

5.5 SNP Master Data

Master data is fundamental data, such as data about products, locations, resources, and production process models (PPMs). You must create a supply chain model in order to execute the planning process. Moreover, you have to create special master data for the planning methods used in SNP. For example, to carry out extended safety stock planning, you need to enter specific data (such as safety stock, safety stock method, service level) on the **Lot Size** tab of the product master.

To use master data in SAP APO, it can also be transferred out of SAP ERP via the APO Core Interface (CIF). Master data is usually created and processed in the executing system. You can also use the transferred master data in other SCM components such as the Inventory Collaboration Hub (ICH). You carry out the data transfer before you start working in SAP APO in order to create a consistent planning situation between both systems.

The following sections provide you with information about the master data of the different planning methods that you need to take into account in your planning processes.

5.5.1 Locations

First, you need to create locations. A *location* is a logical or physical place where quantity-based administration of products or resources is carried out.

The standard location types are as follows:

- Production plant (1001)
- Distribution center (1002)
- Transportation zone (1005)
- Stock transfer point (1006)
- Storage location / MRP area (1007)
- Customer (1010)
- Supplier (1011)
- Subcontractor (1050)

▶ Transportation service provider (1020)

▶ Terminal (1030)

▶ Geographical area (1031)

▶ Branch (1040)

In the location master data, you must specify the following: a storage and handling resource for resource planning on the location level; the production and shipping calendar; and the Available-to-Deploy (ATD) category groups. You also must assign the relevant time zone to the location. The time zone and the assigned calendar are used for scheduling purposes.

5.5.2   Products

Next, you create the required product master data. Some master data overlaps with the master data already in SAP ERP. The latter data is automatically transferred from SAP ERP to SAP APO via the CIF. Therefore, you don't need to maintain this data twice. You also have to save the SAP APO-specific information in the master data.

To do this, you need to maintain two types of data. First, maintain the location-independent global product master data, including product properties (such as weight, volume, shelf life) and units of measure (such as algorithms for converting volumes to the base unit of measure). The global product master data is normally automatically transferred from the SAP ERP system.

Secondly, maintain the location-specific master data. You need to do this in different views of the relevant tabs:

▶ **Demand**
Maintain the demand strategy, demand allocation, and stock types.

▶ **Lot Size**
Maintain the lot size settings, such as lot size procedure and safety stock methods.

▶ **Procurement**
Maintain the procurement type (internal or external procurement) and planned delivery time. You also have to maintain other data specially for SNP optimization, such as the following:

  ▶ Cost function (with external procurement)

  ▶ Procurement costs

- ▸ Product-specific storage costs

- ▸ Penalty costs if minimum safety stock level is not maintained

▸ **GR/GI**

Maintain usage levels of handling and storage capacity so that SNP can carry out capacity planning (see Figure 5.2). To use the TLB, maintain TLB-specific data such as loading group, shipment upsizing, and maximum coverage.

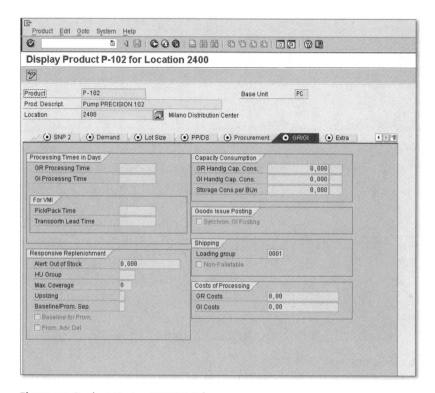

Figure 5.2 Product Master, "GR/GI" Tab

▸ **SNP 1**

In this view, maintain the SNP-relevant penalty costs for SNP optimization (see Figure 5.3).

The following fields exist in both location-specific and location-independent forms, and in forms specific to customer demand, demand forecast, and corrected demand forecast:

- ▸ **No Del. Penalty (penalty for non-delivery)**
  The penalty per day for non-delivery of the required product quantities.

▷ **Delay Penalty**
The penalty per day that is applied by the Optimizer to gauge the severity of a product delivery delay after the planned delivery date/time.

▷ **Maximum Delay**
The maximum number of days that a product can be delayed.

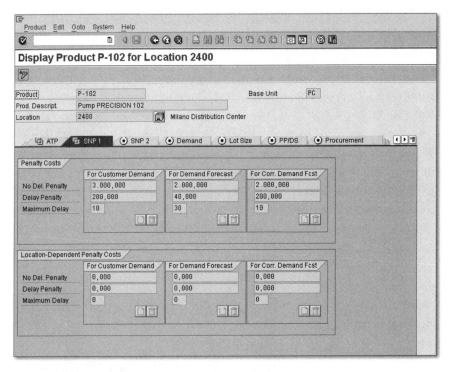

Figure 5.3 Product Master, "SNP 1" Tab

▶ **SNP 2**
Maintain the data on this tab as shown in Figure 5.4.

▷ **Demand Profile**
How the system calculates demand.

▷ **Forecast Horizon**
A period in calendar days in which the forecast is not taken into account as a component of the overall demand.

▷ **Pull Deployment Horizon (Pull Depl. Hor.)**
Number of days for which the distribution demand is taken into account in the deployment calculation.

▶ **Period Split**
How planning data is temporally disaggregated when you release the demand plan from DP to SNP.

▶ **VMI Promotion Lead Time (VMI Promo. LTime)**
Like the target range, which refers to the total demand without VMI promotions and is specified in the lot size profile, this lead time refers to the number of days that are required to fulfill the demand, and, in particular, to VMI customer promotions before their due date.

▶ **Supply Profile**
How supply is calculated by the system. This is done in key figures such as production and distribution receipt.

▶ **SNP Production Horizon (SNP Prod. Hor.)**
Where SNP ends and Production Planning and Detailed Scheduling (PP/DS) begins.

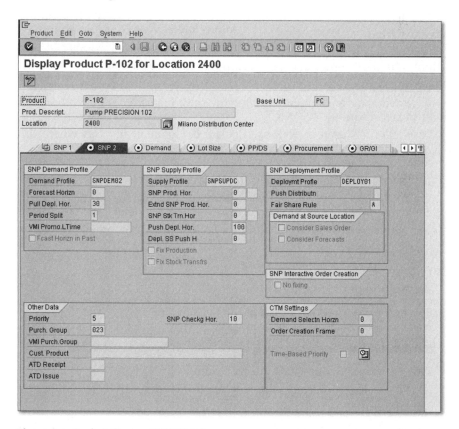

Figure 5.4 Product Master, "SNP 2" Tab

▶ **SNP Stock Transfer Horizon (SNP Stk. Trn.Hor.)**
Number of days on which the system is not planning any stock transfers (this time period begins with the start of the heuristics run). The system does not generate any planned distribution receipts within this horizon; instead, it moves them to the first day after the stock transfer horizon.

▶ **Push Deployment Horizon (Push Depl. Hor.)**
Quantity that is available for a distribution in the future. Receipts after this time period are too uncertain to be confirmed by deployment.

▶ **Deployment Safety Stock Push Horizon (Depl. SS Push H)**
The push horizon for deployment when safety stock is used.

▶ **Fix Production**
This checkbox specifies that the production time period should be outside the planning time period.

▶ **Fix Stock Transfers**
This checkbox specifies that the transport should be outside the planning time period.

▶ **Deployment Profile**
Logic that the system uses in deployment calculations in order to create distribution proposals.

▶ **Push Distribution**
Push rules are used in SNP to calculate deployment in cases where the ATD quantity fulfills demand.

▶ **Fair Share Rule**
If demand exceeds supply, the system can use fair-share logic to calculate deployment using the ATD quantity. This logic enables planners to use alternative procedures for assigning a limited product supply to the originators of the demand.

▶ **Priority**
The priority of the product.

▶ **Purchaser Group (Purch. Group)**
ID of a purchaser or group of purchasers that is responsible for specific purchasing activities.

▶ **VMI Purchaser Group (VMI Purch. Group)**
ID of a purchaser or group of purchasers that is responsible for purchasing activities associated with the VMI product.

▶ **Customer Product (Cust. Product)**
Material number that the customer uses for this product.

► **ATD Receipt**

This field is relevant for deployment and the TLB in SNP. The ATD receipt category group specifies which order categories contribute to increasing the ATD quantity or other quantity that is available to build the transports (e.g., EE stands for SNP planned orders).

► **ATD Issue**

The ATD issue category group specifies which order categories contribute to decreasing the ATD quantity or other quantity that is available to build the transports (e.g., BM stands for sales orders).

5.5.3 Resources

Resource master data consists of data on plant capacities, machines, persons, means of transport, warehouses, and resource-specific planning parameters for SNP, Capable-to-Match (CTM), and PP/DS. Resource data is relevant for planning order dates and times in conjunction with work hours and available resource capacities. You create a resource in the system independently of any particular supply chain model or planning version, and assign all planning-relevant resources to a model. When this happens, the system also automatically copies the resources to all planning versions in this model.

When you create a planning version for a supply chain model, the system creates a planning version-specific copy for every resource that you have assigned to the model. If you want to modify the planning data of the resource retroactively, you may have to make these modifications in every planning-specific copy of the resource.

Work centers can be transferred to SAP APO from the SAP ERP system via the SAP APO Core Interface (CIF). This maps the capacities of the work center in SAP ERP to each resource in the SAP APO system.

The following general resource types can be created for SNP:

► Single-mixed resource

► Multimixed resource

► Bucket resource

► Transportation resource

Mixed resources have SNP bucket capacity as well as time-continuous capacity and PP/DS bucket capacity. Only one activity can be executed for a single-activity resource at any one time, while multiple activities can be executed for a multi-activity resource. An SNP bucket capacity is an SNP resource with quantity-based available capacity. The most detailed level that can be planned for this capacity is the day level (periods or "buckets"). You can define the available capacity of bucket resources as follows:

▶ **Quantity (non-time-based)**
Allows you to define the transportation capacity of a truck or the storage capacity of a warehouse, for example.

▶ **Rate (time-based quantity)**
Allows you to define the consumption or production capacity of a resource; in other words, the quantity of the resource that is consumed or produced on a working day.

The bucket resource is identical to the transportation resource. You can derive the SNP bucket capacities of the mixed resources from the time-continuous capacity, or define these independently. You define the parameters required for this in the **SNP Bucket Capacity (SNP Bucket Cap.)** tab.

When calculating the SNP bucket capacity from the time-continuous capacity, the system calculates an available bucket capacity with the time dimension for a *single-mixed resource* by multiplying the working time by the loss factor.

In this case, you cannot assign a dimension or unit of measure to the time-continuous capacity of a *multimixed resource*. The SNP bucket capacity is calculated from the time-continuous capacity with the time dimension using the following formula:

(Working time of resource) x (Time-continuous capacity) x (Loss factor)

You use the loss factor in each case to ensure that neither sequence-dependent setup activities nor activity relationships are factored in SNP.

You can derive the available bucket capacity of mixed resources and vehicle resources from the time-continuous capacity and, if needed, specify a loss factor (for repair or setup periods, for example), or define one using specific parameters. It is possible to define the available bucket capacity for bucket resources only using parameters.

To display the input fields of these capacity parameters, select the **SNP Bucket Cap.** tab. The screen shown in Figure 5.5 opens.

A list of the available bucket capacities is shown in the upper part of the screen. In the lower part of the screen, you see the planning parameters for the resource selected in the upper part. The available bucket capacities are as follows:

▶ **Bucket-Oriented Dim.**
Enter the dimension in which you want to plan, such as time.

▶ **Period Type** (such as day)

▶ **Number of Periods**

▶ **Bucket Capacity**
Enter the number of dimensions (if the time dimension is used) that the bucket contains.

▶ **Bucket Util. Rate %**
For transportation resources, you also need to enter the volume of the resource.

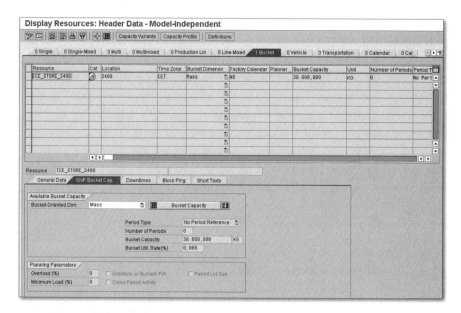

Figure 5.5 SNP Bucket Capacities

You must also set the following planning parameters:

▶ **Overload (%)**
Percentage value by which the resource load can exceed the resource capacity. In the planning process, the system interprets a resource load that exceeds this value as a resource overload, and may trigger an alert.

- **Minimum Load (%)**
  Percentage by which the capacity load may fall below the available capacity of the resource.

- **Schedule on Buckets Prfl.**
  Specifies that activities have to start at the start of a bucket.

- **Cross-Period Activity**
  Specifies that activities on a resource can start in one bucket (such as on a particular day) and end in another (such as on another day).

- **Period Lot Size**
  The SNP optimization process executes cross-period lot size planning on this resource.

You can specify multiple variants of available capacity and use a status indicator to flag the available capacity of these variants as normal, maximum, or minimum capacity. You can also specify costs that the SNP Optimizer takes into account in the planning process in relation to use of normal or maximum capacity and the non-fulfillment of the minimum capacity. You do this when defining quantities or rates, or in the capacity profile of the resource. However, the minimum capacity and the costs that you define for a capacity variant with "Normal capacity" status are taken into account by the SNP Optimizer only for product resources. For time periods for which you have not defined any capacity variant, the system uses the standard available capacity. If the normal capacity is less than the minimum capacity, the system uses the normal capacity as the minimum capacity, and if the normal capacity is greater than the minimum capacity, the system uses the normal capacity as the maximum capacity.

5.5.4 Production Process Model (PPM)

Production process models (PPMs) and production data structures are used in SAP APO as sources of supply for in-house production. Using a source of supply for in-house production, the planning applications in SAP APO can create a planned order within the demand planning process that provides this product. The PPM plan is the basis of a production process model.

The PPM plan describes without reference to a specific order the work steps and components required to manufacture the output products of the plan. A PPM plan comprises bill of material data and routing data from SAP ERP. In the case of operations and their associated activities, you use the PPM plan to define the production process and assign the required components and resources. You also define activity relationships between the activities, as shown in Figure 5.6.

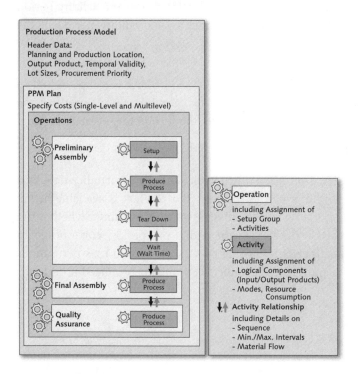

Figure 5.6 PPM Diagram

Lastly, for every output product in a PPM plan, you need to define a PPM in which you specify the validity conditions for using the PPM plan.

Header Data

Make the following settings in the *header data* of the PPM plan (see Figure 5.7):

▸ **Single Level Costs**
This contains only the costs for the production steps defined in this plan.

▸ **Multilevel Costs**
These costs also include the costs of providing the required components.

▸ **Lot Size Margin (Lot Size from—to)**
The procurement quantity for the main product of the planned order has to fall within the lot size interval that you defined in the PPM of the product.

▶ **Temporal Validity**

The availability date/time of the planned order has to fall within the validity period of the PPMs. The system automatically uses the validity period that you specified for the output product as the validity period of the PPM.

▶ **Planning Location**

The location in which you create the planned order has to be entered in the PPM as the planning location. A PPM is therefore always valid for one specific location only. The system creates the receipt for the main product in the planning location.

▶ **Bucket Offset**

Factor that the SNP Optimizer uses to calculate the availability date of a receipt element within a period (bucket). If a product is available in the middle of a period, the system has to have information about whether the product can be used at the start or the end of this period (corresponds to the start of the next period). For that reason, the system uses two rounding limits, one for transported products and one for produced products.

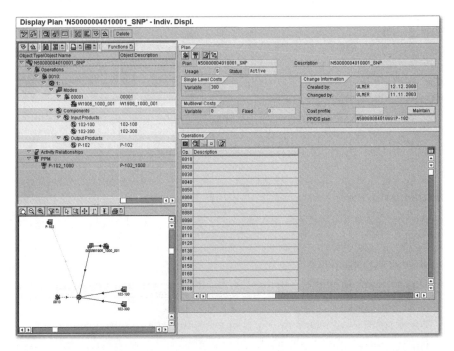

Figure 5.7 PPM Header Data

Operations

In an *operation*, you specify which setup status is required for this operation on the primary resource, and which activities are required.

Activities

In SNP, every *activity* has to have a duration of at least one day or a multiple of one day. Every operation can contain only one activity.

You need to define the following for every activity:

▶ What type of activity it is; for example, a setup activity or a processing activity.

▶ If the activity has the type "Process" or "Wait," the scrap that results from this activity has to be defined as a percentage value. You can define scrap as time-specific or plan version-specific.

▶ Which products are used or manufactured by the activity. You need to define the following for every activity:

  ▶ Which logical components are required or produced. Under the logical components, enter the "real" input or output product—that is, the one that is defined in the system—as an alternative component. You can assign multiple alternative components that are different in terms of their temporal validity or material consumption. You can also define the material consumption as a time-specific and plan version-specific parameter for every alternative component.

  ▶ The resources on which the activity is executed (modes). In SNP, you can define only one mode per activity. The unit of measure for SNP has to be *day*, and the duration is fixed. A primary resource, location, and the resource consumption are required only if they are associated with PPM resources. If you can use different resources for this activity, create a specific mode for every possible combination. For example, in the optimization process, the system can automatically switch to an alternative mode if a particular mode is not available.

Activity Relationships

Activity relationships define the temporal sequence of activities. In SNP, you only need to define the operation name and the activity number between the activities.

5.5.5 Production Data Structure (PDS)

In SNP, you can use the production data structure (PDS) as an alternative to the PPM. Similar to the PPM, the PDS is a combination of routing data and bill of material data. It differs from PPM in that it provides more flexible options for combining and reusing individual routings and bills of material. The information already given on SNP-PPM also applies to SNP-PDS.

SNP-PDS is supported by all SNP planning processes except supply and demand propagation. One other restriction applies to the function for **deleting transaction data**—you cannot select and delete objects based on specific production data structures.

There are two ways of creating an SNP PDS:

▶ **Generate an SNP PDS from iPPE Data**
  You can either create the Integrated Product and Process Engineering (iPPE) data in a connected Discrete Industries/Mill Products (DIMP) system and transfer it to an SAP SCM system via the CIF, or create it directly in the SAP SCM system. You should note that for SNP you must use an SNP routing in the iPPE data. Then create a product version for the iPPE data and, from that, generate an SNP PDS.

  In the production versions, specify the validity period of the routing data for a product and a location, as in a PPM or an SAP ERP production version. You can also define costs and co-products here. In the production version, you can also specify a PP/DS production version, which is then factored by PP/DS when SNP is implemented in PP/DS orders.

▶ **Generate an SNP PDS from SAP ERP Data**
  To use this option, generate the SNP PDS in the SAP ERP system directly from the routing, bill of material, and production version data. In our example, to do this, you have to select "SNP" or "SNP subcontracting" as the PDS type in the CIF integration model. The corresponding SAP ERP data is then transferred to the SAP SCM system, and an SNP PDS is automatically created from that data in the SAP SCM system.

  If you select "SNP subcontracting," the product master data (for components too) is automatically created in the subcontractor location. Also, the transportation lane is automatically created between plant and subcontractor (although this is not possible if you are using an SNP PPM).

After the SNP PDS is generated, you can only display this source of supply. If you want to make changes, you have to do this in the iPPE or SAP ERP data. Then, you will have to regenerate the PDS.

Like the SNP PPM, the SNP PDS is used as a planning basis in SNP. The source determination process takes into account all existing sources of supply, regardless of whether each one is an SNP PPM or an SNP PDS.

5.5.6 Transportation Lanes

You need transportation lanes for planning distribution and demand across various locations. Products can be procured only if there are transportation lanes between the potential locations.

Stock Transfers Between Locations

You can use transportation lanes to plan stock transfers between locations in SAP APO. You have the following options for doing this:

▶ Manually create a transportation lane in SAP APO

▶ Create a special procurement type in the material master record in SAP ERP

When a material master record with this kind of special procurement type is transferred via CIF, the relevant transportation lane from the supplier plant to the customer plant can be automatically created in the SAP APO system.

External Procurement Relationships

In the SAP ERP system, the business relationship between a supplier and a customer takes the form of a purchasing info record or an outline agreement (contract or scheduling agreement). If you transfer this purchasing data to SAP APO, the system automatically creates external procurement relationships. At the same time, the system also creates a transportation lane from the supplier plant to the customer plant. The external procurement relationship and the transportation lane are assigned to each other.

You can also manually assign an external procurement relationship to a transportation lane. For example, in subcontracting with third-party provision of components, you have to manually create the transportation lane from the supplier to the contractor in SAP APO.

Sales Scheduling Agreements

In the SAP ERP system, the business relationship between a plant (supplier) and a customer exists in the system in the form of a sales scheduling agreement. If you have transferred these sales scheduling agreements from Sales (SD) to the APO system, the system automatically creates sales scheduling agreements there. At the same time, the system also creates a transportation lane from the supplier plant to the customer plant. The sales scheduling agreement and the transportation lane are also assigned to each other.

A transportation lane can be more precisely specified using the following additional information:

▶ The products that can be procured via this transportation lane

▶ The means of transport that can be used in transporting the goods to be procured

You can create a transportation lane for any of the following:

▶ A specific product

▶ All products

▶ A specific mass selection

Note here that mass selection can be used only for products that exist both in the source and the target location.

Figure 5.8 illustrates a transportation lane. To create a transportation lane, select **Advanced Planner & Optimizer • Master Data • Transportation Lane** from the menu. Then enter the locations in question and click on **Enter**. The screen shown in Figure 5.8 opens.

The upper part of the screen shows the **Product-Specific Transportation Lane**. This lists all the products to which this transportation lane applies, and includes product-specific data such as minimum and maximum lot size, priority, and start and end dates. The product procurement parameters are used for source determination and are also maintained here.

The middle part of the screen contains the **Means of Transport** that are available. Goods can be transported between locations of a transportation lane via truck, ship, and aircraft, for example. What you need to do here is to assign a means of transport to a transportation lane and specify the relevant parameters such as the duration, distance, and costs of the transport. The system can calculate the distance directly from the geographical coordinates of the locations. If multiple means of transport are assigned to a transportation lane, the SNP Optimizer can use the transport duration, transport costs, and penalty costs for delays as a basis for selecting the most appropriate means of transport. In the above example (see Figure 5.8), both products (P-102 and P-103) can be transported by **truck**. This involves specific transport costs.

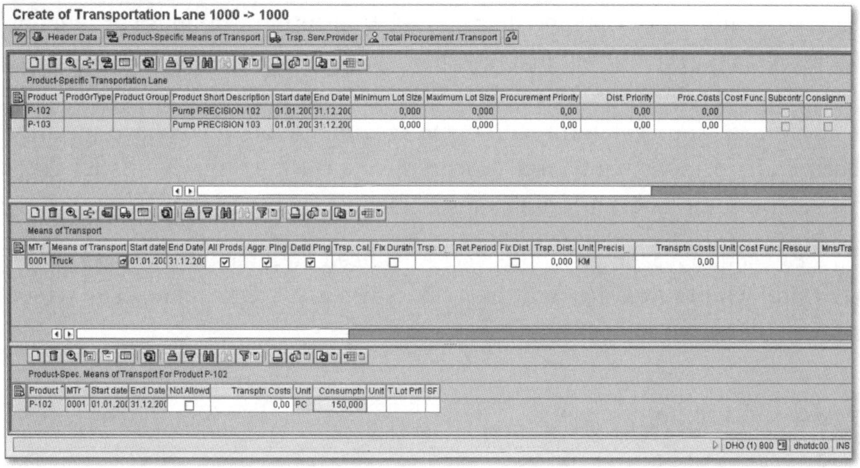

Create of Transportation Lane 1000 -> 1000

Product-Specific Transportation Lane

Product	ProdGrType	Product Group	Product Short Description	Start date	End Date	Minimum Lot Size	Maximum Lot Size	Procurement Priority	Dist. Priority	Proc.Costs	Cost Func	Subcontr	Consignm
P-102			Pump PRECISION 102	01.01.200	31.12.200	0,000	0,000	0,00	0,00	0,00			
P-103			Pump PRECISION 103	01.01.200	31.12.200	0,000	0,000	0,00	0,00	0,00			

Means of Transport

MTr	Means of Transport	Start date	End Date	All Prods	Aggr. Plng	Detld Plng	Trsp. Cal	Fix Duratn	Trsp. D.	Ret.Period	Fix Dist	Trsp. Dist.	Unit	Precisi	Transptn Costs	Unit	Cost Func	Resour	Mns/Tra
0001	Truck	01.01.200	31.12.200	☑	☑	☑						0,000	KM		0,00				

Product-Spec. Means of Transport For Product P-102

Product	MTr	Start date	End Date	Not Allowd	Transptn Costs	Unit	Consumptn	Unit	T Lot Prfl	SF
P-102	0001	01.01.200	31.12.200		0,00	PC	150,000			

DHO (1) 800 dhotdc00 INS

Figure 5.8 Transportation Lane

The lower part of the screen shows product-specific settings for each means of transport (e.g., **Product-Specific Means of Transport for Product P-102**). You can assign a product-specific means of transport to one or more products, having first defined this means of transport in the list of means of transport. You can assign a means of transport in the following ways:

▶ **You can assign a specific means of transport or all existing means of transport to a product.**
To do this, select a product in the **Product-Specific Transportation Lane** list and select **Create** from the **Product-Specific Transport Means of Transport** list.

▶ **You can assign one product, or all existing products, to a means of transport.**
To do this, select a means of transport in the **Means of Transport** list and select **Create** from the **Product-Specific Transport Means of Transport** list.

As you can see in the above example, differing costs for product transport can be specified for a specific means of transport. Therefore, the system can reflect settings for transport costs that are specific to a certain means of transport, such as higher costs for air transport.

Quota Arrangements

You create quota arrangements in the Supply Chain Engineer (SCE) or in the quota arrangement master data. Quota arrangements can be defined on the level of location, external procurement relationships, or in-house production (PPM). If you have not defined any quota arrangements, you must specify a procurement priority in the **Product-Specific Transportation Lane** or in PPM for automatic source determination. On the other hand, if you have specified both quota arrangements and procurement priorities, the heuristics takes into account the quota arrangements.

To create a quota arrangement, select **Advanced Planner & Optimizer • Master Data • Quota Arrangement** from the SAP Easy Access menu. The screen shown in Figure 5.9 opens.

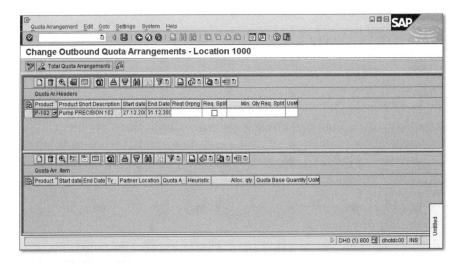

Figure 5.9 Quota Arrangements

The upper part of the screen shows the header data of the quota arrangement (**Quota Ar. Headers**). Here, you assign the relevant products for the quota arrangement.

The lower part of the screen shows the item data of the quota arrangement (**Quota Arr. Item**). Here, you assign the partner location and the quota arrangement type (such as the quota arrangement percentage) by making the corresponding entries in each field.

5.5.7   Master Data for Hierarchical Planning

Because, in hierarchical planning, you execute the SNP heuristics or the SNP Optimizer on the product group level, you first have to specify the relevant master data. You also have to consider some peculiarities intrinsic to master data maintenance in hierarchical planning:

▶ **Creating Location Groups**
Hierarchical planning is carried out on the basis of a location product group. To create this location product group, you first have to create a product group and a location group. These groups each consist of individual products and locations that are grouped using hierarchies. You create all levels of these hierarchies as independent products and locations in the product and location master data. The header location product of the location product hierarchy is the location product group on the basis of which you will carry out the hierarchical planning process.

▶ **Unifying Product Groups in All Locations**
If you want to carry out planning for multiple levels (locations) of your network, the same product groups should be defined in all locations.

▶ **Unifying Lot Size Parameters within Product Group**
SNP disaggregation takes into account the rounding values and lot size parameters that are specified for the individual products and product groups. If you want to ensure that no remainders are left on the product group level in SNP disaggregation, the rounding values specified on the product level must be the same within the same group. Also, the rounding value of the product group has to be a multiple of the value of the product level. Lastly, the minimum lot size on the group level should be greater than or equal to the minimum lot size on the product level.

▶ **Unifying the Procurement Type within the Product Group**
The procurement type that is specified on the product group level should also exist on the product level.

▶ **Unifying the Planning Horizon within the Product Group**
The same (extended) SNP production horizon and SNP stock transfer horizon should be defined for all products of the product group (including the header product or header product group).

▶ **Creating Resources for a Product Group for Capacity Planning**
You also always have to create a resource on the product group level for optimization-based planning. With hierarchical planning, the SNP Optimizer uses the resource and the costs that were specified on the product group level. Resource creation is optional for SNP heuristics.

▶ **Reconciling Resource Parameters within the Product Group**
The resource capacity on the product group level should amount to the sum of the resource capacities specified on the product level. If you are using multiple PPMs or production data structures on the product level, the resource consumption of the PPMs or production data structures on the product group level should also amount to the sum of the resource consumption of the various PPMs or production data structures on the product level.

▶ **Unifying Transportation Lanes within the Product Group**
Because SNP disaggregation uses the source determination decisions of the product group level, in external procurement, the same transportation lanes have to apply for product group and the individual products.

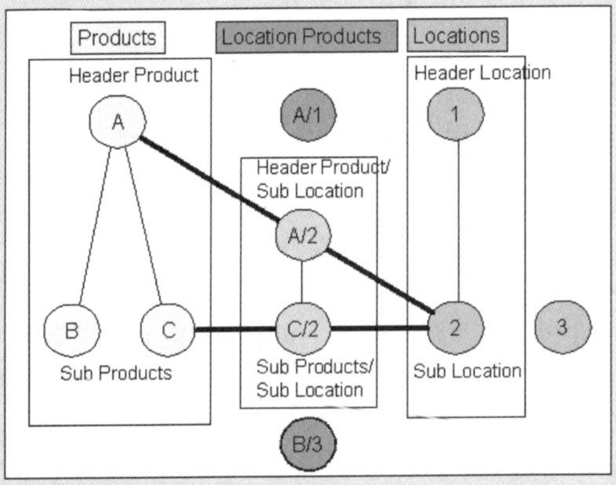

Figure 5.10 Example of a Location Product Hierarchy

In this example, the product hierarchy consists of product group A and sub-products B and C. The location hierarchy consists of location group 1 and sub-location 2. There are also the location products A/1, A/2, C/2, and B/3 and location 3. The generated location product hierarchy consists of the levels product group/location (level 1) and product/location (level 2). Level 1 contains A/2, while level 2 contains C/2. C/2 is a component of A/2. A/1 is not a component of the generated location product hierarchy, as the product group/location group level is not specified in the generated hierarchy. B/3 is not a component of the hierarchy, as location 3 is not a component of the location hierarchy, nor does a product group/location node exist for B/3 (which would then have to be called A/3).

Also, in the case of in-house production, you have to create a PPM or PDS hierarchy on the product group level for every PPM or PDS, as SNP disaggregation uses the source supply decisions from the product group level. The PPM or PDS hierarchy should be consistent with the location product hierarchy.

5.5.8 Setting Up the SCM Model

In this step of the process, you create a model name and assign the model to a planning version. To do this, open the **Advanced Planner & Optimizer menu** and choose **Master Data • Planning Version Management • Model and Version Management**. The screen shown in Figure 5.11 opens.

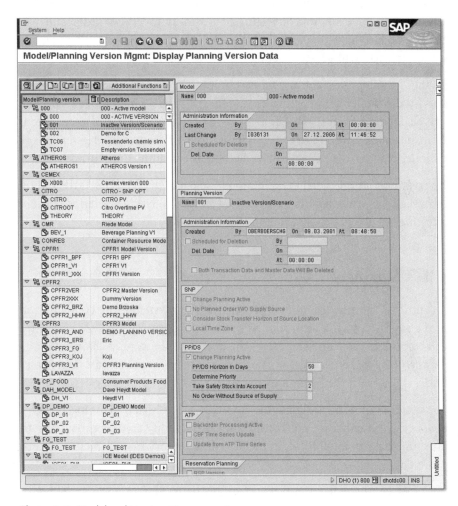

Figure 5.11 Model and Version Management

First, create a model name and enter a description. Then, assign the model to at least one planning version. As before, give the planning version a name and a description.

If you are using SNP planning, you need to activate (check) the **Change Planning Active** option in the **SNP** section of the screen. If you are using Production Planning and Detailed Scheduling (the **PP/DS** section of the screen), you need to activate the **Change Planning Active** option in both the **PP/DS** and the **SNP** sections. This makes it possible to trigger automatic planning, or to create planning file entries if planning-relevant changes are made. This checkbox is relevant for converting SNP orders to PP/DS order and vice versa. You also have to check this checkbox for the target-planning version; otherwise, you will have to manually plan all orders.

In the next step, you can model the supply chain in the SCE. You need to specify the model name before setting up the supply chain model. The supply chain model consists of individual nodes (locations) and connections (transportation lanes). You can assign multiple different planning versions to a model. You can also create multiple models for simulation purposes.

By creating multiple versions of a model, you are giving yourself the option of executing simulative planning and creating simulation scenarios without affecting the actual supply chain model.

5.6 Summary

A central factor in successfully implementing the system is the configuration of the supply network. This involves structural decisions that are very difficult to reverse later on. Therefore, the design of the supply chain—with its master data, locations, and transportation lanes—requires care and attention, especially in the beginning.

The configuration of the planning interface—that is, the planning books—holds great potential for enhancing software usability and for exhausting all the optimization possibilities in the area of inventory management and procurement.

Now that you have been introduced to this basic configuration of SNP with SAP APO, we will describe its application in the next chapter.

This chapter focuses on the application of inventory planning with SAP APO-SNP and will address such questions as the following: What planning methods, safety stock calculations, and optimization possibilities are there? What is the process from the original planning to delivery to the customer?

6 Inventory Planning with SAP APO-SNP—Implementation

The SAP Advanced Planner and Optimizer (SAP APO) component *Supply Network Planning* (SNP) allows activities to be synchronized and the material flow to be planned throughout the entire supply chain. In this way, feasible plans can be prepared for procurement, production, warehouse stock, and transport, while supply and demand can be precisely coordinated. Three different planning methods are available for inventory planning in SAP APO: heuristics with capacity leveling, the SNP Optimizer, and Capable-to-Match (CTM). The functions for distribution planning comprise the deployment and the Transport Load Builder (TLB) and support you while dynamically customizing and optimizing your distribution network. You can also decide how and when the distribution of the warehouse stocks should take place.

First we'll describe the planning desktop; then we'll look at the various planning methods.

6.1 Desktop for Interactive SNP Planning

On the desktop for interactive planning[1] provided in Supply Network Planning (SNP), you can display planning information (both aggregated and detailed) and make manual changes to your data. You can also execute the SNP planning runs (such as the heuristic- or optimization-based planning, for example) directly from this screen.

---

[1] You can also carry out the planning process in the background (see Chapter 4, *Demand Planning with SAP APO-DP—Implementation*).

The desktop for the interactive planning consists of two key components: the selection area and the work area. You call up the interactive SNP planning using the menu path **Supply Network Planning • Planning • Supply Network Planning interactive (all books)**.

6.1.1 Selection Area

The selection area is the most important tool for searching, sorting, and organizing information. Figure 6.1 shows the standard SNP planning book.

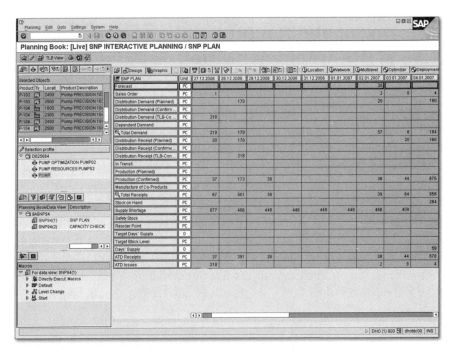

Figure 6.1 SNP Standard Planning Book

The selection area is on the left of the SNP standard planning book and comprises the following four areas (from top to bottom):

▶ **InfoObjects (with shuffler)**
The InfoObjects area displays all characteristic values for which data can be planned and read. InfoObjects in Supply Network Planning include, for instance, particular products, locations, resources, production process models (PPMs) or transportation lanes. The shuffler contains the table in which you select the InfoObjects you want to plan.

▶ **Selection Profile**
The selection profile shows the selection IDs with which the current planner is working. The selection profile allows the Supply Chain Planner to quickly access frequently used selections.

▶ **Planning Book/Data View**
In the **Data Views** area, you select your planning books and data views. In Supply Network Planning, the system also provides standard planning books and data views according to the various planning types. Specifically, these are:

  ▶ **Network Planning interactive**
  First, this includes the standard planning book **9ASNP94** with the views **SNP94(1) – SNP Plan** and **SNP94(2) – Capacity Check** (capacity view) in the data view area. Secondly, this includes the planning book **SNP94**, which offers standard functions for running the interactive supply network planning.

  ▶ **Sales & Operations Planning (SOP)**
  This includes the standard planning book **9ASOP** with the views **SOP(1) – SOP Location Products, SOP(2) – Lanes, SOP(3) – SOP PPM** and **SOP(4) – SOP Resource** in the **Data View** area.

  ▶ **Distribution Resource Planning (DRP)**
  This includes the standard planning book **9ADRP** with the view **DRP(1) – DRP** in the **Data View** area. This user interface is almost identical to that of the interactive supply network planning; however, here you can also display the distribution receipts and issues.

  ▶ **Transport Load Builder (TLB)**
  The Transport Load Builder (TLB) offers the standard functions of interactive TLB planning in the standard planning book **9ASNP94**.

  ▶ **VMI interactive**
  This includes the standard planning book **9AVMI** with the view **9AVMI(1) – VMI** in the **Data View** area. In addition to the typical SNP data, here you can also display the values for your Vendor-Managed Inventory (VMI) receipts and requirements (planned, confirmed, and TLB-confirmed).

  ▶ **Delivery schedules interactive**
  This brings you to the planning book **9ASA** with the view **SA(1)**. In this planning book, you can display all relevant data on the delivery schedule processing and change it.

▶ **Macros**

The **Macros** area shows components that are active both for all data views in this planning book and for this data view.

6.1.2 Work Area

The work area is used for display and planning purposes. It is located on the right of the screen and consists of one or several tables (depending on the planning book and data view) and a graphic. Only the tables are displayed by default.

The work area has a function toolbar with symbols for various functions, some of which are supported by Supply Network Planning (SNP) and the demand planning (DP). The functions here are specifically designed for SNP (see Figure 6.2).

Figure 6.2 SNP Function Toolbar

Table 6.1 indicates the functions of the SNP function toolbar.

Symbol	Function
Location	Execute location heuristic
Network	Execute network heuristic
Multilevel	Execute multilevel heuristic
Optimizer	Execute Optimizer
Deployment Optimizer	Execute deployment run
Deployment	Make (or change) deployment settings

Table 6.1 Explanation of the SNP Function Toolbar

If you place the cursor on a cell in the planning book from Figure 6.1 and choose **Display detail** in the context menu (or call the detail view by double-clicking on it), you will get another table with the order details for the selected cell. This table shows the individual orders (e.g., sales orders) with data such as the quantity, the source of supply, and the availability/requirements date of the order. In the table you can additionally set the firming indicator, change the quantity, date and time of orders, and assign alternative sources of supply to orders. Note that an order can be shifted into another period if you change the date and time, and that it can then disappear from the current (cell-related) detail screen.

In the following sections, we will describe the three planning methods that SAP APO offers for inventory planning: heuristic-based planning with capacity leveling, optimization in the SNP planning, and the CTM method.

6.2 Planning Method: Heuristic-Based Planning

The heuristic is used as part of, also comprises the capacity leveling and the deployment (see Section 6.8). The heuristic run processes the individual planning locations in sequence and determines the sourcing requirements. The heuristic processing groups all of the requirements that exist for a product in a location into a total requirement for the period. The heuristic run then determines the valid sources of supply and the corresponding quantity on the basis of predefined percentage rates for each source of supply (quota arrangements) or procurement priorities for transportation lanes and production process models (PPMs) or production data structures (PDS). The requirements are then passed through the supply chain to calculate a plan. However, this plan cannot necessarily also be run, because the existing real capacity situation has not yet been addressed. Using the capacity leveling, the planner can then adjust the plan and draw up a viable plan.

The key figures on which the heuristic is based, as well as the planning period, are determined by the planning book. You can also use macros to define how general key figures such as total requirement and warehouse stock or product-specific key figures such as safety stock, reorder point, and target stock level are calculated.

6.2.1 Operation of the Heuristic Run

Figure 6.3 shows the schematic sequence of heuristic run processing.

The SNP heuristic plans all distribution requirements for all locations within the distribution network, before the BOM is exploded and the secondary requirement is processed in the production locations. The system only explodes the BOM if you choose a multilevel heuristic run. Thus initially, all products of the highest location level are planned, before all products of the next location level are scheduled. The heuristic therefore plans low-level code for low-level code downwards. The low-level code indicates on what level of the BOM a location product is situated, and in what location in the supply chain. The system determines the low-level code based on the position of the products in the BOM and the location to which the product is assigned. The highest low-level code, that is the code 0, is given to a finished product that is assigned to the last location in the supply chain (e.g., a customer location). The next-lowest low-level code (1) is given to the finished product in the second-last location (e.g., a distribution center), etc. In the same way, the system assigns the low-level codes to the individual components on the various BOM levels.

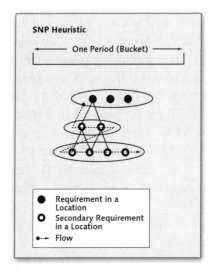

Figure 6.3 Processing the Heuristic Run

The SNP heuristic then schedules the location products in the sequence of the low-level codes, that is, it begins with the location product with low-level code 0, etc.

The following factors are considered during processing:

► Scrap
► Requirements profile
► Low-level codes of the location products
► Lead times
► Valid Production Process Models (PPMs)
► Valid transportation lanes
► Calendar
► Component availability

▸ Location products

▸ Lot-size rules

▸ SNP requirements profile

▸ SNP capacity profile

▸ Quota arrangements or procurement priorities

6.2.2   Heuristic Profiles

The heuristic profiles contain the product master data settings required for the heuristic-based SNP planning on the one hand, and the Customizing setting on the other. Thanks to the assignment of the profiles to the product master, you only have to maintain one field instead of many individual fields. You can define the settings for the individual profiles using an ABC/XYZ analysis.

Table 6.2 describes the profiles that are used by the SNP heuristic. You can define some of these profiles in the location product master and some in the Customizing or in the current Supply Network Planning (SNP) settings.

Profile	Usage in the Heuristic Planning Run
SNP requirements profile (product master)	Defines how the requirement is calculated by the system.
SNP capacity profile (product master)	Defines how the capacity is calculated by the system, that is, key figures such as, for example, production and distribution receipt.
SNP rounding profile (Customizing)	Defines how order default quantities are rounded by the system into deliverable units.
Lot-size profile (product master)	Defines what lot-sizing procedure will be used during planning. This profile also allows you to define additional restrictions such as for example minimal or maximum lot sizes or a rounding value.
SNP lot-size profile (transportation lanes)	In this profile, you can define minimum and maximum lot sizes for the transport. You then specify the profile in the transportation lane in the section **Product-specific transport** for a particular product. This allows you to define minimum and maximum transport lot sizes for particular products. If you only want to transport whole-number multiples of a transport lot size, you can also define the transport lot size as a rounding value in this profile.

Table 6.2 Explaining the Heuristic Profiles

Profile	Usage in the Heuristic Planning Run
SNP requirements strategy (current settings)	Defines how the forecast volumes in the demand planning are produced and how sales orders are cleared against the requirements forecast.
SNP planning profile (current settings)	In this profile you can make basic settings for the various SNP planning procedures such as, for instance, the heuristic, Optimizer, deployment heuristic, deployment optimizer, and Transport Load Builder (TLB).
	The SNP planning profile, which you have activated in the Customizing of the SNP under **Maintain global SNP settings**, applies globally for all SNP planning methods. With some planning methods, you can overwrite the settings of the active profile by setting a different SNP planning profile in the background when you execute the planning.

Table 6.2 Explaining the Heuristic Profiles (cont.)

6.2.3 Capacity Leveling

The capacity leveling function represents an addition to heuristic-based planning in Supply Network Planning. The SNP heuristic run is an infinite planning that does not take any capacities into account and can therefore lead to resource overloads. The SNP capacity leveling allows you to balance the load placed on production and transport resources by shifting orders or subquantities of orders into preceding or subsequent periods using backward or forward scheduling. You can also transfer orders to alternative resources in the same period. The capacity leveling only takes SNP planned orders and SNP stock transfers into account. Deployment rearrangements, TLB transports, and production planning and detailed scheduling orders (PP/DS orders) are not aligned by the system; however, the resource load caused by these orders is considered.

The SNP capacity leveling is designed to stabilize certain bottleneck resources. It is run locally on a resource in a fixed period, that is, dependencies on other resources are not taken into account. A capacity leveling across the entire supply chain would correspond to a rescheduling and therefore exceeds the scope of this function.

You can exercise the capacity leveling function both in the interactive SNP planning and in the background. The advantage of interactive planning is that you can directly display the resource load before and after the leveling. If you run the capacity leveling in the background, you can choose several resources for the leveling (which are then processed in sequence). You can also use a selection profile. Running in the background is also very well suited for large data volumes and complex models. You receive a detailed log for both types of execution.

Since the leveling is only run on a local resource, it can lead to an overloading of other resources and to the formation of additional stocks or the creation of missing quantities. If you want to include the capacities of all resources simultaneously, you must run the SNP optimization (see Section 6.3).

You can specify that the capacity leveling also include alternative resources. This means that the system will include production process models (PPMs) or production data structures (PDS) that produce the same location product with alternative resources.

Capacity Leveling Profile

You can control the capacity leveling using various parameters, which you can define in a profile and later specify when you execute the capacity leveling in the interactive planning or in the background. You can also indicate the parameters manually before each execution of the capacity leveling or overwrite individual parameters of the profile. You define the capacity leveling profile in Figure 6.4 in the SAP APO Easy Access menu under **Supply Network Planning • Environment • Curr. Settings • Profiles • Define capacity leveling profiles**.

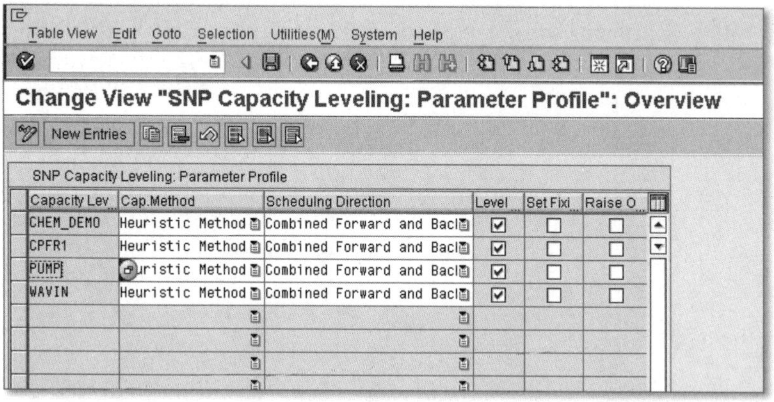

Figure 6.4 Capacity Leveling Profile

You can define the following specific parameters using the profile:

▶ Capacity leveling method (Heuristic, Optimizer, or BAdI)

▶ Scheduling Direction (forward, backward, or combined)

▶ Prioritizing of orders (i.e., which orders are processed first during the capacity leveling)

▶ Handling of fixed orders and fixing of orders during the capacity leveling

▶ Maximum resource load

▶ Maximum runtime of the capacity leveling

The capacity leveling generates alerts using macros, which you can then display in the Alert Monitor.

6.2.4 Sample SNP Heuristic Planning with Capacity Leveling

The initial situation in our example shows a forecast requirement in the SNP planning book totaling 120,000 for the product CPG-FG1 for the customer US-CUS1 in the calendar week of May 1st, 2007 (weekly periods are set) (see Figure 6.5).

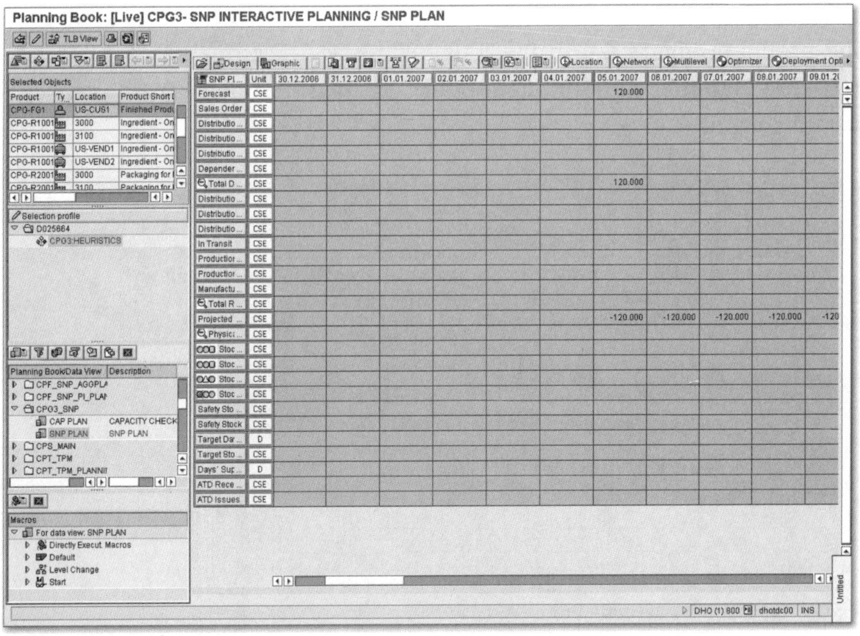

Figure 6.5 Example "Heuristic Planning," Initial Situation

1. Press the **Multilevel** button to implement the multilevel heuristic planning. The result is displayed in Figure 6.6.

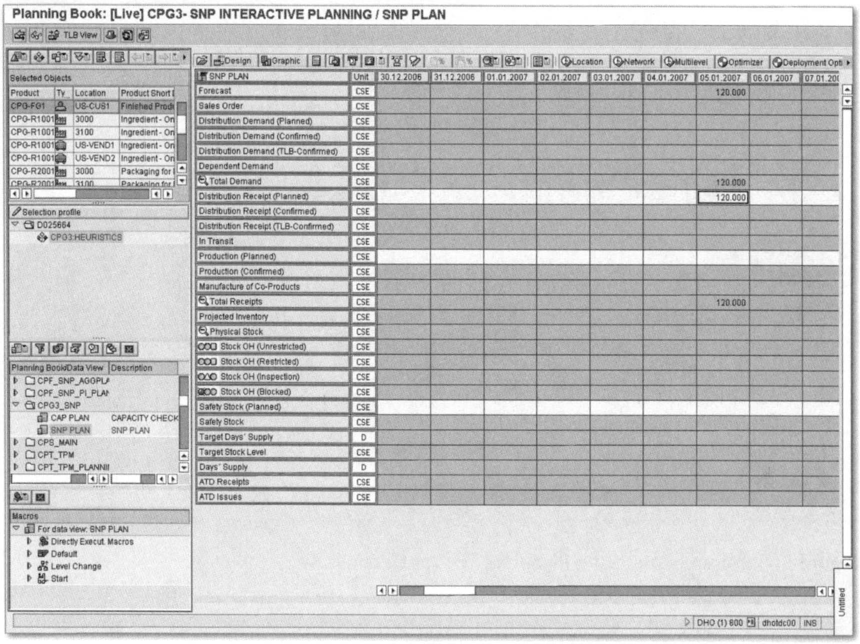

Figure 6.6 Example "Heuristic Planning," Result of the Heuristic: Level 1

2. The planning has generated a distribution receipt (distribution receipt key figure) on the customer location in the amount of the entire requirement. When you double-click on the distribution receipt (**Distribution Receipt (Planned)**), the detail view for the receipt will appear in the lower part of the screen (see Figure 6.7).

3. In the detail view, you can now see that the distribution receipt, due to a previously established quota arrangement, is covered by two purchase requisitions with 80 % (96,000) from the distribution center 3500 and 20 % (24,000) from the distribution center 3700. By double-clicking on the source 3500, you can see that in this location there is a distribution requirement of 96,000 and receipts, in turn, divided by the quota arrangements, of 60 % (57,600) from location 3000 and 40 % (38,400) from location 3100 (see Figure 6.8, bottom screen).

This is now run until the lowest level, the supplier, so that the multi-level heuristic has scheduled all levels and has therefore used the previously created quota arrangements for the planning.

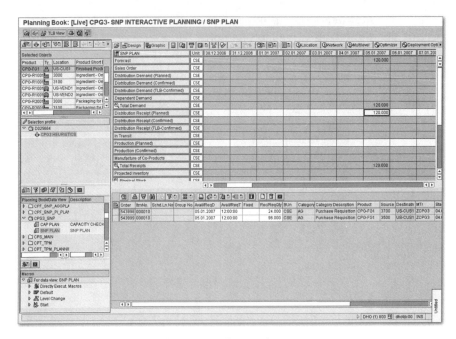

Figure 6.7 Example "Heuristic Planning," Order Detail View

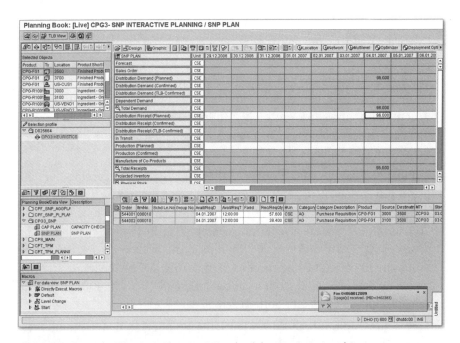

Figure 6.8 Example "Heuristic Planning," Result of the Heuristic: Level 2

4. In our next step, we can now run the capacity leveling. To do this, select the relevant planning book for the capacity scheduling and the resources you want to level, by using the shuffler. You can see the result of the heuristic planning as a capacity view in Figure 6.9.

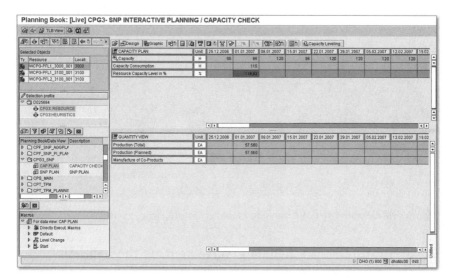

Figure 6.9 Example "Heuristic Planning," Capacity View

5. In the upper part of the screen, you can identify the available capacity and the capacity consumption on the selected resource (shown in hours in the example above). In the lower part of the screen, you can see the quantities belonging to the consumption. You now run the capacity leveling by clicking on the **Capacity Leveling** button. The result of the capacity leveling is shown in Figure 6.10.

6. The capacity consumption was restricted to max. 100% per period. The remaining 30% is distributed onto the next period (in the above example by forward scheduling). The quantities (which can be seen in the bottom screen) have also been distributed accordingly.

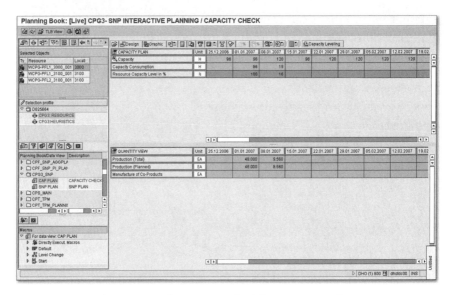

Figure 6.10 Example "Heuristic Planning," Result of the Capacity Leveling

6.2.5 Procurement Scheduling Agreements in the Heuristic-Based SNP Planning

Scheduling agreements for procuring products are also taken into account within the heuristic-based planning in Supply Network Planning. Scheduling agreements allow you to improve cooperation with your suppliers. Since your suppliers are better informed of requirement times and volumes, you can shorten the processing times. You can also include the volumes confirmed by the suppliers in your planning in the form of maximum vendor capacities.

As possible sources of supply, the SNP heuristic considers procurement scheduling agreements that are created in an online transaction processing (OLTP) system and are transferred through a corresponding interface (SAP ERP system: APO Core Interface (CIF)) into the SAP APO system.

Process

For the delivery schedule processing, you can choose between four different processes that you set for APO delivery schedules in the external procurement relationship:

▶ Process with expected confirmations
▶ Process without confirmations

▶ Process with confirmations in exceptional cases

▶ Process without calls

The sample process described below is the process with extended confirmations. For the options *process without confirmations* or *process with confirmations in exceptional cases*, the information given below still essentially applies, with the exception that because of the scheduling agreement release creation in SAP APO, scheduling agreement delivery schedules are created automatically in the OLTP system.

The *process without calls* represents a simplification of the process described in Figure 6.11. It is especially suitable for scenarios where the supplier makes the confirmations for the collaborative inventory planning via the Internet. He then dispenses with Step 3—the creation of scheduling agreement releases. During this process, the vendor (using an Internet-based planning book) sees only the schedule lines and then confirms these directly. Alternatively, the manufacturer can also enter the confirmations in the interactive SNP planning.

The following special prerequisite applies to this simplified process. You should choose a confirmation profile with a tolerance check, so that alerts inform you of any major deviations between the desired and confirmed quantity (in the Customizing of the Supply Chain planning, choose **Collaborative procurement • Procurement scheduling agreement • Receipt of order acknowledgement • Maintain confirmation profiles for receipt of order acknowledgement**.

Sample Process for the SNP Scheduling Agreement Processing (Process with Expected Confirmations)

Figure 6.11 describes a sample process for the scheduling agreement processing in Supply Network Planning. This is the process with expected confirmations. The process relates to the heuristic-based SNP planning, taking into account APO scheduling agreements. Delivery schedules and scheduling agreement releases are generated in the OLTP system. You can also display these schedule lines and scheduling agreement releases in the interactive SNP planning.

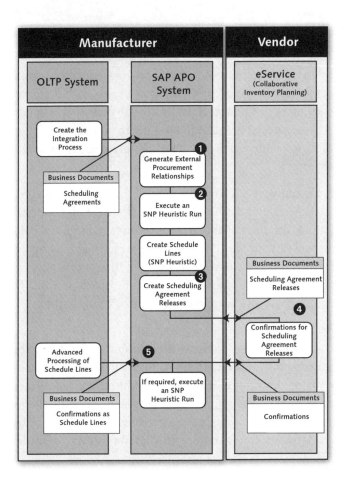

Figure 6.11 Sample Process for SNP Scheduling Agreement Processing (Process with Expected Confirmations)

1. The SAP APO system initially generates external procurement relationships. If you transfer scheduling agreements and purchasing info records from an OLTP system through an interface in SAP APO, this data is created as external procurement relationships in the SAP APO system. A separate external procurement relationship is created for each scheduling agreement item. An external procurement relationship is product-specific and is assigned to a transportation lane. Transportation lanes are created automatically in SAP APO if you copy data from the OLTP system. The external procurement relationship therefore contains the contractual details of the relationship between a source location (vendor or delivering plant) and a target location (plant). You must then also assign a means of transport to the transportation lane.

2. You then perform a heuristic-based planning at location product level in Supply Network Planning. The SNP heuristic considers the delivery schedules transferred from the OLTP system as possible sources of supply. The system applies the normal rules of source of supply determination in the SNP heuristic, that is, the delivery schedules are considered by procurement priority or by quota arrangement according to the source of supply determination.

You can initially execute this heuristic without capacity (infinitely), that is, without factoring for vendor capacity. In this case, you may include the vendor capacity in a later planning run, which you can execute after you have received the confirmations for your scheduling agreement releases from the vendor.

During the planning run, the SNP heuristic creates schedule lines to the scheduling agreements included as sources of supply, through which the total quantity of a scheduling agreement item is subdivided into various subquantities with the corresponding delivery dates. You can display the schedule lines, like the entire planning result, in the interactive planning (planning book 9ASA; in the SAP APO Easy Access menu, choose **Supply Network Planning • Planning • Delivery schedules (procurement) • Delivery schedules interactive**).

3. You now manually or automatically create delivery schedule releases with which you notify the vendors to deliver the products on the dates listed in the schedule lines.

4. The vendor notifies you of her capacities, for example, via the collaborative inventory planning. In the planning book 9ASAS, your vendor can display the schedule lines and scheduling agreement releases and specify in the key figure **Confirmation** what volumes she can deliver. Furthermore, in the key figure **Capacity**, she can also indicate her total capacity, which you can also derive from the confirmation quantities (e.g., using macros). The vendor can also specify the capacity for the transportation lanes for a scheduling agreement item and thereby restrict the capacity of the means of transport. Alternatively, you can also enter the capacities that the vendo has notified you about via email, for instance, in the interactive planning (planning book 9ASA or 9ASAS). The confirmations are automatically transferred by the system as scheduling agreement schedule lines into the OLTP system.

5. If the confirmed quantity falls below the release quantity, you can run a new SNP planning in the background to schedule the requirement quanti-

ties that are still open. During this planning, you can include the capacity notified by the vendor (see Step 4) as a maximum vendor capacity. As described in Step 2, you should enter the corresponding planning book and key figures here.

6.2.6 Direct Delivery from the Production Plant to the Customer

If you are delivering larger volumes of a finished product to a particular customer (e.g., for promotions), it may be useful to deliver these quantities directly from the production plant to the customer. Direct delivery is not linked to a location type, such as the production or customer location, for example. Because there is no detour via a distribution center, you can save on transportation and storage costs, for instance.

For the heuristic-based planning in SNP, you can set the system to preferentially deliver certain products directly. The system then uses the Transport Load Builder (TLB) (Section 6.9) to check what product volumes can be delivered directly with what means of transport. The system handles any remaining quantities with the normal source determination.

In most cases, only a small percentage of the products to be scheduled would be considered for direct delivery (e.g., approximately 2–3 for promotional products). For performance reasons, it is advisable that you don't select a larger number of products for direct delivery.

The process described below is an example:

1. You run an SNP heuristic interactively or in the background. The SNP heuristic first tries to cover the requirement quantities of the customer location via the transportation lanes that you flagged for the direct delivery (DL). If there are several DL transportation lanes for a product, the system factors in the procurement priorities of the transportation lanes. The system does not include any quota arrangements in this step.

2. The Transport Load Builder uses the settings made in the TLB profile to determine what product volumes can be delivered with what means of transport through the indicated transportation lanes. Unlike the normal TLB run, the TLB does not create any TLB transports in this process. The SNP heuristic creates SNP stock transfers as usual.

3. The SNP heuristic checks whether there are remaining quantities. The heuristic performs a normal supply source determination for these remaining quantities.

4. Consequently, in the interactive SNP planning, you can display what product volumes are delivered through what transportation lanes. With regard to a normal SNP heuristic run, the result log contains the created SNP stock transfers and any error messages.

6.3 Planning Method: Optimization in the SNP Planning

In addition to the SNP heuristic, the SAP APO component *Supply Network Planning* provides linear and mixed integer linear optimization approaches that are solved using simplex algorithms and branch-and-bound methods. The Optimizer compares alternative solutions for a problem and recommends the best allowable solution. In so doing, it considers all restrictions that were defined in the system.

6.3.1 Introduction to SNP Optimization

The SNP Optimizer allows you to perform a cost-based planning. This means that it tries to search all allowable plans to find the plan that is the most favorable in terms of the total costs evaluation. The total costs are composed as follows:

- ▶ Costs for production, procurement, storage and transport
- ▶ Costs for boosting the production, storage, transport and handling capacity
- ▶ Costs for the shortfall in the safety stock
- ▶ Costs for delayed delivery
- ▶ Stockout costs

A plan is permissible from the point of view of the Optimizer if it meets all of the constraints of the supply chain model that you have activated in the SNP optimization profile. The admissibility of a solution may include, for example, due date or safety stock constraints being violated. Due dates and safety stocks, for instance, are *soft constraints*, that is, restrictions whose violation to which you assign costs. The Optimizer will only propose a plan that violates soft constraints if the plan represents the most cost-efficient plan, according to the costs specified in the system.

The Optimizer also makes sourcing decisions in the context of an optimization-based planning. In other words, it decides the following, under a cost viewpoint:

- ▶ What products and what volumes are produced, transported, procured, stored and delivered (product mix)
- ▶ What resources and what production process models (PPMs) or production data structures (PDS) are to be used (technology mix)
- ▶ When you are to produce, transport, procure, store, and deliver
- ▶ Where production, procurement, storage, and delivery will take place, and from what location to what location the transportation will run

Because you can enter production process models (PPMs) or production data structures (PDS) with fixed resource consumption in the master data, you can also handle setup operations in the Supply Network Planning. In this way, you can also use the SNP Optimizer for a lot-size planning. The Optimizer also supports a cross-period lot-size planning if you need to group orders into large lots due to high setup expenses.

The Optimizer uses the linear programming method to include all conditions relevant for the planning problem simultaneously in an optimal solution. The more constraints that are activated, the more complex the optimization problem becomes, and the more CPU time the system will require to solve the problem. The optimization should therefore generally be run as a background job.

The Optimizer differentiates between *continuous linear* and *discrete* optimization problems.

Linear Optimization

Three methods are available to solve continuous linear optimization problems with the Optimizer. You can select from among these methods in the SNP optimization profile:

- ▶ Primal simplex method
- ▶ Dual simplex method
- ▶ Inner point method

All three methods produce an optimal solution. The main difference in the application of these methods can be in the runtime. However, there is no general rule for choosing the best method for a given problem (other than to test each individual method). Benchmarking provides a good evaluation for the application based on a test scenario, because an optimal choice of method essentially depends on the structure of the supply chain and less on the input data. This is why a daily benchmarking is not required in a production environment.

Discrete Optimization

In Supply Network Planning, a problem is not *continuous*, that is, *discrete*, if the model contains the following:

▶ Discrete (whole-number) lot sizes for transport or PPMs/PDS

▶ Discrete means of transport

▶ Discrete increase in production capacity

▶ Minimum lot sizes for transport or PPMs/PDS

▶ Piece-by-piece linear cost functions for transport, production, or procurement (fixed-costs term)

▶ Fixed PPM/PDS resource consumption

▶ Fixed PPM/PDS material consumption

▶ Cross-period lot-size planning

If the Optimizer is to consider one of these restrictions, you must apply a discrete optimization method, which you can choose in the SNP Optimizer profile:

We distinguish between two important cases for the piece-by-piece *linear cost function*, which you can define in the master data: *Convex cost function* (costs per unit increase for higher volumes, e.g., modeling of overtime or night shifts) and *concave cost function* (costs per unit decline for higher volumes, e.g., modeling of freight rates).

Convex cost functions don't complicate the planning problem and can be efficiently solved; however, they can also be modeled without using the piece-by-piece linear cost functions via using alternative modes.

Alternatively, concave piecemeal linear cost functions cannot be solved by an LP (linear programming) solver, but only by discretization methods (mixed-integer linear programming). If linear functions are modeled piece by piece, but the Optimizer is executed without discretization, the Optimizer takes into account the linear costs that are specified in addition to the piecemeal linear cost function.

Applying the discrete optimization method can dramatically increase the runtime requirements. Note that the Supply Network Planning is a medium-term planning function whose emphasis should not be on solving whole-number problems (i.e., the application of the discrete optimization method).

The discrete optimization method cannot be used together with the strict prioritization.

Prioritization

The Optimizer can decide between the *priority of sales orders* and the *priority of forecast demand*. During a *strict prioritization*, sales orders always have the priority 1, the corrected requirements forecast the priority 5, and the requirements forecast the priority 6. Within each priority class, the system uses all available cost information to determine the ultimate solution. If the *cost-based prioritization* is applied, the Optimizer uses penalty costs information from the product master data (tab **SNP 1**, see Figure 5.3) to determine the optimal solution.

Decomposition

The *decomposition* is a flexible tool to level out the discrepancy between the optimization quality and the required runtime (or computing time). While the SNP Optimizer generally does return a better solution (i.e., the optimal solution) for any given runtime without decomposition, if we have a given fixed runtime, it may find a better solution with the decomposition. Furthermore, the decomposition may be a way for the Optimizer, if it has major discrete problems, to find a permissible solution if one exists.

With the decomposition methods that you define in the SNP Optimizer profile, you can reduce the runtime and memory requirements of the optimization. Time, product, and resource decomposition are available as decomposition methods.

The *time decomposition* accelerates the solution process by subdividing the initial problem into subproblems that succeed each other in time. The system then solves these subproblems sequentially.

The *product decomposition* accelerates the solution process by forming product groups. During the product decomposition, the sequence of the planning is usually in line with the non-delivery costs and the overall requirements quantity of the products. The priority profile allows you to assign priorities for important products and thereby manage the sequence of the planning. The rule of thumb here is that the smaller the time window, the faster the system will find a solution; the larger the time window, the better the quality of the solution found.

The *resource decomposition* accelerates the solution process by first determining a sequence of the resources via analyzing the material flow and the basic decisions of the Optimizer regarding production, procurement, transport, etc. The Optimizer can then form subproblems for the individual resources, which it solves sequentially. In each of these subproblems, a resource will be booked or consumed so that no other order can use the same resource at the same time.

During the resource decomposition, the sequence of the planning is generally determined by the production process models (PPMs) or production data structures (PDS) (see Section 5.5.4 and Section 5.5.5). If this sequence is not clear, or you want another sequence, you can change it by assigning priorities to the resources. In this way, you ca, for example, reverse the standard sequence by which the system first plans the production of the assemblies and then that of the finished products, or plan important resources that must be utilized for cost reasons first. Resource decomposition is particularly suitable if the resources are always occupied in a similar sequence through the production processes.

For the product and resource decomposition, you can define priorities with the SNP priority profile, that is, you can change the sequence in which the Optimizer groups products and resources into subproblems and plans them. There are three options for this in SAP APO-SNP: vertical or horizontal aggregated planning and incremental optimization.

Aggregated Planning—Vertical

To reduce the size of the model to be optimized, the Optimizer can restrict the planning to the level of the location product groups (provided you have defined the requirements on the lower level). Plans are distributed onto the products of lower levels according to the requirement for these products. You must define hierarchies for products and locations in the hierarchy master in order to be able to plan on the product group level. This data is used to generate the location product hierarchy. You must also define the PPMs or PDS for the product groups and create the PPM or PDS hierarchy in the hierarchy master.

Aggregated Planning—Horizontal

This function allows you to plan a subgroup of your supply chain. You can restrict the products or locations that are included during the optimization run. For example, if the optimization is only run up to the plant level, but the forecasts are run up at the customer level, the Optimizer can total the requirements at the plant level and use this value during the optimization run. Furthermore, the transport times, for example, from the plant to the distribution center and to the customer, as well as the duration of the PPMs or PDS, are taken into account.

Incremental Optimization

If you only execute the optimization-based planning for a part of the model or based on an existing plan, this is described as an incremental optimization. With this form of optimization, the plan may be unfulfillable, because the Optimizer cannot plan any receipts for shortages that have arisen through fixed orders from previous planning runs. It may also happen that the input products defined in PPMs or PDS, or products that are available for procurement through a transportation lane in a source location (source location products), and their stocks, may not be considered.

To avoid this, in the SNP Optimizer profile, you can define that the stocks for unselected input or source location products should be included by the Optimizer. You may also define for the secondary and distribution requirement for fixed orders that it should be handled in the same way as a planned independent requirement, that is, that the Optimizer allows shortages against the calculation of non-delivery costs. You can set these non-delivery costs in the product master data for the individual requirement types customer requirement, requirements forecast, and corrected requirements forecast. You can also set for the secondary and distribution requirement for fixed orders and for the stocks of unselected input or source location products that they should be included by the Optimizer as "pseudo-hard restrictions." This means that shortages are possible against the calculation of penalty costs that are internally fixed in the Optimizer and correspond to infinitely high costs. In this way, you can ensure that the Optimizer will only allow shortages if it could not otherwise find any permissible solution.

6.3.2 Processing the Optimization Run

As you can see in Figure 6.12, the Optimizer plans all distribution requirements for all locations within the distribution network before the BOM is exploded and the secondary requirement is processed in the production locations.

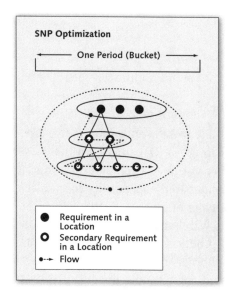

Figure 6.12 Processing Logic of the SNP Optimizer

The SNP Optimizer considers the following factors during the processing:

▶ Valid transportation lanes

▶ Lead times

▶ Transport capacity

▶ Transportation costs

▶ Handling capacity

▶ Handling costs

▶ Production capacity

▶ Production costs

▶ Storage capacity

▶ Storage costs

▶ Time stream (location master data)

▶ Lot size (minimum and maximum lot size and rounding value)

- ▶ Scrap
- ▶ Alternative resources
- ▶ Penalty costs for non-coverage of the requirement
- ▶ Penalty costs for non-adherence to the safety stock
- ▶ Procurement costs
- ▶ Shelf life
- ▶ Cost multiplicators
- ▶ Location products
- ▶ Fixed PPM/PDS resource consumption
- ▶ Fixed PPM/PDS material consumption

The Optimizer considers the entire capacity and the entire alternative capacity, which is available globally (in all locations). Depending on the chosen system settings, the Optimizer can either not offer a solution for a capacity overload situation, or increase the capacity based on a penalty costs calculation. The Optimizer considers all active types of capacity restrictions, including transport, production, handling, and warehouse constraints. To a limited extent, it also considers the shelf life of products. The result of the optimization run does not include the pegging of orders back to the original individual requirement, because the requirements are periodized.

6.3.3 Finite Planning with the SNP Optimizer

Finite planning using the SNP Optimizer is especially suitable if the capacity of your company resources is limited and this limited capacity has an impact on your production and distribution planning. With finite planning, you can already include the capacities in Supply Network Planning (SNP), to make it easier to create executable plans for the subsequent detailed scheduling (e.g., with SAP APO Production Planning and Detailed Scheduling, PP/DS).

Furthermore, during the finite planning with the SNP Optimizer, you can also include a possible expansion of your capacities in your planning, against the calculation of additional costs.

You can finitely schedule the following resource types with the SNP Optimizer:

- ▶ **Resource types**
  - ▷ Production resources
  - ▷ Transport resources

- ▷ Handling resources
- ▷ Warehouse resources
- ▶ **Resource types**
  - ▷ Single and multi-mixed resources
  - ▷ Bucket resources
  - ▷ Transport resources

Characteristics of Finite Planning

The SNP Optimizer always includes all of the model's restrictions at the same time. This means that during the finite planning, the Optimizer considers the available capacities of all resources at the same time. In this way, during a multilevel production, for instance, all production levels are included in the planning at the same time.

You can define what capacity restrictions (production, transport, handling or storage capacity) should be considered by the Optimizer in the SNP Optimizer profile. The SNP Optimizer will only include the net available capacity, in other words, it checks whether the capacity available in SNP is already consumed by other application areas of the system (e.g., PP/DS, Deployment, TLB) or fixed SNP orders.

> **Example**
>
> The SNP Optimizer subtracts the capacity consumed by PP/DS, for instance, from the available capacity in SNP. If the capacity consumption by PP/DS exceeds the aggregated capacity offering in a bucket (period) in SNP, the Optimizer assumes an available capacity of 0 in the corresponding bucket and does not plan any additional capacity consumption in this bucket.

You have the option of defining several available capacity variants for resources and of flagging these as minimal, normal, or maximum available capacities. In this way, you can leave the decision up to the Optimizer to increase the capacity or to cause a shortfall to the minimum capacity against the calculation of additional costs. Since the Optimizer will always choose the lowest-cost solution, it will only increase the capacity or fall below the minimum capacity if this results in the most favorable overall solution, despite the additional costs. You define the costs for the possible variants with minimal, normal, or maximum offering in the resource master data in the quantity/rate definition or in the quotation profile.

Production Resources

Capacity Consumption

The SNP Optimizer takes into account the capacity consumption of a production resource that you define in the mode of the production process model (PPM). A PPM can consume several resources and a resource can be consumed by several PPMs. The duration of an SNP-PPM (i.e., the total of all durations of the activities of the PPM) is fixed. It has no effect on the resource consumption, but rather is used only for the scheduling of the PPM. The resource consumption that is fixed for each activity is distributed evenly across the activity length. This means that the Optimizer ignores the consumption type defined for the activity and always assumes a continuous consumption (consumption type C).

If you use the linear optimization method, the Optimizer includes only the variable resource consumption defined in the PPM. If you also want the Optimizer to include the fixed resource consumption, you must choose the discrete optimization in the SNP Optimizer profile and define a discretization horizon for the fixed material and resource consumption (see Figure 6.13). This is necessary, for instance, if you want to map setup times using the fixed resource consumption during the lot-size planning with the SNP Optimizer.

The Optimizer also includes time-dependent resource consumptions that you have defined in the PPM. You can use these time-dependent consumptions to map different consumptions over the time of the buckets. In this way, you can include in your planning, for example, that a machine should show a higher consumption of lubricants at the start of production than towards the end of production.

In Figure 6.13, you can see the corresponding settings of the fixed and variable resource consumption circled in the PPM. You can get to this screen by choosing the SAP APO menu under **Master data • PPM • PPM**.

Available Capacity

For the maximum available capacity variant of production resources, you can define that the Optimizer can either increase by the entire capacity offering of this variant (e.g., a whole level), or not increase at all. In this case, the Optimizer will then also only include the entire increase costs or no costs at all.

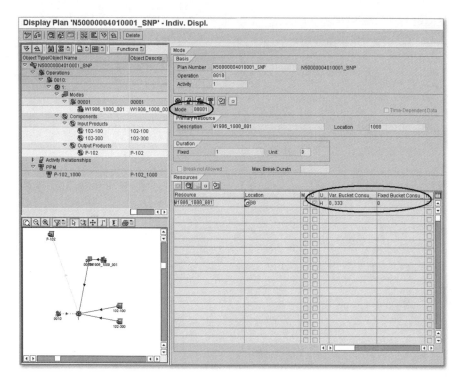

Figure 6.13 Production Resource, Capacity Consumption

Capacity Costs
You can also fix the costs for increasing the capacity of production resources time-dependently. For example, you can specify that for a planning buckets profile in daily periods, the increase will cost more on Mondays than on Tuesdays.

For production resources, you can also define costs (optional) for the normal available capacity variant (standard capacity). You can specify these costs (also time-dependent) for each capacity unit and bucket. The costs are accrued in proportion to the resource usage.

Transport Resources

Capacity Consumption
The SNP Optimizer only takes into account the variable capacity consumption (per day) of the means of transport that you have defined in the transportation lane in the **Consumption** field in the section **Product-Specific**

259

Means of Transport (see Figure 6.14). In the SAP APO menu, choose **Master data** · **Transportation lanes** · **Transportation lanes**.

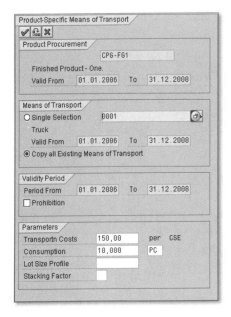

Figure 6.14 Transport Resource, Capacity Consumption

You specify this consumption in each case for the product specified in this section. The consumption depends on the transport duration. If the transport duration is 0, no resource consumption exists.

Available Capacity

You can assign transport resources to several transportation lanes and thereby limit the transport capacity on these lanes. To do this, enter a transport resource in the transportation lane in the **Resource** field in the section **Means of Transport** (cannot be seen in the figure).

In the SNP Optimizer profile, you can set that the available means of transport should be considered as discrete, i.e., as not divisible. In this case, the means of transport are considered discretely for each transportation lane. You define the means of transport capacity in the resource master data in the **Dimension** field. You can use this option, for example, to map the means of transport available in your company (e.g., a truck). If you commission external transportation providers, the discrete handling of means of transport will not be particularly relevant to you.

Capacity Costs

The transportation costs included by the Optimizer comprise the product-specific transportation costs (i.e., the transportation costs you have entered in the transportation lane in the section **Product-Specific Means of Transport**) and the transportation costs for the means of transport (i.e., the transportation costs entered in the **Parameters** section, see Figure 6.14). The means of transport costs depend on the transport resource consumption for all products that are transported on the transportation lane, as well as by the distance between the start and target location defined for the transportation lane. You can define the means of transport costs either as costs per transport resource unit or as costs per means of transport. For instance, if you want to map discount scales, you can apply the cost functions. The application of cost functions is particularly suitable for the collaboration with external service providers.

Handling Resources

Capacity Consumption

You can assign handling resources of a location in the location master data (**Resources** tab) as **Resource inbound** or **Resource outbound** (see Figure 6.15). In the SAP APO menu, choose **Master data · Location master · Location master**.

The handling-in resource is consumed during the goods receipt processing time by incoming transports (SNP stock transfers) and external procurement; the handling-out resource is debited during the goods issue processing time by outgoing transports.

You can define the capacity consumption of the handling-inbound and handling-outbound resources for the relevant location product in the location product master data (**GR/GI** tab) (see Figure 6.16). In the SAP APO menu, go to **Master data · Product master · Product master**.

The resource consumption relates to the handling operation and is therefore proportional to the quantity, but not to the time.

Warehouse Resources

Capacity Consumption

The Optimizer considers the capacity consumption of the warehouse resource you define for the relevant location product in the location product master data (**GR/GI** tab) (see Figure 6.16).

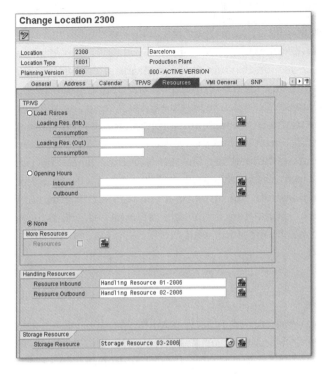

Figure 6.15 Assigning Handling Resources to the Location

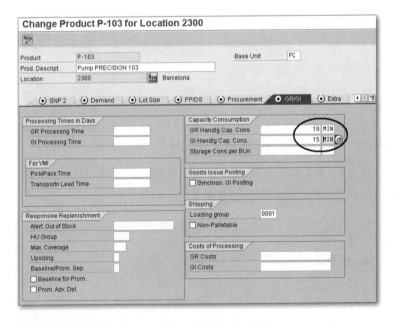

Figure 6.16 Handling Resource, Capacity Consumption

Available Capacity

The warehouse capacity restriction is a soft constraint for the Optimizer, that is, the restriction can be violated by the Optimizer against the charging of penalty costs. The warehouse capacity is defined as a soft constraint because the Supply Network Planning is integrated with APO-PP/DS and the SAP ERP system. As a result of the integration, there may be initial warehouse stocks or fixed material receipts (e.g., from PP/DS) that cannot be reduced within a bucket and exceed the warehouse capacity. To find a solution, the Optimizer can violate the restriction of the warehouse capacity against the charging of penalty costs. However, due to the high penalty costs, the Optimizer will always try to adhere to the warehouse capacity.

The capacity offering of the warehouse resource is not aggregated by bucket, as it is for the other resource types. The Optimizer always considers the capacity offering that is available on the last day of a bucket.

In addition to the capacity of the warehouse resource, you have the option of setting a product-specific upper limit for the warehouse stock in the location product master. The Optimizer observes this upper limit if you activate the **Maximum product-specific warehouse quantity** key figure in the SNP Optimizer profile. You can also define a time-dependent upper inventory limit.

6.3.4 Determining the Supply Source with the SNP Optimizer

If there are alternative procurement options in your company that are associated with different costs, you can use the Optimizer in Supply Network Planning to solve the following problems:

- When you are to produce, procure, store, and deliver (e.g., including deciding on in-house production versus external procurement)
- What products and what volumes are produced, transported, procured, stored, and delivered (product mix)
- What resources and what production process models (PPMs) or production data structures (PDS) are to be used (technology mix)
- When you are to produce, transport, procure, store, and deliver
- From what location to what location you want to transport (e.g., *production plant → distribution center* or *distribution center → customer*)

Unlike the heuristic-based planning and the Capable-to-Match (CTM) planning, the SNP Optimizer does not determine the sources of supply on the basis of predefined quotas or rules, but makes its decisions via sources of supply based on costs. Two sources of supply are relevant to the Optimizer: transportation lanes and production process models/production data systems.

The goal of an optimal supply source determination using the SNP Optimizer is, in particular, to define the production locations in such a way that the number of stock transfers and therefore also the costs of the stock transfers are reduced.

The SNP Optimizer does not consider any quotas or procurement priorities. However, it can be used to create quotas for subsequent heuristic-based planning runs. In this way, for example, following a longer-term optimization-based planning (e.g., on a monthly basis), you can run shorter-term heuristic planning runs. Here, the quotas created in the optimization-planning run serve as the basis for the heuristic planning runs.

Since the Optimizer does not take into account any quotas, nor does it support any even distribution of the production onto different locations (with regard to the resource utilization or quota on a quantity basis).

Furthermore, the Optimizer does not consider any external procurement relationships (i.e., any delivery schedules, contracts or purchasing info records) as sources of supply. If you have assigned a means of transport to the transportation lane generated from the external procurement relationship, this transportation lane is included by the Optimizer. However, the Optimizer does not create any orders for the delivery schedules during the planning (it only includes existing orders as fixed orders).

Controlling the Source of Supply Determination through Costs

Since the SNP Optimizer takes all conditions of a model into account at the same time, to find an optimal solution (i.e., the most cost-effective solution) you can essentially only affect the Optimizer's selection of the sources of supply through the costs. For instance, you can achieve a certain prioritization of the sources of supply through steering costs, for example, by reducing the production costs in the preferred location. However, you should also note here that the Optimizer will always include all influencing factors.

▶ **Prioritizing the production resources through the production costs**
You can influence the Optimizer's decision as to where to produce and with what resources by defining the production costs accordingly in the PPM/PDS. For example, if you want to define the priorities of three differ-

ent PPMs/PDS, you can set the lowest production costs for the PPM/PDS with the highest priority, higher costs for the PPM/PDS with the second-highest priority, and the highest costs in the PPM/PDS for the PPM/PDS with the lowest priority. To do this, define the single-level production costs or a cost function in the PPM/PDS (see Figure 6.17). You can get to this screen through the SAP APO menu **Master data • PPM • PPM**.

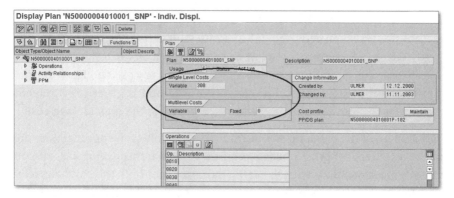

Figure 6.17 Production Costs in the PPM

However, note that in making its decision, in addition to the production costs, the Optimizer will consider the warehouse costs of the products involved in the PPM/PDS, as well as the capacity offering of the resources required for the PPM/PDS.

▶ **Prioritizing the procurement location through the transportation costs**
You can influence the Optimizer's decision regarding from which locations from the system it should procure by defining the costs accordingly in the transportation lane. For instance, if you want to define the priorities of two different procurement locations, you enter lower transportation costs for the transportation lane of the preferred location than you would enter for the other transportation lane. The transportation costs comprise the means of transport costs (**Costs** in the subscreen **Means of transport of the transportation lane**) and the product-specific means of transport costs (**Costs** in the section **Product-specific means of transport**) (see Figure 6.14). Note however, that in making its decision, the Optimizer also includes other influencing factors aside from the transportation costs, such as the warehouse costs and production costs of the location.

6.3.5 Lot-Size Planning with the SNP Optimizer

Within the lot-size planning, you define in which periods what requirements quantities are provided. You essentially have two options available:

▶ You procure or produce the exact requirements quantities for a product. The order size corresponds to the requirements quantity here. The main advantage of this method is the low warehouse costs, however, the disadvantage lies in the high procurement and setup costs.

▶ You group several requirement quantities for a product from successive periods into larger procurement or production lots. With this procedure, you procure or produce in advance and use the cost savings from the economies of scale. The advantage of this method is lower procurement and setup costs; however, the disadvantage lies in the high storage costs.

Based on all of the costs, the SNP Optimizer determines the optimal (i.e., the most cost-effective) procurement, production, and transport lot sizes. If you run a finite scheduling with the SNP Optimizer, not only the costs are relevant for the lot-size planning, however, but the available capacities as well.

In the context of the integration with the downstream production planning and detailed scheduling (e.g., SAP APO Production Planning and Detailed Scheduling, PP/DS), we can already take into account larger setup consumptions and/or costs during the planning and preliminary planning in Supply Network Planning (SNP). This makes it easier for production planning and detailed scheduling to create executable plans.

Lot-Size Planning in Production

For the lot-size planning in production using the SNP Optimizer you can map both setup consumptions and setup costs in the system. You can also influence the lot-size planning by setting minimum and maximum lot sizes and discrete (whole-number) lot sizes.

Consumptions for Setup Times

You essentially have three possibilities available for mapping setup consumptions in the system:

▶ If the amount of the setup consumptions per period is known from the history, you can map the remaining consumption by reducing the capacity offering of the production resource accordingly. If the setup consumption remains the same across the different periods, you can reduce the rate of resource utilization in the resource master data. For example, for a setup consumption of 20%, enter a rate of utilization for the bucket capacity (period capacity) of 80% (see Figure 6.18). To do this, in the SAP APO menu, choose **Master data • Resource • Resource**.

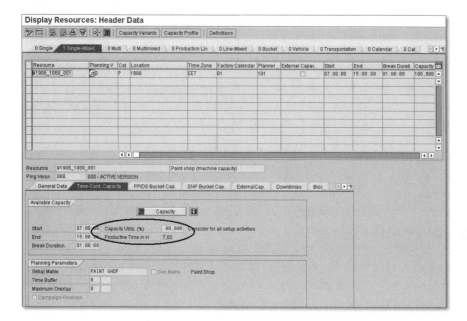

Figure 6.18 Rate of Utilization

▶ If the setup consumption fluctuates across the various periods, you can reduce the standard capacity for the individual periods accordingly. In this case, you can select the linear optimization method for the optimization run, that is, no discretization is required.

▶ If the amount of the setup consumptions is not known, but the setup consumption is relatively low in comparison with the bucket capacity, you can define the setup consumption as a fixed bucket resource consumption in the PPM (see Figure 6.13). To allow the Optimizer to consider the fixed bucket resource consumption defined in the PPM, you must define a discretization horizon (see Figure 6.21) in the SNP Optimizer profile in the field **Fixed material and resource consumption**. You must also choose the discrete optimization method in this profile.

▶ If the amount of the setup consumptions is not known, but the setup consumption is relatively high in comparison with the bucket capacity, you can run a lot-size planning for all periods.

Setup Costs

The Optimizer primarily determines the optimal lot sizes and the number of lots based on the setup and storage costs. If there are high setup costs and low storage costs, the Optimizer will most likely schedule large lots, while it will tend to schedule small lots if there are low setup costs and high storage costs.

You can define the setup costs in the PPM as fixed costs within the cost function. You must also choose the discrete optimization method in the SNP Optimizer profile and enter a discretization horizon in the **PPM/PDS Execution** field on the **Discrete Constraints** tab (see Figure 6.21).

Integration

If you run an integrated SNP- and PP/DS planning (i.e., there is a link between SNP PPM and PP/DS PPM), the Optimizer considers setup statuses from the production planning and detailed scheduling. This means that the Optimizer ignores setup consumptions and costs if there is already a PP/DS order for the corresponding PP/DS-PPM in the corresponding bucket. Here you must activate the key figure **Lot-size planning for all periods (for a cross-period lot-size planning)** or the key figure **Non-cross-period lot-size planning (for a lot-size planning that does not cover all periods)** in the SNP Optimizer profile on the **Integration** tab.

Minimum/Maximum Lot Sizes

If a minimum or maximum lot size is required for your production, for example, due to technical restrictions (e.g., you always have to produce at least a whole tank of active agent), you can define minimum and maximum lot sizes. You essentially have two options for defining these minimum and maximum lot sizes:

▶ You define the minimum and maximum **Lot Size** in the PPM (see Figure 6.19). In the SAP APO menu, go to **Master data • PPM • PPM**.

▶ You define the minimum lot size in the location product master data on the **Lot Size** tab in conjunction with the lot-size procedures **Fixed lot size** or **Exact lot size** (see Figure 6.24). In the SAP APO menu, choose **Master data • PPM • PPM**.

 ▷ **Fixed lot size**
 The value you specify as a fixed lot size is considered by the SNP Optimizer as a minimum lot size. For each execution of the PPM, the output quantity of the PPM (i.e., the quantity of the output component) then corresponds to this fixed lot size.

▶ **Exact lot size**

The Optimizer considers the minimum lot size defined in the location product master as the minimum lot size.

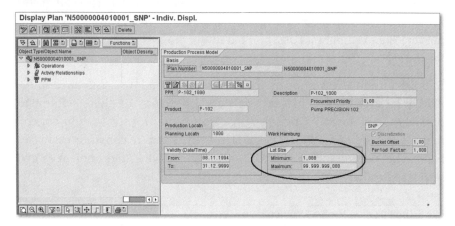

Figure 6.19 Lot Sizes in the PPM

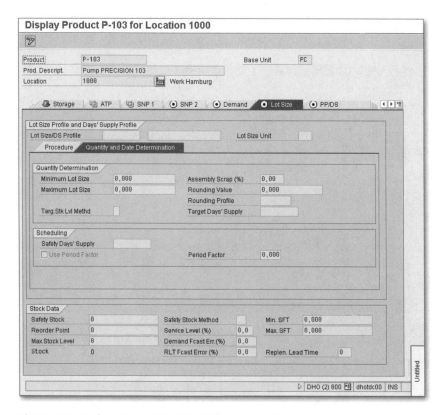

Figure 6.20 Product Master, "Lot Size" Tab

These settings are taken into account by the SNP Optimizer for integration reasons (e.g., with PP/DS). The minimum lot size defined in the product master applies for all production process models that use this product as header material. If the minimum lot size in the product master is larger than the minimum lot size in the PPM, the Optimizer uses the value from the product master. The maximum lot size defined in the product master is not relevant for the SNP Optimizer.

In order for the SNP Optimizer to use the minimum lot sizes defined in the PPM or location product master, you must also choose the discrete optimization method in the SNP Optimizer profile and enter a discretization horizon in the field **Minimum PPM/PDS Lot Size** on the **Discrete Constraints** tab (see Figure 6.21). Here, in the SAP APO menu go to **SNP • Environment • Curr. settings • Profiles • SNP Optimization profile**.

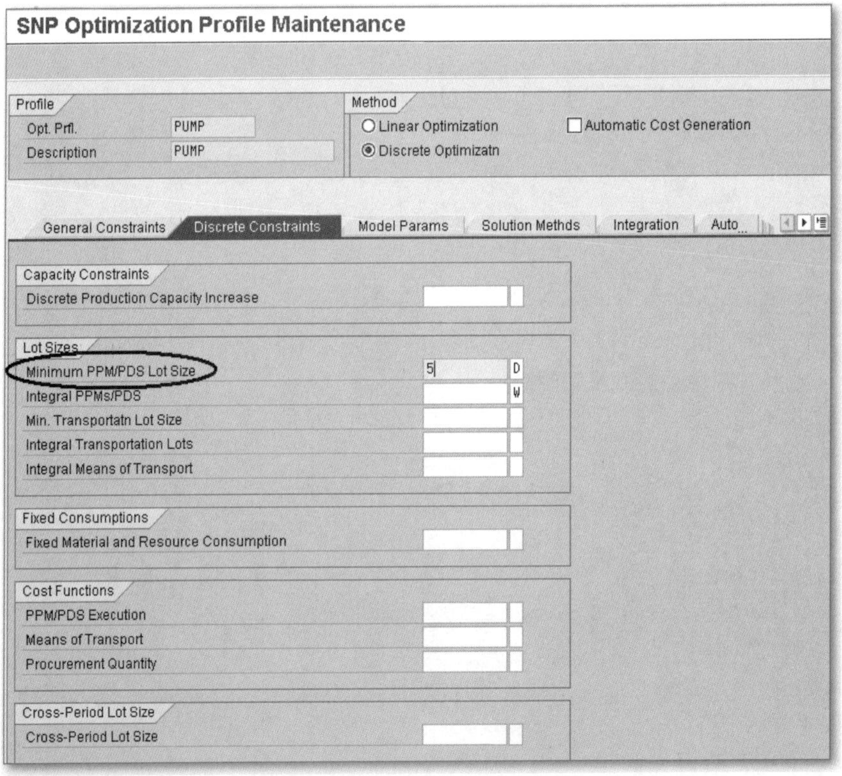

Figure 6.21 SNP Optimization Profile, "Minimum PPM/PDS Lot Size" Field

The maximum PPM lot size defined in the production process model is also taken into account by the Optimizer in choosing the linear optimization method. For this you must activate the key figure **Maximum PPM/PDS Lot Size** in the SNP Optimizer profile on the **General Constraints** tab (see Figure 6.22). To do this, in the SAP APO menu choose **SNP • Environment • Curr. settings • Profiles • SNP Optimization profile**.

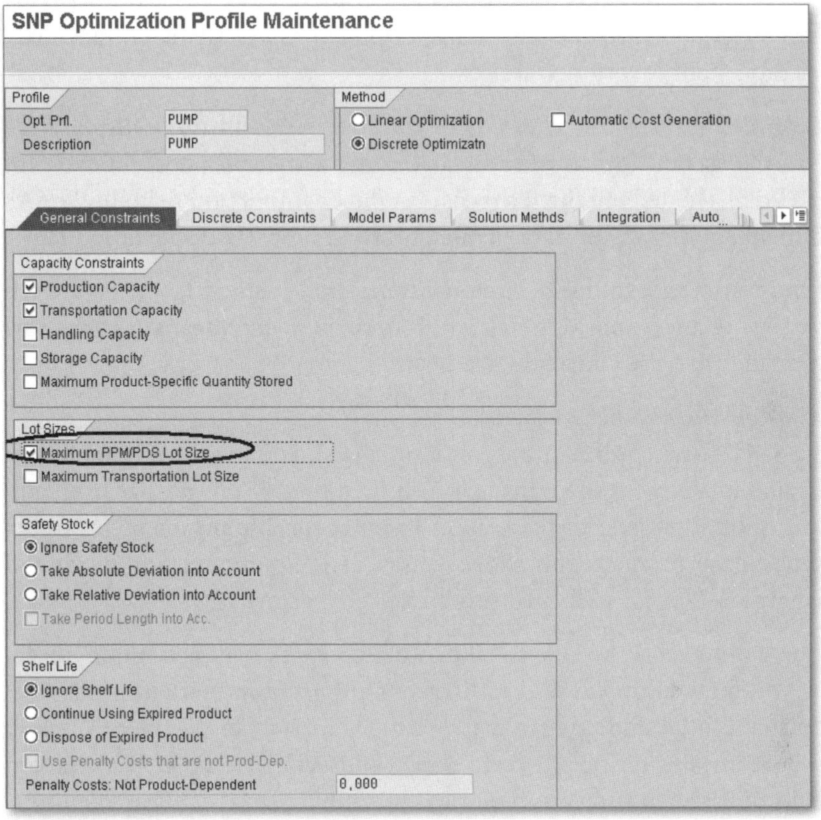

Figure 6.22 SNP Optimization Profile, "Maximum PPM/PDS Lot Size" Field

Discrete (Integer) Lot Sizes

If you can only produce whole-number multiples of a lot, for example, due to technical restrictions in your factory (e.g., you can only produce full tanks of an agent, so you cannot produce 1.5 tanks), activate the Discretization key figure in the PPM. To allow this key figure to also be observed by the Optimizer, you must also choose the discrete optimization method in the SNP Optimizer profile and enter a discretization horizon in the **Integral PPMs/PDS** field on the **Discrete Constraints** tab. In this case, the Optimizer will always plan production in whole-number multiples of the output component quantity.

Lot-Size Planning in Transportation

Fixed Means of Transport Costs

In the same way as the setup costs in production were handled, the SNP Optimizer mainly determines the optimal lot sizes in the transport based on the fixed costs of the means of transport. If these costs are high, the Optimizer will tend to schedule large transport lots (i.e., less frequent transports, for example, only every two weeks).

You can define these fixed means of transport costs in the transportation lane in the section **Means of transport**. Enter a transport cost function for which you have defined the fixed costs in the **Cost function** field. In the SAP APO menu, go to **Master data • Transportation lane • Transportation lane**.

You must also choose the **Discrete Optimization** method in the SNP Optimizer profile and enter a discretization horizon in the **Means of transport** field on the **Discrete Constraints** tab.

Maximum/Maximum Lot Sizes

In the SNP lot-size profile (transportation lanes), you can set minimum and maximum lot sizes for the transport. You then specify this lot-size profile in the transportation lane in the section **Product-specific means of transport** for a particular product. This allows you to define minimum and maximum transport lot sizes for particular products.

For the Optimizer to be able to take into account the defined minimum lot sizes, you must also choose the **Discrete Optimization** method in the SNP Optimizer profile and enter a discretization horizon in the field **Minimal transport lot size** on the **Discrete Constraints** tab. The defined maximum transport lot size is also considered by the Optimizer in selecting the linear optimization method, if you activate the key figure **Maximum Transportation Lot Size** in the SNP Optimizer profile on the **General Constraints** tab.

Discrete (Integer) Transport Lots and Means of Transport

If you only want to transport whole-number multiples of a transport lot size (e.g., only entire pallets of a product), you can define that the Optimizer should take this into account during the planning by choosing the **Discrete Optimization** method in the SNP Optimizer profile and entering a discretization horizon in the field **Integral Transportation Lots** on the **Discrete Constraints** tab. You normally define the transport lot size as a rounding value in the SNP lot-size profile (transportation lanes). Alternatively, however, you can set in the Customizing of the SNP under **Maintain global SNP settings** that the Optimizer should use the rounding value defined in the location product master of the target location as the transport lot size.

You can equally define that the Optimizer should only plan whole-number means of transport, so, for example, only an entire truck in each case for the transport. To do this, enter a discretization horizon in the field **Integral Means of Transport**.

Lot-Size Planning in Procurement

Fixed Procurement Costs
Like the setup costs in production and the fixed means of transport costs in the transport, the SNP Optimizer primarily determines the optimal lot sizes in the procurement based on the fixed procurement costs. If these costs are high, the Optimizer will tend to schedule large procurement lots, (i.e., less frequent procurement operations, for example, only every two weeks).

You can define these fixed procurement costs in the location product master on the **Procurement** tab. Enter a procurement cost function in the **Cost Function** field, for which you have defined the fixed costs. You must also choose the discrete optimization method in the SNP Optimizer profile and enter a discretization horizon in the **Procurement Quantity** field on the **Discrete Constraints** tab.

Minimum/Maximum and Integer Lot Sizes
Minimum/maximum and integral or discrete procurement lot sizes cannot currently be taken into account by the SNP Optimizer during the lot-size planning. However, there is a solution to help you map these lot-size restrictions:

1. First, enter your supplier as a location in your model.
2. Secondly, create a transportation lane between the supplier and the requirement location.
3. Third, map the procurement lot-size restrictions as transport lot-size restrictions (see the section *Lot-Size Planning in Transportation*).

6.3.6 Inventory Planning

Warehouse stock serves to protect a company against uncertainties and fluctuations in requirements. If you hold too much warehouse stock, however, too much capacity is tied up and the warehouse costs are correspondingly high. Alternatively, if warehouse stocks are too low, there may be a risk, for example, that you won't be able to cover an unforeseen requirement.

The primary goal when using the SNP Optimizer in the area of inventory planning is therefore to hold the warehouse stock between certain upper and lower limits.

When planning the warehouse stock, the SNP Optimizer takes into account goods receipts and issues caused by other application areas of the system (e.g., production planning and detailed scheduling, deployment, Transport Load Builder) or fixed SNP orders.

You can first define whether the SNP Optimizer, when calculating the storage costs, should interpret the warehouse stock for each bucket (period) as an average warehouse stock per bucket or as the warehouse stock at the end of the bucket:

▶ **Average warehouse stock**
The Optimizer calculates the warehouse costs by multiplying the warehouse stock, the storage costs defined in the location product master, and the number of days in the bucket with each other. This option is well suited for constant receipts and issues in the course of a bucket.

▶ **Closing stock balance for month**
The Optimizer calculates the storage costs by multiplying the warehouse stock with the storage costs defined in the location product master. This option is well suited for more irregular receipts and issues in the course of a bucket.

In each case, you define the storage costs in the location product master data on the **Procurement** tab in the **Product Storage Costs** field (see Figure 6.23) for a specific product in a particular location. As a matter of principle, you should always define the storage costs because this allows you to ensure that the SNP Optimizer does not schedule any unnecessary preproduction. The storage costs allow you to guarantee that production, procurement, and transport will always run as close to the requirements as possible. Since the storage costs are defined product-specifically, you can use them to help you control where, that is, in what locations, a product is stored.

Adhering to a Lower Stock Limit with the Safety Stock Planning

The SNP Optimizer decides whether and how the safety stock of a product is built in particular locations. The desired amount of the safety stock must be specified to the Optimizer. You can either define this amount directly based on your experience from the past in the location product master, or allow the system to determine it using the enhanced safety stock planning. The safety stock is a soft constraint for the Optimizer, that is, the restriction can be violated against the charging of penalty costs. You can define the penalty costs for infringing on the safety stock in the location product master on the **Procurement** tab in the **Safety Stock Penalty** field so that the Optimizer can take the safety stock into account (see Figure 6.23). In the SAP APO menu, go to **Master data • Product master • Product master**.

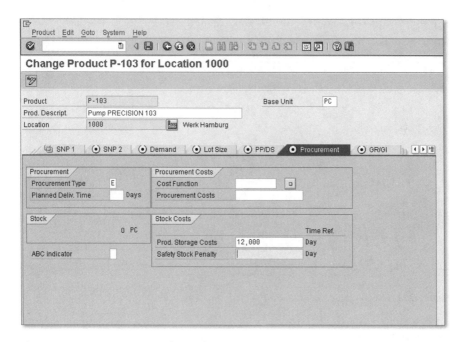

Figure 6.23 Inventory Costs in the Product Master, "Procurement" Tab

These costs must be higher than the storage costs; otherwise, the Optimizer would not plan any safety stock.

The amount of the safety stock cannot exceed the product-specific upper inventory limit defined in the location product master (**Maximum Stock Level** field on the **Lot Size** tab) (see Figure 6.24). For this, in the SAP APO menu choose **Master data • Product master • Product master**.

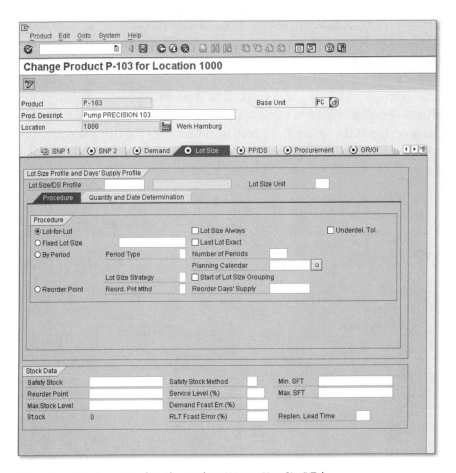

Figure 6.24 Maximum Stock in the Product Master, "Lot Size" Tab

Adhering to a Lower Stock Limit with the Days' Supply Planning

You can also run a static days' supply planning with the SNP Optimizer using the safety stock. Here you should ensure that at any time, there is at least as much of a product in stock as is required within a days' supply period.

Here you should define a safety stock method (**SZ**, **MZ**, **SM**, or **MM**, see Section 6.7) for the corresponding product in the location product master on the **Lot Size** tab and enter a fixed, period-independent safety days' supply (see Figure 6.25). In the SAP APO menu, go to **Master data • Product master • Product master**.

You can also set the safety days' supply period-dependently in the planning table of the interactive planning. The SNP Optimizer uses the results of the days' supply planning as the basis for building the safety stock.

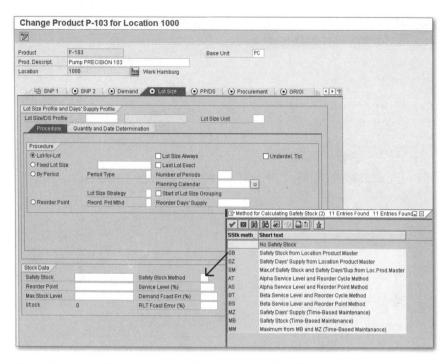

Figure 6.25 Safety Days' Supply in the Product Master, "Lot Size" Tab

Adhering to an Upper Stock Limit with a Static Upper Stock Limit

You can define a product-specific upper stock limit for a location product in the location product master data. To do this, enter a value on the **Lot Size** tab in the **Maximum Stock Level** field (see Figure 6.24). The SNP Optimizer will take this upper limit into account during the planning. The upper stock limit is a soft restriction for the Optimizer, that is, the restriction can be violated against the charging of penalty costs. Furthermore, you can also define a time-dependent upper stock limit in the interactive SNP planning for a product.

You can set an upper stock limit for all products by defining the available capacity of a storage resource in the resource master data. The SNP Optimizer includes this upper limit during planning.

Adhering to an Upper Stock Limit with a Dynamic Upper Stock Limit

You can also use the shelf life functionality to set a dynamic upper stock limit for the optimization-based planning. To do this, you must activate the key figure **Planning with Shelf Life (Plng with Shelf Life)** in the product master data on the **Properties** tab and enter a period in the corresponding field (i.e.,

Shelf Life field) (see Figure 6.26). In the SAP APO menu, go to **Master data ·
Product master · Product master.**

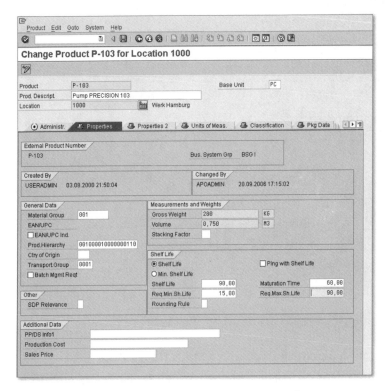

Figure 6.26 Shelf Life in the Product Master, "Properties" Tab

During the planning, the Optimizer then guarantees that at no time is there more warehouse stock for this product than is needed in the specified period.

For instance, if you enter a shelf life of one week, you define that prior to this period no material receipts should be planned for the requirement that exists in this week, that is, that warehouse stock should not be held any longer than one week in advance for the requirement.

The Optimizer then plans the continued use of the product for products with an exceeded shelf life date, though it calculates penalty costs for this.

Shelf-Life of a Product

The SNP Optimizer can also consider the shelf life of a product to a limited extent. Here, the Optimizer tries to ensure that at no time does it plan more warehouse stock for this product than is needed in the corresponding period. If a larger volume of the product than is consumed in the period must be stored, the Optimizer considers these surplus volumes as volumes that must be disposed of against penalty costs.

You should note the following restrictions of the SNP Optimizer:

▶ When you create orders at the end of the optimization run, the system does not differentiate between the volumes that are regarded by the Optimizer as disposable and the remaining planned volumes. This means that the total of both quantities is displayed as the planning result (e.g., in the interactive planning).

▶ The shelf life of the product defined in the product master data is not inherited beyond the production levels, i.e., the shelf life of an input component does not affect the shelf life of an output component. For example, if you define the shelf life of an agent, the system does not transfer this shelf life onto the later tablets and packaging.

▶ The shelf life of the product defined in the product master data is also not passed on across multiple locations during transport (similar to production). In other words, if a product is transported from one location to another, the defined shelf life period begins once again. Consequently, in the event of cycles in the distribution network (i.e., you can transport a product from one location through another and back again to the start location) through a round transport, products become durable again. In this case, the Optimizer can reuse a product that will be disposed of.

6.3.7 Optimization Profiles

Table 6.3 describes the profiles used by the SNP Optimizer. To access the individual profiles, in the SAP Easy Access menu, choose **Supply Network Planning • Environment • Curr. Settings • Profiles**.

Profile	Usage in the Optimization Planning Run
SNP Optimizer profile	In this profile, you define the optimization method to be used during the optimization run (linear or discrete optimization) and the restrictions to be considered.
SNP cost profile	In this profile, you define the weighting of the various cost types in the target function, in other words, you compare and determine the relationship of the costs to each other.

Table 6.3 Optimization Profiles of the SNP Optimizer

Profile	Usage in the Optimization Planning Run
	We recommend that you change only the standard settings for test purposes in the context of the modeling. In production systems, you should, if possible, not change the standard setting 1.0, which corresponds to the costs entered in the cost maintenance, because this can lead to unintended effects.
SNP lot-size profile (transportation lanes)	In this profile, you can define minimum and maximum lot sizes for the transport. You then specify the profile in the transportation lane in the section **Product-specific transport** for a particular product. This allows you to define minimum and maximum transport lot sizes for particular products.
	If you only want to transport whole-number multiples of a transport lot size, you can also define the transport lot size as a rounding value in this profile.
	To allow the Optimizer to include the defined minimum lot sizes and rounding values, you must choose the **Discrete Optimization** method in the SNP Optimizer profile.
SNP Optimization limit profile	If you want to run a rescheduling after a planning run of the SNP Optimizer, you can increase the planning stability using this profile by restricting the possible deviations in the decision variables from the previous optimization plan. For instance, you can allow lower deviations at the start of the planning period and then extend these towards the end of the horizon, in order to avoid major short-term planning changes.
	As the basis for the rescheduling, you can choose not only the last optimization run to be executed, but also previous optimization runs.
SNP priority profile	For the product and resource decomposition, you can define priorities with the SNP priority profile, that is, you can change the sequence in which the Optimizer groups products and resources into subproblems and plans them.
SNP planning profile	In this profile, you can make basic settings for the various SNP planning procedures such as, for instance, the heuristic, Optimizer, deployment heuristic, deployment optimizer, and Transport Load Builder (TLB).
	The SNP planning profile, which you have activated in the Customizing of the SNP under **Maintain global SNP settings**, applies globally for all SNP planning methods. With some planning methods, you can overwrite the settings of the active profile by specifying a different SNP planning profile in the background when you execute the planning.
Parallel processing profile	This profile allows you to determine what background jobs are divided into parallel processes. You can set the number of processes running in parallel, the number of objects per processing block, and the server group. In each case, you define the profile for a particular application function, such as the SNP Optimizer, for example.

Table 6.3 Optimization Profiles of the SNP Optimizer (cont.)

6.3.8 Executing the Optimizer in the Interactive Planning (Example)

We will now describe a system example for applying the SNP Optimizer in detail. The Optimizer proposes a plan based on the minimal procurement, storage, transport, and production costs for several products at the same time, without overloading resources.

1. In the SAP Easy Access menu, choose **Advanced Planning and Optimization • Supply Network Planning • Planning • Supply Network Planning interactive**. The screen shown in Figure 6.27 is displayed. Use the shuffler to select the location products to be scheduled.

2. Select the location products to be planned. Figure 6.27 shows you the requirements and stock situation prior to the optimization.

Planning Book: [Live] CPG3- SNP INTERACTIVE PLANNING / SNP PLAN

SNP PLAN	Unit	05.01.2007	06.01.2007	07.01.2007	08.01.2007	09.01.2007	10.01.2007	11.01.2007	12.01.2007	13.01.2007	14.01.2007	15.01.2007	22.01.2007
Forecast	CSE	6.000							6.000			12.000	
Sales Order	CSE												
Distribution Demand (Planned)	CSE												
Distribution Demand (Confirmed)	CSE												
Distribution Demand (TLB-Confirmed)	CSE												
Dependent Demand	CSE												
Total Demand	CSE	6.000							6.000			12.000	
Distribution Receipt (Planned)	CSE												
Distribution Receipt (Confirmed)	CSE												
Distribution Receipt (TLB-Confirmed)	CSE												
In Transit	CSE												
Production (Planned)	CSE												
Production (Confirmed)	CSE												
Manufacture of Co-Products	CSE												
Total Receipts	CSE												
Projected Inventory	CSE	-6.000	-6.000	-6.000	-6.000	-6.000	-6.000	-6.000	-12.000	-12.000	-12.000	-24.000	-24.000
Physical Stock	CSE												
Stock OH (Unrestricted)	CSE												
Stock OH (Restricted)	CSE												
Stock OH (Inspection)	CSE												
Stock OH (Blocked)	CSE												
Safety Stock (Planned)	CSE												
Safety Stock	CSE												
Target Days' Supply	D												
Target Stock Level	CSE												
Days' Supply	D												
ATD Receipts	CSE												
ATD Issues	CSE												

Figure 6.27 "SNP Optimization" Example, Initial Situation

3. Call the **Optimizer** with the button of the same name. The **Optimization** tab in the **SNP Optimizer** window will be displayed (see Figure 6.28).

4. On the **Optimization** tab (see Figure 6.28), you can select one of your predefined SNP Optimizer cost and optimization limit profiles. From here, you can also branch into the maintenance screens for the SNP Optimizer, cost and optimization limit profiles, for example, to make changes to existing profiles. Figure 6.29 shows the selected cost profile for the SNP Optimizer.

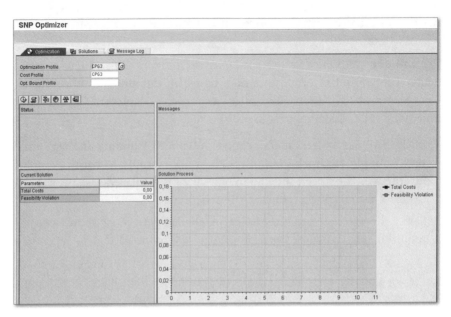

Figure 6.28 "SNP Optimization" Example, "Optimization" Tab

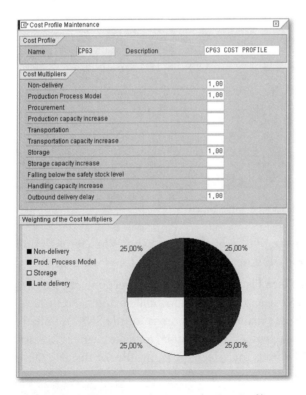

Figure 6.29 "SNP Optimization" Example, Cost Profile

5. Choose **Execute** to start the optimization run. In the area **Current Solution** on the **Optimization** tab, you will get a list of the resulting costs determined by the Optimizer for the current solution (see Figure 6.30).

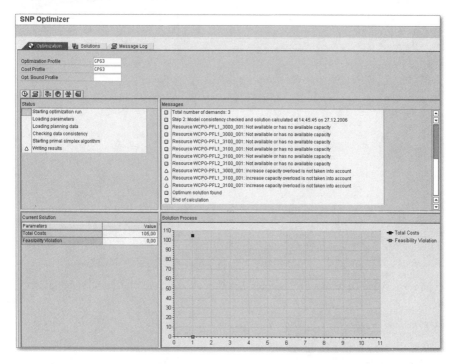

Figure 6.30 "SNP Optimization" Example, Interactive View of the SNP Optimizer

6. During the optimization run, the system displays the individual steps of the optimization process in the **Status** area.

7. Select the **Solutions** tab to display information on previous optimization runs. The solution found by the SNP Optimizer is shown in the **Solution selected** area (see Figure 6.31). When you select a solution in the right area of the screen, the corresponding data appears on the left.

8. Select the **Message Log** tab to display messages on previous optimization runs. If you select an optimization run in the left area of the screen, the corresponding messages are displayed in the area on the right. In addition, the **Message Text** area also displays messages on the current optimization run (see Figure 6.32).

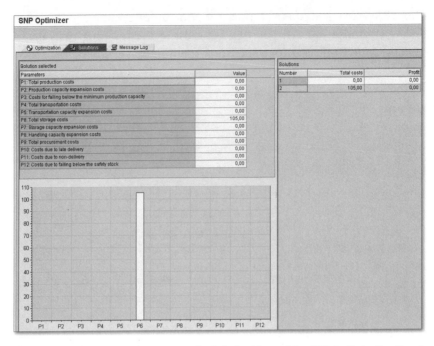

Figure 6.31 "SNP Optimization" Example, Solution View of the SNP Optimization Result

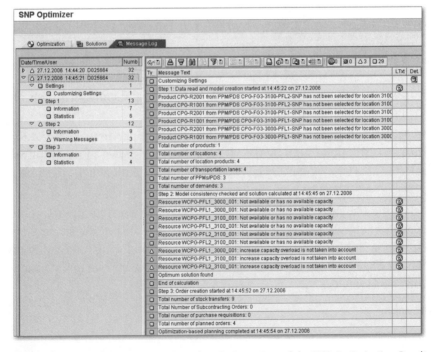

Figure 6.32 "SNP Optimization" Example, Message View of the SNP Optimization Result

During the SNP optimization run, a range of restrictions are taken into account, such as the capacity restrictions that were defined for the resources. Generally, in the SNP Optimizer profile, you define what restrictions the Optimizer needs to consider during the optimization run. In certain cases, however, it may be necessary to define the restrictions time-dependently, for example, if the quantity of a product provided by a vendor fluctuates from period to period. You can define such time-dependent restrictions in the interactive planning and set the following limit values:

- Upper limit for external procurement (at product/location level)
- Upper limit for warehouse stock (at product/location level)
- Upper limit for production (at product/PPM level)
- Upper limit for transport (at product/transportation lane level)

You cannot determine any time-dependent lower limits, because this could result in the Optimizer not finding any permissible solution. An exception is the warehouse stock, for which you can define a lower limit time-dependently via the safety stock.

The result of the SNP Optimizer can now be analyzed in the interactive view (see Figure 6.33).

SNP PLAN	Unit	04.01.2007	05.01.2007	06.01.2007	07.01.2007	08.01.2007	09.01.2007	10.01.2007	11.01.2007	12.01.2007	13.01.2007	14.01.2007	15.01.2007
Forecast	CSE		6.000							6.000			12.000
Sales Order	CSE												
Distribution Demand (Planned)	CSE												
Distribution Demand (Confirmed)	CSE												
Distribution Demand (TLB-Confirmed)	CSE												
Dependent Demand	CSE												
Total Demand	CSE		6.000							6.000			12.000
Distribution Receipt (Planned)	CSE	6.000							6.000			6.000	6.000
Distribution Receipt (Confirmed)	CSE												
Distribution Receipt (TLB-Confirmed)	CSE												
In Transit	CSE												
Production (Planned)	CSE												
Production (Confirmed)	CSE												
Manufacture of Co-Products	CSE												
Total Receipts	CSE	8.000							8.000			8.000	6.000
Projected Inventory	CSE	8.000							6.000			8.000	
Physical Stock	CSE												
Stock OH (Unrestricted)	CSE												
Stock OH (Restricted)	CSE												
Stock OH (Inspection)	CSE												
Stock OH (Blocked)	CSE												
Safety Stock (Planned)	CSE		7.000					3.000					
Safety Stock	CSE												
Target Days' Supply	D												
Target Stock Level	CSE												
Days' Supply	D	1								1		4	
ATD Receipts	CSE												
ATD Issues	CSE												

Figure 6.33 "SNP Optimization" Example, Result of the SNP Optimizer in the Interactive SNP Planning

Automatic Cost Generation

Costs play a major role for optimization-based planning in *Supply Network Planning* (SNP). The Optimizer selects the plan with the lowest total costs from among all of the permissible production and distribution plans. This means that the Optimizer also makes operational business decisions, such as covering a requirement at a particular time, based on the associated costs.

To provide the costs for the planning to the Optimizer, you can define your actual costs such as production and transport costs in the system. You can also define steering costs that correspond to your operational business objectives; however, converting operational business objectives into steering costs is not easy for the planner. This is because the planner doesn't have the information on the amount of the steering costs and the relationships can be exceptionally complex.

With the automatic cost generation function, it is very straightforward to get the system to generate all steering costs that are relevant for the Optimizer (i.e., the cost model). The system generates these costs automatically based on the operational business goals you have defined. Maximizing the service level is assumed to be the primary objective. You can also define the following goals:

▶ Consideration of requirement and product priorities

▶ Consideration of procurement priorities

This function also allows you to easily and quickly prepare an optimization-based production plan. To create a finite (capacity-based) production plan, you only have to make a few additional settings (such as for example, taking capacities into account).

The system generates the following steering costs:

▶ Storage costs

▶ Production costs, that is, costs for the production process model (PPM) or the production data structure (PDS)

▶ Product-specific transport costs

▶ Procurement costs

▶ Penalty costs for safety stock shortfalls

▶ Penalty costs for non-delivery

▶ Penalty costs for delayed delivery

The system calculates the amount of the costs based on the operational business objectives you have defined. If you want to draw up an optimization-based production plan with the function **Automatic cost generation**, you must first define your business goals for the planning. The system then uses these goals to automatically generate the corresponding steering costs, which determine the Optimizer's planning decisions. You can define priorities for the safety stock and three different priority classes of the requirement:

▸ Customer requirement

▸ Corrected requirements forecast

▸ Requirements forecast

You can also specify that the system should consider the priority of products. You can specify this priority in the master data of the location product on the tab **SNP 2** (see Figure 5.4). The product priority is taken into account by the system along with the requirements priority.

Cost Maintenance

Costs play a major role for optimization-based planning in Supply Network Planning. The Optimizer selects the plan with the lowest total costs from among all of the permissible production plans.

To call the function, in the SAP Easy Access menu choose **Advanced Planning and Optimization • Master data • Application-specific master data • Supply Network Planning • Cost maintenance (directory)** or **Cost maintenance (tabular)** (see also Figure 6.29).

You can define the following costs:

▸ Production costs

▸ Storage costs

▸ Handling costs

▸ Transportation costs

▸ Procurement costs

▸ Costs for delayed delivery

▸ Costs for non-delivery

▸ Costs for using the available capacity of resources

▸ Cost function

6.4   Planning Method: Capable-to-Match (CTM)

The Capable-to-Match (CTM) functions adjust multiple prioritized customer requirements and forecasts with a range of categorized offerings and also take into account the current production and transport options in a multi-level production environment.

6.4.1   Possible Applications of CTM Planning

This function allows you to run a multilevel, finite planning of the requirements in your supply chain. Unlike the Optimizer of Supply Network Planning (SNP), which runs a cost-based planning, the CTM planning uses a heuristic procedure. In other words, CTM does not perform an optimization of the costs. Instead you can use priorities, for instance, to influence the sequence of the requirements and the selection of procurement alternatives. The CTM planning does not consider the individual production and distribution stages in sequence, as is the case with the classical Material Requirements Planning (MRP) run for example, but instead looks at them at the same time. This ensures that the CTM planning creates a viable plan that is on time.

Unlike the production planning and detailed scheduling (PP/DS), which covers the short-term planning, the CTM planning is geared towards medium- to long-term planning. The CTM planning therefore does not support detailed scheduling strategies such as sequence-dependent setup activities or the synchronization of multi-activity resources.

Since CTM runs the actual planning on a separate server, just as is the case with the SNP Optimizer, CTM is suited to more complex planning problems with a large volume of data.

See below for an overview of the CTM functions:

▶ **Finite Planning Through Several Locations**
The CTM planning creates procurement proposals for in-house production sources of supply and transportation lanes. In doing this, it includes CTM resources and material capacities at all levels in the supply chain. You can assign the sequence in which CTM should evaluate procurement alternatives yourself. If the production capacity on a resource is not sufficient to cover the total requirement, CTM evaluates another procurement alternative for the remaining quantity.

▶ **Strategies for Deleting and Selecting Requirements and Receipts**
With the strategies for deleting and selecting requirements and receipts, you can run a complete rescheduling and perform a net change planning. You can also restrict the planning scope in terms of time or location product-specifically.

▶ **Requirements Prioritization**
You can prioritize the requirements that are relevant for the planning based on predefined and descriptive characteristics. CTM then plans the requirements in order of their priority.

▶ **Stock Categorization**
You can assign the receipts and stocks that are relevant for the planning to various categories. The search strategy allows you to define the sequence in which CTM should consume the receipts during the planning.

▶ **Stock Control**
The planning with safety stock or target days' supply guarantees that CTM also covers unforeseen requirements. Within the inventory control, CTM provides functions with which you can avoid building stocks that are too large.

▶ **Master Data Selection and Order Selection**
With the master data selection and the order selection, you can flexibly define subgroups of master data and thereby restrict the planning to certain areas of your supply chain. This means that it is relatively easy for you to split the overall planning process into smaller planning steps that CTM executes one after the other.

▶ **CTM Planning with Rules**
Taking into account SAP ERP attributes or descriptive characteristics of customer or forecast requirements, you can derive rules with requirements coverage strategies and product replacements requirements-dependently for the CTM planning.

▶ **Fixed Pegging Relationships**
CTM can create fixed pegging relationships automatically. If you use fixed pegging relationships automatically, you can also identify after the CTM planning run for what requirement CTM has created a particular order.

▶ **Master Data Check**
You can check the consistency of the master data for the CTM planning run. The system checks both the master data itself and the semantics of the data.

6.4.2 CTM Planning Process

Figure 6.34 shows the entire CTM planning process:

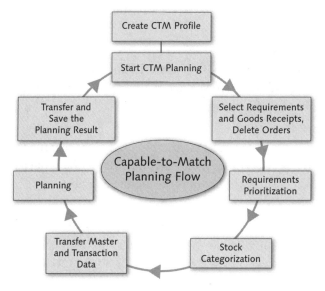

Figure 6.34 CTM Planning Process (Source: SAP)

1. You create a CTM profile.

2. You start the CTM planning run directly from the CTM profile or run it in the background.

3. The system selects the requirements and receipts in the planning period. Depending on the planning and deletion mode you have set in the CTM profile, the system does not delete all fixed orders, for example.

4. The system prioritizes the requirements based on the criteria you have given.

5. The system assigns the receipts and stocks to the requirement categories.

6. The system selects the master and transaction data that is required for the planning. The system copies the data to the CTM planning machine on the optimization server.

7. The CTM planning runs the following planning steps:

   ▶ Choose procurement alternative

   ▶ Run scheduling

   ▶ Create orders

   ▶ Consume receipts and stocks

8. The CTM planning copies the planning result to the SAP liveCache, that is, the system saves the orders and pegging relationships in the SAP liveCache.

6.4.3 Settings for the CTM Planning

You use the Capable-to-Match profile (CTM profile) to control what and how you plan. You can create several CTM profiles to simulate various different planning situations or to subdivide the overall planning process into several planning runs. To create a CTM profile, in the SAP APO menu choose • **Multi Supply and Demand Matching (CTM)** • **Planning** • **Planning Capable-to-Match (CTM)**. This will then bring you into the CTM profile maintenance (see Figure 6.35).

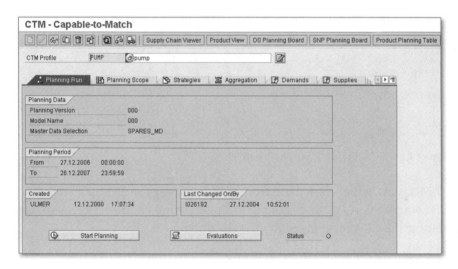

Figure 6.35 CTM Profile, "Planning Run" Tab

The basic structure for the CTM planning is formed by the data that CTM is to use for the planning, and the timeframe for the planning. In the CTM profile, you specify the planning version that the CTM planning is to be based on in the **Planning Run** tab (see Figure 6.35). From the planning version, CTM determines the corresponding Supply Chain model.

Furthermore, in the CTM profile, you make all of the settings that CTM requires for the planning, for example, master data, the order and stock selection, planning and deletion mode, settings for the requirements prioritization, and stock categorization.

Defining Master Data for the Selection

You enter the relevant master data on the **Planning Scope** tab (see Figure 6.36) for the CTM planning with this profile.

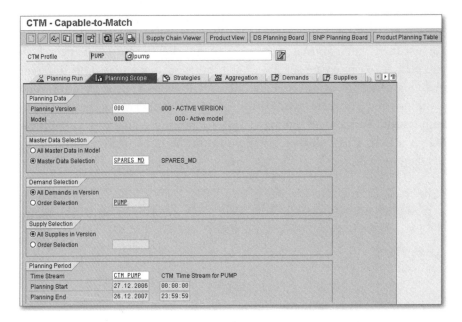

Figure 6.36 CTM Profile, "Planning Scope" Tab

CTM draws on the selected master data of the model and all order data of the planning version for the planning. In the **Planning Period** area, you define this for the CTM planning with the **Time Stream**.

Since the Capable-to-Match planning (CTM planning) is always based on a supply chain model, but you don't always want to schedule with all of the master data in the model, you can exclude master data from the planning with the **Master Data Selection** function. You can also use the master data selection, for example, to limit the CTM planning to only a particular BOM level of your product.

You can include the following master data of the specified supply chain model in the master data selection according to particular criteria or exclude them from the selection:

▶ **Location Products**
  The CTM planning can only create or delete orders for location products that are contained in the master data selection. If a planned order has a

component for a location product that is not contained in the master data selection, the entire order for CTM is considered as fixed. The system cannot delete this order, unless you have set the key figure **Do not check order details** in the CTM profile on the tab **Settings • Basic settings**. In this case, CTM deletes the order, even if not all of its components are contained in the master data selection.

▶ **External Procurement Sources of Supply (Transportation Lanes)**
If you exclude a transportation lane from the planning, a CTM cannot create any more stock transfers between the corresponding locations. However, the system can delete existing stock transfers if the orders are not fixed. If you use the master data selection to exclude all transportation lanes for a location product with procurement type "External procurement (E)," CTM creates a purchase requisition without a source location.

▶ **In-house Production Sources of Supply**
If you exclude an in-house production source of supply from the planning, CTM cannot create any orders for this in-house production source of supply. However, the system can delete existing orders for this in-house production source of supply if the orders are not fixed. If you exclude all in-house production sources of supply for a location product with procurement type "In-house production (I)," CTM can now only cover a requirement by consuming existing stocks. If there are no stocks available, CTM cannot cover the requirement.

In order for the CTM planning to use an in-house production source of supply, the location components of all components of the in-house production source of supply must be contained in the master data selection.

You can also allow the system to select all of the master data that is needed to cover a requirement.

Order and Stock Selection

You can run order selections for the requirements selection and the stock selection of the CTM planning, as shown in Figure 6.36 on the **Planning Scope** tab. The CTM planning run then selects requirements or receipts and stocks for the products that are contained both in the master data and in the order selection.

You can use the following criteria to further restrict the selection of the orders:

► **Selection Period**
Normally the system selects all orders within the planning period defined in the CTM profile. You can further restrict this period through the order selection. For instance, you can limit the selection of orders to two months, while CTM can create new orders for the next three months.

► **ATP Categories**
You can restrict the selection of orders to particular Available-to-Promise (ATP) categories. For instance, you can set the system to only schedule sales orders and not forecast requirements. If you don't enter any particular ATP categories here, CTM selects orders for all ATP categories.

Requirements Prioritization

For the system to be able to run a requirements prioritization, you must define the sort sequence. You enter the criteria by which the CTM planning is to sort the requirements in a certain sequence. The CTM planning initially sorts the requirements by the first criterion. Only those requirements that have been sorted by the first criterion and that show the same value are also subsequently sorted by the second criterion, etc.

You can define for each criterion whether an ascending or descending sorting, or a special sorting, should be used to sort the requirements. To do this, you must define the criteria and their sort sequence in the CTM profile on the **Demands** tab (see Figure 6.37).

The position of the individual criteria in this table determines the sequence in the sorting. With the special sorting, you can assign priorities for the various values of a criterion.

Example
You assign the following priorities for the criterion *Customer*: ► Priority 1: Customer B ► Priority 2: Customer A ► Priority 3: Customer C

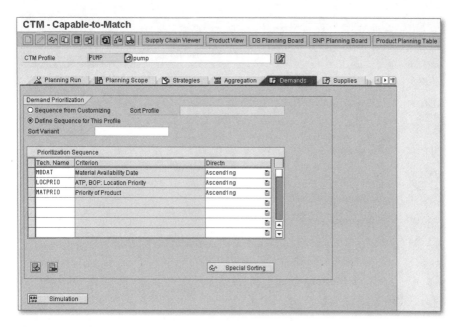

Figure 6.37 CTM Profile, "Demands" Tab

The CTM planning supports the special sorting for the criteria mentioned in Table 6.4.

Criterion	Description	Ascending/ Descending Sorting	Special Sorting
ANTLF	Maximum number of permitted subdeliveries per item	Yes	No
ATPCAT	Category of stock/receipt/requirement/forecast	No	Yes
BMENG	Confirmed Quantity	Yes	No
CNFPART	ATP, BOP (Back Order Processing): confirmation portion	Yes	No
CTMQTY	CTM quantity	Yes	No
DELNR	Number of the order/MRP element	Yes	No
DELPS	Position of the order/MRP element	Yes	No
ERTMS	Date on which the order was added	No	No
GMENG	Receipt or requirement quantity	Yes	No

Table 6.4 Possible Sort Criteria of the Requirements Elements in the CTM

Criterion	Description	Ascending/ Descending Sorting	Special Sorting
GRKOR	Delivery group (items are delivered together)	Yes	Yes
KUNNR	Customer	Yes	Yes
LFTMS	ATP, BOP: delivery date	No	No
LIFPRIO	Delivery priority	Yes	No
LOCNO	Location	Yes	Yes
LOCPRIO	Priority of the location	Yes	No
MATNR	Product number	Yes	Yes
MATPRIO	Priority of the product (time- and version-dependent maintenance can be performed for this criterion)	Yes	No
MBDAT	Material provision date	Yes	No
MRANK	Enhanced product priority	Yes	No
ORDPRIO	Order priority, e.g., determined from a previous CTM run, especially for dependent requirements	Yes	No
PSTYV	Item category of the sales and distribution document	No	Yes
USEREXIT	ATP, BOP: user-exit priority	Yes	No
VBTYP	Sales and distribution document type	No	Yes
WMENG	Desired quantity	Yes	No

Table 6.4 Possible Sort Criteria of the Requirements Elements in the CTM (cont.)

Instead of specifying a sort criterion, you can also call a user exit on each sort level. The user exit allows you to evaluate combinations of criteria, for example. One application case for this would be, for instance: only if the requirement is based on a sales order (criterion "Sales and distribution document type") should the system sort according to the criterion "Delivery priority of the order item."

Once you have run the requirement prioritization, you can simulate the requirements contained in the system to display the priority sequence. To do this, first click on the **Simulation** button and then call the simulated sequence with the **Requirements** button. Figure 6.38 shows the requirements prioritization as the result.

CTM: Display Prioritized Demand

Requirement Info | Product View

Requirements for Profile PUMP - Version 000 - Run No. 0001

Object ID	Product	Location	PlngSegTyp	Acct Assgt	Ct	Date	Time	Quantity	Pr.	Cat	Subloc	Strategy	Delay	Frame	Earliness	PartFulfil	Part Fulf	Pegging
19	102-300	1000			DR	27.12.2006	14:53:12	9,000-	0	AY	0100	D	999	999	999	☑	☑	1
20	102-400	1000			DR	27.12.2006	14:53:12	9,000-	0	AY	0100	D	999	999	999	☑	☑	1
21	102-200	1000			DR	27.12.2006	14:53:12	9,000-	0	AY	0100	D	999	999	999	☑	☑	1
22	102-100	1000			DR	27.12.2006	14:53:12	9,000-	0	AY	0100	D	999	999	999	☑	☑	1
23	102-300	1000			DR	27.12.2006	14:54:07	4,000-	1	AY	0100	D	999	999	999	☑	☑	1
24	102-300	1000			DR	27.12.2006	14:54:07	9,000-	1	AY	0100	D	999	999	999	☑	☑	1
25	102-300	2300			DR	27.12.2006	14:54:07	24,000-	1	AY	0001	D	999	999	999	☑	☑	1
26	102-400	1000			DR	27.12.2006	14:54:07	9,000-	1	AY	0100	D	999	999	999	☑	☑	1
27	102-400	1000			DR	27.12.2006	14:54:07	4,000-	1	AY	0100	D	999	999	999	☑	☑	1
28	102-400	2300			DR	27.12.2006	14:54:07	24,000-	1	AY	0001	D	999	999	999	☑	☑	1
29	102-200	1000			DR	27.12.2006	14:54:07	4,000-	1	AY	0100	D	999	999	999	☑	☑	1
30	102-200	1000			DR	27.12.2006	14:54:07	9,000-	1	AY	0100	D	999	999	999	☑	☑	1
31	102-200	2300			DR	27.12.2006	14:54:07	24,000-	1	AY	0001	D	999	999	999	☑	☑	1
32	102-100	1000			DR	27.12.2006	14:54:07	9,000-	1	AY	0100	D	999	999	999	☑	☑	1
33	102-100	1000			DR	27.12.2006	14:54:07	4,000-	1	AY	0100	D	999	999	999	☑	☑	1
34	102-100	2300			DR	27.12.2006	14:54:07	24,000-	1	AY	0001	D	999	999	999	☑	☑	1

Figure 6.38 CTM Profile, Simulation of the Requirements Prioritization

Requirements Categorization

The Capable-to-Match planning categorizes all receipts and stocks available for the CTM planning prior to each planning run. You can group the receipts and stocks according to various criteria and assign individual stock categories. If you don't define any separate stock categories or specify any categorization profile, the system assigns all receipts and stocks to stock category 00.

You can choose between two stock categorization options:

▶ **Categorization with ATP Categories**
You assign existing ATP categories or category groups to stock categories of the CTM planning. In the search strategy, you assign a sequence in which the system is to consume the receipts and stocks of the various stock categories. For example, you want the system to consume all fixed orders (e.g., category 1) prior to the planned orders (e.g., category 2).

▶ **Categorization with Stock Limits**
You define various intervals for the stock and receipt quantity of a location product using stock limits. You can define several intervals and assign a different stock category to each interval. In the search strategy you can exclude a stock category, that is, the system may not consume the quantity defined for the stock category.

You can set one of your stock categories as a standard category. The system uses the standard category for all receipts and stocks that you have not categorized.

You make the settings and assignments for the stock categorization in the categorization profile. In the CTM profile, choose the **Supplies** tab (see Figure 6.39).

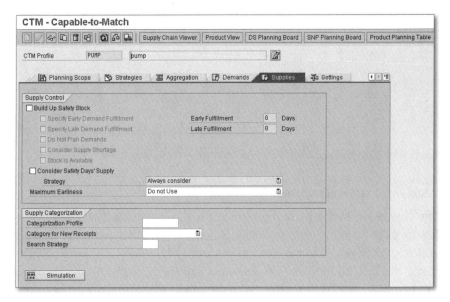

Figure 6.39 CTM Profile, Stock Categorization on the "Supplies" Tab

Once you have run the stock categorization, you can simulate the supplies contained in the system to display the categories. To do this, first click on the **Simulation** button and then call the simulated sequence with the **Stocks** button (see Figure 6.39). Figure 6.40 shows the stock categorization as the result.

Search Strategy

The search strategy follows, on the one hand, an internal system sequence that you have no influence over, and alternatively, a sequence specified by you.

The system always runs the search strategy locally for a location product. In covering the requirement for a particular location product, the receipts and stocks for other location products do not initially play any role. To cover a dependent requirement, the system also runs the search strategy locally for the corresponding location product.

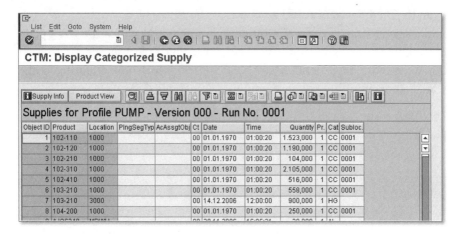

Figure 6.40 CTM Profile, Simulation of the Stock Categorization

System-Internal Sequence

If you don't specify any search strategy, or if you use a search strategy in which you have not entered any stock categories, the system runs the program-internal search strategy as shown in Table 6.5.

Sequence	Category	System Behavior
1	00	Consume receipts and stocks for the predefined standard category
2	00	Replace receipts and stocks of the standard category 00
3		Run source determination
4		Create purchase requisition

Table 6.5 System-Internal Sequence of the CTM Search Strategy

Here the system first finds receipts and stocks for the predefined standard category 00. The system has assigned all receipts and stocks that you have not assigned to any stock category to the standard category 00 during the stock categorization. If there is no receipt of the standard category 00 for the (original) location product, the system evaluates existing rules. Here, the system can also only replace receipts with the standard category 00.

If the system does not find any receipt for the standard category 00 or cannot use the receipt found to cover the requirement on time, the CTM planning runs a source determination based on the procurement type of the location product. If no sources of supply exist for the location product, CTM creates a purchase requisition in the case of external procurement.

User-Defined Sequence

In the search strategy, you can define the sequence in which the CTM planning should use the receipts and stocks to cover the requirements. To do this, you must have defined stock categories, which you indicate in the search strategy in the sequence you want (see Table 6.6).

The CTM planning can only use the receipts and stocks of stock categories that are contained in the search strategy. The system can always use receipts and stocks of the standard category 00.

Sequence	Category	System Behavior
1	00	Consume receipts and stocks for the predefined standard category
2	01	**Consume receipts and stocks of the stock category 01**
3	00	Replace receipts and stocks of the standard category 00
4	01	Replace receipts and stocks of the stock category 01
5		Run source determination
6	02	**Consume receipts and stocks of the stock category 02**
7		Create purchase requisition

Table 6.6 Example for a User-Defined Sequence (the steps highlighted in bold are user-defined)

If you apply rules in the CTM planning, the replacements are always made directly prior to the source determination. Here, the system processes receipts and stocks for the replacement product in the same sequence as receipts and stocks of the original product, prior to generating planned orders or stock transfers.

The system also assigns receipts that the system creates during the planning, but does not immediately completely use to cover a requirement (e.g., when using lot sizes or co-products) to a stock category. If you do not assign any stock category for these receipts, the system assigns the receipts to the standard category 00. The system also applies the search strategy for these receipts accordingly.

The system always generates purchase requisitions as the last step, after checking all stock categories.

The example shown in Figure 6.41 illustrates the local application of the search strategy:

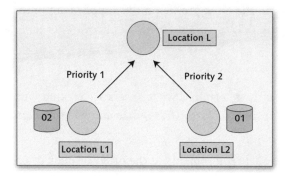

Figure 6.41 Search Strategy Example in the CTM Planning (Source: SAP)

You have a requirement for location *L* and can procure the corresponding receipt both from *Location L1* and from *Location L2*. The transportation lane between *Location L* and *Location L1* has the higher priority. On *Location L1*, there is a stock of stock category *02*; on *Location L2*, there is a stock of stock category *01*.

In the system, you have defined a search strategy as shown in Table 6.7 (see also Figure 6.39).

Sequence	Category	Stock Category Description
1	01	Stock category 01
2	02	Stock category 02
3	***	*** Source determination ***

Table 6.7 Search Strategy for the Stock Determination—"*" indicates that no more stocks (stock categories) are selected here; instead, the source determination is triggered.

In this example, the CTM planning first runs the search strategy on *Location L*. Since there are no receipts and stocks on Location L, the system performs a supply source determination. Based on the priorities of the transportation lanes, the system chooses *Location L1*. The CTM planning now runs the search strategy locally for *Location L1*. The system uses the existing stock of the stock category *02*, although a stock with stock category *01* exists on *Location L2*.

If you don't assign any priorities for the transportation lanes, you cannot affect the choice of location. The system does not take into account the stock categories for the individual locations during the source determination.

You create the search strategy in the CTM profile on the **Supplies** tab in the **Search Strategy** field (see Figure 6.39).

6.4.4 Planning Algorithm

The planning algorithm ultimately determines what orders are created with what quantity and for what Capable-to-Match (CTM) date and what receipts and stocks CTM consumes.

CTM now processes the individual requirements in the order of their priority. The CTM planning applies the search strategy for each requirement and performs the source determination and scheduling for the requirement and the corresponding dependent requirements.

When CTM has covered the requirements, the system transfers the orders and pegging relationships that CTM has created to the SAP liveCache.

Source Determination

If you have entered a search strategy in the CTM profile, CTM first evaluates this search strategy, that is, the system first finds existing receipts and stocks for the specified stock categories. If the system cannot meet the requirement from existing receipts and stocks, or you have stipulated the source determination in the first place in the search strategy, the system proceeds as follows in determining the relevant source of supply:

1. **Timely Requirements Coverage**
   The CTM planning always first tries to meet the requirement on time. This also applies if the system cannot include the specified quota arrangement or procurement priority.

> **Example**
>
> You have entered procurement priority 1 for source of supply A and procurement priority 2 for source of supply B. The system can only belatedly cover the requirement with source of supply A, whereas the system can cover the requirement with source of supply B on time. In this case, the CTM planning chooses the source of supply with the lower procurement priority so that it can cover the requirement on time.

2. **Quota Arrangement or Procurement Priority**
   If all sources of supply can meet the requirement on time, the system either takes into account the defined quota arrangement or the values for the procurement priority.

▶ **Quota Arrangement**

For this you must have defined at least one quota arrangement for the location. If this is the case, the system does not take into account any additional settings such as the procurement priority, for example. If the system cannot clearly determine the source of supply through the quota arrangement, the system determines a random result.

▶ **Procurement Priority**

If you have specified *in-house production* as the procurement type in the location product master, the system considers the procurement priority in the PPM or in the PDS.

If you have specified *external procurement* as the procurement type, the system considers the procurement priority in the transportation lane.

For the procurement type in-house production or external procurement, the system compares the procurement priority from the transportation lane with the procurement priority in the PPM or in the PDS.

The source of supply with the lower value for the procurement priority takes precedence over the source of supply with the higher value. The highest procurement priority is the value 0.

If the CTM planning has to choose from among several sources of supply with the same procurement priority, the system compares (a) the costs of the means of transport with each other for transportation lanes, (b) for PPM or PDS, the fixed multilevel costs with each other and (c) for the transportation lane and PPM or PDS, the costs of the means of transport with the fixed multilevel costs.

The end result is that CTM chooses the source of supply with the lowest costs.

3. **Valid-from Date and Valid-to Date**

For the same value for quota arrangement, procurement priority and costs, the system takes into account the validity of the source of supply. If the CTM planning works with backward scheduling, the system chooses the source of supply whose validity is as close as possible to the requirements date. With forward scheduling, the system chooses the source of supply with the earliest validity start date.

4. **Lot-Size Specifications**

If a further differentiation is required, the system considers the lot-size specifications for in-house production sources of supply.

The system only takes into account in-house production sources of supply whose value for the minimum lot size is smaller than the requirements quantity, or whose value is lower than the value for the minimum lot size in the location product master.

If the requirements quantity is larger than the value for the maximum lot size of all in-house production sources of supply that are involved, the system chooses the in-house production source of supply with the highest value for the maximum lot size.

If the system determines several such in-house production sources of supply, it chooses the in-house production source of supply with the lowest value for the minimum lot size.

If the CTM planning has to split the order, the system will only perform the source determination again for the remaining quantity if the value for the minimum lot size is higher than the remaining quantity. If this is not the case, the system follows the sequence of the source determination that has already been run in order to determine the source of supply for the remaining quantity.

Scheduling

The planning period for the Capable-to-Match planning is determined by the **Time Stream** in the CTM profile (see Figure 6.36). With these periods and horizons, you can define a period in which CTM chooses the requirements and receipts for the planning, and a period in which CTM creates or deletes the orders.

The CTM planning will always try to cover a requirement on time. If CTM cannot schedule a receipt prior to the requirements date, the requirement is considered as not covered. For delayed requirements coverages, CTM tries to cover the requirement by the end of the planning period. If you have entered a value for the maximum delay in the CTM Customizing, the delayed requirements coverage ends accordingly prior to the end of the planning period.

In the CTM Customizing under **SAP SCM Implementation guide • SAP APO • Supply Network Planning • Multi Supply & Demand Matching (SDM) • Capable-to-Match (CTM) • Define global values and default values** on the tab **Demand-Dependent Constraints**, you can choose between two basic strategies for the late demand fulfillment: the **Domino Strategy** and the **Airline Strategy** (see Figure 6.42):

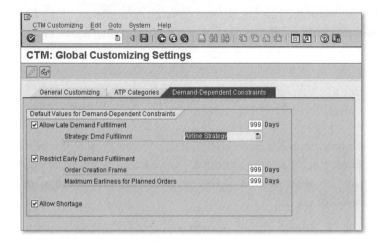

Figure 6.42 CTM Customizing—Scheduling Strategy

▶ With the *Domino Strategy*, CTM uses the late demand fulfillment for each demand when the requirements date is passed.

▶ With the *Airline Strategy*, CTM proceeds as follows: The system shifts requirements that CTM cannot cover on time to the end of the requirements prioritization. Only when CTM has been able to cover all other requirements does CTM begin with the late demand fulfillment for the demands that the system was not able to cover on time.

6.5   Analyzing Planning Results

Once you have made all of the settings required for CTM planning, you can start the planning run from the CTM profile on the **Planning Run** tab by clicking on the **Start Planning** button.

The CTM planning runs the following planning steps:

1. Choose procurement alternative
2. Execute scheduling
3. Create orders
4. Consume receipts and stocks

The CTM planning copies the planning result to the SAP liveCache, that is, the system saves the orders and pegging relationships in the SAP liveCache. You can then analyze the planning results. There are two aspects involved with analyzing the results from the CTM planning run: ensuring that the technical side of the planning run has been successfully completed, and evaluating the actual planning results in the various tools and interactive tables of SAP APO.

6.5.1 Technical Aspects of the CTM Planning Run

Messages

Once the CTM planning run has been completed, you can display the messages that have been created for the various CTM planning steps of the current run (e.g., for the order selection, the requirements prioritization or uploading master data).

To do this, in the CTM profile, choose **Results analysis • CTM Log**. You will get the display in Figure 6.43.

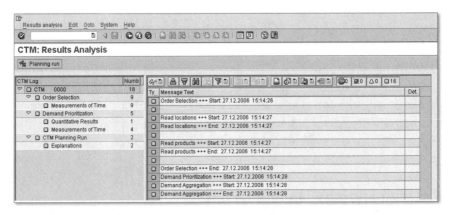

Figure 6.43 CTM Evaluations—Messages

One of the following colored symbols appears in the **Planning run view of the CTM profile** to the right beside the button **Evaluations** and informs you on the presence of any messages.

▶ **Color "Green"**
The CTM run has been successfully completed.

▶ **Color "Yellow"**
There is at least one warning.

▶ **Color "Red"**
There is at least one liveCache error. The planning result must therefore be corrected.

Normally, the messages for the current run are deleted once you exit the CTM profile; however, you can save the messages for each run in the Explanation Log, which you can then call again.

Log Files

When searching for the error, you can display the log files for your planning runs that contain the history and the status of all optimization runs (see Figure 6.44). In the CTM profile, choose **Results analysis • Display LogFiles**.

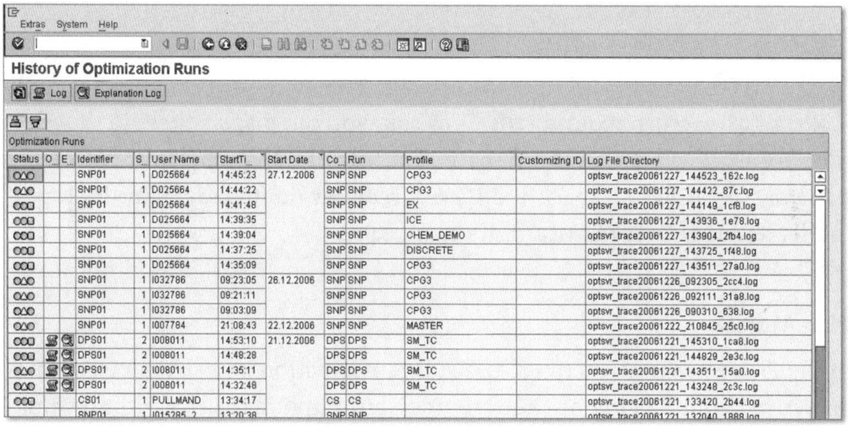

Figure 6.44 CTM Evaluations, Log Files

qRFC Monitor

If you write the orders created by CTM asynchronously into the SAP live-Cache and you notice that the liveCache processing slows down, you can call the qRFC monitor and display the outbound queues and their destinations and entries.

6.5.2 Evaluating the CTM Planning Results

Requirements

You can display a list of all requirements that the CTM planning has tried to cover, as well as further details on the corresponding requirements-dependent constraints and the replacement rules that were used for the coverage. To do this, click on the **Requirements Info** button on the **Demands** tab of the CTM profile. Figure 6.38 illustrates the results.

CTM Messages

The CTM messages give you a rough overview of the information in the current CTM planning run. In this way, you can see precisely, for instance, how many orders have been deleted, how many requirements or stocks have been copied to the CTM engine, or how many orders and pegging relationships have been created. If you use the requirements distribution, you can also see how many orders have been created.

To display the CTM messages, click on the **Evaluations** button on the **Planning Run** tab of the CTM profile. Figure 6.43 illustrates the results.

Alert Monitor

If alerts have occurred during the CTM run, you can display these in the Alert Monitor.Click on the **Evaluations** button on the **Planning Run** tab of the CTM profile. You will reach the **CTM screen: evaluate result**. In the top of the screen, the **Alert Monitor** button appears.

Plan Monitor

In the Plan Monitor, you can also display information on key figures, such as delays in requirements or the resource consumption. Click on the **Evaluations** button on the **Planning Run** tab of the CTM profile. The screen **CTM: Evaluate result** opens. The **Plan Monitor** button appears in the upper part of the screen. The prerequisite here is that you must have set a key figure schema on the **Settings** tab of the CTM profile.

Supply Chain Viewer

The Supply Chain Viewer is a tool that you can use to analyze the results of the CTM planning run, for example. You can display both information on the orders created by CTM and information on orders created by other applications (see Figure 6.45).

The Supply Chain Viewer provides you with an order-oriented display of your entire supply chain. You can graphically display the process of reconciling offers and requirements through several levels in your supply chain. To call the Supply Chain Viewer, from the CTM screen choose: **Evaluate result** from the **Supply Chain Viewer** menu (see Figure 6.43).

Once you have selected a particular requirement on the left subscreen by double-clicking on it, the relevant information for this requirement is dis-

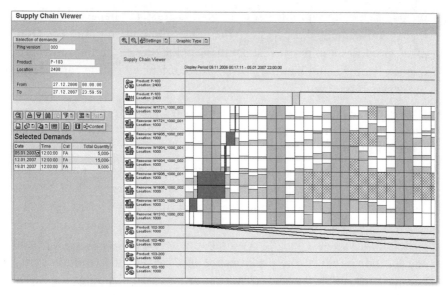

Figure 6.45 CTM Evaluations, Supply Chain Viewer

played across the entire supply chain in the Gantt diagram on the right side of the screen. You can also display information on the original requirement (product, location, quantity, and time) or through an activity (such as resource, location, quantity, and time) in the dialog window. You can also show and hide the pegging relationships between the planning objects, by clicking on the **Settings** button and then selecting **Display Supply Tree**.

Product View

In the product view, you can display requirements and stock information on your location products. You can also query pegging structures, period views, and detailed order information.

6.6 Comparing the Planning Methods

The following is a comparison of the most important aspects of the various SNP planning methods:

▶ The heuristic is a rapid, infinite planning method that generates alerts in the absence of material availability or resource overloads.

▶ The optimization-based planning takes into account the material and resource availability simultaneously. Using the linear programming, it can include all possibly problematic relevant factors simultaneously, that is, there is no sequential processing when determining a solution. The Optimizer proposes a minimal cost solution by looking at the transport, production, storage, and handling costs, in accordance with the corresponding constraints.

▶ CTM is a rule-based procedure with extensive prioritization options and finite, global planning for the production resources. CTM is an order-related planning.

▶ The speed at which you can perform the three planning methods can roughly be divided as follows. The heuristic is the fastest method, CTM is somewhere in the middle, and the optimization-based planning is the most complex and slowest method. But, this is only an approximate rule of thumb. If you schedule a very large number of orders for each period and location product, the performance of CTM and the Optimizer may become comparable, because CTM runs order-based planning.

▶ The quality of the planning result of the heuristic is the lowest (infinite!), then comes CTM (rules), and we expect the best planning result using the Optimizer.

▶ Production resources are included in a global, finite way by the Optimizer and CTM, while the infinite planning result of the heuristic must be subsequently processed interactively.

▶ Transport, storage, and handling resources can only be globally and finitely included by the Optimizer.

▶ Priorities control CTM. Priorities for the Optimizer can be set using penalty costs for late delivery and non-delivery of the location products.

The question now is what planning method is the right one for a particular customer problem. There is no generally valid answer to this question. You always have to consider the individual underlying conditions and the business processes. Nevertheless, here are some rough recommendations for the various methods:

▶ **Recommendation for using the heuristic as the planning strategy:**

  ▷ An infinite planning (without taking into account capacities) focusing on the mid- to long-term area is sufficient.

  ▷ Resources play a minor role in the planning process and can be disregarded.

  ▷ The cost of performing the planning strategy should be kept low.

▶ **Recommendation for using the optimization-based planning:**

  ▷ For customers, there are alternatives with regard to their production sites and sources of supply.

  ▷ Resources are used together, that is, several products are produced at the same time on a resource.

  ▷ Resources for production, transport, and storage play a key role for the customer in his planning process, that is, the customer's resources restrict him heavily in his planning process, and a resource expansion can be accomplished only by incurring heavy financial expenses.

▶ **Recommendation for using the Capable-to-Match as a planning strategy:**

  ▷ A priority-controlled planning in terms of the procurement and customer side is vital for the customer.

  ▷ The customer's business processes demand a so-called down-binning procedure based on product replacements.

  ▷ Using ATP replacement rules, CTM can use a product of higher quality to cover a requirement for a product of lower quality. In the CTM planning run, the system uses the freely available receipts and stocks of the higher-value product as replacement stock.

6.7 Safety Stock Planning

Supply chain planning is influenced by a number of factors that can't be forecast with absolute certainty.For example, when forecasting customer requirements, there is generally an uncertainty with regard to the quantity. In addition, disturbances and fluctuations in production cause deviations in the planned replenishment lead time. You can take various planning measures to protect yourself against such insecurities in planning. Here we will deal in particular with the safety stocks and their impact on the delivery service.

In this context, from sales and distribution, we often get a stipulation for a complete service level, that is, it is assumed that each incoming customer request must be met without any time delay. In this case, the service level is 100 %. However, actual operating practice must usually assume that the costs required to produce 100 % service level cannot be justified. The higher the desired service level is chosen, the lower are the possible missing part costs, and the higher are the storage costs necessitated by the higher stocks.

If a warehouse were to be 100 % ready to deliver a given material at all times, it would mean that inevitable forecast errors would require storing a considerable amount of safety stock, which would also cost a great deal. The amount of safety stock depends on the following:

▶ Service level

▶ Replenishment lead time

▶ Forecast quality

To keep the safety stock and therefore the storage costs as low as possible, in practice the Material Requirements Planning (MRP) Controller defines a specific service level for each material. When formulated mathematically, this service level represents the probability that no stockout will occur during the replenishment lead time of the relevant material. If you select a relatively high service level, the system will calculate just as high a level of safety stock; if you choose a low service level, the safety stock will also be low.

The replenishment lead time describes the in-house production time for in-house production, and the planned delivery time in the case of external procurement. It involves the period between the start of the procurement process and the storage of the material. The MRP Controller defines the replenishment lead time. Because the probability of stockouts is higher in a longer period, the safety stock must also be higher for longer replenishment lead times.

Safety stock therefore protects against various deviations. Examples include delivery date variances (the replenishment lead time varies), requirement variances (the forecast is inaccurate), delivery quantity variances (the vendor delivers too little or something of poor quality), and inventory variances (inventory-taking recognizes a deviation between the plan and actual inventory) (see Figure 6.46).

Figure 6.47 illustrates the relationship between the service level and the storage costs for the safety stock.

The optimal service level is determined from the optimum of the stockout costs and the service costs: the safety stock costs in this case. The total costs for the service level can be shown in a convex curve progression, if the safety stock costs increase for an increasing service level and the stockout costs decrease.

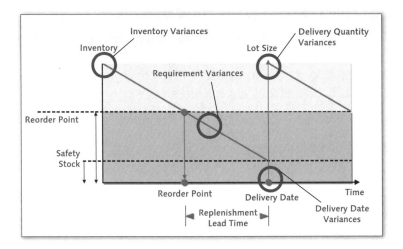

Figure 6.46 Reasons for the Safety Stock (Source: SAP)

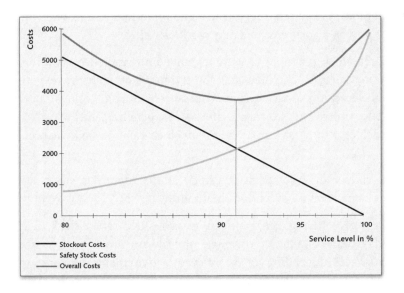

Figure 6.47 Relationship Between Safety Stock Costs and Service Level

If you chose a service level that is too high, you must deal with large stocks that tie up a great deal of capital and involve high storage costs. If the service level is too low, you incur unduly high stockout costs for loss of sales, default penalties, and special drives such as overtime or additional shifts. You can see in Figure 6.47 that the last 5 % of the service level accounts for around 50 % of the inventory costs. You must therefore carefully consider how much each additional percentage point of service level is worth to you.

6.7.1 Simple and Enhanced Safety Stock Methods

Because safety stocks are generally required for products in various production plants or distribution centers, you can select a safety stock method for each location product in the product master. The various methods here are subdivided into standard methods and enhanced methods.

SAP APO provides two methods of safety stock planning:

▸ Standard Safety Stock Planning

▸ Enhanced Safety Stock Planning

In the standard methods, the planner must directly specify the required information to calculate the safety stock. In the enhanced method, however, the safety stock is determined automatically, based on the service level, the current requirements forecast, and historical data.

The standard methods are based solely on the planner's experience. With the enhanced methods, the system suggests the amount of safety stock based on scientifically proven algorithms for safety stock planning.

Standard safety stock planning is used to build up warehouse inventory according to the safety stock values that you set, based on your past experience with the location product master. You can select from various safety stock methods. Unlike the enhanced safety stock planning, this approach does not consider a forecast error. The safety stock value is static or time-dependent.

Figure 6.48 shows an absolute safety stock at the top. It is static and describes the same level for all periods that follow.

In the lower part of the screen, you can see a relative safety stock. It is defined in days (target range of coverage) and always procures the same amount of material, depending on the relevant requirements situation, to cover the target range of coverage, say, in the form of 10 days. In other words, orders are always for enough material to fill inventory for 10 days.

As you can see in Figure 6.49, with the enhanced methods, first the deviation range between the actual sales and the demand forecast is compiled. Secondly, the requirements for the safety stock are added to the overall requirements, in accordance with the mean absolute deviation (MAD). The safety stock is therefore dynamically adjusted to the MAD.

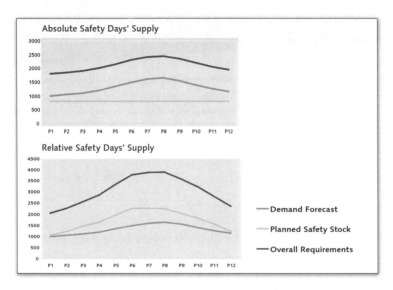

Figure 6.48 Simple Methods of Safety Stock Planning

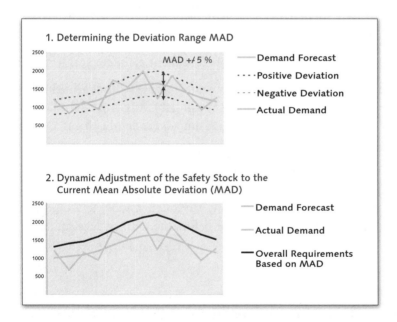

Figure 6.49 Enhanced Methods of Safety Stock Planning

6.7.2 Standard Safety Stock Planning in SAP APO

You can also change the safety stock values manually on the desktop of the interactive planning of Supply Network Planning.

The standard methods are distinguished by their consideration of time and are based on the planner directly specifying the information on the safety stock to the system:

	Time-Independent (Static)	Time-Dependent (Dynamic)
Safety Stock	SB	MB
Safety days' supply	SZ	MZ
Max (safety stock, safety days' supply)	SM	MM

Table 6.8 Standard Methods for Safety Stock Planning in SAP APO

The following standard methods are available (see also Table 6.8):

▶ SB—Safety stock from the location product master
▶ SZ—Safety range from the location product master
▶ SM—Maximum from SB and SZ from the location product master
▶ MB—Safety stock (time-dependent maintenance)
▶ MZ—Safety range (time-dependent maintenance)
▶ MM—Maximum from SB and SZ (time-dependent maintenance)

SB, SZ, and SM are static methods. Their parameters are set independently of time in the location's product master (**Lot Size** tab). MB, MZ, and MM are dynamic methods. Their parameters are set time-dependently, that is, during interactive SNP safety stock planning.

You can define the safety stock directly with a safety range of coverage, or as a maximum from the safety stock and the safety range. If you create a maximum, you can adjust the amount of safety stock dynamically to the flow of requirements as long as it does not fall below the defined level of safety stock.

Static Methods in SAP APO

SB—Safety stock from the location product master
This method is used in the production planning area if the **Safety Stock** and **SB Methods** fields are maintained in the location product master.

To do this, go into the SAP APO menu, choose **SAP APO • Master data • Product • Product** and in the product master, go to the **Lot Size** tab. There you enter the key figure **SB** in the **SB Method** field (see Figure 6.50).

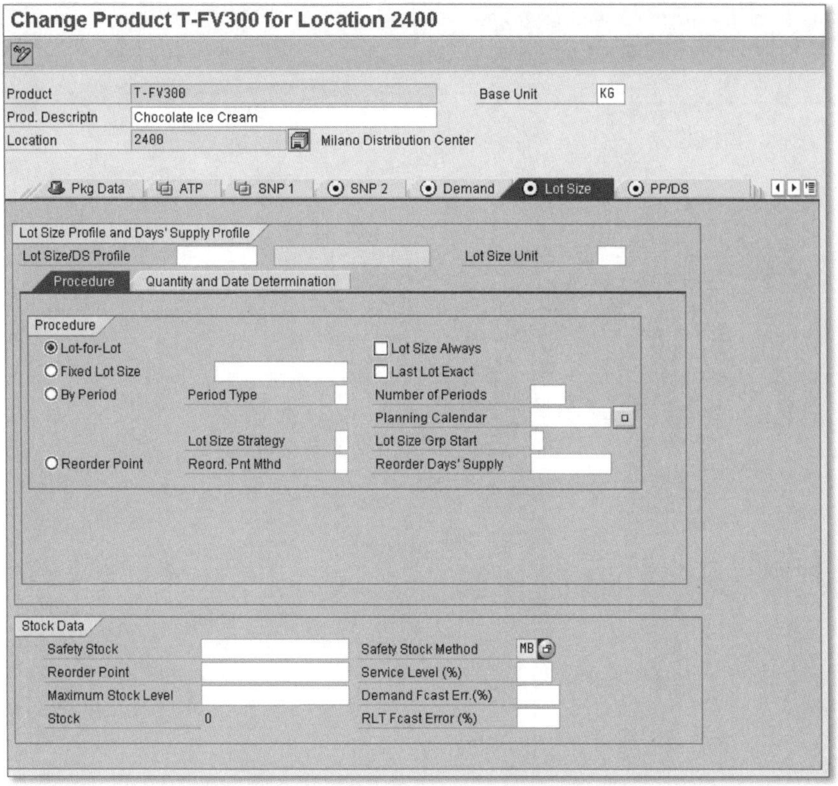

Figure 6.50 Product Master, "Lot Size" Tab, Safety Stock Method

In the model/plan version administrator in the plan version in the **PP/DS** subscreen, in the field **Take Safety Stock into Account**, you must also specify for the safety stock to be included in the PP/DS planning (see Figure 6.51). To do this you must call the menu **APO • Master data • Planning version management • Model and planning version management**.

The safety stock is the quantity that should cover unexpectedly high requirements in the coverage period. The purpose of the safety stock is to reduce the risk of missing quantities occurring.

It is interpreted as a requirement. To cover the requirement, planning creates a planned order in the amount of the safety stock. The start date of the planned order is the current date, provided the strategy settings allow this. The system does not consider the offset from the strategy settings. When the order is created, capacities on resources may be taken into account if there is a corresponding strategy. You can generate an excess coverage alert during safety stock planning.

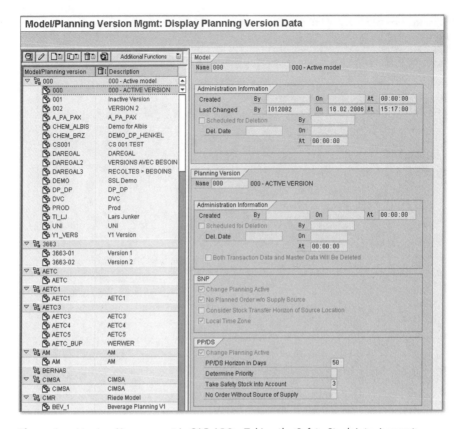

Figure 6.51 Version Management in SAP APO—Taking the Safety Stock into Account

SZ—Safety range from the location product master

Maintenance of the fields **SafetyRW** and **SB Method** is a prerequisite for taking this standard method into account. You must select SZ as the Safety Stock Method (see Figure 6.50).

The safety days' supply is the number of business days between the availability date of a newly created receipt element and the requirements date of a requirements element.

In SAP ERP, you can only define entire days as safety days' supply. But in SAP APO, you can specify fractions of days. Two decimal points are permitted. For example, you can specify 0.5 days for 12 hours or 0.33 days for around 8 hours (or more precisely, 7 hours, 55 minutes, 12 seconds). (A business (work) day corresponds to 24 hours.) The production calendar from the location serves as the basis for scheduling.

During planning, the requirements elements are pushed into the past (virtually) by the amount of the safety days' supply. This new situation serves as the basis for order generation.

Periodic lot sizes are based on the original dates of the requirements, that is, the safety days' supply is not used to distribute the requirements over the periods. However, the generated requirements coverage is moved by the amount of the safety days' supply. Nevertheless, for technical reasons, planning with continuous requirements considers the safety days' supply during the distribution of the requirements (or requirements polygon curve sections) across the periods.

SM — Maximum from SB and SZ from the location product master

Production planning and detailed scheduling with this safety stock method uses the SB and SZ methods. No "maximum" is created from both procedures. As a prerequisite for executing the methods, you must also maintain the **Safety Stock** and **SafetyRW** fields, as well as the SB method (see Figure 6.50).

In technical terms, the safety stock is determined first and the safety days' supply is considered next because the safety stock should also be moved by the amount of the safety days' supply.

Dynamic Methods in SAP APO

The dynamic methods analyze period-related safety ranges and safety stocks. The data is mapped in SNP as key figures. In production planning and detailed scheduling (PP/DS), the dynamic methods can only access these key figures if you have specified the SNP planning area that contains the key figures in the SAP APO Customizing of the production planning and detailed scheduling in the **Display Global Parameters and Default Values** screen (see Figure 6.52).

MB — Safety stock (time-dependent maintenance)

The safety stock is determined as for the method SB, but instead of the **Safety Stock** field from the location master data, the period-dependent value is used (see Figure 6.50).

If the dynamic safety stock in a period is greater than in the previous period, a virtual requirement is generated that represents the difference quantity. An appropriate receipt element covers the virtual requirement in the planning run.

Display Global Parameters and Default Values

| Planning | Execute | ATP Categories |

Logging — Only Errors, Terminations, and Warnin..

Create/Change Orders

☑ Use Number Range		Number Range Number	01
Heuristic for Change Quantity	SAP_PP_001	□ Heuristic Conversion SNP->PP/DS	ZDVC	□
Plan Explosion	Explode Production Process Model		
Planning Area	9ASNP02		
Remove Orders from ProdCampaign	No Restrictions		
Transfer to R/3 In-House Production	Always Create Transfer Events (Default)		
Transfer to R/3 Ext. Procurement	Always Create Transfer Events (Default)		
Activate Fixed Pegging	Fixed Pegging is Inactive		

Schedule Orders: Strategy Profiles

Interactive Planning	SAP002	Conversion SNP -> PP/DS	SAP002
Integrated DS Plng Board	SAP001	Conversion ATP -> PP/DS	SAP002
Planning Run	SAP002	Capable-to-Promise	Z_KAINDL
R/3 Integration	SAPINTR3	Planned Ord. Management	SAP002
BAPI	SAP002		

Schedule Orders

| Propagation Range | SAPALL |
| Sched. Horizon for ATP Tree Structures | 30,00 |

Figure 6.52 SAP APO Customizing, Display Global Parameters and Default Values

If the dynamic safety stock from one period to the next becomes smaller, fewer receipt elements are created for the requirements elements in the period with the smaller amount of safety stock—corresponding to the difference quantity. In the product view, you can see that the requirements are partially covered from the excess safety stock.

Figure 6.53 illustrates the dynamic safety stock in interactive SNP planning in the **Safety Stock (Planned)** field. Here you must choose the menu **SAP APO • Supply Network Planning • Planning • Supply Network Planning interactive**.

In the **Forecast** line you see a requirement of 267 Pcs. on 13.12. and in the line **Safety Stock (planned)** of 100 Pcs. And you can see the related receipt in the **Distribution Receipt** (Planned) row of a total of 367 (267 + 100).

In calendar week 52, the requirement is 333, and the safety stock has increased by 100 to a total of 200. You therefore see a total receipt of 433 (333 + 100). The inventory stock in the **Inventory Stock** line is now 200 Pcs.

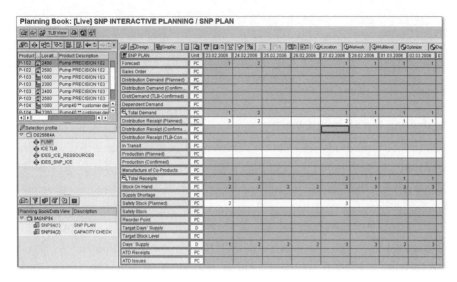

Figure 6.53 SAP APO Interactive Supply Network Planning (SNP) with Key Figures for Dynamic Safety Stock

MZ—Safety range (time-dependent maintenance)

The safety stock here is determined much like it is in the SZ method, but the period-dependent safety ranges are used instead of the safety ranges from the location product master.

Execution is similar to that of the SZ method, but the requirements of a period are moved by the period-dependent safety days' supply.

MM—Maximum of MB and MZ (time-dependent maintenance)

Like the SM safety stock method, here the MB and MZ methods are run consecutively.

In the production planning and detailed scheduling, first the MB method is considered and then the MZ method.

Process in the system

1. You enter the relevant data in the fields **Safety Stock, SB Method** (available methods: SB, SZ, SM, MZ, MB or MM) and **Safety Days' Supply** on the **Lot Size** tab in the location product master (see Figure 6.50).

2. If you want to use methods MZ, MB, or MM, you must use the SNP standard planning area 9ASNP05 and the standard planning session 9ASNP_ SSP (or a planning area and planning session based on them) that contain

the key figures "9ASAFETY—Safety Stock (planned)" and "9ASVTTY—Safety Days' Supply" (see Figure 6.53).

3. If needed, you can also modify the safety stock values after the planning run on the desktop of interactive planning in supply network planning.

Evaluating the Standard Methods

The standard methods are relatively uncomplicated algorithms that planners will find easy to understand and use. The planner can easily digest the results and is usually already familiar with these methods.

However, there are also a number of disadvantages with the standard methods: to use the standard methods, planners must store the appropriate parameters in the material master data. If the planner is responsible for a relatively large number of materials, a huge amount of maintenance is required, which the planner usually cannot cope with. The parameters would of course have to be checked periodically and updated as required. Because the planner usually doesn't have time for this kind of micro-management, she will not maintain and monitor the parameters for the individual materials, but instead will form material groups. All materials in a material group are now supplied with the same parameters. If a stockout then occurs for a material, to make her work easier, the planner will simply increase all of the parameters (i.e., the reorder point or safety stocks) for the entire material group, even if no stockout has occurred for the other materials in this material group. This then leads to a creeping stock increase.

An additional disadvantage is that the safety stocks depend entirely on the estimate of the planner. This approach is not supported by the IT system that was implemented with great effort.

6.7.3 Enhanced Safety Stock Planning in SAP APO

The standard methods are based completely on the experience of the planner. With the enhanced methods, the system suggests the amount of safety stock based on scientifically proven algorithms for safety stock planning. These enhanced methods are based on the following assumptions:

▶ The requirement is regular, that is

  ▷ It appears in almost every period.

  ▷ The requirement quantities are significantly higher than zero.

▷ The requirement quantities don't fluctuate too wildly.

(rule of thumb: *standard deviation/mean value < 0.5*)

Given this assumption, you can presume that a normal distribution of forecast errors will occur. Typically, the assumption doesn't apply to spare parts, because they usually have requirements that are only sporadic.

▶ Stockouts can be resupplied later. In other words, no requirements are lost.

▶ Upstream links in the supply chain can always fully supply downstream links. Planners can take alternative measures to avoid potential stockouts that are not covered by a safety stock (e.g., rush transports).

▶ All uncertainties within the supply chain are statistically independent of each other.

▶ The average value of a forecast error is practically zero. Generally, overestimates and underestimates counterbalance each other. For that reason, the forecast procedures in use may not show any significant, systematic error.

If one or more of the aforementioned assumptions don't apply or apply only partially in your scenario, the calculated safety stocks can deviate from the correct values. Consequently, the actual service level can deviate from the target service level.

Safety stock planning in supply network planning therefore allows you to think about the supply side of your supply chain. In other words, not only do you have an option to consider the forecast and actual requirements (consumption), but also the deviations between the order (replenishment lead time) and the actual delivery (the supplier's delivery reliability).

Time-independent warehouse stock basically depends on the following elements:

Safety Stock Planning Methods

The target service level is based either on the percentage of the orders fulfilled or on the order volume fulfilled. For example, if you want to define the target safety stock as a percentage of fulfilled orders, a partial fulfillment is unacceptable and is regarded as an unfulfilled order. But the target warehouse stock is calculated based on the assumption that backorders can cover unfilled orders so that no sales are lost and the requirements are regular and not sporadic.

Furthermore, the replenishment procedure in use does not influence safety stock planning. The replenishment procedure is set in the location product master. If you select a reorder point method, the reorder point quantity is calculated based on the target days' supply from the location product master. If you select an order cycle method, the target days' supply is regarded as an order cycle.

Forecast Requirements and Historic Variability of the Requirements

The requirement for a product in a location is the total amount of the primary requirements in the location and the secondary requirements in all downstream locations.

Calculation of the safety stock considers the forecast from demand planning and the requirements variability derived from the historical forecasts and the realized requirements (forecast error of the requirement). Alternatively, the system also considers the forecast error of the requirements that you might have defined in the location product master.

During the creation of the safety stock for finished products, safety stock planning follows the requirements from the location (such as a distribution center) to the customer level. The system considers incoming quota arrangements here.

During the creation of the safety stock for components, the system calculates requirements based on the explosion of the BOM components and the primary requirements for the finished products.

Anticipated Replenishment Lead Time and Historical Variability of the Replenishment Lead Time

The replenishment lead time (RLT) for a product in a location is the RLT for the replenishment from an upstream safety stock location. Safety stock calculation considers the expected replenishment lead time based on the production time, the time needed to process goods issues, transportation time, and the time needed to process goods receipts. In addition, the system also considers the variability of the replenishment lead time determined in the past.

Safety stock planning considers the replenishment path from the location where the safety stock is stored up to the next upstream safety stock location. The critical replenishment path is the path with the longest replenishment time because the safety stock in one location should cover the variability or the replenishment lead time in the most unfavorable case.

The variability of the RLT (forecast error of the RLT) is calculated on the basis of two of the key figures that you defined. One key figure is the RLT planned in the past; the other is the actual RLT. The system also considers the forecast error of the RLT that you might have defined in the location product master.

Safety stock is calculated for each period. The safety stock is planned only for location products.

Service Level

The starting point is the service level that you should maintain by carrying the amount of safety stock you have calculated. You can interpret it as follows, depending on the business process:

▶ **Stockout occurrence-oriented (Alpha Service Level)**
The service level in % indicates that no stockout is anticipated in x% of the periods within the planning period.

▶ **Stockouts-oriented (Beta Service Level)**
The service level percentage states that x % of the expected total customer requirements can be satisfied within the planning period.

Table 6.9 contains a sample for calculating the stockout or occurrence of a stockout in enhanced safety stock planning in SAP APO.

Period	1	2	3	4	5	6	7	8	9	10
Expected requirements	100	100	100	100	100	100	100	100	100	100
Stockout	0	0	0	0	0	10	0	0	0	10
Occurrence of a stockout	–	–	–	–	–	Yes	–	–	–	Yes

Table 6.9 Sample Calculation of a Stockout in Enhanced Safety Stock Planning in SAP APO

The formula for calculating the stockout is:

Total of stockouts: 20 → Beta service level: 1-(20/1 000) = 98 %

The formula for calculating the occurrence of a stockout is as follows:

Total of stockout occurrences: 2 → Alpha service level: 1-(2/10) = 80 %

Some support for deciding what service level to use is whether or not subsequent delivery of a stockout involves stockout-dependent or stockout-independent costs. If the majority of the costs of a subsequent delivery are stockout-independent (fixed) costs, we recommend an alpha service level. If the majority of the costs of a subsequent delivery are stockout-independent (variable), we recommend a beta service level.

Forecast Quality

Along with the service level, the forecast quality is important for the calculation of the safety stock. You can consider a forecast error on the requirements side and on the supply side. The key figures in Table 6.10 form the starting point for calculating a forecast error.

Requirements Side	Supply Side
Key figure for the planned requirements quantity	Key figure for the planned procurement time
Key figure for the actual requirements quantity	Key figure for the actual procurement time

Table 6.10 Key Figures for Determining the Forecast Error

The forecast error is calculated by determining the plan–actual deviation of the related key figures. The standard deviation of the plan–actual deviations is interpreted as the forecast error. With this approach, a forecast error is determined from the historical data and assumed for future forecasts. To deal properly with the dynamics of future processes, it helps to interpret the forecast error as a relative error. In other words, the relationship of the forecast error and the forecast (variation coefficient) is recorded—instead of just the forecast error. The example in Table 6.11 illustrates what this approach means.

Period	1	2	3	4	5
Requirements forecast	100	1000	1000	100	100
Forecast error if the standard deviation is constant	10	10	10	10	10
Forecast error if the variation coefficient is constant	10	100	100	10	10

Table 6.11 Calculating the Forecast Error; Mean Value of the Planned Requirements Quantity: 100, Standard Deviation of the Planned-Actual Deviations: 10

If the forecast error does not depend on the forecast, an upward forecast leads to the unexpected result that the level of safety stock goes down—because the forecast error decreases in relation to the forecast. A relative forecast error therefore makes more sense in a dynamic environment than a constant forecast error does.

If a forecast error exists in terms of procurement (forecast error of the RLT), the forecast error of the requirement is adjusted with the assumption that the two forecast errors are independent of each other.

You can also enter the forecast error of requirements and the replenishment lead time directly into the location product master. We recommend direct entry in the following cases:

▶ No historical data exists (because a new product is involved, for example).
▶ The scope of the historical data is so small that you cannot calculate a statistically significant forecast error.
▶ The forecast error can effectively be seen as a constant.

The forecast error can also be calculated as a measurement of the exactness of the forecast. The forecast error describes the expected deviations between the forecast requirements quantity and the requirements quantity actually realized. The calculation is based on historical forecast quantities and actual quantities. The historical forecast error that you determine is projected onto future forecasts. It is referred to as a mean absolute forecast error or mean absolute deviation (MAD).

To deal properly with the dynamics of future forecasts, it helps to interpret this forecast error as a relative error. In other words, the relationship of the forecast error and the forecast is recorded, instead of just recording the forecast error.

This forecast error is known as the *Mean Absolute Percentage Error* (MAPE) (also mean relative deviation, variation coefficient). The relative forecast error is weighted with the amount of the requirements forecast and thereby converted into an absolute forecast error.

Calculating the Safety Stock Based on the Forecast Quality

Calculating the safety stock here follows the example of the Alpha Service Level (AS) policy, as shown in Table 6.12. The result is the following formula for calculating the safety stock:

Service Level	Safety Factor	RLT	Rel. Forecast Error	Safety Stock
50.01 %	0,0003	1	100	0.04
80.00 %	0,8416	1	100	119.02
90.00 %	1,2816	1	100	181.24

Table 6.12 Calculating the Safety Stock

Service Level	Safety Factor	RLT	Rel. Forecast Error	Safety Stock
95.00 %	1,6449	1	100	232.62
98.00 %	2,0537	1	100	290.44
99.00 %	2,3263	1	100	329.00
99.50 %	2,5758	1	100	364.28
99.90 %	3,0903	1	100	437.03
99.99 %	3,7191	1	100	525.96

Table 6.12 Calculating the Safety Stock (cont.)

Effect of a falling forecast error on the safety stock

Assuming that the forecast error and the replenishment lead time remain constant (a constant of k and s), a decreasing forecast error directly affects the safety stock. This is expressed in a restatement of the formula for calculating the safety stock:

$$\sigma_{rel} = \frac{sb}{k \cdot \sqrt{\lambda + 1}}$$

$$\sigma_{rel} = \frac{sb}{const}$$

$$\sigma_{rel}\downarrow = \frac{sb\downarrow}{const}$$

Figure 6.54 illustrates the results: A change in the forecast error results in a proportional change in the safety stock.

A reduction in the forecast error by 20 % also reduces the safety stock by 20 %.

Inventory policy

The inventory policy used in SNP requirements planning also has a significant influence on the algorithm for calculating the safety stock. That's why you must distinguish between two different inventory policies, as shown in Figure 6.55:

▶ **Order cycle policy (black)**
An order decision is made depending on the time: procurement can be triggered only for all t periods.

▶ **Reorder point policy (gray)**
A reorder point decision is made depending on the warehouse stock. In other words, procurement can be triggered if warehouse stock goes below a specific level, s (reorder point).

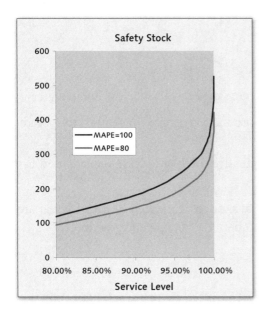

Figure 6.54 Effect of the Forecast Error on the Safety Stock

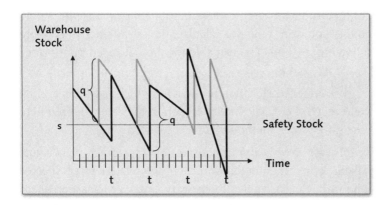

Figure 6.55 Inventory Policy (Source: SAP)

Four safety stock methods with model support result from both interpretations of the service level:

	Order Cycle Policy	Reorder Point Policy
Alpha Service Level	AT	AS
Beta Service Level	BT	BS

Table 6.13 Enhanced Safety Stock Methods in SAP APO

The preconditions for the use of these methods include the following:

▶ The requirements trend of the products is regular (in contrast to sporadic requirements).

▶ Stockouts are delivered subsequently: "back order case" (as opposed to a "lost sales case").

In the context of these preconditions, safety stocks can be calculated at any link in the supply chain or for each period of the planning period.

Process

Setting the Master Data for the Enhanced Safety Stock Planning

1. Go into the SAP APO menu, choose **SAP APO · Master Data · Product · Product** and switch into the product master. In the **SB Method** field on the **Lot Size** tab of the product master, use the input help to choose the safety stock method that you want to use to calculate the safety stock (see Figure 6.50). The following methods are available for the enhanced safety stock planning: **AT**, **AS**, **BT**, and **BS**.

2. Enter the service level for the location product for which you are planning in the **Service Level (%)** field. The interpretation of the value entered here depends on the safety stock method you have selected.

3. If the relative forecast error is almost constant or if historical plan–actual data is unavailable, you can enter an estimate of the relative forecast error in the location product master data. If necessary, enter a forecast error for the requirement in the **Forecast Error Requirements (%)** field and the replenishment lead time in the **Forecast Error RLT (%)** field.

You can calculate such an estimate with the following formula:

*Sigma_D / Mue_P * 100 %*

Sigma_D is the standard deviation of the time series (forecast value vs. actual value). The variable Mue_P is the average value of the forecast values.

However, as far as possible, you should let the system calculate this forecast error from historical data if it is available.

4. In the **Target Range** field, enter the number of days that the warehouse inventory and planned stock receipts of a product should cover the known requirements. If you select an order cycle method, this value is interpreted as an order cycle.

Running the Enhanced Safety Stock Planning

To execute the enhanced safety stock planning, choose from the SAP APO Easy Access menu **Supply Network Planning** • **Planning** • **Safety Stock Planning**; the **Safety Stock Planning** screen opens. Because of the size, the screen is displayed in two parts here (see Figure 6.56 and Figure 6.57).

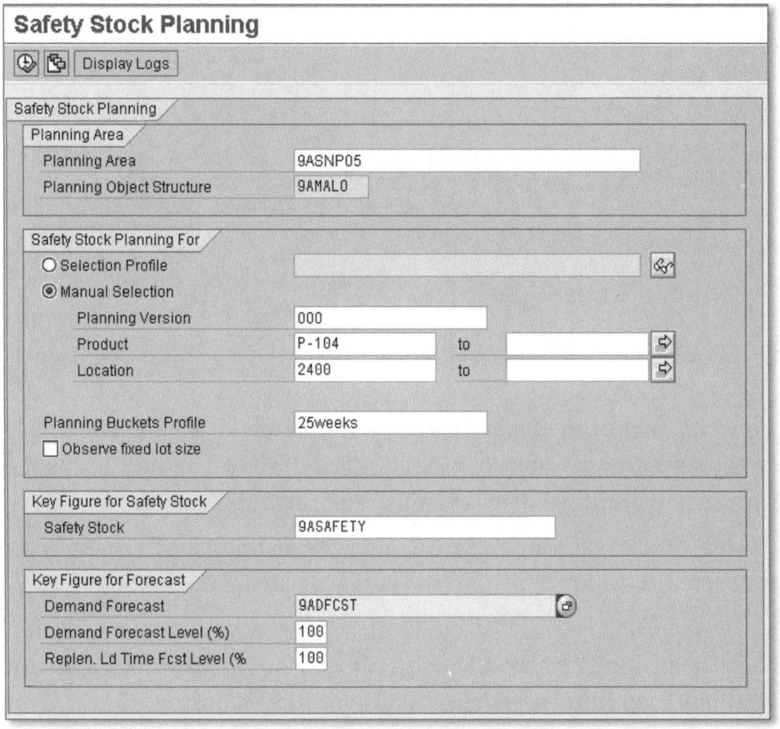

Figure 6.56 Enhanced Safety Stock Planning, Part 1

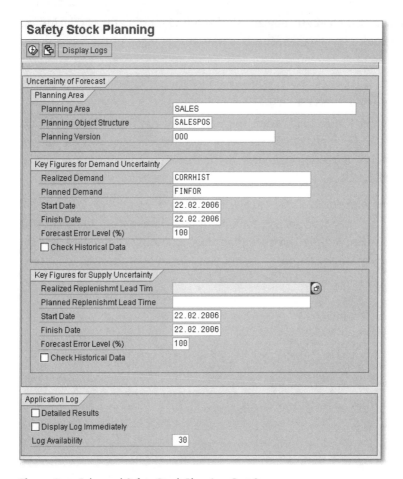

Figure 6.57 Enhanced Safety Stock Planning, Part 2

▶ The upper portion of the **Safety Stock Planning** screen includes the filter criteria for selecting the objects used in safety stock planning such as the planning area, planning object structure, and planning version.

▶ In the **Safety Stock Planning For** area, enter the planning objects you want to plan for: for example, which products should be planned in which locations.

▶ If you use safety stock method BS, you can activate the **Observe fixed lot size** checkbox to indicate whether the system should consider the fixed lot size in the location product master when determining the procurement quantities.

▶ In the **Safety Stock** field, select the key figure to store the results of safety stock planning (the calculated safety stock).

▶ In the **Demand Forecast** field, select the key figure that contains the forecast demand. (This is the demand that covers the safety stock planning.) The key figure is normally 9ADFCST, which must be assigned to planning object structure 9AMALO.

▶ In the **Demand Forecast Level (%)** field, you can correct the requirements forecast that you want to use to calculate the safety stock. For example, if you have information indicating that the forecast created in sales planning is too high or too low, you can increase or lower the level of the forecast accordingly.

▶ In the **Replenishment Lead Time Forecast Level (Replen. Ld Time Fcst Level (%)** field, you can correct the replenishment lead time forecast that was calculated by the safety stock planning. You can find this value in the log. For example, if you have information that the replenishment lead time forecast is too high or too low, you can increase or lower the level of the forecast accordingly.

The lower portion of the window contains information on the sources used to calculate the uncertainties.

Here too, you must first set the filter criteria to select the planning area, the planning structure, and the planning version.

▶ In the **Realized Demand** field, select a key figure that contains the actual realized demand. Based on the data of this key figure, safety stock planning valuates the uncertainty of past requirement forecasts. An entry in this field is optional. The system considers the key figure entered only if you have not defined a forecast error for the requirement in the location product master.

▶ In the **Planned Demand** field, select a key figure that contains forecast figures generated in the past. An entry in this field is optional. The system considers the key figure entered only if you have not defined a forecast error of the requirement in the location product master.

▶ The difference between the realized and planned demand helps determine the variability of the demand forecast.

▶ In the **Start Date** and **Finish Date** fields, enter the horizon for which the forecast error should be calculated.

▶ If you assume that your forecast accuracy will improve in the future, you can enter a percentage in the **Forecast Error Level (%)** that corresponds to the forecast level. For example, you can determine that the forecast error in the future will be only 80 % of the past forecast error.

- ▸ If you activate the **Check Historical Data** checkbox, the system checks to see what periods of historical data are available from the specific key figure when calculating the forecast error in the specified period. The system then considers the historical data only after this period when calculating the forecast error.

- ▸ In the **Realized Replenishment Lead Time** field, enter a key figure that contains the actual replenishment lead time. Safety stock planning must also valuate the uncertainty of the expected replenishment lead time. An entry in this field is optional. The system considers the key figure entered only if you have not defined a forecast error of the requirements lead time in the location product master. If you do not enter a key figure here and have not set a forecast error, the system assumes that the replenishment lead time does not involve any uncertainty.

- ▸ In the **Planned Replenishment Lead Time** field, enter a key figure that contains the replenishment lead time planned in the past. An entry in this field is optional. Additionally, the same comments apply here as for the **Realized Replenishment Lead Time** field.

- ▸ Set the desired key figure in the **Application Log** area, if you want to display a log of the results.

You can display the calculated safety stock as a key figure in interactive SNP planning and, if needed, change it manually or copy it into another planning version. You can also use the calculated safety stock in production planning and detailed scheduling (PP/DS) and in Capable-to-Match (CTM) planning.

In terms of the demand side, the system first determines all the location products that are supplied from the location product that carries safety stock. The second step then projects all forecasts and forecast errors onto the location product that carries safety stock to calculate the safety stock, while considering all quantities and time relationships.

In terms of the supply side, the system first determines all the location products that supply the location product that carries safety stock. That step is repeated until a location product that carries safety stock or an external supply in the supply chain is reached. A second step determines the critical supply path by calculating the maximum replenishment lead time. Finally, all the forecasts and forecast errors along the critical path are projected onto the location product that carries safety stock to plan the safety stock.

Evaluating the Enhanced Methods

The enhanced methods for determining the safety stock have the following advantages:

▸ The safety stocks can be optimally adjusted to various levels of demand. The safety stock is no longer stored statically in the master data. It is intended to meet actual demand. This approach means that fluctuating demand and procurement situations are automatically taken into account.

▸ No more laborious configuration or master data maintenance processes are necessary. The system makes the optimal setting individually for each material master.

▸ Current replenishment lead times that are used in the enhanced safety stock planning are considered.

The disadvantages of these enhanced methods include the following:

▸ The planner cannot immediately understand the result. Planners must work with the result more intensively. Moreover, because the procedure is usually new for planners, they need more time to familiarize themselves with it.

▸ To understand the results, planners must understand the enhanced methods and their relationship with the forecast accuracy.

6.7.4 Conclusion

When used correctly, the enhanced methods of safety stock planning have considerable potential for the stock optimization, which is why they are highly recommended.

Safety stock planning also enables you to achieve a specific service level by creating safety stock for all semifinished and finished products in the corresponding plants and distribution centers across the entire supply chain.

Two key questions must be answered where a safety stock planning is concerned:

▸ At what levels within the supply chain should safety stock be carried?

▸ How high should the safety stock be at a level that carries safety stock?

A simple supply chain consists of a supplier, two production plants, two distribution centers, and a customer. Even with a simple supply chain, it's clear that the question regarding the levels on which safety stock should be carried—given the many different possible combinations (2 to the power of n

possibilities)—presents a highly complex decision-making problem (in this example, there are already 64 possibilities). The large number of options means that you should take advantage of the planners' experience and allow them to simulate selected planning scenarios.

In general, dynamic, multilevel safety stock planning for any supply chain structures poses a very complex decision-making problem. For that very reason, you should use high-performance heuristics. Such heuristics focus on algorithms for single-level, time-independent safety stock planning, which can be linked to multilevel, time-dependent supply chain planning by adjusting the input parameters.

Consequently, the system must adjust the forecast and the forecast error for the demand and procurement sides.

6.8   Deployment/Replenishment

After production has been completed, deployment (also called replenishment planning) determines which requirements can be covered by the supply that is actually available. If the available quantities are not sufficient to cover the requirement, or if they exceed the requirement, deployment makes adjustments to the plan created by the SNP run. The deployment run generates deployment stock transfers based on the SNP stock transfers created by the SNP run. Using the deployment stock transfers, the Transport Load Builder (TLB) then groups transport loads and generates TLB shipments (see Section 6.9). There are three deployment planning strategies:

▶ Deployment heuristic

▶ Real-time deployment

▶ Deployment optimization

6.8.1   Deployment Heuristic

The deployment heuristic creates a distribution plan for *one* product in *one* location of the supply chain model. After production has been completed, the system first checks which product quantities are actually available in the source locations (locations with stock). The total of these product quantities is called the Available-to-Deploy (ATD) quantity. The system then determines how the ATD quantity must be distributed to the destination locations (locations with requirements). The system then takes into account the different distribution rules for a situation where the available product quantities may exceed or fall short of the requirement (fair share and push rules). You can define these rules in the **SNP Deployment Profile** or on the **SNP 2** tab of the location product master. To do this, go to **Master Data • Product • Product Master** in the SAP APO menu and select the **SNP 2** tab (see Figure 6.58).

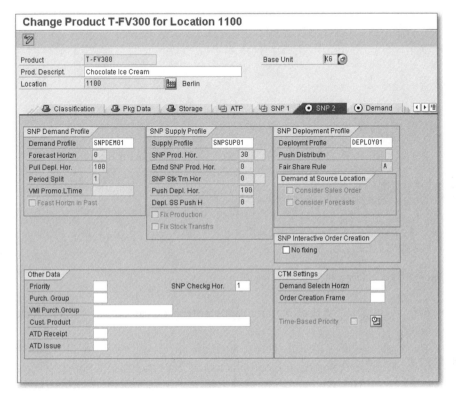

Figure 6.58 Deployment Profile in the Product Master

In addition, deployment considers a number of deployment horizons that you can also define in the location product master.

Distribution Rules for the Deployment Heuristic

Fair Share Rules
If demand exceeds supply, the system can use fair share rules to calculate the deployment based on the ATD quantity. Fair share rules enable planners to use alternative procedures for assigning a limited product supply to the pegged requirements. The following rules are available:

▶ **Fair share rule A: Proportional distribution based on requirements**
The goal of fair share rule A is to distribute the stock proportionally to all requirement locations in accordance with the planned distribution requirement (see Figure 6.59).

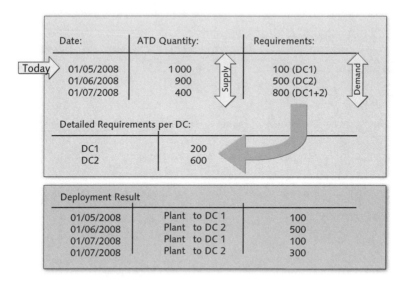

Figure 6.59 Deployment, Fair Share Rule A

▶ **Fair share rule B: Proportional distribution based on the target stock level**
The goal of fair share rule B is to increase the stock levels in all requirement locations to approximately the same percentage as that of the target stock level. The percentage for each destination location is defined as

deployment-relevant stock (this equals the warehouse stock minus the SNP stock transfers) divided by the target stock level

If there is a negative deployment-relevant stock, the system first tries to increase the warehouse stock in these destination locations to zero. The system then attempts to increase the warehouse stock in all destination locations to the same percentage of the target stock level (see Figure 6.60).

▶ **Fair share rule C: Distribution by percentage based on quota arrangements**
The goal of fair share rule C is to distribute the stock in accordance with the quota arrangements in the requirement locations (see Figure 6.61). To be able to use rule C, you must define the outbound quota arrangements for source location products in the Supply Chain Engineer.

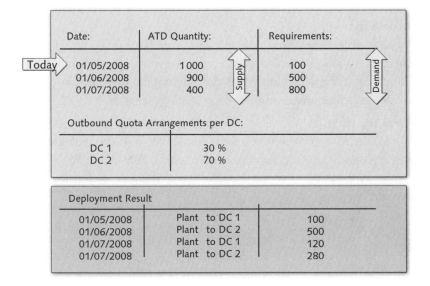

ATD Quantity in Plant = 300

Distrib. Center	Planned Stock	Target Stock	% Target Stock	Allo-cation	% Target Stock
DC	50	500	10	200	50 %
DC 2	500	700	71.4	0	71.4%
DC 3	0	200	0	100	50 %

deployment-relevant stock (this equals the warehouse stock minus the SNP stock transfers) divided by the target stock level

Figure 6.60 Deployment, Fair Share Rule B

Date:	ATD Quantity:	Requirements:
Today 01/05/2008	1 000	100
01/06/2008	900	500
01/07/2008	400	800

Supply — Demand

Outbound Quota Arrangements per DC:

DC 1	30 %
DC 2	70 %

Deployment Result

01/05/2008	Plant to DC 1	100
01/06/2008	Plant to DC 2	500
01/07/2008	Plant to DC 1	120
01/07/2008	Plant to DC 2	280

Figure 6.61 Deployment, Fair Share Rule C

► **Fair share rule D: Distribution based on the distribution priority**
The goal of fair share rule D is to distribute the stock in accordance with the priorities that you defined in the outbound transportation lanes of the source location (distribution priority). If a fair share situation occurs, the system tries to cover all requirements from the current date onward until the ATD quantity has been depleted.

Push Rules

SNP uses push rules to calculate deployment when the ATD quantity covers the requirement. The following rules are available:

▸ **Pull Distribution**
Deployment covers the entire demand within the pull deployment horizon. Stock is distributed in accordance with the due dates defined in the individual requirement locations. The system does not distribute any supply to the pegged requirement before the requirements date.

▸ **Pull/Push Distribution**
The system distributes the entire supply immediately to the requirement locations (without considering the requirements dates defined by the requirement locations) to cover the whole requirement within the pull deployment horizon.

▸ **Push Distribution By Demands**
The system immediately distributes the entire supply for the whole planning horizon to the requirement locations to ensure that all demands are covered. The pull deployment horizon in this case is ignored.

▸ **Push Distribution By Quota Arrangement**
The system distributes the entire supply immediately in accordance with the quota arrangements specified for the requirement locations. The demand situation in the destination locations is ignored in this case.

▸ **Push Distribution Taking into Account the Safety Stock Horizon**
The system confirms planned goods issues, for which you would only have to use the safety stock in the source location to cover these goods issues if the difference between the requirements date and the deploy date is lower than the safety stock horizon. This means that the system only falls below the safety stock that you specified in the **Lot Size** tab of the location product master if the demand to be covered is in the safety stock horizon. Note that the safety stock horizon rolls with the planning.

The example in Figure 6.62 illustrates how the three push rules *Pull Distribution*, *Pull/Push Distribution*, and *Push Distribution* are used for demand:

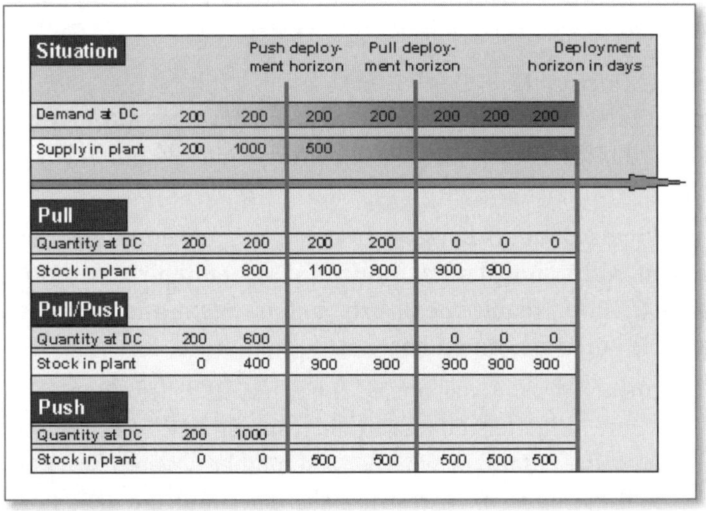

Situation	Push deployment horizon		Pull deployment horizon		Deployment horizon in days		
Demand at DC	200	200	200	200	200	200	200
Supply in plant	200	1000	500				
Pull							
Quantity at DC	200	200	200	200	0	0	0
Stock in plant	0	800	1100	900	900	900	
Pull/Push							
Quantity at DC	200	600			0	0	0
Stock in plant	0	400	900	900	900	900	900
Push							
Quantity at DC	200	1000					
Stock in plant	0	0	500	500	500	500	500

Figure 6.62 Deployment According to Pull/Push Distribution

▶ **Pull Distribution**
On each day when the requirement is within the pull horizon (four days in the future), a quantity of 200 pieces is distributed to the distribution centres.

▶ **Pull/Push Distribution**
On the first day when the supply has 200 pieces, a quantity of 200 pieces is distributed. On the second day, a quantity of 600 pieces is distributed. Although the supply is 1,000 pieces, the requirement within the pull horizon only amounts to 600 pieces; therefore, only 600 pieces are distributed.

▶ **Push Distribution By Demands**
On the first day when supply is 200 pieces, 200 pieces are distributed. On the second day when supply is 1,000 pieces, 1,000 pieces are distributed. Since the requirement in the system amounts to 1,400 pieces, the entire supply can be distributed. A requirement of 200 pieces at the end of the planning horizon remains uncovered due to supply that is too low within the push horizon. If the requirement in the system were 800 pieces, only 800 pieces would be distributed on the second day.

Deployment Horizons for the Deployment Heuristic

The deployment heuristic takes into consideration four different deployment horizons that you define on the **SNP 2** tab of the location product master, as shown in Figure 6.58:

▶ **Pull Deployment Horizon (Pull Depl. Hor.)**
This horizon indicates the period when the deployment takes into account the planned distribution requirement. The period begins with the date of the current day.

During the deployment run, the system tries to cover the entire distribution requirement within this defined horizon. Distribution starts on the first day that distribution requirements exist in the system, and ends with the last day of the pull deployment horizon.

The pull deployment horizon is also used for the push distribution. This horizon then specifies whether the requirement should be covered immediately (pull/push distribution), or whether it should be covered based on the due date (pull distribution). It restricts the date until the SNP stock transfers are considered relevant for the deployment. Only a planned requirement within this horizon, which was confirmed, is covered by the deployment.

▶ **Push Deployment Horizon (Push Depl. Hor.)**
This horizon specifies the period when deployment takes into account goods receipts that were defined in the category group for the ATD receipt. The period begins with the date of the current day.

If the push distribution was specified (if the distribution requirement is lower than the supply and the warehouse stock), this horizon determines whether the warehouse stock is distributed before the due date of the distribution requirement in accordance with the defined push rule. Only warehouse stock within the push deployment horizon is included for push deployment, that is, for a deployment before the actual requirements date.

▶ **Safety Stock Horizon**
This horizon is only used for the push rule push distribution, taking into account the safety stock horizon.

▶ **SNP Checking Horizon (SNP Checkg. Hor.)**
Deployment uses this horizon to calculate the quantity available for distribution to the requirement locations. It restricts the quantity available within the push deployment horizon. Within the SNP checking horizon, deployment calculates the ATD quantity for a period in which it adds the

ATD goods receipts of the current periods and previous periods and sub-stracts all ATD goods issues within the SNP checking horizon.

Example for a Deployment Heuristic

To implement a deployment heuristic, select the menu options **SAP APO · SNP · Planning · SNP in Background · Deployment**. Enter the corresponding selection data here. In addition to the version, product, and location details, also specify the deployment horizon as shown in Figure 6.63. In this case, we want to implement deployment in a horizon of 100 days.

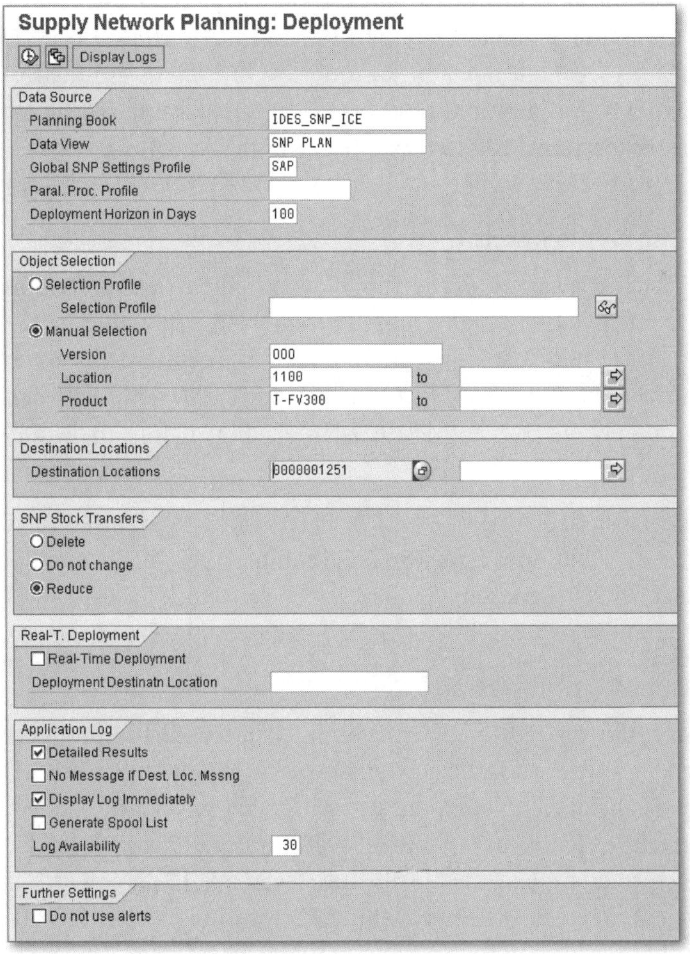

Figure 6.63 Deployment Heuristic, Selection Screen

The results of the deployment planning are shown in Figure 6.64.

Product	Start Loc.	Dest. Location	Push	FS	Demand Date	ATD Qty	Roll Fwd	Conf.Qty	DistDemand	StorageQty	Target Stk	Unit
T-FV100	1100	0000001250		A	25.12.2006	10000,000	1000,000	4927,048	5419,753	0,000	0,000	KG
T-FV100	1100	0000001251		A	25.12.2006	10000,000	1000,000	5072,952	5580,247	0,000	0,000	KG
T-FV100	1100	0000001250		A	01.01.2007	0,000	1000,000	0,000	0,000	0,000	0,000	KG
T-FV100	1100	0000001251		A	01.01.2007	0,000	1000,000	0,000	0,000	0,000	0,000	KG

Figure 6.64 Deployment Heuristic, Results

There is a demand of 10,000 pieces for material T-FV100 on 25.12.2006 at the location 1250 and 1251. However, the ATD quantity on this day is 10,000 pieces in the location 1100. The full ATD quantity can be distributed from location 1100 to the demand locations 1250 and 1251. The entire ATD quantity is distributed to both demand locations. 4,927 pieces are distributed from location 1100 to location 1250 on 25.12.2006 and 5,072 pieces are distributed from location 1100 to location 1251.

6.8.2 Real-Time Deployment

Real-time deployment is a variant of the deployment heuristic and is used to implement deployment based on the most current results possible of the SNP run. In this case, the system considers the present requirements situation in the destination locations by first implementing an SNP run between the source location and the relevant destination locations before the actual deployment run.

When fair share rule B (see Section 6.8.1) in particular is being used, it is important that the distribution is based on (as accurate as possible) a calculation of the target stock level and the planned warehouse stock levels.

6.8.3 Deployment Optimization

The deployment optimizer creates a distribution plan for all the products that you selected in all the chosen locations of your supply chain model. After production has been completed, the system first checks which product quantities are actually available in the source locations (locations with stock). The total of these product quantities is called the available-to-deploy (ATD) quantity. The system then determines how the ATD quantity must be distributed to the destination locations (locations with requirements). The optimizer mainly considers the following factors in this case:

▶ **Distribution Rules**
for a situation where the available product quantities exceed or fall short of the requirement, such as fair share and push rules

▶ **Costs**
all costs defined in the supply chain model, such as transport costs, storage costs, and penalty costs for non-delivery

▶ **Constraints**
such as transportation and storage capacities and transportation lot sizes

You define constraints and distribution rules in the SNP deployment optimization profile. In this profile, you can also define other parameters (such as decomposition methods, for example) for the deployment optimization to improve runtimes.

The purpose of the deployment optimizer is to find the plan among all *feasible* plans (these are plans where all the specified constraints are taken into consideration) that is the most favorable in terms of evaluating the total cost.

Distribution Rules for Deployment Optimization

Supply Shortage
If the deployment optimizer establishes that the ATD quantity falls short of the requirement for the destination locations, it uses the rule that you specified in the SNP deployment optimization profile if a supply shortage occurs. You can access the SNP deployment optimization profile by selecting the menu options **SAP APO • SNP • Environment • Current Settings • Profiles • SNP Deployment Optimization Profile** (see Figure 6.65).

The following rules are available:

▶ **Distribution Based on Lowest Costs**
When calculating the product quantities to be distributed, the deployment optimizer only considers the costs defined in the supply chain model and the constraints specified in the SNP deployment optimization profile. The calculated distribution plan then corresponds to the plan with the lowest overall costs.

With this option, the demand of a location may not actually be covered, for example, because the demand of another location can be covered more cost-effectively.

- ▶ **Fair Share Distribution By Demands**
  The main goal of the deployment optimizer is to distribute the ATD quantity evenly according to the demand of the destination locations (sales orders and forecasts).

  When distributing the calculated quantities, the system also includes the costs defined in the supply chain model. If the transport costs are high, the optimizer can therefore decide not to distribute the allocated quantity directly to a destination location, but to distribute the quantity to this destination location indirectly through another location. If the calculated fair share quantities cannot be distributed to individual locations due to specified constraints, these quantities are distributed to the other destination locations based on cost factors.

- ▶ **Earliest Delivery**
  Together with the **Fair Share Distribution By Demands** option, you can specify that the deployment optimizer for the fair share distribution first covers the earliest demand as fully as possible before it plans the coverage of later demand. If you do not select this option, the optimizer will try to distribute the ATD quantity evenly across the demand in the different periods.

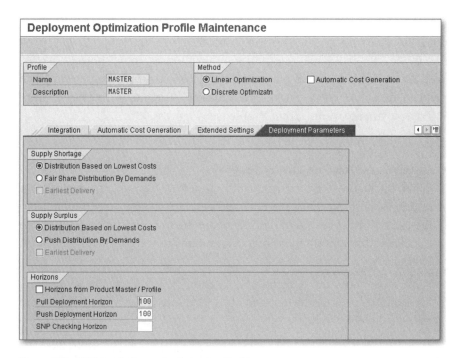

Figure 6.65 SNP Deployment Optimization Profile

Supply Surplus

If the deployment optimizer establishes that the ATD quantity exceeds demand for the destination locations, it uses the rule that you specified in the SNP deployment optimization profile if a supply surplus occurs. The following rules are available:

▶ **Distribution Based on Lowest Costs**
When calculating the product quantities to be distributed, the deployment optimizer only considers the costs defined in the supply chain model and the constraints specified in the SNP deployment optimization profile. However, the system generally covers the entire demand of destination locations, since high non-delivery costs prevent a demand from not being satisfied. The optimizer distributes excess stock to the location with the lowest costs. This does not necessarily have to be a location with a demand.

▶ **Push Distribution By Demands**
The main goal of the deployment optimizer is to evenly distribute the ATD quantity according to the demand of the destination locations. Since the ATD quantity exceeds the demand quantity, the calculated percentage is over 100 % compared to the fair share situation (this means that the destination locations may receive a quantity that exceeds their demand).

As is the case with fair share distribution, the system also considers the costs specified in the supply chain model when it distributes the calculated quantities and it may allow diversions in the supply chain if this means that the overall costs can be reduced.

▶ **Earliest Delivery**
In conjunction with the **Push Distribution By Demands** option, you can specify that the deployment optimizer distributes the entire available ATD quantity to the destination locations at the earliest requirements date for the push distribution. If you do not select this option, the optimizer tries to distribute the ATD quantity evenly across the demand in the different periods.

Taking Costs into Account

The deployment optimizer takes into account the following costs defined in the supply chain model:

▶ Storage and transportation costs
▶ Costs for increasing storage, transportation, and handling capacities

▶ Penalty costs if there is a shortage in the safety stock level

▶ Penalty costs for delayed delivery

▶ Penalty costs for non-delivery

You can access the SNP cost profile by selecting the menu options **SAP APO • SNP • Environment • Current Settings • Profiles • SNP Cost Profile** (see Figure 6.66). You can use the SNP cost profile to set the relative importance of the different cost types. This means that you don't specify the actual cost, but instead specify the penalty costs in relation to each other.

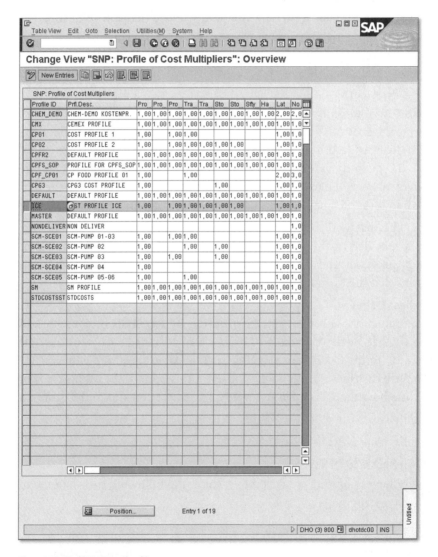

Figure 6.66 SNP Cost Profile

However, the system can also determine the costs by generating the costs automatically. To do this, you must set the **Automatic Cost Generation** tab in the SNP deployment optimization profile (see Figure 6.65).

Automatic Cost Generation

Costs play an important role for optimization-based planning in Supply Network Planning (SNP). The optimizer selects the plan with the lowest overall costs from among all feasible production and distribution plans. This means that the optimizer also makes business decisions such as covering requirements for a certain period based on the associated costs, for example.

For the optimizer to be able to specify the planning costs, you can define your actual costs, such as production and transportation costs in the system. However, you can also define steering costs that correspond to your business objectives. Nevertheless, it is not easy for the planner to convert operational business objectives into steering costs.

You can use the Automatic Cost Generation function to enable the system to generate all the relevant steering costs (i.e., the cost model) easily for the optimizer. You can also use this function to create an optimization-based production plan simply and quickly. To create a finite (capacity-based) production plan, you only have to implement a few additional settings (e.g., considering capacities).

Generating the Cost Model
The system generates the following steering costs:

▶ Storage costs
▶ Production costs, this is, costs of the production process model (PPM) or the production data structure (PDS)
▶ Product-specific transportation costs
▶ Procurement costs
▶ Penalty costs if there is a shortage in the safety stock level
▶ Penalty costs for non-delivery
▶ Penalty costs for delayed delivery

To enable the system to calculate the costs for a delayed delivery, you must specify a maximum delay on the **SNP 1** tab in the product master data.

The system ignores all costs that you may have specified in the master data. They also remain unchanged in the system after the costs are generated.

The system does not generate subsequent costs, since the planner would need to provide additional information, or the costs are only relevant for complex scenarios:

▶ Cost functions (production, transportation, procurement)

▶ Costs for means of transport

▶ Costs for using the available capacity of resources (costs for using the normal and maximum supply or for a shortage in the minimum supply)

In addition, the system does not consider the cost profile for weighting costs that you can define for optimization-based planning.

Properties of the Generated Cost Model

The system ensures that the generated cost model has the following features:

▶ **The model does not indicate any anomalies.**
The system defines the amount of costs in such a way that any unwanted effects such as the following, for example, do not occur:

  ▷ Non-coverage of a requirement due to low penalty costs for a non-delivery

  ▷ Planning a transport due to low costs in the destination location

  ▷ Planning a transport to save storage costs

▶ **The model is stable.**
The costs do not depend on the lengths of periods and transaction data.

▶ **The model in itself is logical.**
The transportation costs grow proportionally for the length of the transport, and the value of products increases with production intensity.

The system automatically accepts the value 1 as the value of raw products (products without input products). If the system is to take the actual storage costs as the basis for calculating the product value, you can select this on the **Automatic Cost Generation** tab in the SNP or deployment optimization profile.

With the exception of storage costs possibly being considered, the generated cost model does not depend on the costs defined in the master data. The system does not support a combination of these two cost models (e.g., the integration of the master data cost model).

Defining Business Objectives

If you want to create an optimized-based production plan using the **Automatic Cost Generation** function, first define your business objects for the planning. The system then uses these objectives to generate the corresponding steering costs automatically, which the optimizer then uses to make its planning decisions.

The main purpose of planning is to maximize the level of service. You can also define the following additional objectives:

▶ Taking requirement and product priorities into account

▶ Taking procurement priorities into account

You define these objectives in the SNP or deployment optimization profile. To do this, select the menu options **SAP APO • SNP • Environment • Current Settings • Profiles • SNP Deployment Optimization Profile** and choose the **Automatic Cost Generation** tab (see Figure 6.67).

Figure 6.67 SNP Deployment Optimization Profile, "Automatic Cost Generation" Tab

Taking Demand and Product Priorities into Account

You can define priorities for the safety stock and three different priority classes for the demand:

- ▸ Customer Requirement
- ▸ Corrected Demand Forecast
- ▸ Demand Forecast

The standard setting is that all the priority classes and the safety stock have the same priority.

You can also specify that the system also considers the priority of products. You can specify this priority on the **SNP 2** tab in the master data of the location product (see Figure 6.58). The system takes into account the product priority, combined with the demand priority. You can determine which priority is more important and should be considered by the system first.

To simplify this combination from both priority types, you must still also divide the product priorities into three classes of A, B and C products.

Figure 6.68 shows exactly how the system proceeds if the demand priority is more important than the product priority or vice versa.

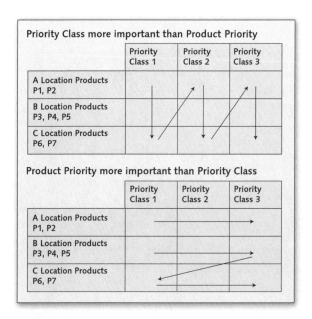

Figure 6.68 Business Objectives for Deployment Optimization

If the demand priority is more important than the product priority, the system first covers all the demand of priority class 1 (e.g., customer requirement) for all location products. It then covers all the demand of priority class 2, and so on. If the product priority is more important, the system first covers all the demand of all priority classes for the location products of class A, then all the demand for the location products of class B, and so on.

Taking Procurement Priorities into Account

You can specify that the system considers the procurement priorities of production process models (PPMs) or production data structures (PDS) as well as transportation lanes. You define this priority in the master data of the PPMs/PDS and transportation lanes (on a product-specific basis). The procurement priority of sources of supply for in-house production is always more important in this case than the sources of supply for external procurement (similar to the procedure for SNP heuristics).

The system first always covers all the demand of a period with goods receipts from all sources of supply available in this period (in the procurement priority sequence for these sources of supply). Only then does the system try to cover the demand with goods receipts from sources of supply of an earlier period. If the system has to revert to an earlier or later period, it may no longer necessarily adhere to the prescribed principle in this period.

Taking Constraints into Account

From the point of view of the deployment optimizer, a plan is feasible if it fulfills all the constraints of the supply chain model that you defined in the SNP deployment optimization profile. The feasibility of a solution can involve violations of the due dates or safety stocks constraints. These are soft constraints, that is, constraints to which you assign violation costs. The optimizer only proposes a plan that violates soft constraints if this plan is the most cost-effective one, based on the costs specified in the system.

The deployment optimizer uses linear programming methods to include all relevant conditions for the planning problem simultaneously in an optimum solution. The higher the number of constraints activated, the more complex the optimization problem, which means that even more time is required to solve the problem. You should therefore generally execute the optimization as a background job.

The optimizer differentiates between continuous linear optimization problems and discrete optimization problems (see Section 6.3.1). The information already provided in Section 6.3.1 also applies to decomposition, the main focus of which is to reduce the runtime and memory requirements of optimization.

Prioritization

The deployment optimizer can differentiate between the priority of sales orders and that of demand forecasts. In the case of strict prioritization, sales orders always have priority 1; the corrected demand forecast has priority 5, and the demand forecast has priority 6. The system uses all available cost information within each priority class to determine the ultimate solution. If you apply cost-based prioritization, the optimizer uses penalty cost information from the product master data to determine the best solution. For this purpose, select the menu options **SAP APO • Master Data • Product • Product** and choose the **SNP 1** tab (see Figure 6.69).

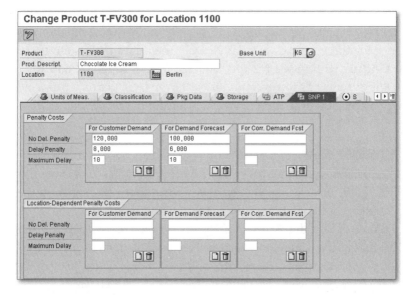

Figure 6.69 Product Master Data, "SNP 1" Tab

6.9 Transport Load Builder (TLB)

The Transport Load Builder (TLB) enables you to compile transport loads for certain means of transport and it also ensures that the capacity for the mode of transport is loaded to its maximum capacity. The main objectives of TLB planning include:

▸ Grouping transports that are within user-defined parameter limits (e.g., weight or volumes)

▸ Ensuring uniform loadings for means of transport or loadings for means of transport based on products

TLB groups deployment stock transfers or replenishment orders, which were generated for individual products in previous planning runs, with TLB shipments.

You can use TLB in SAP Inventory Collaboration Hub (SAP ICH) or in Supply Network Planning (SNP). SAP ICH also contains functions that go beyond the range of SNP-TLB functions, although these will not be discussed here.

6.9.1 Grouping Transport Loads Using TLB

TLB first groups the deployment stock transfers or replenishment orders of the current period to TLB shipments. In this case, TLB tries to load the transports up to the maximum upper limit of the parameters that you specified in the TLB profile for the means of transport.

TLB also uses the loading method that you defined in the transportation lane for the means of transport. It loads the transports with the same products or with products of the same loading group (loading based on products), or it distributes the products evenly to all grouped transports (uniform loading). Note however that TLB does not apply optimization methods; therefore, an optimum solution cannot be guaranteed. The Transport Load Builder specifically considers the loading methods as follows:

► **Loading by Product**
TLB first sorts the loading groups alphabetically and then sorts the products again within the loading group. In the second step, TLB distributes the loading groups and products to the transports in their sorted sequence. If a loading group can only be partially loaded onto a transport, TLB loads the remainder of the loading group onto the next transport. Consequently, a loading group may therefore be too large or too small for a transport.

► **Uniform Loading**
TLB tries to distribute the products to transports in such a way that their percentage is the same on each transport. In this case, TLB adds a rounding value of the product in question to a transport that indicates the lowest ratio between the quantity already loaded and the total requirement of the product. If the relationships of all products are the same, TLB adds a rounding value of a randomly selected product to the transport.

If all TLB shipments are within the valid parameter limits, TLB terminates the planning run.

6.9.2 Procedure for Remaining Quantities

You may have a situation where TLB with the deployment stock transfers or replenishment orders of the current period could not load one of the TLB shipments up to the defined lower limits. If the Transport Load Builder (TLB) with the deployment stock transfers or replenishment orders of the current period could not load one of the TLB shipments up to the defined lower limits, TLB first redistributes the product quantities. TLB now tries to ensure that all transports are within the valid upper and lower limits of the parameters by loading some transports up to the defined lower limits only. This means that TLB groups all transports again, taking into account the loading method.

If TLB still cannot find a valid solution using this approach, it uses the following methods for changing transport quantities:

- **Upsizing transport quantities**
  TLB upsizes the product quantities to be transported by implementing additional deployment stock transfers or replenishment orders that are within the pull-in horizon. TLB also sorts the stock transfers within this horizon according to their range of coverage.

  You can also define a coverage period for a product in the master data of the location product. TLB must only select as many deployment stock transfers of the product as are required to cover the requirement of this period. You can also exclude upsizing transport quantities for a product.

  TLB upsizes the transport quantities with the individual rounding values of the product until all transports are within the valid upper and lower parameter limits.

- **Reducing transport quanitities**
  TLB reduces the product quantities to be transported by prioritizing and reducing the deployment stock transfers or replenishment orders of the current period, taking into account their range of coverage.

The decision as to whether TLB upsizes or reduces transport quantities for remaining quantities is made based on a threshold value and decisions for changing the transport quantities. In SAP Inventory Collaboration Hub (SAP ICH), TLB can also base its decision on costs. You implement these settings in the transportation lane for the means of transport.

You can also fine-tune the settings for changing transport quantities by creating your own profile for the basic TLB settings in SAP ICH Customizing or Supply Network Planning (SNP) Customizing. When you upsize the transport quantities, for instance, you can specify that the transports are loaded up to the upper limit parameter.

6.9.3 Setting Up the Master Data for TLB

The TLB-specific master data described below provides an overview of the TLB settings.

Product Master Data

You can access the master data by selecting the menu options **SAP APO · Master Data · Product · Product**. You implement the following settings on the relevant tabs in the master data of the product or location product:

▶ **"Properties" tab** (see Figure 6.70)
The **Stacking Factor** field (**Measurements and Weights** field group) is relevant if you want to use the "Pallet Stacking" TLB parameter in the TLB profile. The stacking factor specifies the number of pallets of a product that can be stacked on top of each other by the system. With mixed pallets, the system uses the lowest stacking factor of all products.

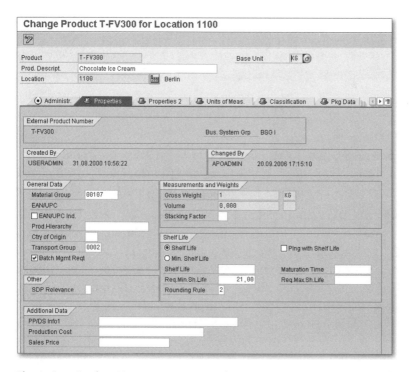

Figure 6.70 Product Master, "Properties" Tab

▶ **"Units of Meas."** tab (see Figure 6.71)

For the Weight, Volumes and Pallet Stacking (SNP-TLB only) parameters
that you use in the TLB profile, you must define a conversion of the units
of measure of the parameter in the basic unit of measure of the product.

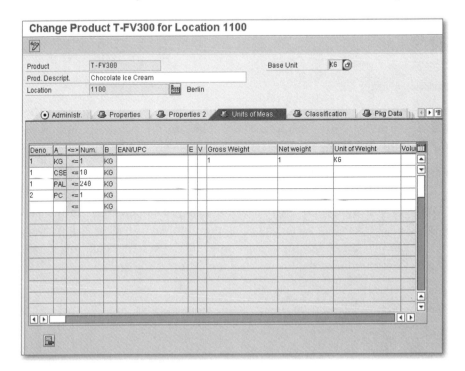

Figure 6.71 Product Master, "Units of Meas." Tab

▶ **"SNP 2"** tab (see Figure 6.72)

When you maintain the **VMI Purch.Group** field (**Other Data** field group),
the Transport Load Builder can distribute the TLB shipments to individual
orders in accordance with the purchasing group of the VMI customers.

SNP-TLB only takes into account the **ATD Receipt** and **ATD Issue** fields
(**Other Data** field group). You can enter category groups that you defined
in SNP Customizing under **Basic Settings • Maintain Category Groups**.
You can use the category groups to define which order categories contribute to the quantity available for grouping transports. If you don't enter a
value here, the system uses the value from the location master data, or it
uses the standard ATR and ATI category groups.

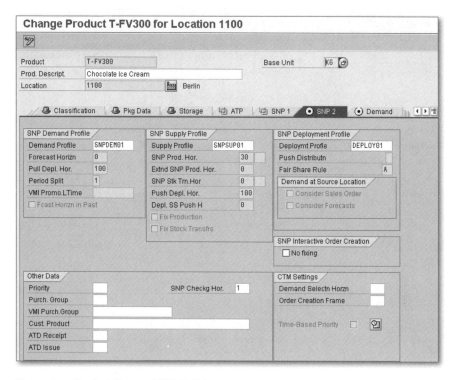

Figure 6.72 Product Master, "SNP 2" Tab

- **"Lot Size" tab** (see Figure 6.73)

  TLB uses the **rounding value** when grouping transport loads. However, it first includes the value that you defined in the transportation lane, that is, in the lot size profile (SNP) or set of transportation guidelines (SAP ICH) specified in the transportation lane. If you did not assign a value in the transportation lane, TLB uses the value entered here or the value 1. To ensure that SNP-TLB can use this rounding value, you must set the corresponding indicator in SNP Customizing under **Basic Settings • Maintain Global SNP Settings**. Otherwise, SNP-TLB only uses the rounding value from the transportation lane.

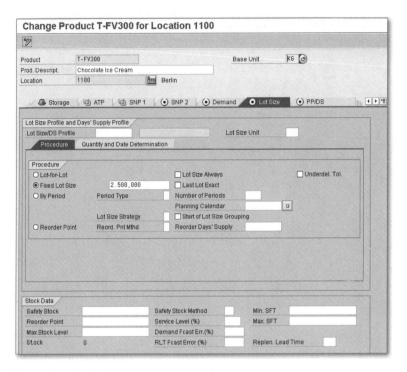

Figure 6.73 Product Master, "Lot Size" Tab

▶ **"GR/GI" tab** (see Figure 6.74)

TLB must only pack products of the same **HU Group (Responsive Replenishment** field group) together in the same handling unit (HU). This field is valid for pallets in the TLB, which does not use any handling units. Other fields to be maintained include:

▷ **Max. Coverage ("Responsive Replenishment" field group)**
TLB takes into account the maximum coverage period when upsizing transport quantities. The system only uses as many deployment stock transfers of the product as are required to cover requirements for this period.

▷ **Upsizing (upsizing transport quantities in the "Responsive Replenishment" field group)**
You specify whether transport quantities can be upsized for the location product, and whether this is allowed beyond the maximum coverage period.

▷ **Loading group ("Shipping" field group)**
TLB takes the loading group into account when it applies the loading method for loading by product.

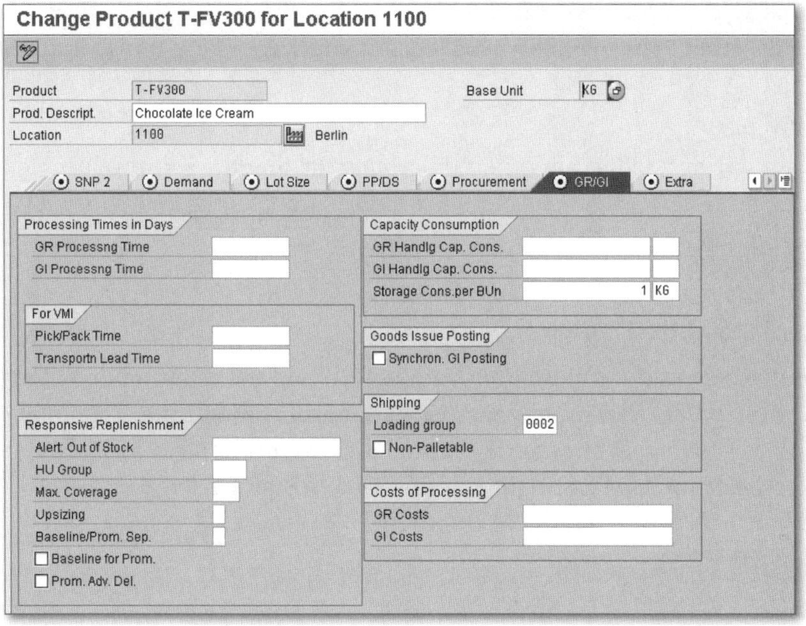

Figure 6.74 Product Master, "GR/GI" Tab (for TLB)

Location Master Data

You can access the master data by selecting the menu options **SAP APO · Master Data · Location · Location**. Go to the **SNP** tab in the master data of the location and implement the following settings there (see Figure 6.75).

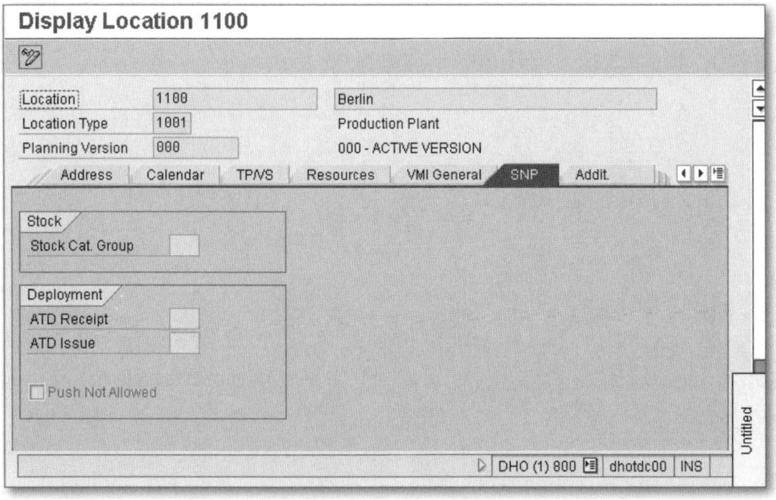

Figure 6.75 Location Master, "SNP" Tab

▶ **Initial screen, "Address" tab**

The **Location Type** field here is relevant if you want to use transportation zones.

▶ **"SNP" tab**

If you did not define any category groups for the location product (see product master), SNP-TLB uses the category groups specified under **ATD Receipt** and **ATD Issue**.

Master Data of the Transportation Lane

You can access the transportation lane by selecting the menu options **SAP APO • Master Data • Transportation Lane • Transportation Lane**. You implement the following settings for the means of transport in the master data of the transportation lane (see right half of screen in Figure 6.77):

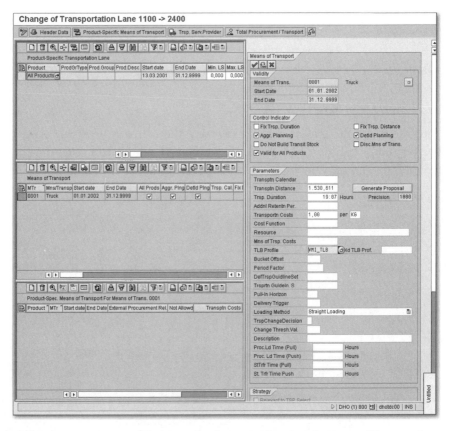

Figure 6.76 Master Data of Transportation Lane, "Product-Specific Means of Transport" Section

▶ **"Product-Specific Means of Transport"** section (see Figure 6.77)
TLB only considers the **Lot Size Profile** field (**Min. LS** and **Max. LS**—lot size profile transportation lane). You can specify a profile here that you previously created in SNP Customizing under **Basic Settings • Profiles • SNP Lot Size Profiles (Transportation Lane)**. TLB uses the rounding value defined in this profile (see product master, **SNP 2** tab).

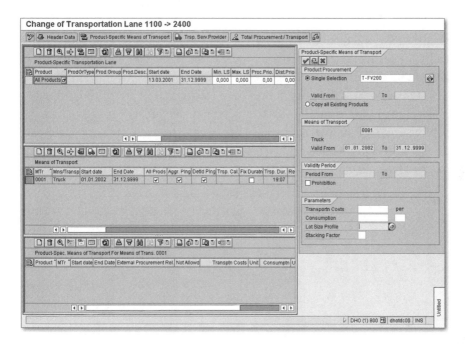

Figure 6.77 Master Data of Transportation Lane, "Means of Transport" Section

▶ **"Means of Transport" section**

▷ **TLB Profile**
You must assign a TLB profile that you previously created.

▷ **Loading Method**
Specify whether you want TLB to use the loading method for loading by product or for uniform loading.

▷ **Pull-In Horizon**
TLB uses the pull-in horizon when it upsizes transport quantities.

▷ **TrspChangeDecision and Change Thresh.Val.**
In the **TrspChangeDecision** field (the basis of a transportation decision), you define how TLB calculates the value that it uses to change a transport quantity. The system compares the calculated basic value

with the value that you specified in the **Change Thresh.Val.** field as a threshold value for changing a transport quantity. It then upsizes or reduces the transport quantity.

Executing TLB and Checking the Results

You can start the Transport Load Builder as a background job or from the interactive TLB planning. After you perform the TLB run, you can display the results in the interactive TLB planning and then change the transports manually. To do this, select the menu options **SAP APO · SNP · Planning · Interactive SNP Planning**, choose the corresponding materials in the shuffler and then select the **TLB Planning** button (see Figure 6.1). A list of the generated TLB shipments (see middle part of screen in Figure 6.78) as well as the deployment stock transfers that have not been processed (see right-hand part of screen in Figure 6.78) are then displayed and you can remove deployment stock transfers from the TLB shipments or add new ones to these transports.

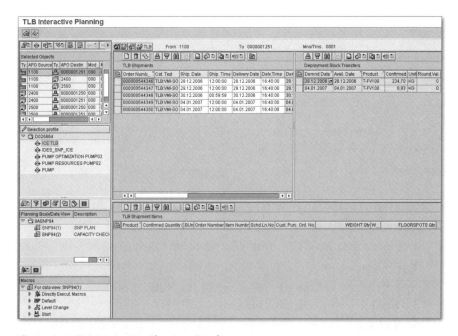

Figure 6.78 TLB Interactive Planning, Results

You can also display the results of the TLB run in the Application Log generated during the run.

6.10   Aggregated SNP Planning

Aggregated planning within Supply Network Planning (SNP) supports planning scenarios where you perform heuristic-based or optimization-based planning at the level of the header location product of a location product hierarchy. You then disaggregate the planning results on the individual subproducts of this two-tier hierarchy. You can use this type of planning for:

▶ Improving performance

▶ Simplifying the planning process

▶ Simplifying the supply chain model to be planned (option to plan larger models)

▶ Making planning decisions at aggregated level (such as selecting sources of supply, taking into account capacities or defining lot sizes)

After the SNP planning run and the SNP disaggregation, you can display and change the data in the interactive SNP planning. You can also display the resource consumption at header and subproduct level in the capacity view of the interactive planning and perform capacity leveling for the resources of the subproducts.

6.10.1   Prerequisites for Aggregated Planning

You can use the following standard planning books to perform aggregated planning in Supply Network Planning (SNP):

▶ For aggregated planning and planning with aggregated resources, SAP provides the 9ASNPAGGR standard planning book along with the SNP-AGGR(1) and SNPAGGR(2) data views based on standard planning area 9ASNP02. This planning area and the planning book contain the key figures required for aggregated planning as well as the assignment of key figure attributes of the **Aggregation** indicator, for example, and of key figure functions 9001 to 9026. The **Aggregation** indicator specifies whether the aggregated value or the normal value is calculated and displayed at the level of header location product in a key figure. The indicator also controls whether the value is retained or deleted at subproduct level after the aggregation. However, you can also create your own planning area and planning book based on the standard planning area and standard planning book.

▶ If you use the 9ASNP02 standard planning area, it has already been assigned hierarchy structures by SAP. You establish the basis for the hierarchies that you create yourself. Nevertheless, you can also create your own hierarchy structures for location products, resources, and production process models (PPMs) or production data structures (PDS) and assign these to the planning area that you use (**Aggregated Planning** tab).

▶ The 9ASNPAGGR standard planning book also contains the NETDM auxiliary key figure that is used by SNP disaggregation as the basis for determining product requirements. The system calculates the net requirements saved in this key figure at subproduct level using the **Net Requirements (Disaggregation)** macro while taking into account the warehouse stock. Rather than considering the requirements from earlier periods in this case (**Supply Shortage** key figure), the system instead only takes into account requirements as of the period in which the disaggregated value is available. If you want another calculation of the product requirement for the SNP disaggregation, you can also create your own requirements key figure as an auxiliary key figure for the planning book and you can calculate the net requirements using a macro. Assign the key figure function 9010 (**Aggregated Planning: Disaggregation Requirement**) to this key figure.

The following prerequisites must be met in relation to master data and the Customizing settings for the aggregated planning:

▶ You must implement the master data settings and other settings required for executing the SNP heuristic or SNP Optimizer. You must also consider special features when defining master data for the aggregated planning .

▶ You must specify the value **Delete at Subproduct Level** in SNP Customizing by selecting the menu options **Basic Settings** • **Maintain Global SNP Settings** in the **Aggr: Old Orders** field (this only applies for the sample process described under Aggregated Planning—see Step 4). If you want to use order groups, you must also define the value **Use Order Group** in the **Aggr: Order Group** field. The system takes the order group into account for the aggregation and disaggregation. You can also determine the connection between the orders at header and subproduct level as well as the connection between the individual orders at subproduct level. To do this, you can use the order group after the data has been disaggregated from header to subproduct level.

▶ You must release the forecast data from Demand Planning (DP) or from an OLTP system to the subproduct level in SNP. Planning data must be at subproduct level for aggregated planning.

6.10.2 Aggregated Safety Stock Planning

As part of aggregated planning in Supply Network Planning (SNP), you can perform safety stock planning based on aggregated data as a preliminary stage of the actual SNP planning. Since the safety stock is planned at the level of header location product, all the required data such as master data, requirements data, and historical data must also be at this level. You can aggregate some of this data automatically from sublevel to header level; however, you can also prepare this data at header level.

Below we describe which data you can aggregate and which settings you must implement for this aggregation.

Standard Safety Stock Planning

You can aggregate master data and requirements data for standard safety stock planning at aggregated level as follows:

▸ **Safety stock and safety days' supply**
You define this data on a time-independent basis in the master data of the location product, or on a time-dependent basis in the interactive SNP planning. At the level of header location product in the master data of the location product hierarchy, you can specify that the system aggregates the data automatically from the level of sublocation products to the level of header location product (**Agg. S.Days'Supply** and **Agg. S.Stock** fields). You can use different methods such as a mean value and a total, for example, for the aggregation. For the system to be able to aggregate the time-dependent data automatically, you must save this data in time series key figures in the SAP liveCache. The data is only aggregated temporarily; therefore, the aggregated data is not saved permanently. The aggregated data is only available for the SNP planning procedure, SNP heuristic, SNP Optimizer, and for the SNP mode of Capable-to-Match planning (CTM). Production Planning and Details Scheduling (PP/DS) and the PP/DS mode of CTM planning cannot access the data. You must manually prepare the data at the level of header location product for these applications.

▸ **Requirements Data**
The requirements data is used by the safety stock methods that are based on the safety days' supply (SZ, SM, MZ and MM). You make this data available in an order key figure in the SAP liveCache. On the **Key Figures** tab in the planning area, you can specify that the data saved in the key figure is automatically aggregated from the level of the sublocation product

to the level of the header location product. Define a value of 1 or 2 in the **Aggregation** field for this purpose.

▶ **Safety Stock Methods**
You cannot aggregate this master data automatically, in other words, you must define this data for the header location product. If you want to plan data both at aggregated and detailed level in an SNP planning process, you should define the safety stock methods in exactly the same way at both levels. This is not necessary if you only plan at aggregated level because the system only uses the data of the header location product.

Enhanced Safety Stock Planning

You can aggregate demand forecast data and historical data as follows for enhanced safety stock planning at aggregated level:

▶ **Demand Forecast Data**
The planner makes the demand forecast data available in an order key figure in the SAP liveCache . On the **Key Figures** tab in the planning area, you can specify that the data saved in the key figure is automatically aggregated from the level of the subproduct to the level of the header location product. Define a value of 1 or 2 in the **Aggregation** field for this purpose.

▶ **Historical Data**
The planner makes the historical requirements data and the data for replenishment lead times (RLT) available in time series key figures in the SAP liveCache. At the level of the header location product in the master data of the location product hierarchy, you can specify that the system aggregates the data automatically from the level of sublocation products to the level of header location product (**Hist.Data Req.** and **Hist.Data RLT** fields). The data is aggregated by periodically accumulating the demand forecasts or actual requirements, or by periodically calculating mean values of the RLT forecasts or actual RLT.

▶ **Master Data of Location Product**
You cannot automatically aggregate the master data of the service level, target days' supply and forecast errors, or the safety stock methods; you must define this master data for the header location product.

6.10.3 Single-Level Assignment of Receipts and Requirements

Before you perform aggregated planning in Supply Network Planning (SNP), you can use this function to assign receipts, which are directly assigned to a location product with a transportation lane, to the corresponding requirements. This enables you to prevent the system from assigning receipts to incorrect requirements during the aggregated planning, since detailed information will no longer be available at aggregated level.

A single-level assignment means that the system only uses the receipts from a level of the distribution network.

The system takes the aggregated receipt and requirements situation into account for SNP planning at aggregated level. If the available receipts were not already assigned to the corresponding requirements at subproduct level, the system may use the receipt for a specific sublocation product to cover the requirement for another sublocation product. The system does not subsequently create a new receipt that could cover the requirement of the sublocation product after the disaggregation. For instance, the receipt for a red T-shirt could therefore cover the requirement for a blue T-shirt.

To prevent this type of scenario, you can perform a single-level assignment of receipts and requirements at subproduct level before the aggregation. The system first checks the transportation lanes assigned directly to the location product for available receipts. It then creates fixed SNP stock transfers that can be used in the aggregated SNP planning run and cannot be deleted.

Since this is a single-level assignment, it can fail if the receipts are not available in the source of supply for external procurement that is assigned directly to the location product.

6.10.4 SNP Disaggregation

You can execute this function as part of aggregated planning in Supply Network Planning (SNP). The heuristic-based or optimization-based planning, performed on the level of the header location product, and the results are disaggregated to the level of individual subproducts. Both the header location product and the subproduct belong to the same product location hierarchy.

The SNP disaggregation disaggregates the planning result, which was saved in the key figures **Distribution Receipt (Planned)**, **Distribution Requirement (Planned)**, **Production (Planned)** or **Dependent Requirement,** on the individual subproducts. After the disaggregation, the aggregated value for the header location product is displayed in the key figures **Aggregated Distribution Receipt** or **Aggregated Distribution Requirement (Planned)** and **Aggre-**

gated **Production (Planned)** or **Aggregated Dependent Requirement** in the interactive SNP planning. The disaggregated value for the individual subproducts is displayed again in each case in the non-aggregated key figures, such as, **Distribution Receipt (Planned),** and so on (when you select the individual subproduct).

When you right-click to see the detailed view for the aggregated key figures, a list of the orders that the system created for the subproducts of the header product is displayed. You can change this order data.

Disaggregation Methods

You can choose between two disaggregation methods and you can also combine the methods.

▶ **Disaggregation By Requirements**
The values are disaggregated from header product level to subproduct level in accordance with the principles of fair share distribution or push distribution, which also use the deployment. If demand exceeds supply, with fair share distribution the system distributes the supply evenly to the individual subproducts according to their requirements. The procedure is similar for push distribution, but where supply exceeds demand in this case. The SNP disaggregation determines the disaggregation requirement, that is, the requirement of the subproducts, based on the NETDM auxiliary key figure or on a user-defined auxiliary key figure. The system uses the **Net Requirement (Disaggregation)** macro to calculate the net requirement saved in the NETDM key figure, taking into account the warehouse stock. Rather than considering the requirements from earlier periods in this case (**Supply Shortage** key figure), the system only looks at the requirements starting with the period that contains the value to be disaggregated.

▶ **Disaggregation By Quota Arrangement**
The values from header product level to subproduct level are disaggregated by quota arrangement that you defined for the subproducts. You define these quota arrangements either on a time-independent basis in the master data of the product hierarchy or location product hierarchy, or on a time-dependent basis in a time series key figure. You specify the time series key figure in the settings for the disaggregation. You can either use an existing (previously unused) key figure of your planning area, or you can create a new key figure and assign it to your planning area and plan-

ning book. For more information, refer to the administration details of the planning area.

▶ **Combining the Methods**
You select the **Disaggregation By Quota Arrangement** method and specify a horizon. For orders within the horizon, the system performs disaggregation by requirements. For orders outside the horizon, the system performs disaggregation by quota arrangement. This is useful if you want to have more precise requirement information for a short-term period than for a later period.

Disaggregation Modes

You can define how the system processes the orders within a period (bucket) during the disaggregation. The following disaggregation modes are available:

▶ **Period-Oriented (Bucket-Oriented) Disaggregation**
Within a period, the system accumulates all order quantities of orders at header product level that have the same source of supply, and it disaggregates this total quantity on the subproducts. The system uses the minimum lot sizes and the rounding values on the total quantity of a period in this case.

▶ **Order-Oriented Disaggregation**
The system individually disaggregates all orders that are available at header product level on the subproducts. It uses the minimum lot sizes and rounding values on the order quantity of each individual order. When orders are created at subproduct level, the order-oriented disaggregation mode creates a unique reference to the source order at header product level. This reference is identified by the order group number, which is displayed in the detail view of the interactive planning for the orders so you can use it to identify what the orders relate to in each case. To do this, however, you must have specified in SNP Customizing that the system can use the order group. You can also change the order group number for an order and, in doing so, assign the order to a different order group. Data such as firming indicators and availability dates are subsequently adjusted automatically to the data of the order group.

Planning Scope

When you perform the disaggregation in aggregated planning, there are two options you can use:

- ▶ **Location Disaggregation**
  The value saved at header product level is only disaggregated for the selected products in the selected locations.

- ▶ **Network Disaggregation**
  The value saved at header product level is automatically disaggregated in all the locations of the distribution network that contain the selected header product and subproducts.

If you determined the MRP levels before you performed a network or location disaggregation, the system automatically processes the locations in a specific sequence in order to calculate the disaggregation requirements accurately. The system starts with the location that represents the end of the supply chain and where the requirement is contained at subproduct level (e.g., a distribution center).

Period of Disaggregation

You can define a special disaggregation horizon. This means you can specify the period when the system reads the aggregated orders at header product level and creates the disaggregated orders at subproduct level. The period begins on the start date of the disaggregation.

The SNP disaggregation, SNP heuristic, and SNP Optimizer take into account the following SNP horizons (periods) of the header location product:

- ▶ SNP production horizon
- ▶ Extended SNP production horizon
- ▶ SNP stock transfer horizon

For this reason, you should always perform the SNP disaggregation on the same day as the SNP planning run (heuristic or optimizer). Otherwise, the receipts generated in the planning run could move into horizons where the system can no longer disaggregate them. There is however one exception here—if you enter a start date for the disaggregation (or this is specified by a user exit). The horizons in this situation are ignored for the disaggregation.

Deleting Orders at Header Level

You can implement a setting to specify how the system should proceed with the orders at the level of header location product after the disaggregation. These are the values that were saved in the key figures **Distribution Receipt** or **Distribution Requirement (Planned)** and **Production (Planned)** or **Dependent Requirement**. You can specify that the system deletes, reduces, or does not change the orders. Note the following in this case:

▶ **Orders Are Reduced**
The system reduces the orders at header product level by the sum of the disaggregated orders at subproduct level in the relevant period. If you defined different rounding values or minimum lot sizes for the subproducts and the header product in the product master data, a residual value may remain. This residual value is then displayed in the key figures **Distribution Receipt** or **Distribution Requirement (Planned)** and **Production (Planned)** or **Dependent Requirement** in the interactive planning.

▶ **Orders Are Not Changed**
The values that were saved in the key figures **Distribution Receipt** or **Distribution Requirement (Planned)** and **Production (planned)** or **Dependent Requirement** are retained. The system subsequently includes these values when it calculates the total receipts or total requirement, and therefore calculates these values twice. This can cause problems at a later stage when the data is processed further. For instance, problems may occur in other locations.

The system deletes or reduces the orders in each case in the disaggregation horizon. The option to retain orders should be used primarily for simulation purposes.

Log

The system creates an application log when you perform SNP disaggregation in the background. This log includes detailed information on the disaggregated planned orders and stock transfers.

6.10.5 SNP Aggregation

After aggregated planning has been performed in Supply Network Planning (SNP) and a subsequent SNP disaggregation has been completed, you can use this function to aggregate the created stock transfers and planned orders again at header level. This can be useful, for example, if you want to change certain location products at header level. You can then perform another disaggregation.

You can only use this function for SNP planned orders and SNP stock transfers. You cannot use this function for stock transfers and planned orders of the subcontracting and delivery schedule type, or for product substitution orders.

Aggregation Process

The system uses the following aggregation processes, depending on whether the orders have an order group number:

▶ **Orders With an Order Group Number**
The system combines the orders according to their order group and aggregates all suborders of an order group into a header order of the same order group. As a prerequisite, you must have made the relevant setting in SNP Customizing to specify that order groups can be used. The order group number for the orders is displayed in the detail view of the interactive planning.

▶ **Orders Without an Order Group Number**
If the orders don't have an order group number (i.e., if in accordance with the Customizing setting, you don't use order groups or if these are orders that were not created by SNP), the system groups these orders according to the period and the source of supply.

You can change the header order after the aggregation and disaggregate the changes again on the suborders with the SNP disaggregation. If you want to ensure that the system uses the reference (which was created by the order group) again for the disaggregation, select the order-oriented disaggregation mode. If you performed the aggregation according to the period and source of supply, you can create a parallel process by selecting the period-oriented disaggregation. For more information on disaggregation modes, see Section 6.10.4.

For the aggregation, the system uses the lot sizes defined for the header location product, provided these lot sizes don't conflict with the aggregation. Otherwise, the system ignores the lot sizes. This is the case, for example, if the sublevel quantity is 180 and the lot size at header level is 100.

Planning Scope

When you perform aggregated planning, you can execute a location or network aggregation:

▶ **Network Aggregation**

The system aggregates the orders for the selected products in all the locations of the distribution network that contain the products. The order in which the processing is performed is based on the logic used in the SNP network heuristic.

▶ **Location Aggregation**

The system aggregates only those orders for the selected products in the selected locations.

To make specific changes, for example, you can also use the aggregation, but only on a particular header location product.

Aggregation Period

You can define a special aggregation horizon. This means that you can specify a period when the system reads the orders at subproduct level and creates the aggregated orders at header product level. The period begins on the start date of the aggregation.

You can also define a time delay. The horizon will then only begin after this time delay, which is calculated from the start date. The system does not take into account any other horizons, such as SNP production horizons and SNP stock transfer horizons.

Deleting Orders at Sublevel

You can specify how the system should proceed with the orders available at sublevel after the aggregation. The options here are either to delete the orders, or to not change the orders. The default setting is to delete the orders. If you specify that the system should not change the orders, the system copies these orders during the aggregation. You should only use this setting for simulation purposes, since the order quantities and resource consumption are duplicated in this case. The system deletes each order in the aggregation horizon.

Log

The system creates an application log when you perform SNP aggregation in the background. This log includes detailed information on the aggregated planned orders and stock transfers.

6.11 Product Interchangeability in SNP Planning

In Supply Network Planning (SNP), the interchangeability of products is examined both for heuristic-based planning and optimization-based planning. Therefore, in the SNP planning run, you can transfer requirements for a product, which is to be discontinued, to a follow-up product, or you can use existing stock for a product to cover the requirement for the follow-up product.

SNP supports the following types of product interchanges:

▸ **Discontinuation of products**

▸ **Supersession chain**

Different forms of supersession chains are possible in SNP, for example:

▹ A → B ↔ C

▹ A → B → A (e.g., for promotional measures such as promotions)

▹ A → B → C → D → A → B → C → D (e.g., for seasonal product changes)

The arrows above represent the direction of interchangeability of the products. You can interchange products in a forward direction (→) or in a full direction (↔).

▸ **Form-Fit-Function Class (FFF class)**

In order to take into account the product interchangeability for SNP planning, you must use the standard 9ASNP_PS planning book with the PROD_SUBST data view. This planning book contains the required key figures **Substitition Requirement** and **Substitution Receipt** and a modified macro (which takes these key figures into account) for calculating the stock balance. You can also create your own planning book based on the standard planning book.

The SNP planned orders and stock transfers generated during the planning are transferred into a connected SAP ERP system; however, you cannot transfer the SNP product substitution orders also created and linked to these orders. In other words, the product substitution data during the SNP planning cannot be displayed in the SAP ERP system. Nevertheless, you can integrate the SNP product substitution data with SAP ERP via Production Planning and Detailed Scheduling (PP/DS).

The following section describes examples of the different options you can use to interchange products in SNP.

6.11.1 Discontinuation of Products

A product (A) is replaced by a follow-up product (B) at a certain time. All requirements that exist for this product are transferred to the follow-up product in the planning run as of this date, which was defined as the valid-from date in the master data for the product interchangeability. You can specify that existing stock from A can still be consumed by setting the **Consume** indicator for A in the master data for the product interchangeability. You can also specify a date up to which stock from A is still to be used.

If the system determines a requirement for A during the planning run and if it establishes that A is no longer valid, the system creates a receipt (an SNP product substitution order) for A in the **Substitution Receipt** key figure to offset the requirement for A. The system also creates a requirement for B in the **Substitution Requirement** key figure to transfer the requirement to B. The requirement for B will then be covered as normal by the planning run (e.g., by creating an SNP planned order in the **Production (Planned)** key figure). If you set the **Consume** indicator for A, stock from A can also be used after the discontinuation date to cover the requirement for A until it is depleted or until the specified consumption date has been reached.

6.11.2 Supersession Chain

A product (A) is replaced by a follow-up product (B) at a certain time. In the planning run, requirements for A are transferred to B as of this date. However, requirements for B cannot be transferred to A because you selected the *Forward Interchangeability* direction for A. Product B is then replaced by product C at a later date. Requirements for B are transferred to C as of this date. Since the *Full Interchangeability* direction was specified for B, requirements for C are also covered with excess warehouse stock from B.

To replace A with B, the system first proceeds as described in Section 6.11.1. If the system establishes that there is a requirement for B and B is no longer valid, it creates a substitution receipt for B to offset the requirement for B. The system also creates a substitution requirement for C to transfer the requirement to C. If the system determined a requirement for C and had already detected that there is still surplus stock for B, it creates a substitution receipt for C and a substitution requirement for B. The system first uses the surplus stock from B to cover the requirements for B up to the next consumption date. The system only covers requirements from C if there is still stock available from B.

6.11.3 Form-Fit-Function Class (FFF Class)

Various products that do not differ regarding all of their technically relevant properties are grouped in an FFF class and FFF subgroup (based on a specific location). Only the product of the FFF subgroup identified as the leading product may be procured. In SNP, all requirements that exist for the other products of the FFF subgroup are transferred to the leading product. If there is insufficient stock available for the leading product, the stock of the other products of the FFF subgroup is used. The leading product is only procured (produced in-house or procured externally) if none of the products have sufficient stock.

If the system determines a requirement for a product other than the leading product and this product does not have sufficient stock, the system creates a substitution receipt for this product to offset the requirement. The system also creates a substitution requirement for the leading product to transfer the requirement to this product.

6.11.4 Special Features When Using the SNP Optimizer

Besides the details mentioned above, the following special features still apply when you use the SNP Optimizer:

▶ The Optimizer generally makes its decisions based on the costs defined for the supply chain model (e.g., costs for storage, transportation, production, and procurement). The Optimizer always identifies the most cost-effective solution.

▶ The Optimizer does not calculate any costs for interchanging one product with another product in the same location.

▶ Unlike the heuristic, the Optimizer does not just look at the product in one location, but in all locations of the model.

The following example shows how these special features can affect the interchangeability of products:

Example

Product A in location C is to be replaced by product B in location C. There is no more stock for product A in location C. If a requirement were now received for product A, the SNP heuristic would transfer the requirement to product B. However, the Optimizer checks whether there is still stock available for product A in other locations of the model.

If there is still sufficient stock in location D, for example, the Optimizer checks the costs associated with a stock transfer of product A from location D to location C. If this is the most cost-effective solution (because the storage costs in D are higher than the transportation costs to C, for example), the Optimizer plans the transfer of stock from D to C. The requirement for product A is then covered by the transferred stock.

6.12   Transferring SNP Planning Results

6.12.1   Releasing SNP Planning to Demand Planning

You can use this function to release the final SNP plan back to demand planning again to ensure that the demand planner can compare the unconstrained demand plan with the constraint-based SNP plan. You also use this report if you want to perform sales and operations planning (SOP).

In a technical sense, the report is used to transfer data that was saved in orders into time series. This is necessary, since the data used in sales and operations planning must be saved in time series. You must therefore transfer the relevant order categories (from Supply Network Planning) into the corresponding time series key figures (in SOP).

6.12.2   Converting SNP Orders for Production Planning and Procurement into PP/DS Orders

If, in production planning and detailed scheduling (PP/DS), you want to plan in detail receipts that you created with Supply Network Planning, you must convert the SNP orders into PP/DS orders. This conversion involves the system generating PP/DS orders from SNP orders and then deleting the SNP orders. You can use the following options for converting orders:

▶ Use mass conversion to convert all SNP orders that begin in the PP/DS horizon or in a larger conversion horizon.

▶ In interactive planning, you can convert specific individual SNP orders that are inside or outside the PP/DS horizon.

▶ Implement the conversion within a planning version. When creating the PP/DS orders, the system takes into account the current propagation area.

Procurement Quantity Calculation

To determine the procurement quantities of the PP/DS orders from the receipt quantity of an SNP/CTM order, PP/DS calculates the procurement quantity ("lot creation") for the conversion. There are different options available for this purpose. For example, you can implement a 1:1 conversion, or you can determine the procurement quantities again, independently of SNP using the lot size settings from the location product master.

Determining the Source of Supply

The sources of supply that PP/DS uses to create PP/DS orders depends on the procedure you select. You have the following options:

▶ PP/DS determines the sources of supply independently of SNP using the automatic PP/DS function for determining sources of supply.

▶ PP/DS determines the source of supply from the SNP order to be converted.

Order Status

In the settings, you can specify the status that you want the system to use to create the PP/DS orders. You can use the following options in this case:

▶ The PP/DS orders are assigned the **Output Firmed** indicator. You can only manually change the receipt quantities of PP/DS orders with the **Output Firmed** indicator.

▶ The system sets the conversion indicator for the PP/DS orders. Immediately after the orders are transferred to a connected SAP ERP system, the system automatically converts planned orders and purchase requisitions with a set conversion indicator into production orders or purchase orders.

If you perform the conversion in active planning version 000, the system runs conversion checks (e.g., an ATP check) defined in the conversion rule before it sets the conversion indictor. The system only sets the conversion indicator if the checks for the PP/DS order are completed successfully without any errors.

Scheduling PP/DS Orders

If you set forward scheduling, the system proceeds by default from the start date of the first activity of the SNP/CTM order. With backward scheduling, the system proceeds by default, from the end date of the period that contains the availability date of the SNP order to be converted.

You can specify a safety time for the backward scheduling. The system then begins the backward scheduling at a correspondingly earlier date rather than at the end of the period.

6.13 Summary

In this chapter, you were introduced to the concept of performing and optimizing demand planning with SAP APO. You learned about the three planning methods in Supply Network Planning in detail and you should now be able to select and use these methods for your own requirements. In addition, you now know what safety stock planning means and how you can use this method of planning. Finally, you learned how to plan deliveries to customers using deployment and the Transport Load Builder.

Demands on supply chains are increasing; they must be able to adapt flexibly and within hours or even minutes to changes in the market. This is where the integration of SAP Supply Chain Management (SAP SCM) with other systems, and its architecture, play an important role. This chapter will familiarize you with both aspects of Supply Chain Management.

7   SAP APO—Integration and Architecture

7.1   Integration with ERP Systems

SAP Supply Chain Management (SAP SCM) contains several components that formed separate systems in previous releases. In particular, SAP SCM 5.0 contains the SAP Advanced Planner and Optimizer (SAP APO) 5.0 component, and also includes the Supply Chain Event Management (SCEM) and Inventory Collaboration Hub (ICH) components.

SAP APO is a standalone SAP solution with its own release cycle. As part of SAP SCM, you can integrate it directly with an ERP system (SAP R/3, SAP R/3 Enterprise, or SAP ECC), SAP Business Intelligence, as well as with legacy systems or external systems. This ensures that all the required transaction data is transferred to the relevant systems and made available there. It also facilitates a complete integration and the retrieval of master data elements and data for warehouse stock and purchase orders, for example. This integration creates a continuous planning cycle where actual data (e.g., orders and deliveries) flows from an SAP ERP system into SAP APO and demand data or planned orders are transferred from Demand Planning (DP) to an SAP ERP system.

SAP provides the interfaces responsible for integrating the SAP ERP system with SAP APO through a corresponding plug-in. The standard interface between an SAP ERP system and SAP APO is called a Core Interface (CIF) and the interface modules that you use to implement a customized integration are known as BAPIs (Business Application Programming Interfaces). Both the CIF and the BAPIs are part of the plug-in. Figure 7.1 illustrates the integration of different SAP components in supply chain planning.

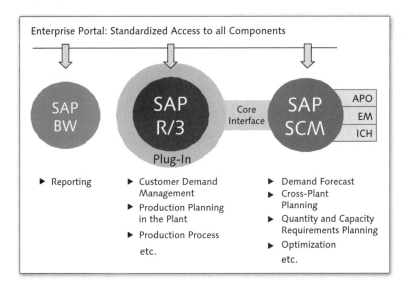

Figure 7.1 SAP Components in Supply Chain Planning (Source: SAP)

When you use SAP SCM, you have two different integration concepts for connecting ERP and APO systems together (see Figure 7.2):

- **The Core Interface (CIF)**
  to connect between APO and one or more SAP ERP systems

- **The Business Application Programming Interface (BAPI)**
  to connect APO and a non-SAP system

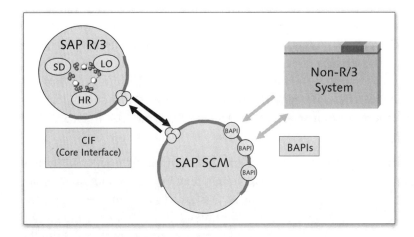

Figure 7.2 Integration Options (Source: SAP)

7.1.1 Plug-In (PI)

SAP R/3 plug-ins are interfaces that enable you to exchange data between one or more SAP R/3 systems and other SAP components. The SAP R/3 plug-ins supply the SAP components from SAP R/3 3.1I to SAP ERP Central Component (SAP ECC) 5.00 with transaction and master data in real time. They allow you to use SAP application components such as SAP APO together with other SAP components. SAP R/3 plug-ins are add-ons to SAP R/3 that you can use to run several SAP components simultaneously (see Figure 7.3).

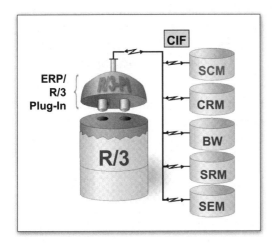

Figure 7.3 Plug-In Technologies for SAP ERP Systems (Source: SAP)

Most plug-ins are add-ons, that is, enhancements made to R/3 standard software by adding extra functions.

You can use the R/3 plug-in to supply different SAP components with transaction and master data. Not only does the CIF supply APO with initial data records (initial data transfer) in this way, for example, but using plug-ins also guarantees a continuous supply with all relevant data changes. R/3 can therefore be integrated with APO as of R/3 Release 3.1I.

To integrate SAP ERP and SAP APO easily, you need to install a relevant plug-in for the R/3 release. Note also that separate support packages are delivered for the plug-ins.

SAP R/3 plug-in 2004.1 is the last plug-in release delivered separately.

In future, new and enhanced interfaces for integrating SAP R/3, SAP R/3 Enterprise, and SAP ECC will no longer be delivered in the form of a separate add-on (SAP R/3 plug-in).

This means that:

- SAP ECC 6.00 and later releases will contain all required interfaces for technical integration with other SAP components that were previously part of the SAP R/3 plug-in.

- Customers who use SAP R/3 4.6C, SAP R/3 Enterprise 47x100 and 47x200, and SAP ECC 5.00 will receive additional integration interfaces in a support package for SAP R/3 plug-in 2004.1. This is included in their maintenance and will be synchronized with the future SAP Business Suite delivery. The delivery for 2005 was made in November 2005 with support package 10 of SAP R/3 plug-in 2004.1. This regulation applies only to customers with SAP R/3 plug-in 2004.1. Customers with SAP R/3 plug-in 2003.1 or older must upgrade to SAP R/3 plug-in 2004.1 or SAP ECC 6.00, if necessary.

- Customers who use SAP R/3 3.1I up to 4.6B will not receive any additional interfaces for new SAP component releases.

7.1.2   Core Interface (CIF)

As a subcomponent of the SAP R/3 plug-in, the Core Interface (CIF) is a real-time interface through which the initial data (initial transfer of data) as well as the APO system are supplied with data changes (change transfer). The CIF consists of the following parts:

- Integration model
- Active data channel
- Message serialization
- Event channel

The integration model contains the integration variants that are created as master data and transaction data in the CIF. This data has been selected from the SAP ERP system in advance and transferred to the APO system through an active data channel. The message serialization supports the communication (e.g., a change transfer of transaction data) of the systems through parallel channels. The function of the event channel is to accept change requests from the APO system. It also determines the recipient and controls the transfer technique (synchronous, asynchronous, BAPI).

Technically, an SAP ERP system is connected to an SAP APO system using a Remote Function Call (RFC) connection (see Figure 7.4). The data selected using the CIF is transferred through this connection. Not all the available master data and transaction data in the SAP ERP system is generally required for planning in SAP APO. By generating an integration model, you define which data objects in SAP ERP are selected from the total quantity of data for the transfer to SAP APO. The CIF enables and controls this internal data transfer between the SAP ERP and SAP APO systems.

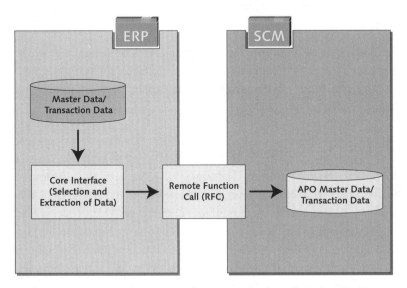

Figure 7.4 Integration of SAP ERP and APO Systems through CIF by RFC (Source: SAP)

The central tasks of the CIF include determining the source and target systems in complex system environments, supplying SAP APO with relevant master data and transaction data (e.g., bills of material and task lists), forwarding data changes automatically, and returning the planning results received to the executing system (SAP ERP system or an external system).

A special feature is the close linking of SAP APO to the SAP ERP system as already mentioned. This linking is made using prompt and error-tolerant communication technology. If, during the transfer, technical errors (e.g., a network is not connected) or application-based errors (e.g., the incorrect data is selected) occur when you transfer data using the SAP APO Core Interface, you should find the cause of the error, correct it, and transfer the data again. The data is transferred asynchronously through the SAP APO Core Interface (qRFC—queued Remote Function Call). This means that either the data from the sending system is first buffered and then transferred (outbound queue), or that it is transferred and buffered by the receiving system (inbound queue). Incorrect queues cause a data channel to become blocked and they prevent additional transfers.

SAP APO can use the RFC technology to implement planning in real time since changes, for example, to a sales order (where purchase order items are enhanced or an order is deleted) are registered within the shortest time in the APO system and a new planning run occurs. This difference between this technology and previous Advanced Planning & Scheduling (APS) systems is that information is processed more on a real-time basis rather than on a batch-oriented basis.

The special feature of maintaining data is that an SAP ERP system already in use is always the system that contains the master data and that only the APO master data, for which there is no corresponding data in the SAP ERP system, is saved separately in the liveCache.

7.1.3 Business Application Programming Interface (BAPI)

Business Application Programming Interfaces (BAPIs) are object-oriented interfaces that you can use to connect external systems to SAP APO. BAPIs are a part of SAP Business Objects that enable external systems to access SAP ERP functions through the Internet and using Component Object Model/Distributed Component Object Model (COM/DCOM) or Common Object Request Broker Architecture (CORBA). Data, processes, and integrated business chains are represented on an object-oriented basis through Business Objects (BO). A BO therefore means a business object such as a customer, vendor, order, restrictions, or item.

Therefore, SAP APO is no longer necessarily connected to the SAP ERP system but, by using BAPIs, it can instead also directly connect to any other ERP systems of third-party providers or can allow the standard CIF to be enhanced to meet a customer's individual requirements.

From a technical point of view, BAPIs are implemented as RFC-enabled function modules, that is, data is transferred asynchronously (between an R/3 system and an APO system, for example) using the definition of the source and target systems. BAPIs therefore represent a flexible alternative to support access through the Internet. There are currently over a thousand different BAPIs and their numbers continue to grow with each new development. The main programming languages used for providing this channel are C++, Java, Visual Basic, and so on.

7.2   Integration with SAP NetWeaver BI

A complete Business Information Warehouse (SAP NetWeaver BI, in former Releases SAP BW) is integrated into SAP APO. Together with the SAP live-Cache, this contributes to the processes for demand planning being executed efficiently. SAP APO uses the integrated SAP NetWeaver BI architecture for technical planning reasons. This means that the integrated SAP NetWeaver BI is designed for saving data relevant for planning and for creating simple reports. To create comprehensive reports, we recommend that you use a separate SAP NetWeaver BI system because a memory-intensive creation of reports could substantially reduce the speed and flexibility of the planning component for SAP APO.

SAP APO Demand Planning (SAP APO-DP) supports the use of InfoCubes, which have the same data structures as the InfoCubes used in SAP NetWeaver BI. This means that data can be exchanged easily between both applications. There are several benefits to this type of integration; for example, market research data such as data from AC Nielsen can be saved in SAP NetWeaver BI in this way. This data is then analyzed in SAP APO-DP to determine which data should be used for causal analyses. Consensus-based forecasts can then be created in SAP SCM Demand Planning and transferred to SAP NetWeaver BI. There, you can process forecasts for reports and ad-hoc evaluations that will contribute to the business objectives being implemented successfully. You can also use SAP NetWeaver BI to request data from several heterogeneous data sources.

InfoCubes are also used for integrated demand planning, marketing planning, requirements planning, and inventory planning. An InfoCube describes an integrated stock of plans. By defining planning books, you can display integrated data for demand planning, marketing planning, requirements planning, and inventory planning in planning tables and charts. You can also define threshold values to ensure that alerts are automatically created in the alert monitor if plans appear outside the user-defined tolerance limits. By integrating costs and prices into the InfoCubes, you can display the information sorted according to sales, costs, profit, and volumes.

7.3 Architecture and System Landscape

One of the foundations on which the IT architecture of all SAP SCM solutions is based is the secure, scaleable, reliable three-tier client-server architecture of SAP. This architecture consists of a presentation client, an application server, and a database server. A typical SAP SCM landscape comprises one or more OLTP systems, for example, SAP R/3, SAP R/2, or systems from other suppliers, and an SAP APO solution. The OLTP system can also act as an execution system in this case. SAP ERP is based on a three-tier client-server architecture. In addition to this architecture, you also need SAP liveCache to execute SAP APO.

The two central solutions—SAP Quick Sizer and SAP liveCache—will be explained in more detail in the following sections.

7.3.1 SAP Quick Sizer

The SAP Quick Sizer is an Internet-based tool that you can use to calculate the resources you require for SAP SCM quickly and simply. This tool was developed by SAP in close cooperation with its hardware partners and is made available to customers free of charge. You can use the Quick Sizer to turn business requirements into technical requirements. Based on the results determined by the Quick Sizer, you can select a system that matches both the budget and the business objectives of your company. The relevant questionnaire is available online and is based on current, business-oriented figures. The Quick Sizer calculates the expected workload on the CPU, disk space, and memory based on the estimated data throughput, and the number of users working with the different SAP SCM components. As part of the SAP GoingLive Check, SAP also checks the sizing of a SAP SCM system that is necessary for starting production successfully. Sizing methods and benchmarks for SAP SCM are available in the SAP Service Marketplace. Together with the Quick Sizer, which provides an initial approximate sizing of the SAP SCM solution, these methods support companies in finding the best size for their SAP SCM system.

7.3.2 SAP liveCache

The performance of a planning solution is critically important if users want to take advantage of the available information. The SAP liveCache is the core element of the processing functions in SAP APO. SAP liveCache is a database engine for management complex objects such as the Supply Chain Management solution of SAP: SAP APO. You must always be able to access and change large quantities of data for this type of solution. The relational database system was therefore enhanced to such a degree that the data structures and data streams (such as networks and relationships) can be mapped more easily and more efficiently. SAP liveCache works based on objects and, unlike MaxDB, operates exclusively with its data in the main memory of the database system for an optimum configuration.

Contrary to strategic planning, which uses historical data and analyses from the Business Information Warehouse, the emphasis for operational and tactical planning is on the up-to-date status of the available data. SAP liveCache guarantees this up-to-date status using a high-performance main memory with a very high computing power. Bottlenecks that may occur between a hard disk and a working memory when you transfer data are avoided, and you can implement extensive and complex calculations (planning runs) almost in real time. Data between an SAP ERP system, a non-SAP system, and SAP APO is exchanged through the OLTP (Online Transaction Processing).

The architecture of the system is based on ABAP, whose access is slower compared to C++; therefore, C++ was used as the programming language for the SAP liveCache. Consequently, the speed at which the data that is exchanged between the liveCache server and the liveCache in the main memory is accessed is a matter of nanoseconds.

Time-consuming planning runs can be updated as a batch process to prevent the performance of the online system from being affected. The planner can schedule the execution of a job for a specific time (e.g., over night or on the weekend) to ensure that large quantities of data can be processed by exception-based management. In this case, the planner simply has to check the alerts generated by the system and can then take any necessary measures.

7.4   Summary

The SAP APO Core Interface is the interface that enables data to be exchanged between SAP APO and the SAP ERP system. The SAP liveCache is a key component of the technical infrastructure and a prerequisite for implementing a SAP SCM scenario with SAP APO. SAP NetWeaver BI is a component of SAP APO that is used to better integrate the actual data relevant for the planning. For this reason, not only does SAP APO have a very modern technical Basis architecture, it also has a real-time interface to the ERP system, which is an essential planning tool. Its other integration components (e.g., SAP NetWeaver BI and BAPIs) only add to making SAP APO a very flexible instrument and the tool best equipped to deal with the varied aspects of Supply Chain Management.

This chapter provides an overview of the important steps you must follow to implement the SAP APO-DP and APO-SNP components successfully.

8 Implementation Process

8.1 Project Methodology

The procedure in the project is based on the methods developed by SAP for providing support when a system is installed: AcceleratedSAP (ASAP). The application components of ASAP are as follows:

- A procedure model (roadmap) with step-by-step instructions and recommendations for each activity
- Tools and examples, templates/forms, and checklists (e.g., for areas such as tests, end-user training, transport systems, data collection, SAPscript, and authorizations)
- SAP implementation tools as the basis for many activities, for example, configuring business processes
- Service and support products such as EarlyWatch, OSS, GoingLive Check

Figure 8.1 shows the ASAP Roadmap with its five phases:

1. Project Preparation
2. Business Blueprint
3. Realization
4. Final Preparation
5. Go Live & Support

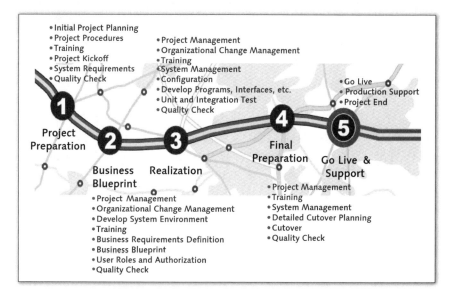

Figure 8.1 ASAP Roadmap

8.1.1 Project Preparation

The purpose of the project preparation is to define the general conditions for implementing the project successfully. The main activities required to do this include the following:

▶ Defining the goals and objectives of the project

▶ Establishing the project organization (personnel)

▶ Creating the project plan (time-frame)

▶ Determining the project standards (e.g., documentation standards, change request procedure)

▶ Implementing training for the project team

▶ Setting up the system landscape for the implementation

▶ Creating a communication plan for uniform communication for the project participants who are planning and implementing the kick-off meeting

8.1.2 Business Blueprint

In the Business Blueprint phase, you create a business blueprint that you want to implement with SAP Supply Chain Management (SAP SCM). First you develop the detail of the analysis results from the specification sheet and you evaluate the key processes and applications. Analysis workshops on the following topics are held in this phase:

► Central demand planning

► Forecast

► Safety stock planning

► Cross-plant inventory planning

► Production planning

► Cross-application coordination of subplans in a rolling, capacity-based demand planning

► Subcontracting

► Replenishment planning and distribution

► Estimated transportation planning

► Reporting and monitoring

The following topics are dealt with in these analysis workshops to detail the relevant subjects (e.g., Forecast):

► Process analysis

► Master data analysis

► System metrics

► System and application analysis

► Interface requirements

► Future requirements for the process and functions

The results of the workshops are documented in a log. At the end of this phase, the important requirements are documented and prioritized in detail for all relevant processes. This log is then used as the basis for the requirements for the solution.

You need the system metrics to estimate the subsequent system sizing, and to structure the design in such a way that you can ensure that the business processes are developed efficiently and in a user-friendly manner. The system metrics in the SAP Advanced Planner and Optimizer (SAP APO) environment must contain the following important information:

► Number of characteristic combinations, key figures, and planning versions in demand planning

► Number of locations/sites (plants, distribution centers, storage locations, vendors, customers, and so on)

- Number of sales orders each year for each business area
- Number of replenishment orders each year for each business area
- Number of products to be planned
- Number of BOM levels to be planned
- Number of capacities to be considered

The solution (also called the business blueprint) is then created. The requirements developed in the analysis phase are implemented into a combined uniform process and function design. To do this, the following activities are carried out:

- Process design is created
- Application and function design is created
- Integration design is created
- Solution is documented
- SAP APO prototype (optional) is created
- Authorization concept for SAP APO is created
- Archiving concept for SAP APO is created

You can use an SAP APO prototype to implement the solution clearly and to observe the consequences. Changes resulting from this analysis phase are incorporated into the solution iteratively. The process and function solution forms the basis for the next project phase, the Realization (Implementation) phase.

The completion of the Blueprint phase and the start of the realization phase that follows it represent the formal acceptance of the blueprint (or solution) by the customer. The key user of the customer accepts the processes, organizational structure, user interface design, interfaces, and migration designs (mapping logic), and the system metrics. From a technical point of view, the technical contact person must approve the user interfaces and the interface and migration designs. The technical contact person also approves the security and performance concept, the guidelines for developing, correcting and modifying data, the overall technical architecture and solution descriptions, and the user concept. The Realization phase only starts after the details of the previous phase have been accepted.

8.1.3   Realization

The purpose of this phase is to implement an SAP APO client into the development system for Customizing settings and to perform initial tests. During this phase, the predefined processes (Customizing) are configured and the system enhancements are developed (e.g., user exits, reports, forms, workflows). If necessary, required modifications are made, interface and migration programs are created, and test migrations are performed. Both the configuration and the development occur iteratively in individual interdependent (i.e., built upon each other) cycles. In addition, the test and training concepts created in the Blueprint phase are refined.

The quality of implementing the planned concept defined in the blueprint is checked using several user acceptance and integration tests.

The activities of this phase include the following:

▶ Configuring the Administrator Workbench and the Supply and Demand Planning (S&DP) administration

▶ Executing the Customizing for the basic and master data relevant for SAP-APO such as characteristic combinations in demand planning and the product master data and location master data in the Supply Network Planning (SNP) module, for example

▶ Implementing the processes/functions documented in the blueprint into SAP APO applications

▶ Implementing the system integration using the Core Interface (CIF) and, if necessary, BAPIs for connecting to external systems

▶ Setting up the test environment

▶ Integrating the first set of data of the relevant SAP APO master data and transaction data into the development and test system

▶ Testing functions and interfaces including the CIF monitoring

▶ Training the project team for the relevant SAP APO processes

▶ Setting up the live environment

▶ Organizing the system administration

The test scenarios and test organization should be documented to ensure that any errors that may occur can be traced and reproduced at any time and corrected. When the tests are being implemented, a knowledge transfer takes place between the external consultant and the customer's project team members on the one hand, and the customer's internal departments on the other.

While the SAP APO system is being configured, the project team members create the documentation and training materials for the end users.

8.1.4   Final Preparation

The goal of this phase is to complete the final preparation of a live SAP SCM system. To do this, the following steps are required:

▶ **Data is loaded into the live system**
  - ▷ CIF monitoring is carried out
  - ▷ liveCache operating concept is created

▶ **Live system is accepted**
  - ▷ Key users train the end users
  - ▷ Stress and mass tests are performed
  - ▷ Cutover planning and implementation is fulfilled (the sequence in which the system settings, programming scope, master data and transaction data are transferred into the live environment is defined here)
  - ▷ Customer signs off (approves) the fully installed system and the production start date and official activation of the live system are agreed on

8.1.5   Go Live & Support

The key users and external consultants must offer the end users professional support for a period of four weeks after a system has gone live. In this phase, the project is also officially handed over to the maintenance and support team and the project results are documented.

8.2   SAP Solution Manager

The individual project activities described in detail in the ASAP methodology are greatly supported by the SAP Solution Manager tool, which SAP recommends you use to support you with the implementation activities.[1] The SAP Solution Manager is available free of licensing costs and provides tools, contents, and procedures that can be used beyond the implementation itself, as well as across several systems for the productive operation of the system and

---

[1] For more information, see also Marc O. Schäfer, Matthias Melich: *SAP Solution Manager.* SAP PRESS 2007.

the continued improvement of SAP solutions. The connected SAP system landscape can therefore consist of any SAP solutions (e.g., SAP IS-Mill, SAP SCM, SAP NetWeaver BI) with their relevant subsystems (e.g., development, test, production, training, and migration systems).

The advantages of using the Solution Manager include the following:

▶ Central work platform for all project members

▶ Transparency in implementing and operating SAP solutions

▶ Integration of Knowledge Warehouse for storing documents

▶ Business process orientation beyond the SAP software lifecycle

▶ No licensing costs

▶ Contents can be reused for future projects

▶ Delivery of predefined contents (e.g., roadmaps) that can be updated regularly

The SAP Solution Manager can therefore be integrated into the project flow as follows (see Figure 8.2):

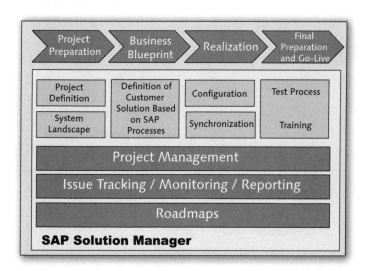

Figure 8.2 Integrating the SAP Solution Manager into the Individual Project Phases

The roadmaps delivered by SAP, which can be updated irrespective of the system, contain a phase-driven standard procedure in the delivery status for implementing the project functionally and technically, and for operating the system with links to corresponding accelerators. Project-specific roadmaps can be generated based on the standard roadmaps. The SAP Solution Manager provides graphic-based maintenance for the project-specific roadmaps and gives you an overview of the status of the particular roadmap.

▶ **Phase 1: Project Preparation**
   In the Project Preparation phase, you can define projects as templates for subsequent projects. You can enter corresponding administrative data for each project. The project definition in subsequent phases also allows you to display the project status and the period of the project. A description of the project-specific system landscape is also provided.

▶ **Phase 2: Business Blueprint**
   For the Business Blueprint phase, the SAP Solution Manager creates the tool for documenting cross-system business scenarios and processes, as well as the process steps in each system involved, including the graphical display of processes and templates that can be downloaded from the SAP Service Marketplace. Therefore the business process models that are delivered by SAP and can be updated, regardless of the system, logically represent the starting point for defining customer-specific business processes, which describe the business process implementations already available in the standard delivery of the system.

▶ **Phase 3: Realization**
   During the Realization phase, the SAP Solution Manager provides configuration guidelines for the standard business processes, help for the central configuration of the SAP systems, and tools for synchronizing Customizing between the systems. Moreover, the business process structure entered in the blueprint can be used to maintain documentation, test cases, Customizing, and customer-specific enhancements for the relevant business processes in the system. The test workbench, error messaging system, and status reporting support the implementation of the actual system test.

▶ **Phase 4: GoingLive Preparation and Go Live**
   In the GoingLive Preparation and Go Live phase, the SAP Solution Manager provides tools for maintaining documentation relating to business processes and end-user training materials (e-learning also). The messaging system can be used to establish a requirement for further development, which can be transferred to a controlled process for yet more development. During the Realization phase, services such as the GoingLive Check and EarlyWatch are available with the SAP Solution Manager.

8.3   Project Organization

8.3.1   Project Management

Before the project starts, a customer project manager and a representative must first be named among all participants involved to guarantee direct and effective communication between all parties. As a top project instance, this project management body must have the authority to make decisions to ensure that critical project situations can be addressed quickly and flexibly. Besides producing expert solutions to problems, the customer is also responsible for controlling as well as managing the project (i.e., ensuring that project prerequisites are maintained, progress is monitored, new organization measures are implemented, etc.).

The main roles of the customer project manager include the following:

▸ Defining the technical, specialist, and implementation strategy

▸ Creating the framework plan for the overall project

▸ Selecting appropriate project management tools

▸ Specifying project standards for the overall project

▸ Being responsible for the internal use of resources

▸ Providing the infrastructure required for the overall project

▸ Planning and monitoring dates, work involved, costs and change requests, as well as quality assurance at overall project level

▸ Ensuring that performance results are reviewed on time

▸ Providing risk management for the overall project

▸ Handling organizational change management for the overall project

▸ Clarifying problems across the project

▸ Being responsible for the project concept and for preparing management decisions

▸ Communicating with and providing information to the steering committee and implementing comprehensive decisions

▸ Planning and implementing meetings for project management

▸ Planning and implementing meetings for pilot project management

▸ Planning and implementing meetings for the decision-making body

▸ Planning and implementing meetings for the steering committee

8.3.2 Steering Committee

The steering committee is a steering and decision-making body consisting of representatives from management and project managers from the contract partners. As the steering and decision-making body, the steering committee makes fundamental decisions and exercises control functions. Those representing the steering committee must each have the authority to make decisions for the parties they represent in the steering committee; however, they must not be members of the project team. The steering committee's meetings are scheduled on a monthly basis. The main tasks of the steering committee include the following:

- Creating the goals and objectives of the project
- Accepting and controlling the project planning
- Accepting the milestone results and status reports
- Supporting project management
- Implementing higher-level decisions (in particular, change requests)
- Solving problems across the organization

8.3.3 Project Core Team

The core team, consisting of the customer's team and the external consultant, are required to plan and coordinate active support in each business area but also in other activities throughout the business.

A core team containing competent members with decision-making powers needs to be built. This team must include employees both from the DP area (see Section 8.3.6) and from the user department.

In particular, the tasks of the core team include the following:

- Defining the business processes and mapping them in the SCM system
- Customizing
- Providing end-user documentation and training
- Documenting the project
- Supporting the end user after the system goes live
- Specifying concepts for additional developments

8.3.4 Business Process Owner

The business process owner is responsible for one or more related business processes of a task area relating to planned processing based on the effort and quality involved.

The activities and areas of responsibility of the business process owner are defined as follows:

▶ Being responsible for assigned business processes and for ensuring that the objectives of the company are implemented in an efficient and economically justifiable manner
▶ Being responsible for mapping business processes correctly and fully within the SAP solution
▶ Customizing
▶ Being responsible for defining the planned requirements and related documentation and formulation
▶ Providing support when the planned processes are being created and defined in the course of the business blueprints being created
▶ Identifying weaknesses and risks within the mapped business processes
▶ Making decisions when selecting alternative approaches to solutions
▶ Specifying concepts for additional developments
▶ Setting up acceptance for the end users
▶ Being responsible for defining roles as part of the authorization concept
▶ Contributing towards defining test scenarios and test cases for the area of responsibility
▶ Implementing measures for change management in the user department
▶ Accepting the business blueprints
▶ Accepting the system solution

8.3.5 Key Users

Key users represent the user department and are the link between the process owners, end users, and project team members. Key users reduce the demands of the project work on the process owner and also specify the requirements of the user department for the system.

The activities and areas of responsibility of the key users are defined as follows:

▶ Bringing specialized knowledge to specific business processes and supporting the business process owner

▶ Providing support when the business blueprint is being created and when detailed requirements are being formulated

▶ Providing support for test phases and actively implementing test scenarios

▶ Refining the concepts for master data and document types in close cooperation with the external consultants

▶ Refining the concepts for migration and interfaces in close cooperation with the external consultants

▶ Preparing and implementing training for end users

▶ Contributing towards creating the user documentation

▶ Offering support when legacy data is being cleaned up

▶ Providing first-level support after a system has gone live

8.3.6 Data Processing Team

A data processing team must be formed to develop a data processing system (hardware, software, networks). This team must include primarily employees for the pure SAP Basis part of the project.

The main tasks of the data processing team include the following:

▶ Defining the hardware requirements similar to the system metrics and anticipating how the system will behave

▶ Developing procurement and installation processes

▶ Setting up the SAP APO pilot and live environments

▶ Organizing the technical administration of the system (data backup, recovery/restart, batch development, monitoring)

▶ Defining the user-specific reorganization and archiving

▶ Setting up and operating a transport and correction process that works

▶ Developing an optimum client-server architecture in close cooperation with the selected hardware manufacturer

▶ Programming interfaces on external systems from legacy systems and into the remaining legacy systems

▶ Planning and implementing release upgrades

▶ Importing, testing, and implementing Support Packages (enhancing the functions of existing SAP releases)

8.4   Summary

The key factors for a successful SAP APO project involve developing a good and structured project management process and selecting the right consulting partners. Using the ASAP Implementation Methodology, the SAP Solution Manager (which as a tool supports the implementation from start to finish) and the implementation experience honed by SAP consultants over many years means that implementing SAP APO into your system is no longer a laborious, difficult project. Rather, implementing SAP APO can now be accomplished efficiently and successfully.

Appendix

A   **Literature** 409

B   **List of Acronyms** 411

C   **Glossary** 415

D   **The Author** 433

A   Literature

Armstrong, J.: *Principles of Forecasting. A Handbook for Researchers and Practitioners*. Norwell 2001.

Ballou, R.: *Business Logistics Management*. London 1992.

Dickersbach, J. Th.; Keller, G.; Weihrauch, K.: *Production Planning and Control with SAP*. Bonn 2007.

Gardner, E. S.: *Forecasting with Exponential Smoothing: Some Guidelines for Model Selection*. In: Decision Sciences 11 (1980).

Gardner, E. S.: *The Trade-Offs in Choosing a Time Series Method*. In: Journal of Forecasting 2 (1983).

Hanke, J. E.; Reitsch, A. G.: *Business Forecasting*. Englewood Cliffs et al. 1995.

Harrison, P. J.: *Exponential Smoothing and Short-Term Sales Forecasting*. In: Management Science 13 (1967).

Holt, C. C.: *Forecasting Seasonals and Trends by Exponentially Weighted Moving Averages*. O.N.R. Memorandum No. 52, Carnegie Institute of Technology. Pittsburgh 1957. (Quoted after: Silver, E.A.; Peterson, R.: Decision Systems for Inventory Management and Production Planning. New York 1985.)

Hoppe, M.: *Inventory Optimization with SAP*. Bonn 2006.

Hoppe, M.: *Collaborative Planning and Development*. In: Zeitschrift Supply Chain Management Nr. 2/2003.

Jenkins, G. M.: *Practical Experiences with Modelling and Forecasting Time Series*. St. Helier 1979.

Kaplan, R. S.; Norton, D. P.: *The Balanced Scorecard. Translating Strategy into Action*. Boston 1996.

Makridakis, S.: *Forecasting, Planning and Strategy for the 21st century*. New York 1990.

Makridakis, S.; Wheelwright, S.; Hyndman, R.: *Forecasting, Methods and Applications*. New York 1998.

Martin, A. J.: *Distribution Resource Planning*. New York 1995.

SAP AG: *Advanced Planner and Optimizer, Functions in Detail*. Edition 2003.

SAP AG: *SAP Advanced Planner and Optimizer, Production Planning and Detailed Scheduling*. Edition 2000.

SAP AG: *SAP ERP 2005 Documentation*.

SAP AG: *SAP SCM 5.0 Documentation*.

Seifert, D.: *Collaborative Planning and Replenishment*. Bonn 2002.

Silver, E.; Meal, H.: *A Heuristic for Selecting Lot-Size Quantities*. In: Production and Inventory Management 14, 1973, p. 64–74.

Supply Chain Council: *Supply Chain Council & Supply Chain Operations Reference (SCOR) Model Overview*. *http://www.supply-chain.org/html/scor_overview.cfm*. Pittsburgh 2004.

Tempelmeier, H.: *Materiallogistik*. Berlin 2003.

Wagner, M.: *Demand Planning*. In: Stadtler, H.; Kilger, C.: Supply Chain Management and Advanced Planning. Berlin 2000.

Wikipedia: *http://www.wikipedia.org*

B   List of Acronyms

ALE	Application Link Enabling
APE	Absolute Percentage Error
APE-A	Adjusted Absolute Percentage Error
APO	Advanced Planner and Optimizer (also: Advanced Planning and Optimization)
APS	Advanced Planning & Scheduling Systems (also: Advanced Planning Solutions and Advanced Planning System)
ASAP	AcceleratedSAP
ATD	Available-to-Deploy
ATP	Available-to-Promise
B2C	Business-to-Consumer
BAPI	Business Application Programming Interface
BI	Business Intelligence
BO	Business Objects
BW	Business Information Warehouse
CIF	Core Interface
CLP	Collaborative Planning
COM/DCOM	Component Object Model/Distributed Component Object Model
CORBA	Common Object Request Broker Architecture
CPFR	Collaborative Planning, Forecasting and Replenishment
CRM	Customer Relationship Management
CRP	Capacity Requirement Planning
CTM	Capable-to-Match
DC	Distribution Center
DIMP	Discrete Industries/Mill Products
DP	Demand Planning
DRP	Distribution Requirement Planning

DS	Detailed Scheduling
ECR	Efficient Consumer Response
EDI	Electronic Data Interchange
EDIFACT	Electronic Data Interchange for Administration, Commerce, and Transport
EM	Event Management
ERP	Enterprise Resource Planning
G-ATP	Global Available-To-Promise
GMRAE	Geometric Mean Absolute Error
GUI	Graphical User Interface
HTML	Hypertext Markup Language
http	Hypertext Transfer Protocol
ICH	Inventory Collaboration Hub
IDoc	Intermediate Document
iPPE	Integrated Product and Process Engineering
JIT	Just in Time
KPI	Key Performance Indicator
LES	Logistics Execution System
MAD	Mean Absolute Deviation
MAPE	Arithmetic Mean Absolute Percentage Error
MdAPE	Median of the Absolute Percentage Error
MdRAE	Median of the Relative Absolute Error
MM	Materials Management
MPS	Master Production Scheduling
MRP	Material Requirements Planning
MRP II	Manufacturing Resource Planning
MSE	Mean Square Error
OLTP	Online Transaction Processing
PDS	Production Data Structure
PI	Plug-in
POS	Point of Sale
PP	Production Planning and Control

PP/DS	Production Planning and Detailed Scheduling
PPM	Production Process Model
PPC	Production Planning and Control
qRFC	queued Remote Function Call
RAE	Relative Absolute Error
RFC	Remote Function Call
ROI	Return On Investment
SAP	Systems, Applications, Programs
SC	Supply Chain
SCC	Supply Chain Cockpit
SCD	Supply Chain Design
SCE	Supply Chain Engineer
SCEM	Supply Chain Event Management
SCM	Supply Chain Management
SCOR	Supply Chain Operations Reference Model
SCPEM	Supply Chain Performance Management
SD	Sales and Distribution
SFC	Shop Floor Control
SNP	Supply Network Planning
S&OP	Sales & Operations Planning
TCO	Total Cost of Ownership
TLB	Transport Load Builder
TRA	Transportation Management
VMI	Vendor-Managed Inventory
WM	Warehouse Management
XML	Extensible Markup Language

C   Glossary

Advanced macro A tool in Demand Planning (DP) for quickly and easily performing complex table calculations. The high level of flexibility of advanced macros enables the planner to map the planning environment in accordance with individual business requirements. Specifically, the tool enables planners to do the following:

▶ Create macros that comprise multiple steps

▶ Control the processing of individual macro steps via control statements and conditions

▶ Control the calculation of macro results via control statements

▶ Use a wide range of different functions and operations

▶ Define offsets, which have the effect that the result of a given period is determined by a value in a previous period, for example.

▶ Restrict the horizon in which the macro is executed to one or more specific periods

▶ Write macro results to a row, column, or cell

▶ Write the results of macro steps to a row, column, cell, or variable

▶ Directly analyze forecast and business data using special icons

▶ Create context-specific and user-specific planning views

▶ Generate alerts in the *Alert Monitor*, which informs the planner about specific business situations.

Advanced Planner and Optimizer (APO)
The SAP Advanced Planner & Optimizer is a software solution for dy-
namic supply chain management. With its applications for detailed planning, optimization, and scheduling, it enables users to monitor and control the logistics chain across enterprise boundaries, accurately and on a global level.

Advanced Planning and Scheduling (APS) A software solution for planning processes (flows of information, finance, and materials) across enterprise boundaries that incorporates external partners into the planning process. Planning is carried out for three planning horizons: short-term, medium-term, and long-term.

Aggregation A function that automatically adds up key figure values on the lowest level of detail at runtime and displays them on a higher level.

For example: if a user displays on the planning screen the forecast demand for a particular region, he or she sees the forecast demand for all sales channels, product families, brands, products, and customers in this region. This ensures that the approach to planning is thorough and consistent throughout the entire enterprise.

The aggregation type of a key figure is set in the administration function for Demand Planning and Supply Network Planning. There are the following three options for standard aggregation:

▶ **Minimum (MIN)**
The minimum for all values displayed in this column is specified in this results row.
▶ **Maximum (MAX)**
The maximum for all values displayed in this column is specified in this results row.
▶ **Summation (SUM)**
The sum of all values displayed in this column is specified in this results row.

There are also several possible exceptions in aggregation, such as the following:
▶ **Average (values not equal to 0) (AV0)**
When reference characteristics are drilled down, the average of the column values that are not equal to 0 is specified in the results row.
▶ **Average (all values) (AVG)**
The average of all values.

Alert Monitor   Component of the *Supply Chain Cockpit* that processes generic exceptions and alerts for all APO applications. These exceptions and alerts are events and conditions that trigger alarms that are specified in the planning and scheduling processes in order to ensure that problems are detected automatically. The Alert Monitor highlights factors such as conditions relating to material, capacity, transport, and warehousing, as well as statistics on delivery performance and throughput. The Alert Monitor is used mainly by planners to monitor the status of plans in the system and to develop guidelines for regenerative planning.

Adjusted R square   Statistical calculation method for a multiple linear regression (MLR) model.
The (adjusted) R square measures the percentage variation in the dependent variables that is explained by the independent variables. Unlike the R square, the adjusted R square incorporates the degree of freedom associated with the sums of the squares. Even though the residual sum of squares may decrease or remain the same when new explanatory variables are added, this is not necessarily the case with the residual variance. The adjusted R square is therefore considered a more accurate measure of goodness-of-fit than R square.
Note the following two points when using the adjusted R square:
▶ If the adjusted R square is significantly lower than R square, this usually means that one or more explanatory variables are missing. Without these, the variation in the dependent variables cannot be fully measured.
▶ If you use this measure to compare two models, you must ensure that the same dependent variable is used.

APO   Advanced Planner and Optimizer

Autocorrelation   Statistical state in which the error variables of a regression model are not independent; that is, the values of historical periods in the forecast model influence the values in the current periods. Time series with a marked seasonal or cyclical pattern are often highly correlated.
However, autocorrelation is a negative phenomenon for many forecasting models, as it can distort the forecast. If autocorrelation reaches an unacceptable level, this can mean, among other things, that the classic multiple linear regression (MLR) model has to be adjusted.

Available-to-Deploy quantity (ATD quantity) A quantity that can be used in the deployment process for distributing goods to distribution centers.

Available-to-Promise (ATP) A function that uses certain basic methods to check whether a product can be confirmed. The basic methods are as follows:

▶ **Product availability check**
The availability check is carried out against the ATP quantity. In R/3, this check is known as an availability check using ATP logic.

▶ **Product allocation**
The availability check is carried out against product allocations.

▶ **Forecast check**
The availability check is carried out against planned independent requirements.

As well as the basic methods, APO also contains advanced availability check methods. These are as follows:

▶ **Combination of basic methods**
This is a sequence of basic methods for carrying out the availability check (for example: 1 – product availability check; 2 – product allocation). It is specified in the check instructions.

▶ **Production call**
Either Capable-to-Promise (CTP) or a multilevel ATP check is carried out.

▶ **Rule-based availability check**
In this case, rules are used to control how the system reacts after an availability check is specified in the check instructions, if the required product cannot be confirmed or can be only partially confirmed. The options are product replacement, location determination, and production call.

Bill of material (BOM) List of all the components of a product or assembly. The list is complete for the purpose in question, has a formal structure, and specifies the name, quantity, and unit of measure of the individual components. A comprehensive product lifecycle management (PLM) solution should support the following BOM types: product and requirements structures, material BOMs, document BOMS, equipment BOMS, BOMs for functional location, sales order BOMs, and project BOMs.

Branch-and-bound procedure A mathematical procedure from the field of operations research with the aim of finding the best solution to a given discrete optimization problem. It is part of the decision tree procedure. As the name suggests, the branch-and-bound algorithm has two parts: the branch and the bound(ary). In the worst-case scenario, all possibilities have to be listed. The analyst creating the algorithm tries to keep the solution space to be analyzed as small as possible by designating branches in the expanded decision tree as suboptimal and discarding them. (Source: Wikipedia)

Bucket A time period such as a day or week.

Bullwhip effect A statistical phenomenon that occurs when constant demand becomes increasingly chaotic. It can also be defined as a minor variation in demand on the retail level that intensifies as it proceeds along the supply chain.

Business Application Programming Interface (BAPI) A visible standardized interface through which various components—SAP APO and a third-party system, for example—can be integrated. BAPIs provide an object-oriented view of the business components of the SAP system. They are implemented and stored as RFC-enabled function modules in the Function Builder of the ABAP Workbench.

Business Framework   An open, component-based architecture that allows software components from SAP and other manufacturers to interact and integrate.

Business Information Warehouse (BW)
Business Intelligence (BI)

Business Intelligence (BI)   IT instruments for analyzing enterprise-wide knowledge. The SAP Business Information Warehouse is the core component of SAP NetWeaver 2004s Business Intelligence. BI manages and stores large data quantities and organizes access permissions. It contains search techniques for fast term searches and file searches, and data filters.

Capable-to-Match (CTM)   A supply chain management function that enhances the cross-plant supply chain planning strategies of *Supply Network Planning*.
The CTM engine carries out a fast check of production capacities and transportation options.
It plans cross-plant production processes, taking into account time-specific process parameters such as output quantity and lead time. To optimize the production process, the capacity check is carried out right up to the operations level. Planning strategies control the sequence of stock consumption and the multilevel bill of material explosion.

Capacity leveling   A way of dividing up work for a particular time period that aims to ensure that a process can

be successfully ended, and that machines and employees are not overloaded.

Chart   A part of the interactive planning screen that maps demand planning data in the form of a line chart or bar chart.

Collaboration   A process whereby enterprises work together for a period that extends beyond the horizon of cooperative practice. In a collaborative process, users, employees, customers, suppliers, and business partners work together across enterprise boundaries and use shared resources and content. Collaborative planning enables partners in the logistics chain to exchange information that is relevant to all parties.

Collaborative Planning, Forecasting, and Replenishment (CPFR)   An Internet-based process of collaboration between business partners. CPFR uses the *Demand Planning* (DP) component only. Process optimization enables users to improve the accuracy of forecasts, for example, and to reduce stock levels.

Constraint   Constraints are restrictions or conditions that have to be fulfilled in the production process so that the production plan can be executed; for example, availability of the required components or work centers with sufficient available capacity.

Core Interface (CIF)   The APO Core Interface is the interface between SAP APO and the standard ERP system. The CIF delivers transaction data and master data to SAPAPO in real time. Only the object data, which is relevant for the individual planning and optimization process in SAP APO, is transferred from the complex data records in the ERP system.

The APO Core Interface is a component of an R/3 plug-in from SAP APO Version 2.0A.

Croston method A statistical forecasting technique that is well suited for products with sporadic demand and low sales, and a relatively large quantity of historical data.

Sporadic demand is characterized by its random pattern of occurrence and its frequent periods of no demand (in fact, most periods may have no demand). The distribution of demand shows that each occurrence of demand is relatively independent of the period of time that has elapsed since the last occurrence of demand. Therefore, this kind of demand pattern is known as irregular or sporadic demand. The demand for spare parts is an example of sporadic demand, as spare parts are usually ordered in large quantities to replenish the warehouse.

Poisson distribution and *negative binomial distribution* are not usually suitable for this kind of data, as they regard zero-phases and non-zero-phases as part of the same distribution and connect them accordingly. Croston (1972) suggested mapping this data in a dual-level process: one level for the intervals between demand occurrences, and the other for the level of demand reached in each occurrence. In conjunction with exponential smoothing, Croston's method generates separate forecast values for the mean level of a demand occurrence and the mean duration of the interval between demand occurrences.

Data mart A storage entity that merges and maintains InfoCubes or information, or both.

Days' supply This is calculated as follows: the warehouse stock is divided by daily demand. If the warehouse stock or demand is 0, the days' supply is set at 9999.

Demand horizon Users use this horizon to specify that the system is to calculate overall demand for the three different time horizons (short-term, medium-term, and long-term) by assigning key figures to the demand categories for the three periods. This means, for example, that the user can specify the categories that contribute to the *distribution receipt* key figure in medium-term planning.

Demand plan A plan that specifies demand quantities for future time periods. First and foremost, the demand plan represents the demand potential; that is, it specifies how many units of the product or product group in question can be sold. The demand plan is the starting-point for production planning.

Demand Planning (DP) An application component of the Advanced Planner and Optimizer (APO) that enables enterprises to create demand forecasts for their products on the market. The result of APO Demand Planning is the demand plan.

APO Demand Planning includes a *data mart*, which is where the user stores and maintains all the information that is required to carry out the demand planning process in his or her enterprise. As an extension of this function, user-defined planning layouts and interactive *planning books* can be used to incorporate different departments into the forecast creation process. The statistical forecasting techniques and extended macro techniques available in APO Demand Planning enable users to create forecasts using demand histories and a wide range of different causal factors. The results can then be consolidated in a consensus-based forecast. Market information and management requirements can be included at any time in the form of forecast corrections and promotions (*promotion planning*). Seamless integration with the APO component Supply Network Planning (SNP) further supports an efficient Sales and Operations Planning (SOP) process.

Demand planning version   Versions of a demand plan that can be created and stored in an *InfoCube*. An InfoCube can contain a wide range of different versions of the sales forecast.
Every demand planning version has a 10-figure character string as its description. Actual data always has to be stored in version 0000000000, as this is where the system expects to find actual data when it executes a series of internal tests. This version is created automatically. When version names are assigned, the user needs to ensure that the names selected are clear and comprehensible to a planner or a group of planners.
For example: MGT0000001 could contain the first management version, PRD0000001 the first version of the production planner, MKT0000001 the first marketing version, and CONS000001 the first consolidated version.
Only one version of the demand plan—that is, only one demand planning version—is transferred to *Supply Network Planning*. The demand planning versions are not exactly the same as the versions in Supply Network Planning and *Production Planning and Detailed Scheduling* (PP/DS).
There are two ways of creating a demand planning version:

- In the version management function (**Demand Planning • Proportion/Version Management**.)
- In a selection variant in interactive planning (**Demand Planning • Interactive**)

Demand profile   This specifies how the system calculates total demand in Supply Network Planning and deployment planning runs.

Deployment   Deployment is used to dynamically utilize and optimize the distribution network, particularly the distribution of materials across locations.

Disaggregation   A function that automatically details on the lowest level a key figure value from a higher level. For example: the system may break down the forecast demand for a particular region based on the various distribution channels, product families, brands, products, customers, and so on. This ensures that the approach to planning is thorough and consistent within the entire enterprise.
Key figure values are stored on the lowest level of detail. If you are using aggregates, these are set specially on the aggregates level.
The aggregation type of a key figure is set in the administration function for *Demand Planning* and *Supply Network Planning*.

Distribution center   A type of plant for providing goods on a short-term basis to other plants or customers. Synonymous with "warehouse".

Distribution demand   This demand represents the planned stock transfer orders that are updated in every phase of the SNP process. The planned distribution demand is calculated during the SNP run.

Stock transfers orders that are confirmed in the deployment run represent the confirmed distribution demand. The confirmed distribution demand is calculated during the deployment run.

Distribution receipt This is the distribution quantity calculated by the SNP run. In SNP, the distribution quantity is calculated for every phase of the planning process: SNP run, deployment run, and transport load building (TLB) run.

Distribution requirements planning (DRP) A time-specific process planning approach for moving goods through the distribution network.

Down-binning procedure This is a common practice in the semiconductor industry of downgrading high-value products to low-value products in order to sell slow-moving items and to maintain service levels.

Durbin-h This is a method used in statistics to check for *autocorrelation* in time series where independent variables are delayed by one or more periods.

If Durbin-h is 1.96 or higher, it is very probable that autocorrelation exists. The Durbin-h test is suitable for large samples; that is, samples of 100 or more.

Durbin-Watson Statistical measure used to check for *first-order autocorrelation*; that is, autocorrelation in time series in which independent variables are not delayed.

The Durbin-Watson statistic lies within a value range of 0 to 4. A value of 2 or close to 2 indicates that no first-order

autocorrelation exists. An acceptable range is that between 1.5 and 2.5. In cases of consistently small error differences, Durbin-Watson is low (less than 1.5), which indicates positive autocorrelation. Positive autocorrelation is very common. In cases with consistently large error differences, the Durbin-Watson is high (greater than 2.5), which indicates negative autocorrelation. Negative autocorrelation, for its part, is not very common.

If the Durbin-Watson statistic is greater than the R square, autocorrelation is probably present. If this is the case, this indicates that there is room for improvement in the forecast model.

In time series with delayed variables, the Durbin-Watson statistic is not reliable because it tends towards a value of 2.0.

Electronic Data Interchange (EDI) This is an electronic exchange of structured business data between the applications of partner enterprises, using standardized data exchange formats and communication protocols via telecommunications networks.

Enterprise Resource Planning (ERP) A production planning and production control concept that integrates business areas (such as production, sales, and human resources) within the enterprise. With ERP, planning is carried out on the basis of shared data, and execution uses a successive approach.

Forecast horizon Within this horizon, SNP does not use the forecast to calculate the total demand. Outside this horizon, SNP calculates the total demand using the forecast or the sales orders (depending on which value is higher) and the other requirements (secondary demand and distribution demand, planned and confirmed).

Forecast method A category (or special group) of algorithms that is used in certain data situations, such as trend development or seasonal development.

Forecast model Used to describe the dependencies between model variables. After the incoming model parameters are calculated (using a suitable algorithm), the model is used for the actual forecast.

Forecasting technique A special algorithm that is used in certain data situations, such as trend development or seasonal development.

InfoCube A central data cube in *Demand Planning* (DP). It contains key performance indicators (KPIs) and characteristics in the form of fact tables (KPI) and dimension tables (characteristics).

Interior point method This is a procedure for identifying optimization procedures in the area of linear, non-linear, and quadratic programs. The main characteristic of the interior point method is faster convergence for large, sparsely populated problems.

In-transit This is a quantity calculated by the SNP run that will reach the specified destination during the next period.

Key Performance Indicator (KPI)
Key figures such as sales, delivery time, and capacity utilization that are used to analyze enterprise goals.

Lifecycle management Forecasting techniques that take into account the various phases of the existence of a product: introduction, growth, maturation, saturation, and discontinuation.

In *Demand Planning* (DP), the planner can map the start and the end of a product lifecycle in the form of a product introduction and a product discontinuation, also known as phase-in profile and phase-out profile.

Like modeling A forecasting technique that is based mainly on historical data. Like modeling can be used for new products, products with short lifecycles, and in cases where the available data is not adequate. This modeling technique enables the planner to use historical data of one or more other, similar products ("like products") to create a demand forecast for a particular product. In *Demand Planning* (DP), this kind of forecast is based on what are known as like profiles. These profiles contain information about which like products should be used and how their data should be scaled.

liveCache The SAP liveCache is a tool for processing large data volumes in main memory. It enables data to be exchanged between different applications.

Location (SCM-APO-MD) A location or organizational entity in SAP APO where products or resources are administrated on a quantity basis.
The standard location types include the following:

▶ Production plant
▶ Distribution center
▶ Transportation zone
▶ Stock transfer point
▶ Storage location materials planning
▶ Customer
▶ Vendor
▶ Subcontractor
▶ Transportation provider
▶ Terminal
▶ Geographical area
▶ Branch

Macro *Advanced macro*

Master planning object structure
A summary of characteristics that can be planned in one or more planning areas of *Demand Planning* or *Supply Network Planning*
If the master planning object structure was created for use in bills of material in the Supply Network Planning, characteristics-based forecasting, or Demand Planning areas, it contains standard characteristics.
The existence of a master planning object structure is a prerequisite for the creation of a planning area.
Supply Network Planning comes with the pre-defined master planning object structure 9ASNPBAS.

Negative binomial distribution A discrete probability distribution, which is also known as Pascal distribution. Negative binomial distribution describes the probability distribution of the number of attempts required to achieve a specified number of successes in a Bernoulli process. (Source: Wikipedia.)

OLTP system The APO system usually works with an online transaction processing (OLTP) system. This system provides the APO system with the required data that is relevant to planning. The APO system transfers the planning results back to the OLTP system. In the OLTP system, the planning may be completed, if necessary, and production and planning may be triggered, confirmed, and so on.
The OLTP system can be an ERP system or another system.

Optimization horizon Time period in which planning is to be optimized.
In optimization, only activities that lie completely within the optimization horizon can be re-planned. Activities that are partially or completely outside the optimization horizon cannot be re-planned; in other words, they are fixed. However, through their activity relationships and pegging relationships to the activities within the optimization horizon, these fixed activities determine the extent to which the non-fixed activities can be moved.

Pegging (SCM-APO-PPS) A procedure in Production Planning and Detailed Scheduling that establishes the relationship between the receipt elements and the requirements elements of a product within a location. Pegging is used to assign the relevant receipt element to the requirements. There are two types of pegging:
▶ **Fixed pegging**
Fixed pegging maintains the assignment of a receipt element to a requirements element in the planning process.
▶ **Dynamic pegging**
With dynamic pegging, the assignment of receipt elements to requirements element may change, depending on the planning situation.

Plan Monitor A tool that analyzes the accuracy of a production plan or the detailed scheduling of a production line, or both.
The Plan Monitor is used to analyze production key figures, characteristics key figures, and other key figures that are derived from formula-based calculations. The key figures are analyzed in accordance with a points system, which results in the overall rating. The results can be displayed in a grid in aggregated or detailed form.
The following key figures can be analyzed:
▶ Throughput time, setup time, downtime, processing time, wait

time, Work in Process (WIP) time, number of delayed orders, available capacity, resource utilization, total number of delays per resource, APO location, and APO product.

▸ Planned, partially-confirmed, and fully-confirmed quantities per APO location and APO product.

▸ Stock level for the individual APO locations and APO products.

Planning area A central data structure in *Demand Planning* (DP) and *Supply Network Planning* (SNP).

If you save actual data or other data in an InfoCube, the InfoCube is assigned to a planning area. The planning area is created as part of the process of configuration for Demand Planning or Supply Network Planning, or both. A planning book is based on a planning area, although the end user sees only the planning book.
The planning area specifies the following data:

▸ Quantity in which data is planned

▸ Currency in which data is planned (optional)

▸ Currency conversion type for displaying planning data in other currencies (optional)

▸ Storage buckets profile to determine the periods in which data is stored in this planning area

▸ Aggregate levels on which data can be stored as well as being stored on the lowest detail level, in order to enhance performance.

▸ Key figures that are used in this planning area

▸ Settings that determine how individual key figures are disaggregated, aggregated, and stored

▸ Assignments of key figures to aggregates

Supply Network Planning already contains pre-defined planning areas. You can also define your own planning areas.

Planning book A tool in SAP APO that defines the content and layout of the interactive planning screen. Planning books are used in *Demand Planning* (DP) and *Supply Network Planning*, and enable the planner to design the planning screen in accordance with his or her individual planning requirements. A planning book is based on a planning area, and a planning area can have any number of planning books.
The user defines the following elements in a planning book:

▸ Key figures

▸ Characteristics

▸ Functions and applications that should be directly accessible from the relevant planning book

▸ User-specific planning horizons

▸ User-specific views of the planning book (including initial column, number of grids, option for other users to access the current view) A planning book can have any number of views.

These and other elements of the interactive planning screen (such as position of columns and rows, use of colors and icons in rows, display of rows as visible or hidden, graphics format, and macro recording) can be configured via context menus in interactive design mode. The SNP component comes with the following two standard planning books:

▸ 9ASNP94 for Supply Network Planning

▸ 9ASOP for Sales and Operations Planning

Users can use the standard views in these planning books as templates for creating their own planning books.

Planning horizon Period that is set for net change planning in the planning horizon. With this type of net change planning, only materials are planned in the planning run that have a change relevant to MRP within the period (in work days). The length of the planning horizon should include the following, at a minimum:

▸ Period in which sales orders are received
▸ Delivery times
▸ Total lead times of materials

Planning layout A form that defines the layout of a planning screen.

Planning object structure A structure that contains plannable characteristics for use in one more planning areas. There are four types of planning object structures:

▸ **Master planning object structure**
▸ **Aggregate**
Aggregates in APO are not identical to those in Business Information Warehouse (BW), but they do have the same purpose: fast data access and, thus, higher performance. Data can be stored in aggregates and on the lowest detail level. An aggregate contains a sub-group of the characteristics contained in the master planning object structure. Creating and working with aggregates in APO is optional. The data is always stored on the lowest detail level. If aggregates are used, the system stores the planning data on the defined aggregate levels and on the lowest detail level. The data is thus stored twice, and consistently; in other words, the sum of details is the same as the aggregate value.
▸ **Standard SNP planning level**
This planning level is already predefined in the system for use in Supply Network Planning.

▸ **Freely-defined SNP planning level**

Planning buckets profile Specified periods in which *Demand Planning* data and *Supply Network Planning* data for past and future planning horizons is displayed and planned.
A planning buckets profile contains the following information:

▸ The entire duration of the planning horizon
▸ The periods in which various sections of the planning horizon are displayed.

The system displays the horizons in interactive planning in such a way that planning starts with the shortest period and ends with the longest period. The future horizon starts with the shortest period (at the start date of the planning horizon) and proceeds in a forward direction until the longest period is reached at the end. The future horizon starts with the shortest period (at the start date of the planning horizon) and proceeds in a forward direction until the longest period is reached at the end.
A planning bucket profile is defined as part of the process of defining the view for a planning book.

Plan version A planning data record for an APO supply chain model. The model contains master data only, while the plan version contains master data and transaction data.
It is possible for simulation purposes to create different plan versions for each supply chain model, but only one model (model 000) and one plan version (plan version 000) are active in each case.
The results of the planning activities in various plan versions of a model cannot be copied to the active version; the planning activity has to be repeated in the active plan version.

Poisson distribution A Poisson distribution, which is a term from probability theory, is a discrete probability distribution that results when a Bernoulli experiment is carried out several times. The latter is a random experiment that can have only two possible results (such as "Success" or "Failure"). If you carry out this kind of experiment very frequently and if the probability of success is low, the Poisson distribution is a good approximation of the corresponding probability distribution. The Poisson distribution is therefore sometimes referred to as "a distribution of rare events." (Source: Wikipedia)

Production horizon A horizon within which no production planning activities take place.

Production Planning and Detailed Scheduling (PP/DS) Functionality within SAP SCM that supports customers by optimizing lead times and bottleneck capacities using new scheduling procedures (setup optimization) and online integration between production planning and production control. This creates a transparent overview of the entire order network.

Production Process Model (PPM) A model that is used to generate production plans for one or more products, taking into account the bill of material and the routing data.
It includes the production of co-products (intentional or unintentional creation of by-products during production). This model defines the flow of material and the required capacity profiles.
There can be different production process models for a product.

Promotion planning A complex of functions that enables the planner to

predict the effect that advertising measures—such as vouchers, magazines inserts, TV spots, discounts, advertising by competitors, Internet advertising, and so on—will have on demand. Sales increases that result from promotions add up to form an existing baseline forecast.

Pull deployment horizon In deployment calculations, *Supply Network Planning* takes into account the entire warehouse stock within this horizon. Deployment calculations consider only the demand within this horizon. Distribution starts on the first day for which demand exists in the system, and ends with the last day of the pull deployment horizon.

Pull distribution Distribution logic that is used if supply exceeds demand and pull distribution was specified in the product /material master. The supply surplus is distributed in accordance with the demand of the current day. Any supply that exceeds the demand of the current day is not distributed.

Push deployment horizon In deployment calculations, *Supply Network Planning* takes into account the entire warehouse stock within this horizon.

Push distribution Distribution logic that is used if supply exceeds demand and push distribution was specified in the product /material master. All demands specified in the system are fulfilled by the deployment process. Distribution starts on the first day on which demand exists, and continues until all the demands defined in the system are fulfilled.

Push rule *Supply Network Planning* uses push logic to calculate the deployment process if the Available-to-Deploy (ATD) quantities can satisfactorily fulfill the demand that exists in the system. There are three ways of using push logic:

▶ With *pull distribution*, on the other hand, the deployment process covers all demand within the pull deployment horizon. Distribution is carried out in accordance with the due dates/times defined in the distribution centers.

▶ With *pull distribution* and *push distribution*, deployment immediately fulfills all demand within the pull deployment horizon without taking into account the due dates/times defined in the distribution centers.

▶ With *push distribution*, all demand defined in the system is immediately fulfilled by the deployment process.

Resource A machine, person, plant, warehouse, or means of transport, among other things, with limited capacity to fulfill a specific function. The following can be mapped in SAP APO:

▶ **Resources whose available capacity is determined by means of working time data.** During working times, the capacity of these resources is available on a continuous basis. There is a difference between single-activity resources, which can execute only one activity at a time, and multi-activity resources, which can execute multiple activities at a time. Single-activity resources and multi-activity resources are used for planning with the APO components Capable-to-Match (CTM) and Production Planning and Detailed Scheduling (PP/DS), which plan production dates/times for orders and operations to the second.

▶ **Bucket resources whose available capacity is defined by quantities (such as transportation or warehouse capacity) or by daily rates (such as production rates).** Bucket resources are used in planning with the APO component Supply Network Planning (SNP) and can be planned in great detail on the daily level.

Resource bottleneck A resource bottleneck occurs when materials, raw materials, or personnel become scarce, possibly with very little notice. They restrict throughput in production or the supply chain.

R square An indicator in multiple linear regression of how well a certain combination of X variables (the drivers or independent variables of the model) explains the variation in Y (dependent variable).

The R square lies within the value range of 0 to 1. A value of 0 signifies that the multiple linear regression model cannot explain the variation in Y. A value of 1 signifies that the model is perfectly suitable. A value of 0.75 or higher indicates an acceptable model. R square is also known as the coefficient of determination or measure of goodness of fit.

Note the following two points in relation to R square:

▶ R square is a non-decreasing function of the number of explanatory variables in a model. In other words, if more historical data and explanatory variables (Xs) are added, R square almost always increases and never decreases. This reason for this is that the incorporation of further explanatory variables into the model means that the forecasting errors that occur are not serious ones.

▶ R square assumes that the dataset being examined is the entire population, but in fact, the dataset is only a sample of the population.

Sales forecast A level of sales (expressed as a quantity or a value) that an enterprise believes it can achieve during a defined future period in accordance with a specific marketing plan and with regard to the expected market situation.

Simplex algorithm An optimization procedure in operations research for solving linear programs (LPs). The simplex algorithm either provides an exact solution after a finite number of steps, or it confirms the insolvability or unlimitedness of the problem. (Source: Wikipedia)

Simulation version Set of simulative planning data that is based on a plan version.
You can use a simulation version to run an alternative plan without having to change the data in the plan version. Thus, you can use different simulation versions to test different planning alternatives.
You can reconcile ("refresh") the simulation version of the plan with the actual plan version at any time, or incorporate ("save") the simulative plan into the actual plan version. When you do the latter, the planning in the plan version or simulation version is not simply copied over; rather, the data is merged in a process in which the "hard" data "wins." For example, a confirmation of an operation has a higher priority than a deadline change.

SNP heuristics Carries out demand planning for the entire supply chain network in order to establish how best to fulfill customer or consumer demand. The logistics chain is optimized in accordance with the customer service level, while at the same time, stock

levels are minimized and the material flow in synchronized. Using a correction-based planning approach, heuristics efficiently plans complex distribution networks in multi-plant production environments.

SNP Optimizer Calculates an optimal plan using the SNP planning model, in which it uses the following linear optimization procedures on the basis of *simplex-based algorithms* and *branch-and-bound procedures*:

▸ **Basic Solve**
The Optimizer creates an optimal solution on the basis of all the available data. This method uses the normal simplex procedure, in which only continual variables occur.

▸ **Discrete**
The Optimizer creates an optimal solution on the basis of all the available data. This method is basically the same as the basic solve procedure, except that some variables can be discretized by the profiles. Transportation, for example, is discretized by the lot size profile, and production is discretized by the production process model.

▸ **Time Aggregation**
The Optimizer accelerates the problem-solving process by grouping the data into periods. The problem is solved for the earliest period first, and then sequentially for the remaining periods.

▸ **Product Decomposition**
The Optimizer accelerates the problem-solving process by creating product groups. The problem is solved for each product group in accordance with the values specified in the Window Size field of the SNP Optimizer profile.

▸ **Priority Decomposition**
The Optimizer accelerates the problem-solving process by grouping the

data based on priorities. The Optimizer solves the problem with the highest priority first, and then sequentially for the remaining priority groups.

SNP stock transfer (SCM-APO-SNP)
An order that maps a goods movement that is planned for the medium term to long term between two locations, and creates this movement in an SNP or CTM planning run. The SNP stock transfer can then be transferred to an execution system, where it can be converted to a stock transport requisition in the case of an ERP system, for example.

Sporadic demand Sales history that shows periods of high demand that are either preceded or followed by periods of low demand or no demand.

Example					
Jan 2006	Feb 2006	Mar 2006	April 2006	May 2006	June 2006
0 units	12 units	10 units	0 units	0 units	24 units

Sporadic demand can often occur in the case of replacement parts or devices that are ordered in bulk in order to replenish warehouse stocks.

Stock transfer horizon *Supply Network Planning* does not plan any deliveries within this horizon.

Supply Chain Cockpit (SCC) A central planning application of the Advanced Planner and Optimizer (APO) for supply chain design. The SCC is a graphical console for modeling, navigating, and monitoring the logistics chain. It functions as the highest planning level, and it is from here that the user can obtain an overview of other planning levels within the enterprise, including de-

mand, manufacturing, distribution, and transportation. The SCC has the following three components:
- **Supply Chain Cockpit**
  Provides a detailed, graphical overview of the entire logistics chain.
- **Supply Chain Engineer**
  Used to model and maintain the network model.
- **Alert Monitor**
  Handles general exceptions and problems in all APO applications.

Supply Chain Engineer A component of the *Supply Chain Cockpit* (SCC) that is used to create and maintain in a graphical interface extended supply chain models.

Supply Chain Management (SCM)
SAP's logistics solution, SAP SCM, fulfills all supply chain processes from planning to networking. It is a complete solution that is open and integrated, and was designed right from the beginning for cross-enterprise e-business.

Supply horizon Users use this horizon to specify that the system calculates overall supply for the three different time horizons (short-term, medium-term, and long-term) by assigning key figures to the supply categories for the three periods. This means, for example, that the user can specify the categories that contribute to the *distribution receipt* key figure in medium-term planning.

Supply Network Planning (SNP) An application component of SAP APO that enterprises can use to define sources of supply, production plans, distribution plans, and purchasing plans. To optimize these plans using optimization algorithms, heuristics-based approaches, and procedures for

comparing supply and demand, the system uses data that is universally available in the *liveCache*. The planner also can define his or her own rules and stockholding procedures.

The *deployment function*, an integral part of SNP, enables the user to dynamically balance and optimize the distribution network. It calculates an optimized inbound and outbound distribution of the available capacity in order to fulfill short-term demand, including sales orders, and stock transfer and safety stock requirements. The deployment logic takes into account a wide range of short-term *constraints*, such as transportation, inventory turnover capacity, and calendar.

Supply shortage   Quantity that cannot be delivered on schedule. This quantity is calculated during the Supply Network Planning run.

Total demand   The total required quantity of a specific product. In *Supply Network Planning*, the planned total demand is the sum of forecast, sales orders, secondary requirements, and distribution demand (planned and confirmed).

Total receipts   The sum of production receipts (planned and confirmed), distribution receipts, and *in-transit quantity*.

Transport Load Builder (TLB)   The SNP module that calculates optimal loads for means of transport by grouping products for transport on the basis of *deployment proposals*, and by ensuring that the means of transport are filled to their maximum capacity.

Trend dampening profile   This profile enables planners to include in their plans a trend downturn when a product reaches market maturity.

The system cannot predict this kind of downturn on the basis of historical data. This profile specifies the percentage per period by which the trend should be dampened.

t-test   A statistical test that indicates whether an independent variable correlates with the dependent variable, i.e., it verifies that the independent variable contributes to the explanation of the dependent variable, and determines whether the independent variable should remain in the model.

The t-test does not provide any information about the significance of the size and influence of an explanatory variable. So, a t-test of approximately 4.6 does not have any more significance than a t-test of 2.4. All it means is that the independent variables connected to the t-test are significant in that they explain the difference in the dependent variables. The size of this relationship is measured by the coefficient of the independent variable and its unit of measurement.

The reference value for a t-test is +/– 2.0. This value is used to determine whether an independent variable significantly correlates with the dependent variable at a confidence level of 95 %.

However, empirical tests have shown that a t-test of +/–1.4 or higher is structurally significant at a confidence level of 90 %.

For this reason, SAP recommends that you keep explanatory variables in the model if the t-test is +/–1.4 or higher. If some of the independent variables have a t-test of less than +/–1.4, you should carry out an ex-post forecast, first with these variables, and then without these variables. If the forecast error with the explanatory variables is lower, you should leave them in the model. However, if the t-test for these independent variables returns a value that is less than +/−1.4, the structural analysis is not valid.

Vendor-Managed Inventory (VMI)
The vendor provides goods and replenishment on the customer's behalf.

Winters' method   Strategy in SAP APO for univariate forecasting for products with seasonal fluctuations in demand.

D   The Author

 After finishing his studies in business administration at Fachhochschule Nordostniedersachsen in Lüneburg, Germany, at John Moores University in Liverpool, England, and at Technical University Baumann, Moscow, Marc Hoppe joined CAS AG, Germany, as an SAP developer in the logistics and production planning areas. He later became a logistics consultant and was responsible for implementing national and international SAP R/3 projects.

Since 1998, Marc has worked as a supply chain management (SCM) consultant at SAP SI. He is responsible for the business-relevant and IT-based implementation and optimization of supply chain management processes, as well as the re-engineering of entire supply chain processes. Since 2001, Marc Hoppe has served as the head of a supply chain management consulting team.

Marc provides his services to large corporations such as Siemens, Unilever, Gillette, Philips, Deutsche Telekom, and Philip Morris, but also to medium-sized companies like G+H Isover, Fertiva, Gauselmann Group, and GEA Group. He has published numerous works on inventory optimization. In addition, he has worked as a teacher for supply chain management at Fachhochschule Nordostniedersachsen in Lüneburg, Germany, and at Dresden International University.

Marc Hoppe is the author of the book *Inventory Optimization with SAP*, published by SAP PRESS in 2006.

If you have questions regarding SAP SCM or SAP APO, or if you want to provide your feedback on this book, you can contact the author via the following:

Email: *marc.hoppe@sap.com*
Fax: +49–6227–782–5664

Index

A

Absolute percentage error (APE) 149
AcceleratedSAP (ASAP) 393
Adjusted absolute percent error (APE-A) 151
Adjusted R square 141, 155, 416
Administrator Workbench 43
Advanced Macro 71, 415
Advanced Planning & Scheduling (APS) 18, 415
Aggregated SNP Planning 365
Aggregation 66, 415
Alert Monitor 24, 82, 159, 308, 416
Alpha factor 118
ASAP → AcceleratedSAP
Autocorrelation 416
Automatic cost generation 286
Automatic forecast 88
Automatic model selection 132, 133, 135, 137
Available-to-Deploy quantity(ATD quantity) 417
Available-to-Promise (ATP) 417

B

BAPI 383, 388, 417
Basic planning object structure 53
BasisCube 47
Bill of material (BOM) 417
BOM 183
Bottom-up planning 66
Branch-and-bound procedure 417
Bucket 371, 417
Bullwhip Effect 417
Business Application Programming Interface → BA
Business blueprint 394
Business Content 45
Business Framework 418
Business-to-Consumer (B2C) 29
BW → SAP NetWeaver BI

C

Calculating the safety stock 327
Cannibalization 167
Cannibalization group 177
Capable-to-Match (CTM) 35, 231, 288, 418
Capacity leveling 238, 418
Causal analysis 32, 65
Causal forecast error 155
    adjusted R square 155, 416
    Durbin-h 156, 421
    Durbin-Watson 156, 421
    mean elasticity 157
    R square 155, 427
    t-test 157, 430
Causal model 138
Characteristic combination 54
Characteristics 42
Chart 418
Client-server architecture 390
Collaboration 23, 29, 97, 418
Collaborative demand planning 78, 180
Collaborative Planning (CLP) 180
Collaborative Planning, Forecasting and Replenishment (CPFR) 31, 418
Components 81
Composite forecast 32, 65
Constraint 418
Core Interface (CIF) 418
Cost maintenance 287
Croston method 127, 136, 419
CTM messages 308

D

Data Mart 48, 419
Data Views 65, 80
Days' supply 419
Days' supply planning 276
Decomposition 252
Delphi method 108
Demand horizon 419

Demand plan   419
Demand planning BOM   77
Demand planning version   420
Demand profile   420
Deployment   37, 231, 336, 420
Deployment heuristic   336
Deployment optimization   344
Determining the supply source   263
Dimension key   49
Dimension table   49, 50
Disaggregation   66, 420
Discrete Optimization   251
Distribution center   420
Distribution demand → SAP APO-SNP
Distribution receipt   421
Distribution Requirement Planning (DRP)
   421
Distribution Resource Planning   36
Down-binning procedure   421
Drill-down function   66
Drill-up function   66
Durbin-h   156, 421
Durbin-Watson   156, 421
Dynamic safety stock   319

E

Electronic Data Interchange (EDI)   29,
   421
Enterprise Resource Planning (ERP)   421
Error total   147
Extended macro   31

F

Fact table   49, 50
Fair share rules   337, 345
Finite planning   256
Forecast alert   146, 159
Forecast error   147, 158, 326, 327, 328
Forecast horizon   421
Forecast method   422
Forecast model   422
Forecast procedures
   aggregation and disaggregation   103
Forecast quality   145, 312, 326
Forecast view   82
Forecasting technique   422
   adjusted R square   416, 427

   constant model with exponential smoo-
      thing 1   116
   Croston method   419
   models with exponential smoothing 2nd
      order   115
   moving average model   113
   qualitative forecasting technique   108
   time series analysis   109
   trend/seasonal model with exp. smoo-
      thing 1. O   122
   univariate forecasting technique   109
Forecasting techniques
   adjusted R square   141, 155
   automatic adjustment of the alpha factor
      119
   automatic model selection   131
   causal models   111
   combined forecasting techniques   141
   composite methods   111
   Croston method   127, 136
   Ex-post forecast   143
   manual forecasts   112
   median method   129
   models with 2nd-order exponential smoo-
      thing   121
   Multilinear regression   138
   naïve methods   111
   quantitative forecasting technique   109
   quantitative forecasting techniques   112
   seasonal linear regression   125
   weighted moving average model   114
Forecasts   31
Form-Fit-Function class   378

G

Geometric mean relative absolute error
   (GMRAE)   153
Global Availability Check (G-ATP)   27

H

Heuristic profiles   237
Heuristic with capacity leveling   35, 231,
   235
Historical sales   41
Holt method   121
Horizontal aggregated planning   254

I

Incremental optimization   254
Individual planning book   208
InfoArea   47
InfoCube   41, 43, 48, 50, 389, 422
InfoObject   45, 79, 232
InfoSource   46
Input component   279
Integrated Supply Chain Planning   38
Interactive demand planning   78
Interactive SNP planning   231
Interior point method   422
In-transit   422
Inventory Collaboration Hub (ICH)   383
Inventory planning → SAP APO-DP
Inventory planning → SAP APO-SNP
Inventory policy   328

K

Key figures   41
Key Performance Indicator (KPI)   422

L

Lifecycle management   32, 422
Lifecycle planning   31, 77, 161
Like modeling   170, 172, 422
Like profiles   164
Linear Optimization   250
Linear regression   136
Location   42, 422
Lot-size planning   266
Lot-size planning in procurement   273
   fixed procurement costs   273
   minimum/maximum and integer   273
Lot-size planning in production   266
   discrete (integer) lot sz   271
   integration   268
   minimum/maximum lot sizes   268
   setup consumptions   266
   setup costs   268
Lot-size planning in transportation   272
   discrete (integer) transport   272
   fixed means of transport costs   272
   minimum/maximum lot sizes   272

M

Macro   423
Macro Workbench   72
MacroBuilder   74
Master data   42, 209, 292
Master planning object structure   204, 423
Material requirements planning (MRP)   16
Mean absolute deviation (MAD)   148
Mean absolute percent error (MAPE)   151
Mean elasticity   157
Mean square error (MSE)   148
Median absolute percent error (MdAPE)   152
Median relative absolute error (MdRAE)   153
Memory storage buckets profile   59
Middle-out planning   66
Missing part costs   311
Missing part formula   153
Multi-level planning   31

N

Negative binomial distribution   423
Notes management   95

O

ODS object   47
OLTP system   27, 246, 390, 423
Optimization horizon   423
Optimization methods
   decomposition   252
   discrete optimization   251
   horizontal aggregated planning   254
   incremental optimization   254
   linear optimization   250
   prioritization   252
   vertical aggregated planning   253
Optimization profile   279
Optimizer   35, 231, 249
Order cycle policy   328
Outlier correction   86, 87, 135
Output component   279

P

Pegging 423
Period split 58
Phase-in/-out 163
  Mechanisms 163
  modeling 170
  models 173
  profiles 165
Plan Monitor 308, 423
Plan version 425
Planning algorithm 302
Planning area 42, 46, 58, 61, 424
Planning book 41, 61, 64, 65, 424
Planning bucket profile 61, 204, 425
Planning horizon 61, 425
Planning layout 425
Planning level 42
Planning object 42
Planning object structure 425
Planning time buckets profile 60
Planning version 42
Plug-in (PI) 385
Poisson distribution 426
Prioritization 252
Process areas in SAP SCM 23
  collaboration 29
  coordination 29
  execution 27
  planning 23
Product assignment 170, 173
Product interchangeability 168
Product lifecycle 162
Production data structure (PDS) 263
Production horizon 426
Production Planning and Detailed
  Scheduling (PP/DS) 379, 426
Production process model (PPM) 263,
  426
Project methodology 393
Project preparation 394
Promotion base 179
Promotion planning 33, 65, 77, 100,
  175, 426
Promotion planning view 84, 179
Pull deployment horizon 426
Pull distribution 37, 426
Push deployment horizon 426

Push distribution 37, 426
Push rule 426
Push rules 337, 340, 345

Q

qRFC monitor 307

R

Realignment 56, 170, 172, 196
Real-time deployment 344
Regression analysis 132
Relative absolute error (RAE) 153
Remote function call (RFC) 386
RemoteCube 47
Reorder point policy 329
Replenishment lead time 312, 324, 368
Requirements categorization 297
Requirements prioritization 294
Resource 427
Resource bottleneck 427
Root of the mean square error (RMSE)
  149

S

S&DP Administration Workbench 41,
  52, 203
Safety range of coverage 316
Safety stock 312
Safety stock planning 34, 274, 311, 335
  enhanced 322, 330
Sales forecast 428
SAP APO 21, 415, 419
SAP APO Core Interface (CIF) 383, 386
SAP APO-DP 25, 30, 77, 389, 393, 419
SAP APO-SNP 25, 41, 199, 231, 393
SAP APO-SNP process flow 200
SAP Business Information Warehouse
  (BW) → SAP NetWeaver BI
SAP Collaborative Planning, Forecasting
  and Replenishment (CPFR) 30
SAP ERP 191
SAP liveCache 42, 51, 206, 368, 389,
  390, 422
SAP Materials Management (MM) 23,
  27

SAP NetWeaver BI   25, 44, 48, 389, 418
SAP Production Planning (PP)   28
SAP Production Planning and Detailed
    Scheduling (PP/DS)   26
SAP Quick Sizer   390
SAP Sales and Distribution (SD)   28
SAP SCM   21, 22, 383
SAP solution manager   398
SAP Supply Chain Event Management
    (SCEM)   29
SAP Supply Chain Performance Manage-
    ment (SCPM)   29
SAP Transportation Management (TM)
    28
SAP Warehouse Management (WM)   28
Scheduling   304
Seasonal linear regression   136
Selection profile   80
Sequence of the search strategy
    system-internal   299
    user-defined   300
Service level   311, 312, 325, 330
Shuffler   79
Simplex algorithm   428
Simulation version   428
Sizing   390
SNP heuristics   428
SNP horizon   372
SNP Optimizer   263, 428
SNP stock transfer   429
Source determination   302
Source of supply determination   264
Source system   47
Special sorting   294
Sporadic demand   429
Standard planning book   207
Standard safety stock planning   315
Standard view   82
Star schema   50
Stock transfer horizon   429
Stockout formula
    calculating the occurrence of a stockout
        325
    calculating the stockout   325
Storage bucket profile   42, 203
Storage costs   311
Supplier-Managed Inventory   30
Supply chain   15, 21, 383

Supply Chain Cockpit (SCC)   24, 85, 429
Supply Chain Design (SCD)   24
Supply Chain Engineer (SCE)   24, 429
Supply Chain Event Management (EM)
    383
Supply Chain Management (SCM)   15,
    22, 429
Supply Chain Viewer   308
Supply horizon   429
Supply Network Planning (SNP)   429
Supply shortage   430

T

Theil coefficient   154
Time series object   63
Top-down planning   66
Total demand   430
Total receipts   430
Tracking signal   154
Transaction data   48
Transport Load Builder (TLB)   26, 38,
    231, 336, 354, 430
Trend dampening profile   430

U

Univariate forecast   65
Univariate forecast error
    absolute percent error (APE)   149
    adjusted absolute percent E   151
    error total   147
    geometric mean relative A   153
    Mean absolute deviation (MAD)   148
    mean absolute percent error   151
    Mean square error (MSE)   148
    median absolute P   152
    median relative A   153
    relative absolute error (RAE)   153
    root of the mean square error   149
    Theil coefficent   154
    tracking signal   154
Univariate forecasting methods   32
Upper stock limit
    dynamic   277
    static   277

V

Vendor-Managed Inventory (VMI)   30, 31, 431
Vertical aggregated planning   253

W

Winters' method   122, 431

X

XML   29, 180

Integrate mySAP SRM with other SAP R/3 core components

Obtain key knowledge about strategies, functionalities and methodologies

Gain detailed and practical understanding of mySAP SRM

approx. 400 pp., 69,95 Euro / US$ 69,95
ISBN 978-1-59229-068-0, May 2007

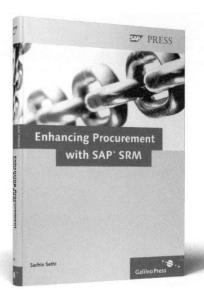

Enhancing Procurement with SAP SRM

www.sap-press.com

Sachin Sethi

Enhancing Procurement with SAP SRM

This book will help readers leverage valuable insights into strategies and methodologies for implementing SAP SRM to enhance procurement in their companies.
Tips and tricks, changes brought about by 5.0 and customization will be woven in throughout the book. It will provide detailed information on integration and dependencies of mySAP SRM with core SAP components like MM, IM, FI and HR.

Maximize the ROI of your SAP GTS implementation

Efficiently solve customs-related issues for your business

Ensure your compliance keeps pace with the global growth of your business

199 pp., 2007, 69,95 Euro / US$ 69,95
ISBN 978-1-59229-096-3

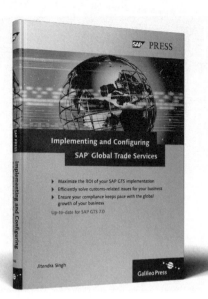

Implementing and Configuring SAP Global Trade Services

www.sap-press.com

Jitendra Singh

Implementing and Configuring SAP Global Trade Services

This detailed reference, covering SAP's Global Trade Services (GTS), examines a wide range of business-related issues in the global trade arena. Comprehensive explanations of major GTS concepts help readers understand each of its modules before proceeding to tackle real-world global trade issues and their resolution with GTS. From implementation to compliance management and customs management, this book helps those involved with SAP GTS get up to speed quickly.

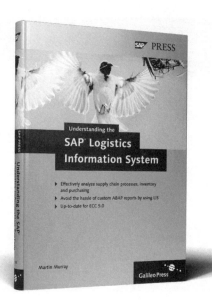

Understanding the SAP Logistics Information System

www.sap-press.com

Martin Murray

Understanding the SAP Logistics Information System

Gain a holistic understanding of LIS and how you can use it effectively in your own company. From standard to flexible analyses and hierarchies and from the Purchasing Information System to Inventory Controlling, this book is full of crucial information and advice.
Learn how to fully use this flexible SAP tool that allows you to collect, consolidate, and utilize data. Learn how to run reports without any ABAP experience thus saving your clients both time and money.

Processes and Customization made easy

Comprehensive details on the APO Core Interface

Extensive coverage of material requirements planning with SAP ECC-MRP

336 pp., 2007, 69,95 Euro / US$ 69.95
ISBN 978-1-59229-113-7

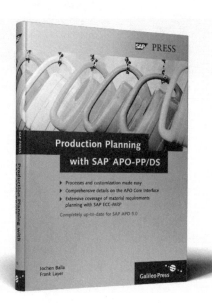

Production Planning with SAP APO-PP/DS

www.sap-press.com

J. Balla, F. Layer

Production Planning with SAP APO-PP/DS

This book provides a profound introduction to the functions, usage, and customization of production planning with SAP APO-PP/DS. The authors teach you, step-by-step, how to use the central functions of APO-PP/DS and everything you need to know to optimally set up data exchange using APO Core Interface (CIF), including extensive details on APO master data. In addition, readers learn how to use the central planning and analysis tools as well as how to create a finite production plan. The book is complemented by a robust appendix, which includes menu paths, SAP Notes, and heuristics, and is guaranteed to be an invaluable reference. The book is based on SAP APO 5.0 but is equally relevant for users of older releases.

Apply SAP SD to your own company's business model and make it work for you

Learn all aspects of SD functionality and essential technical details

365 pp., 69,95 Euro / US$ 69.95
ISBN 978-1-59229-101-4

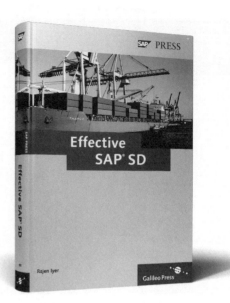

Effective SAP SD

www.sap-press.com

D. Rajen Iyer

Effective SAP SD

Get the Most Out of Your SAP SD Implementation

From important functionalities to the technical aspects of any SD implementation, this book has the answers. Use it to troubleshoot SD-related problems and learn how BAdIs, BAPIs and IDocs work in the Sales and Distribution area. Understand how SAP SD integrates with modules like MM, FI, CO, and Logistics. Whether you're looking for in-depth SD information or need advice on implementation and upgrades, this practical guide is an invaluable reference.

A comprehensive manual
for discrete manufacturing
using SAP PP

Processes and customizing
made easy

All-new 2nd edition—fully updated
and extended for mySAP ERP 2005

477 pp., 2007, 69,95 Euro / US$ 69,95
ISBN 978-1-59229-106-9

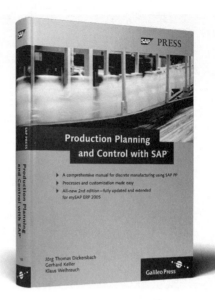

Production Planning and Control with SAP

www.sap-press.com

J.T. Dickersbach, G. Keller, K. Weihrauch

Production Planning and Control with SAP

Basic principles, processes, and complete
customization details

This book provides readers with a concise and easy-
to-follow description of the production planning and
control processes in SAP. Expert insights provided by
the authors help consultants, implementation teams,
and production employees learn how to master the
processes and customizing features of SAP PP
(release mySAP ERP 2005). This comprehensive
reference covers all major production planning and
control aspects as well as key details on mySAP SCM
(APO) integration—all bolstered by volumes of
examples and a complete glossary.

A single source of MM-related
information, including
MM Master data, Purchasing,
Inventory Management and
Financial integration

Understand how MM works and
how it relates to and integrates
with other SAP modules

504 pp., 2006, 69,95 Euro / US$
ISBN 1-59229-072-8

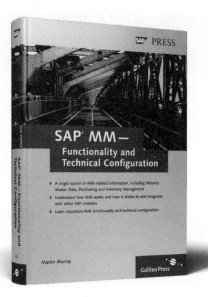

SAP MM—Functionality and Technical Configuration

www.sap-press.com

Martin Murray

SAP MM—Functionality and Technical Configuration

This book includes all aspects of SAP Materials
Management (SAP MM), including MM Master Data,
Purchasing, Inventory Management, and Financial
Integration. The book also addresses cross-application topics that are relevant to MM, such as
document management, batch management, and
classification. Using practical examples and case
studies, this book will give readers a comprehensive
understanding of SAP MM, how it works, and how it
interacts with other SAP modules.

Identify and take advantage
of your full inventory
optimization potential

Reduce inventory costs
without compromising your
ability to deliver

Drastically improve your forecast
and planning accuracy

487 pp., 2006, 69,95 Euro / US$ 69,95
ISBN 1-59229-097-3

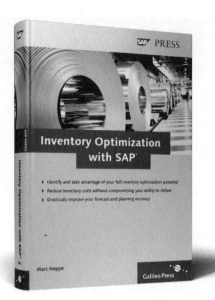

Inventory Optimization with SAP

www.sap-press.com

M. Hoppe

Inventory Optimization with SAP

To protect against shortages, companies tend to
maintain additional inventory at various points in the
supply chain. This book provides readers with a
systematic description of the options and functions
available for mastering inventory management with
mySAP ERP and mySAP SCM. Learn about factors
influencing inventories, inventory analysis, sales
planning and forecasting, disposition, batch sizes,
inventory monitoring, and much more.